Women and Radio

'This book is a celebration of our contribution as women to radio and a clarion call for its powerful voice to be shared equally between women and men.'

Jenni Murray, Presenter, *Woman's Hour*, Radio 4

From the very first days of national broadcasting and the founding of the BBC, through the innovative work of producers such as Hilda Matheson and Olive Shapley, to the breakfast-time antics of Zöe Ball and Sara Cox women have been at the heart of radio, yet marginalised in the official histories.

Women and Radio: airing differences reveals and explains the inequalities experienced by women involved in the industry; yet provides a platform for the many contributions that women have made to radio broadcasting as producers, managers, editors, presenters and consumers. It allows an understanding of feminist approaches to the media and examines 'housewife radio', the relationship between women and music, DJ chatter, the 'female' news agenda and radio as a subversive and empowering medium.

Women and Radio explores the variety of programming from mainstream broadcasts such as *Woman's Hour*, through to radio at the margins as represented by accounts of lesbian radio, feminist pirate broadcasts, local Asian radio and women's community stations. Combining classic work on radio with innovative research, journalism and biography, this book features interviews with DJs, presenters, managers and journalists. Guidelines, advice and helpful information are also offered to women wanting to work in the industry.

Contributors: Margaretta D'Arcy, Stephen Barnard, Sally Feldman, Maria Gibbons, Rosalind Gill, Nicola Godwin, Janet Howarth, Belinda Hollows, Fred Hunter, Anne Karpf, Kate Lacey, Anne McKay, Kim Michaels, Caroline Millington, Caroline Mitchell, Shaun Moores, Sheridan Nye, Karen Qureshi, Olive Shapley, Jo Tacchi, Stephen Wells.

Editor: Caroline Mitchell is principal lecturer in radio at the University of Sunderland. She has been active in the community radio movement in the UK for the last 20 years and jointly set up the first women's radio station in the UK: Fem FM.

Women and radio

Airing differences

Edited by Caroline Mitchell

London and New York

First published 2000
by Routledge
11 New Fetter Lane, London EC4P 4EE

Simultaneously published in the USA and
Canada
by Routledge
29 West 35th Street, New York,
NY 10001

Routledge is an imprint of the Taylor &
Francis Group

© 2000 Caroline Mitchell for introduction
and selection; individual contributions, the
contributors
Typeset in Galliard by Keystroke
Printed and bound in Great Britain by
MPG Books Ltd, Bodmin

*British Library Cataloguing in Publication
Data*
A catalogue record for this book is
available from the British Library

*Library of Congress Cataloging in
Publication Data*
Women and Radio: airing differences /
edited by Caroline Mitchell.
p. cm.
Includes bibliographical references and
index.
1. Women in radio broadcasting.
I. Mitchell, Caroline, 1959– II. Title.
PN1991.8.W65 W66 2001
384.54′082–dc21   00–045042

ISBN 0–415–22071–8 (pbk)
ISBN 0–415–22070–X (hbk)

To Trish, Tony and Caitlin

Contents

List of figures and tables   xi

Notes on contributors   xii

Foreword   xv
Anne Karpf

Acknowledgements   xix

Introduction: On a woman's wavelength?   1
Caroline Mitchell

Part 1

GENDERED RADIO – HIDDEN HISTORIES AND THE
DEVELOPMENT OF PROGRAMMING BY AND FOR WOMEN   9

Introduction   11
Caroline Mitchell

1   **Speaking up: voice amplification and women's struggle
for public expression**   15
Anne McKay

2   **Broadcasting a life**   29
Olive Shapley

3   **Hilda Matheson and the BBC, 1926–1940**   41
Fred Hunter

Contents

4   From *Plauderei* to propaganda: on women's radio in
    Germany 1924–35   48
    Kate Lacey

5   Twin peaks: the staying power of BBC Radio 4's *Woman's Hour*   64
    Sally Feldman

6   Twisting the dials: lesbians on British radio   73
    Sheridan Nye, Nicola Godwin and Belinda Hollows

7   Women's Airwaves Collective   84
    Women's Airwaves survey

8   Sisters are doing it . . . From Fem FM to Viva! A history of
    contemporary women's radio stations in the UK   94
    Caroline Mitchell

Part 2

RADIO TEXTS AND AUDIENCES AND THE RISE OF
FEMINIST RADIO   111

    Introduction   113
    Caroline Mitchell

9   From 'Unruly guest' to 'Good companion': the gendered
    meanings of early radio in the home   116
    Shaun Moores

10 Mother's little helper: programmes, personalities and the
    working day   126
    Stephen Barnard

11 Justifying injustice: broadcasters' accounts of inequality in
    radio   137
    Rosalind Gill

12 Gender, fantasy and radio consumption: an ethnographic
    case study   152
    Jo Tacchi

13 Galway's pirate women   167
    Margaretta D'Arcy

14 Limited talk   182
    Karen Qureshi

15   On air/off air: defining women's radio space in European
     women's community radio   189
     Caroline Mitchell

Part 3
———

WOMEN WORKING IN RADIO   203

     Introduction   205
     Caroline Mitchell

16   Getting in and getting on: women and radio management
     at the BBC   209
     Caroline Millington

17   The long goodbye   219
     Stephen Wells

18   The nature of glass: participation of women in the Irish
     independent radio industry   224
     Maria Gibbons

19   The last bastion: how women become music presenters in
     UK radio   238
     Kim Michaels and Caroline Mitchell

20   Women in radio news: making a difference?   250
     Janet Haworth

21   Sound advice for women who want to work in radio   262
     Caroline Mitchell

Part 4
———

CONTACTS AND RESOURCES   275

     UK women's radio stations, community based training projects
     and support groups   277

     UK radio and training organisations and publications   279

     Women's radio stations and contacts world-wide   281

Index   283

List of figures and tables

Figures

1.1	Women speaking loudly in public	21
8.1	UK Women's radio stations: publicity leaflets	100
13.1	Radio Pirate Woman and Women's Scéal Radio: flyers	168
18.1	Commercial stations – percentage of women and men in different job categories	227
18.2	Community stations – percentage of women and men in different job categories	227
18.3	Routes into radio employment – location of first radio job of commercial radio employees	230

Tables

8.1	UK women's restricted service licences: 1992–2000	98
8.2	UK women's restricted service licences: programming	103
18.1	Proportion of women and men holding selected programme-making jobs	229

Notes on contributors

Margaretta D'Arcy (Irish) was born in the pre-television era, when radio was the waker-up of the imagination. She has been in the theatre since her first job in Dublin at the age of 15. She is author and co-author of twenty-odd plays of all styles and lengths. In 1982, she set up Women in Media & Entertainment. In 1987 she set up an autonomous women's pirate radio (in Galway, Irish Republic).

Stephen Barnard is the author of *On The Radio: Music Radio in Britain* (Open University Press, 1989) and *Studying Radio* (Arnold, 2000), as well as various books on rock music. A full-time freelance writer, he is also a WEA-registered lecturer on broadcasting and popular culture.

Sally Feldman is Dean of the LCP School of Media. At the BBC she was editor of Radio 4's *Woman's Hour*, and was responsible for launching and editing a variety of programmes for Radio 2, 3, 4 and 5 Live. She was previously editor of *Woman's World* magazine and she continues to contribute to a range of publications including the *Standard*, the *Guardian*, the *Times Higher Education Supplement* and *Good Housekeeping*.

Maria Gibbons has a PhD in Zoology from the National University of Ireland, Galway. She works as a freelance media consultant specialising in video production and media-related research. She has a particular interest in alternative media and is presently co-writing a training manual on Community Media.

Rosalind Gill is a lecturer in gender theory at the London School of Economics. Her PhD was concerned with questions about gender and ideology in DJ programmes, and she is currently writing about zoo radio shows. She is author of *Gender and the Media: Representations, Audiences and Cultural Politics* (Polity Press, forthcoming) and editor of *The Gender-Technology Relation: Contemporary Theory and Research* (Taylor & Francis, 1995).

Nicola Godwin studied media and psychology and worked for the BBC for three years before moving into print journalism. She co-edited *Assaults on Convention*, an anthology of essays on lesbian transgression, published by Cassell in 1995.

Janet Haworth is Course Director for the Postgraduate Diploma in Broadcast Journalism at City University, London. She is a former independent local radio news editor and director of the award-winning independent production company, Palace Radio. Her research interests include: Gender and the news agenda, the media image of Horatio Nelson and the impact of new technology on the professional practice of broadcasters.

Belinda Hollows studied audio-visual communications and sociology. She works as a radio studio manager for BBC News and is currently training in Existential Psychotherapy. She co-edited *Assaults on Convention*, an anthology of essays on lesbian transgression, published by Cassell in 1995.

Fred Hunter ran radio propaganda overseas for Central Office of Information 1965–73, then helped found London Broadcasting Company and IRN. He worked fleetingly at ITN before starting Britain's first radio journalism course at London College of Printing. He was awarded the first PhD at City University Journalism Department and retired to research women in media 1840–1990, writing several entries for the new *Dictionary of National Biography*.

Anne Karpf is a journalist, broadcaster, and sociologist. She has been radio critic of *The Listener*, a media columnist for the *New Statesman*, a contributing editor to *Cosmopolitan*, and was the radio critic of *The Guardian* for seven years. She's also written widely on women and radio. A regular contributor to BBC Radios 3 and 4, she is author of *Doctoring the Media: The reporting of health and medicine* (Routledge), and *The War After: Living with the Holocaust* (Minerva).

Kate Lacey is Lecturer in Media Studies in the School of European Studies at the University of Sussex. She is author of *Feminine Frequencies: Gender, German Radio and the Public Sphere 1923–1945* (University of Michigan Press, 1996). Current research focuses on the formative years of broadcasting in ways which connect the public sphere of politics to the 'horizon of experience'.

Kim Michaels works in the radio industry as both a presenter and journalist. She managed '107 The Bridge', a pioneering radio station training women in Washington, Tyne and Wear. She lectures in radio at the University of Sunderland and is currently researching for a PhD concerning women in music radio.

Caroline Millington worked in the BBC from 1970–1999. After 16 years as a producer and editor, she became head of a radio programme department. In 1993 she was appointed Controller of Production for BBC Radio and in 1996 Controller of Multimedia Development in BBC Production. She is now a Non-Executive Director of a Health Authority.

Caroline Mitchell is Principal Lecturer in radio at the University of Sunderland.

She has been active in the community radio movement in the UK for the last 20 years and set up (with Trish Caverly) the first women's station in the UK: Fem FM. She has worked in women's radio development and training across Europe. She is currently doing research about female DJs.

Shaun Moores is Reader in Media and Cultural Studies at the University of Sunderland. He is the author of *Interpreting Audiences: The Ethnography of Media Consumption* (Sage, 1993), *Satellite Television and Everyday Life: Articulating Technology* (John Libbey Media, 1996) and *Media and Everyday Life in Modern Society* (Edinburgh University Press, 2000).

Sheridan Nye worked for the BBC for six years as an engineer and then began working in print journalism. She co-edited *Assaults on Convention*, an anthology of essays on lesbian transgression, published by Cassell in 1995. She now lives in the USA.

Karen Qureshi is a research student and visiting lecturer in the department of Media and Communication at Queen Margaret University College, Edinburgh. Her doctoral research is concerned with the negotiation of identity among second generation Pakistani Scots in Edinburgh.

Olive Shapley (1910–1999) was an inspirational radio producer and presenter who played a major part in bringing working class voices into people's living rooms. In the 1930s she produced pioneering radio features and documentaries about social and cultural issues for the BBC. Her most famous work was *The Classic Soil* (1939). She became presenter of *Woman's Hour* in 1949 and continued to produce TV and radio programmes for the BBC. Later in life, a pioneer to the end, she set up accommodation for single mothers and Vietnamese 'boat people'. Her autobiography *Broadcasting a Life* (Scarlet Press, 1996) was written with the help of her daughter Christina Hart.

Jo Tacchi is Research Fellow in the School of Journalism, Media and Cultural Studies at Cardiff University, Wales. Her publications include 'Radio Texture: Between Self and Others' in *Material Cultures: Why Some Things Matter* (Ed. D. Miller, UCL Press 1998) and 'The Need for Radio Theory in the Digital Age' (*International Journal of Cultural Studies*, 2000).

Steven Wells has been pursuing an essentially unreconstructed punk agenda at the *New Musical Express* for the last eighteen years. He's written for several BBC comedy shows including *The Day Today* and *On the Hour*. He wrote and presented *Dance With the Devil* – a Channel 4 documentary on music censorship. In 1999 he launched his own avant-pulp fiction imprint – Attack! Books – and his first novel, *Tits Out Teenage Terror Totty*, was released to ecstatic reviews.

The Women's Airwaves Collective was set up in Lonon in 1980. It was a feminist radio programme-making group that ran radio training courses for women and also carried out research into the way women were represented both on the radio and as programme makers.

Anne Karpf

Foreword

As cultural shifts go, it is hard to imagine a greater one than that which has befallen women and radio. In under three decades we have moved from a time when executives could still be publicly nervous about the acceptibility of women's voices for broadcasting, with a senior female Radio 1 producer insisting that she would not recommend a 'girl' to front a Radio 1 daytime show (Ross 1977), to one where that network's prestigious breakfast show now has its second successive female presenter, her predecessor having been arraigned for bad language. Radio women, if the tabloid press were to be believed, are all babes and ladettes.

Yet astonishingly, this cultural change has been all but ignored in the academic literature. To my knowledge this is the first substantial volume to deal specifically with the subject of women and radio. In precisely the period during which the field of media studies has exploded, and almost every aspect of mass communications been subjected to theoretical scrutiny, this major area has remained virtually unexamined.

The reasons for its neglect lie partly in the marginal status which radio, accurately dubbed an 'invisible medium', itself occupies in the media studies firmament (Lewis and Booth 1989). Just as television is treated by the press and public as radio's more glamorous, monied sibling, so this hierarchy has been reproduced in academic research, and only recently seriously contested (Lewis 2000).

It is also true that radio, by its very ubiquity, sometimes seems to defy analysis. At times it appears more like a utility – say water or gas – than an art-form or means of communication. At others, attempting to theorise such an inescapable, quotidian medium feels like trying to pin down the air. (Moores in this volume fascinatingly documents just that moment when radio moved from novelty to invisibility.) In addition its simultaneously public and intimate nature, noted in Lacey's chapter, can make it difficult to find the right language and discourse with which to think about it. Yet the very reasons which make the subject so elusive also make it a rich and fertile topic for study.

Hitherto, those interested in it had to trawl through the biographies of female radio pioneers, or extrapolate from television texts. And just as radio seemed an afterthought in media studies, so women have often seemed an afterthought in the emerging field of radio studies.

Caroline Mitchell is to be congratulated for having done so much of the trawling for us, and gathered together a selection of papers, some previously inaccessible, which can serve as markers of the territory.

Whereas radio is often characterised as a female medium, Mitchell found that overall women listen slightly less than men to commercial radio, as well as to Radios 1 and 2; on Radio 5 the disparity is more marked. That network, before its launch and despite its female controller, was disparaged as Radio Bloke, but there are now several other contenders for the title.

I have long thought that the obsession with car radio – the number of programmes called 'drive time' is beyond count – is a scarcely-concealed obsession with men and radio, toys and boys, since only around 20 per cent of radio listening takes place in cars.

Yet this is a particularly interesting moment to be exploring the subject of women and broadcasting. Radio, in its early days seen largely as a means of confirming women in their domestic roles, has come to play a much more complex role in women's lives. With music increasingly a marker of personal identity, and radio the chief source of music, the medium is used by women, and men, as part of the nexus of goods and services through which we construct our social identities. Listeners employ radio to differentiate themselves from their spouse (see Tacchi's chapter), or from parents. Musical taste has become a bridge between the individual and their subculture, a badge of affiliation. Music radio not only, in the argot of marketing, is niched, but also helps us niche ourselves.

The field of women and radio is in its infancy. We have yet to think deeply, for example, about how age affects radio use – how older women, teenage girls and pre-teens use the medium – or ethnic minority women's relationship with national radio. We have barely begun to develop sensitive tools to identify and analyse how different radio stations and programmes address women.

But much has already changed in the field. Feminist discourse has metamorphosed over the past two decades from a preoccupation with stereotyping to an obsession with pleasure (by my reckoning, it was some time in the late 1980s that young female Archers addicts first came out) to a more nuanced understanding of the different dimensions involved in women and radio.

This volume illustrates the sheer breadth of the subject. There are not just many different types of radio – national, local, and community, public service and commercial, permanent and RSLs (Restricted Service Licences) – but also a plethora of different issues. In addition to the employment of women in radio, there is women as audience, and the representation of women by radio – matters which are all linked, albeit not as causally as some early feminist work suggested.

One of this book's chief innovations is to integrate mainstream and community radio as subjects for study, thereby highlighting their similarities and differences (see, for instance, the chapters by Gibbons, and Michaels and Mitchell). These suggest that radio is still a highly gendered culture, where stereotypes about how women can and should sound on air are not being eroded so much as enlarged and defended (see Gill).

Mitchell puts women and community radio – at best usually a footnote in academic analysis – at the core of the book. In two chapters she provides a valuable history of women's radio stations and discusses women's struggle to secure space within community stations, while D'Arcy's chapter provides an evocative account of the Galway women's pirate radio station.

The question of whether women should have cordoned-off spaces on the airwaves, or whether these end up ghettoising women out of the mainstream, refuses to go away. But this volume suggests that historical analysis can illuminate the changing meanings of radio, and the ways in which it has sometimes been deliberately gendered (as described in Lacey's chapter).

The anthology also points to the variety of ways in which the subject can be considered – ethnographically, statistically, historically, and practically. In an area so shamefully underdeveloped theoretically, it marks a significant beginning.

Radio is sharing in the multi-media revolution, part of the vaunted convergence. There's a nostalgic fondness for the old deco sets just at the point where radios (apart from jokey, novelty sets) are looking increasingly like mobile phones, answering-machines, remote controls, and other digital paraphernalia. At a time when women's lives are also undergoing major change – with more women deferring maternity or eschewing it altogether, and a greater than ever number of women living alone – the relationship between women and radio will be a rich and fluid one. May this book excite further debate, critique, and interest in it.

References

Lewis, P. M. and Booth, J. (1989) *The Invisible Medium: Public, Commercial and Community Radio*, London: Macmillan.

Lewis, P. M. (2000) 'Private passion, public neglect: the cultural status of radio', *International Journal of Cultural Studies, Radiocracy issue*, Vol 3 No. 2, 2000.

Ross, M. (1977) 'Radio', in King, J. and Stott, M., *Is This Your Life? Images of Women in the Media*, London: Virago.

Acknowledgements

The idea behind this collection was first conceived in 1994 when I organised a conference called 'On a Woman's Wavelength? – Women and Radio in the 90s' at the University of Sunderland. Many of the contributors to that conference have written for this volume and I am grateful to them, and the other contributors for all their hard work. The School of Arts, Design and Media granted me sabbatical time to prepare and write this book – I am grateful to all my colleagues in the MAC team for shouldering extra administration while I was away. Thanks in particular to Sue Thornham for all her advice and for gently keeping me in touch with academia while I was on maternity leave and to Valerie Alia, Ann Baxter, Kim Michaels, Shaun Moores, Mike O'Brien, Deborah Thomas. Liza Tsaliki and Angela Werndley for their support. I am also grateful to all the students who discussed and shared their ideas with me, particularly those on the women and radio module.

At Routledge, thank you to Rebecca Barden for taking on this book in the first place and to Christopher Cudmore for all his advice, support and patience. Steven Pobjoy from *Marketing* magazine library and Jeff Walden, senior document assistant at the BBC written archives centre were very helpful in tracking down references for me. I am extremely grateful to Helen Baehr, Caroline Beck and Nick Jankowski for reading and commenting on early drafts of my own articles in this volume and to Brian Lister for allowing me to peruse RAJAR figures in his office and for giving me the benefit of his wide experience in the radio industry. Thanks also to Sally Aitchison, Vicki Carter, Julia Darling, Maud Hand, Trisha Jarman, Jude Mallabar, Kate Rich, Margherita Taylor, Sandy Warr and Ami Yesufu who let their professional lives become my case studies.

I would also like to take this opportunity to thank people who have aided and abetted me over the years in my work relating to women and radio, for whom I have the greatest respect. Thanks to Peter Cock, Anne Karpf, Peter Lewis, members of the Radio Studies Network steering group, Anna Reading, Birgitte Jallov, Mary Dowson, the Fem FM steering group, women at the Bridge women's training project in Washington and the Women On Air team in Galway.

Acknowledgements

Several people have given me support in my personal life – over a period when the book was not the only thing to be conceived and given birth to! Particular thanks to Trish Caverly, my partner at Fem FM, Gina Andrewes and Coralie Morton for their friendship, love and encouragement and to Belinda O'Shea and Siobain Bourke for their help with childcare when I needed it. To Peter and Susan Mitchell, my love and thanks for all their support over the years. Finally, to my partner Tony O'Shea, who supported me in every way, from reading and commenting on each draft to holding the baby – all at a time when he had his own PhD to complete – thank you for everything.

The editor would like to thank the following copyright holders for permission to reprint material:

Margaretta D'Arcy, 'Galway's pirate women, a global trawl'. Copyright © Margaretta D'Arcy, 1996. Reprinted by permission of the author.

Stephen Barnard, from chapter 8 'Mother's Little Helper: programmes, personalities and the working day' from *On the Radio: Music Radio in Britain*. Copyright © Stephen Barnard, 1989. Reprinted by permission of the author.

Rosalind Gill, 'Justifying Injustice: Broadcasters' Accounts of Inequality in a Radio Station', from *Discourse Analytic Research: readings and repertoires of texts in action*, edited by Erica Burman and Ian Parker, Copyright © Rosalind Gill, 1993. Reprinted by permission of Taylor and Francis Publishers.

Fred Hunter, 'Hilda Matheson and the BBC, 1926–1940', from *This Working Day World – Women's Lives and Cultures in Britain*, edited by Sally Oldfield. By permission of Taylor and Francis.

Kate Lacey, 'From *Plauderei* to Propaganda: on Women's Radio in Germany 1934–35', from: *Media, Culture and Society*, Vol. 16 (4) 1994. Copyright © Kate Lacey 1994. Reprinted by permission of Sage Publications.

Anne McKay, 'Speaking Up: Voice Amplification and Women's Struggle for Public Expression', from *Technology and Women's Voices*, edited by Cheris Kramarae, Copyright ©1988. Reprinted by permission of Routledge Publishers.

Caroline Mitchell 'On Air/Off Air: Defining women's radio space in European women's community radio.' This chapter will appear in *Community Electronic Media in the Information Age: Perspectives, Findings and Policy*, edited by Nicholas Jankowski (in press). Reprinted by permission of Hampton Press.

Shaun Moores, 'The Box on the Dresser: memories of early radio and everyday life,' from *Media, Culture and Society*, Vol. 10 (1) 1988. Copyright © Shaun Moores 1988. Reprinted by permission of Sage Publications.

Sheridan Nye, Nicola Godwin and Belinda Hollows, 'Twisting the Dial – Lesbians on British Radio', from *Daring to Dissent – Lesbian Culture from margin to mainstream*, edited by Liz Gibbs. Copyright © Liz Gibbs and the authors 1994. Reprinted by permission of Belinda Hollows on behalf of the authors and Cassell publishers.

Olive Shapley, extracts from *Broadcasting a Life*. Copyright © Olive Shapley 1996. By permission of Christina Hart and Scarlett Press.

'Women's Airwaves, Women's Voices', from Local Radio Workshop, *Nothing Local about it, London's Local Radio*. Copyright © Local Radio Workshop 1983. Reprinted by permission of Routledge Publishers.

Stephen Wells, *The Long Goodbye*. Reprinted by permission of the New Musical Express.

Caroline Mitchell

INTRODUCTION: ON A WOMAN'S WAVELENGTH?

Radio is a personal, intimate medium. Allow me to start by indulging in some highly selective moments from my personal 'radio life narrative':

1960s: The large wireless in our drawing room warms up, the lights glow and the sound of the programme fades in. I listen to 'The Clitheroe Kid' – a situation comedy on the Light programme. I love Jimmy Clitheroe's laugh and his 'funny' northern accent; the way he is so naughty, getting into trouble, 'cheeking' his elders. Listening to this programme is an escape into another family, a different class and another gender.

1970s: My school mates and I gather round the small transistor radio on a Sunday evening in the school common room. With mounting anticipation we listen to the 'Top 20 Countdown' on Radio 1. Later, after lights out, I ward off homesickness by listening to my tiny transistor radio. The sound is turned down low so that the matron won't hear and confiscate my radio companion for good.

1980s: As part of my undergraduate studies I carry out a survey about women's employment in local radio. One manager informs me that he won't employ women in technical areas of radio: 'They might get their long hair and fingernails caught in whirling tape spools.' He isn't being ironic. I have short hair and I bite my fingernails. Around that time a Hospital Radio apparatchik tells me not to touch a mixing desk until I have had extensive training: 'It might blow up,' he says.

1990s: Fem FM has been on the air for a week now. History was made when we switched on the transmitter of Britain's first women's station. It's the last programme and we are dancing in the studio. Suddenly the music stops – in our joyous cavorting someone has kicked out the plug powering the transmitter. I push the plug back in – woman power!

2000: I've been in labour for 36 hours. Today for some reason all I can bear to listen to is Radio 2. The music keeps me going. Terry Wogan, Ken Bruce – I can even stand listening to Jimmy Young! But then Steve Wright turns on the smarm. 'Turn it off,' I scream as the next contraction reaches its peak. Our daughter is born early that evening – just in time for 'The Archers'.

Radio is thus entwined into the rhythm of our everyday lives[1] through its texts, genres, discourses, institutions and industry. This volume is the first book to bring together writing and research about women and radio. It combines previously published material with specially commissioned articles and represents some of the key debates in the areas of policy, theory, practice and praxis[2] relating to women and radio. Through a range of personal, historical and theoretical perspectives it consolidates the position of women on the radio research agenda where once they were absent, invisible or marginal. This introduction maps out the core themes in the emerging field of women and radio studies and delineates some boundaries. It briefly outlines the framework of radio in Britain for people who are unfamiliar with its structure.

Women and Radio is divided into three main sections, each with an introduction. The first part, 'Gendered radio – hidden histories and the development of programming by and for women', takes us through personal and historical narratives to explore how radio for, about and by women has developed. Part 2, 'Radio texts and audiences and the rise of feminist radio', is primarily an exploration of the different theoretical and methodological approaches to the study of radio's relationship to female audiences (both 'active' and 'passive') as well as accounts of feminist radio praxis. Part 3, 'Women working in radio', contains contemporary research and case studies about the current position of women working in different roles in the BBC, commercial and community radio sectors. A final section has contacts and resources for those who wish to use academic, vocational, or campaign networks relating to women and radio.

Some of the previously published material in this volume (for instance Local Radio Workshop's survey of sexism on the airwaves and Barnard's review of the relationship between DJs and female audiences) is somewhat dated in the light of subsequent developments in radio employment and practices, but has been included because of its historical and contextual importance for women and radio studies. The book mainly focuses on women and British radio although some interesting examples of European research (i.e. Lacey's historical study of early women's radio in Germany and perspectives on Irish mainstream and pirate radio activity by Gibbons and D'Arcy) are included. The first chapter comes from the United States but its thesis about attitudes towards women's voices in the early days of radio can be applied to British radio.

Catering for 52 per cent? The structure of radio in Britain

The structure of British radio is well-documented elsewhere (Crisell 1997, Barnard 2000).[3] In 1995 radio listening was the third or fourth most popular 'home-based' leisure activity for women (after watching television and visiting /entertaining, alongside listening to recorded music and ahead of reading, gardening and DIY) (Central Statistical Office 1995). Although quantitative research (like that carried out by Radio Joint Audience Research (RAJAR) into when, what and how women listen to the radio is mainly used by industry controllers and managers, a picture of UK radio and its female audience can be revealing.[4] Overall, women listen slightly less than men to commercial radio – the difference mainly coming from national channels.[5] The Radio Advertising Bureau (RAB) has carried out research into how young women use radio and found that 'there are 7.4 million women aged 18–35 in the UK of whom over 78 per cent will listen to commercial radio at some point, for an average of 15 hours a week.' (McLuhan 2000). Two BBC channels, Radio 3 and 4, have roughly the same numbers of men and women listening (men listen to Radio 3 slightly more). Radio 2 is listened to by 24 per cent of men and 21 per cent of women (for roughly the same amount of time). The Controller of Radio 1 recently stated that he wanted to increase the number of women listening to the channel (see Chapter 19). Currently it is listened to by 27 per cent of men and 21 per cent of women, men listening to an average of 10.4 hours a week and women 7.6 hours. The widest 'gender gap' is for Radio 5 Live, which has 19 per cent of the male population listening and 7 per cent of women. It has attempted to woo some women to its sports coverage with specialist programmes but it is not known as 'Radio Bloke' for nothing! Twenty-four per cent of men and 20 per cent of women listen to BBC local radio.

These figures may help schedulers and programmers to provide a better public serve or target consumers more effectively but as important is *how* do women listen? RAB research (2000) has found that men and women require different things from their listening – men consume radio to get specific information, traffic news, football scores etc. and as radio executive Katy Turner claims: 'Women are concerned more with feeling good, being mellow.' (Sullivan 1994: 31).

The female medium?

Anne Karpf has written that radio has a 'special relationship with women's lives, in that it is an explicit accompaniment to them – a commentary, or a counterpoint' (1980: 43). The Radio Advertising Bureau (RAB) has identified that nearly two thirds of 'housewives' (note the quotation marks, the RAB admit that these 'housewives' now include male and pensioner 'main shoppers') listen to commercial radio each week:

> Radio plays an important role in the lives of housewives, relieving their feelings
> of isolation and helping to lighten the spirits while doing chores. It also accounts

for a disproportionately large section of the media day, making radio a dominant medium, in their lives.

(RAB 2000: 8)

Karpf (1987: 169) also talks about the 'gender apartheid' in radio listening where daytime radio women are placed in the private, domestic realm by male presenters who operate in the public realm and assume that men are there too. Defining the 'space' for women on the airwaves is a key concern of this book.[6] The DJs and programme controllers of the 1970s and 1980s consciously or unwittingly colluded in the aforementioned public/private binary. This book documents and celebrates research and practice which places women in a range of spaces in relation to radio, as listeners and practitioners: 'Each of us remains private, we are public at the same time' (D'Arcy 1996: 3).

A summary of early research into women and radio which was mainly influenced by socialist feminist perspectives[7] is necessary before moving onto discussing wider theoretical debates. Women and radio was first put on the academic and political agenda in Britain in 1977 when, in a publication conceived by the campaign group 'Women in Media', Mileva Ross critiqued the British radio industry's attitude to both female listeners and programme makers. Ross concluded that more training was needed to redress the lack of female employees in different sectors of the radio industry. Shortly after this, Anne Karpf (1980) discussed how we should be counteracting the hidden 'anti women' framework behind obnoxious DJ constructed 'strip programming'[8] (which positions women as passive and undemanding listeners). She suggested that there was a need for a wider range of programmes that represented the 'truths' of women's lives – including unashamedly giving feminist-influenced work a fair hearing and creating an industry where women could create their own stations as well as contributing to wider mainstream programming agendas. Baehr and Ryan tried to push policy and practice further through outlining guidelines for change in local commercial radio. They too criticised the limiting 'domestic and sexual boundaries set by the media' (1984: 42) and argued that cheaply made programming that always had an eye on the ratings was anathema to high standards. They recommended that in order to redress the culture of the radio medium of male producers and female consumers, programmers should train more female contributors and generally take more risks with programming. Baehr and Ryan did not recommend the setting up of women's stations in the commercial sector, although they acknowledged that separatist training and programmes for women might increase equal opportunities in the short term.

Women and radio studies

Radio has been called the 'Cinderella' medium (Scannel 1988), and Radio Studies has only recently found a space within Media and Cultural Studies.[9] If radio is Cinderella then women and radio studies still has 'pumpkin' status.

This volume starts to carve out the area of women and radio studies, but is there a coherent, united perspective in the field? Some themes emerge, in particular the dominance of feminist/media and cultural studies approaches to theory, practice and policy; the notion of active audiences and using ethnographic work and critical discourse analysis as methodological tools. Van Zoonen (1994) notes the paucity of studies in feminist media production in cultural and communication studies. One of the strengths of the emerging field of Radio Studies, and also in this volume, is the attention to this area.

Clearly gender, women, feminism and patriarchy are important definers in the debates raised in this book.[10] Inevitably in its nature as a collection of historical and contemporary pieces it is going to be affected by different phases of feminist thought and theory, moving through debates about the 'effect' of sexist radio output on 'passive' audiences, through political economy research about patriarchal employment practices in the radio industries to feminist influenced research in the area of cultural studies, linguistics and anthropology.

Women and radio – old myths and new areas for research

Much of the influence of traditional myths about women's relationship to radio is now disappearing. The well-rehearsed and loudly voiced arguments about women's voices being unsuitable for radio and disliked by listeners have now been more or less smashed.

Women's programming and women's stations have now been tried in practice by mainstream BBC and commercial programmers and by alternative community stations. Many women shy away from having special programmes or stations allocated to them – they say gender is not an important factor in programming. I would argue that this is a rejection of stereotyping, a distrust of the way the radio industry has already packaged femininity in ways that are off-putting to many women. Viva's commercial format failed to address the complexities of working women's identities. Karpf identified the dilemma of a single programme (in this case BBC *Woman's Hour*) representing the range of women's interests: 'It negotiates the conflicts in broadcasting to and for women, at times unsure how far to examine and interrogate the "outside" world' without losing its focus on and validation of the domestic world (Karpf 1987: 175). Stations employing female DJs have begun to address the problems of gender imbalance and limited role models for women in UK music radio. At Radio 1 different audiences are addressed by a wider range of female presenters including music journalists, women with club experience and entertainment DJs.

What we are beginning to see is the development of women's radio expressed in a range of ways. The most conservative, and commercially successful forms are 'soft' programming formats, like that of Heart FM, which attract as many male listeners as female. The audience figures show that men are happy to listen to 'female' formats and programmes (like *Woman's Hour*) but women are not so tolerant of 'male' formats (like Radio Five Live). In the past decade in Britain, women's radio stations including those in the model of 'Fem FM' and occasional feminist pirate radio activity have provided the space for women to express, experiment and raise their voices. Ideas and formats promoted in such relatively 'fringe' media activities are often taken up later in mainstream formats. Sadly what is less likely to change is the patriarchal political economy of the radio industry. We have to look to countries with more imaginative regulatory systems for alternative media cultures to truly thrive. Paradoxically women want it all – difference and equality. They want specialist programmes that without preaching or proselytising validate their gender and/or race, class, sexuality and subculture and they want to be well-represented in different genres in terms of production, management and ownership of all kinds of radio stations.

So what can feminist cultural and media studies scholars contribute to the future of research into women and radio? An interesting line of study is the theoretical notion of voice and space: how at the same time women can be heard and not seen, disembodied when they 'appear' on radio. What also seems to be missing from much of the current research and writing in this area is the nature of the *pleasures*[11] women get from radio. Whether they empathise with, object to, learn from, fantasise over or subvert what they hear and what they make, women can be active consumers and producers of meaning. Women can use radio, as both listeners and programme makers, to subvert, manipulate and play with that space and their identities.

Notes

1 Scannell (1996) describes the way broadcasting relates to everyday routines and events as 'dailiness': 'In modern societies radio and television are part of both the background and foreground of our everyday dealings with each other in a common world' (1996: 5).

2 By 'praxis' I mean practice informed by theory.

3 At the start of 2000 the BBC, which is funded by an annual licence fee, had 5 national networks all based on providing a public service to listeners. Radio 1 is the channel for pop music and youth interest. Radio 2 is for music and light entertainment, mainly aimed at the over 40s. Radio 3 is the channel for arts, culture and classical music. Radio 4 for current affairs, a variety of speech-based programmes, comedy and drama and Radio 5 Live, for news and sport. Each of the British 'regions' (Northern Ireland, Scotland and Wales) has its own radio service and there are 39 local stations and an Asian Radio Network. The Radio Authority grants licences to the commercial sector, which at the start of 2000 has three national stations and 245 local stations as well as 15 cable and 19 satellite services. The Radio Authority also grants short-term licences (Restricted Service Licences) to hundreds of stations each year to cover sporting and cultural events and to test out new formats (often for community-based stations).

4 RAJAR research is for both BBC and commercial sectors. Figures come from weekdays, March 2000 survey, 10 Jan to 26 March 2000. Figures are based on the percentage of all men and women who listen to each station (called the station 'reach') and the average hours they spend listening (in brackets).

5 All Commercial Radio 68% men (15.7) and 65% women (15.3). Source: Radio Joint Audience Research Ltd (RAJAR), conducted by Ipsos – RSL Ltd.

6 A definition and discussion of women's space in the context of feminist revisions of Habermas' (e.g. 1989) public sphere can be found in Chapter 15.

7 See van Zoonen (1994: 12–13) for a useful discussion of typologies of feminism.

8 Music linked by continuous DJ chat and trivia – frequent references being made to landmarks in the listeners' daily domestic routine. Seemingly no end to each 'programme' – one presenter hands over to another and the routine continues.

9 The establishment of the UK Radio Studies Network has been instrumental in highlighting radio as an area for research and study. See Contacts section for details.

10 Natalie Fenton acknowledges the fragmented and contested nature of feminist theory and argues that 'Not only is the concept of "woman" crucial to grasp the gendered nature of the social world, but so is that of patriarchy in order that we do not lose sight of the power relations involved.' (Fenton 1998: 14).

11 Joke Hermes, in the context of her study of women 'reading' women's magazines, talks about how 'it needs to be accepted that readers of all kinds (including we critics) enjoy texts in some contexts that we are critical of in other contexts' (Hermes 1995: 2). She goes on to state that 'post structuralism, psychoanalysis and postmodernism led to the acknowledgement that pleasure was an important study of popular culture in its own right' (op cit.).

References

Baehr, H. and Ryan, M. (1984) *Shut up and Listen! Women and Local Radio*, London: Comedia.

Barnard, S. (2000) *Studying Radio*, London: Arnold.

Central Statistical Office, (1995) *Social Focus on Women*, London.

Crisell, A. (1997) *An Introductory History of British Broadcasting*, London: Routledge.

D'Arcy, M. (1996) *Galway's Pirate Women – A Global Trawl*, Galway: Women's Pirate Press.

Fenton, N. (1998) 'Feminist Media Studies at the junction of modernity and post modernity: caught between a rock and a hard place'. Paper presented at the IAMCR conference, Glasgow.

Habermas, J. (1989) *The Theory of Communicative Action, vol.2*, (translated by T. McCarthy), Boston: Beacon Press.

Hermes, J. (1995) *Reading Women's Magazines*, Cambridge: Polity Press.

Karpf, A. (1980) 'Women and radio' in Baehr, H. *Women and Media*, London: Pergamon Press.

Karpf, A. (1987) 'Radio Times: private women and public men', in Davies, K., J. Dickey and T. Stratford, (eds) *Out of Focus, Writing on Women and the Media*, pp. 168–75, London: The Women's Press.

McLuhan, R. (2000) 'Women demand a fresh perspective'. *Marketing*, 25 May 2000: 36.

Radio Advertising Bureau (2000) *Understanding Radio*, London: Radio Advertising Bureau.

Ross, M. (1977) 'Radio' in King, J. and Stott, M. *Is This Your Life? Images of Women in the Media*, London: Virago.

Scannell, P. (1988) 'Review of books by R. le Roy Bannerman and A. Crisell', *Media, Culture and Society*, 10 (3): 385–88, London: Sage.

Scannell, P. (1996) *Radio, Television and Modern Life*, Oxford: Blackwell.

Sullivan, J. (1994) 'Can programmers target women better?' *Music and Media*, Vol. 11, Issue 42, 15 October 1994.

van Zoonen, L. (1994) *Feminist Media Studies*, London: Sage.

Gendered radio – hidden histories and the development of programming by and for women

It is history writing that has consigned women to the sidelines, not historical events themselves.

(Hilmes 1997: 132)

Media narratives, structures, and audiences are produced in, and themselves help to produce, the same crucible of negotiations of social power that shapes the histories through which we later understand them.

(Hilmes 1997: 289)

Invisible women

There are several weighty and respected 'official histories' of British broadcasting including Asa Brigg's epic chronicles (1961–1995), Scannell and Cardiff's social histories (1991) and Crisell's useful overview (1997). Lewis and Booth's history of public, commercial and community radio (1989) pays the most attention to women's radio. However official histories tend to be 'un-gendered'. Women are rendered invisible through omission, or because their work is hidden, considered inferior or in the background. Occasionally we get a glimpse of women's broadcasting work: a name here, a footnote there. Tim Crook (1998) reveals how Elizabeth Welch may have been Britain's first black woman broadcaster, presenting her own show, *Soft Lights and Sweet Music*, on BBC radio in 1934. However in Briggs (1961) she is only a name on a list, with no mention of her colour. Crook (2000) quotes Susan Okokon who suggests that women such as Welch are 'victims of a kind of cultural amnesia' (Okokon 1998: 11).

This part of the book attempts to represent the 'other' history, missed out in the brief footnotes and fleeting glimpses. It brings together the marginalised histories of radio women – individually and collectively – from BBC, commercial and community broadcasting.

Early voices

When ordinary women spoke formally in public in the 1830s (espousing the causes of the abolition of slavery and equal rights for women) they were vilified for moving out of their 'natural' feminine, domestic sphere of the home, onto public platforms formerly occupied exclusively by male public speakers. Early female public speakers refuted the idea that women's voices were naturally unsuitable for public speaking; they felt that it was the preparation, clarity and confident delivery of the presentation that was important (Lerner 1971). Attitudes associated with the premise that women's voices are not suitable for radio broadcasting, or should be limited to particular areas, are still ingrained in the ideology of the commercial radio industry. In Chapter 1 Ann McKay charts the history of the way that the female voice has been rejected and accepted since women first spoke in public. Her research starts to explain the origins of negative attitudes towards women who present on the radio and she explores the premises on which women's exclusion from radio was founded.

Women shaping the BBC

Of course there were some women working behind the scenes, shaping the early BBC in production and management. Chapters 2 and 3 celebrate the careers of two female producers: Olive Shapley (1910–1999) and Hilda Matheson (1888–1940). Both women were innovators, developing radio techniques that practitioners now take for granted. In Chapter 2 there are three extracts from Olive Shapley's autobiography, documenting her early days at the BBC, her work in the northern region making documentaries about working-class culture (developing new recording and interviewing techniques outside the studio), and her time presenting *Woman's Hour*.

In Chapter 3, Fred Hunter documents how Hilda Matheson, known to Lord Reith as 'The Red Woman', was instrumental in establishing the BBC's News Section in the 1920s and developing the concept of the 'scripted talk'.

Radio for women

In the first two years of the BBC women were encouraged to listen during *Women's Hour* where subject choice was suggested by a Women's Advisory Committee. Minutes of their meetings report that they suggested subjects like '"Women in Public Life", "Openings for Girls with a University Education" (and) "Women in Other Lands"' (Briggs 1961: 245). This title was abandoned in September 1925 and the idea of a separate programme strand for women did not reappear until *Woman's Hour* started in 1946. This does not however mean that women were treated equally. Susan Briggs notes: 'From the start, men patronised women listeners. "It is the little things that so often influence the mind of a woman," wrote Sinclair Russell in 1922' (Briggs 1981: 61).

The origins of female gendered radio are explored by Kate Lacey in Chapter 4 – a fascinating study of the way that *Frauenfunk* (women's radio) developed in Germany between 1924 and 1935 which provides fuel for the anti-essentialist arguments of some women and men against separate programmes for women. Scannell for instance defines women's radio as

a distinctive sector of the audience with particular interests and needs for whom a particular style of address and communicative format were needed to produce a feminized discourse by women for women.

(Scannell 1994: 548)

Lacey charts how the private female discourse of *Plauderei* (Chitchat) became public through radio and how the early concept of daytime scheduling functioned to fit in with the supposed domestic structure of a woman's day. She discusses how women's programming was used by the German authorities as a propaganda tool, reinforcing a reactionary and fascist ideological agenda.

In typical BBC fashion *Woman's Hour* was initially presented by a man. The programme has consistently covered issues of interest to women and subjects from a woman's perspective; during its fifty-year history it has attracted both applause and criticism from all sectors of the audience: feminists, 'housewives' and men (the latter group making up at least thirty per cent of its audience). Sally Feldman was editor of the programme from 1991 to 1997 and in Chapter 5 she combines an historical perspective of *Woman's Hour* with a unique insider insight into a key moment in the programme's history – when the programme's name and timeslot were under threat of change.

Restored histories

Woman's Hour is cited by Chapter 6's authors Sheridan Nye, Nicola Godwin and Belinda Hollows as the earliest programme to refer to lesbianism and the only programme to address lesbian representation head-on by appointing a producer for lesbian issues. 'Twisting the Dials: Lesbians on British Radio' restores a major chunk of British broadcasting history to its rightful place. It covers a wide span of lesbian radio including occasional appearances of lesbians in BBC drama and soap opera, the rise of lesbian and gay programming on BBC Radio Five to recent initiatives from independent production companies and community stations. It should be noted that since 'Twisting the Dials' was published there have been several new programmes, particularly on BBC channels, made by and for lesbian and gay audiences. These include Greater Manchester Radio's 'Gaytalk' and the award winning 'Out this Week' (produced by an independent production company) which ran on BBC Radio Five Live for five years until March 1999, attracting 30–40 thousand listeners a week.

The traditional history of radio includes the rise of local BBC and commercial radio stations in the seventies and eighties. Chapter 7, 'Women's Voices', is a snapshot of the sexism of the output of London's local radio in 1981. It was carried out as part of a non-academic but systematic survey of a week of broadcast output of Capital Radio, London Broadcasting Company (LBC) and BBC Radio London. Women's Airwaves who collectively produced the report were scathing in their polemic about the lack of women reporters and presenters, the sexism of many male DJs and the consistent under representation of women's and feminist perspectives on London's Airwaves.

Another previously unwritten history is included in Chapter 8. This charts the development of women's radio stations in the UK, starting with feminist radio activity first promoted by groups like Women's Airwaves. Compared to the expansive Women's magazine industry it does seem extraordinary that the first time women set up their own station in Britain was almost a century after the invention of radio. This chapter documents the activities of a unique decade of broadcasting when six short-term women's community radio stations broadcast in the UK and the first commercial women's station lasted barely a year. It looks forward to the future of feminist radio in community, pirate and Internet radio stations but is pessimistic about the ability for mainstream stations to cater for the mutiplicity of women's interests and survive commercially.

References

Briggs, A. (1961, 1965, 1970, 1979, 1995) *The History of Broadcasting in the United Kingdom*, vols 1–5, Oxford: Oxford University Press.

Briggs, S. (1981) *Those Radio Times*, London: Weidenfeld and Nicolson.

Crisell, A. (1997) *An Introductory History of British Broadcasting*, London: Routledge.

Crook, T. (1998) 'Was she Britains first female black broadcaster?' Radio Studies List Online posting. Available email *radio-studies@mailbase.ac.uk* 23/12/1998.

Hilmes, M. (1997) *Radio Voices. American Broadcasting, 1922–1952*, Minneapolis: University of Minnesota Press.

Lerner, G. (1971) *The Grimke Sisters from South Carolina, Pioneers for Woman's Rights and Abolition*, New York: Schocken Books.

Lewis, P. and Booth, J. (1989) *The Invisible Medium, Public, Commercial and Community Radio*, London: Macmillan.

Lewis, P. and Pearlman, C (1986) *Media and Power, from Marconi to Murdoch*, London: Camden Press.

Okokon, S. (1998) *Black Londoners 1880–1990*, London: Sutton Publishing Limited.

Scannell, P. (1994) 'Editorial', *Media, Culture and Society*, 16: 547–50.

Scannell, P. and Cardiff, D. (1991) *A Social History of British Broadcasting*, vol. 1, Oxford: Blackwell.

Further reading

Baehr, H. and Ryan, M. (1984) *Shut up and Listen: a view from the inside*, London: Comedia. (*An insight into commercial local radio in the early eighties and recommendations for change.*)

Johnson, L. (1988) *The Unseen Voice: A Cultural Study of Early Australian Radio*, London: Routledge.

Karpf, A. 'Women and Radio', *Women's Studies International Quarterly*, vol. 3 no. 1, 1980, reprinted in H. Baehr (ed.) *Women and Media*, London: Pergamon Press, 1980. (*A picture of British radio and women's employment in the industry in the late nineteen seventies. It contains interviews with senior industry figures revealing attitudes towards female employment as DJs. It offers models of radical women's radio from outside Britain.*)

Matheson, H. (1933) *Broadcasting*, Thornton Butterworth.

Murray, J. (1996) *The Woman's Hour*, London: BBC Books. (*A history of women over the 60 years that Woman's Hour has been on the air. Not a history of Woman's Hour as such although it contains interviews with women about how they related to and used the programme.*)

Chapter I

Anne McKay

SPEAKING UP: VOICE AMPLIFICATION AND WOMEN'S STRUGGLE FOR PUBLIC EXPRESSION

From: Kramarae, C. (1988) *Technology and Woman's Voices*, London: Routledge, pp. 187–206

> If a woman knows her business when she tries to speak before the microphone she can create a most favorable impression.
>
> (Jennie Irene Mix 1924)

Devices for artificial voice amplification were developed in the last quarter of the nineteenth century. They were brought into practical application during World War I, and began to be used for public address and for radio during the 1920s. These devices – the microphone, amplifier and speaker – accomplished for the ear what the microscope and telescope did for the eye. Sounds fainter than the footstep of a fly or the voice of a woman could now be amplified and distributed to unlimited numbers of listeners.

Walter Ong (1967; 1974) has suggested that the technology of voice amplification is significant for women's advancement because it helped to open the world of public participation previously closed to them by natural vocal deficiency and reinforced by custom and lack of training. I have tested Ong's assumption by examining evidence surrounding some related questions.

(1) Are women's voices in fact less powerful than men's? What is the cultural and sociobiological evidence? What is the evidence left by observers of women's public speaking in the era before artificial amplification?
(2) How did women make use of amplification devices when they first appeared, and what was the response to them?

My findings, drawn largely from reports and commentary in newspapers and popular journals, suggest a familiar thesis – that when women used the new technology in support of the goals and activities of established institutions, they were applauded at best or ignored at worst. When they attempted to use it in ways that would lead to change in the traditional order and in women's customary roles, their right to use it at all was challenged.

Are women's voices naturally less powerful than men's?

It has long been assumed that most women's voices without artificial amplification are unequal to the demands of big-time public speaking. Ong (1974) states that, 'the typical male voice can articulate words at a far greater volume than can the typical female voice' (8). Only post-pubertal males, and only exceptional ones among them, are said to have had the vocal power needed to address great open air crowds assembled on battlefields, on town squares, and inside vast churches and other public buildings.

An important consequence is that the style and form of public address and later of formal education were developed with little participation by women, and in many ways most compatible to the needs of men. Education, like public speaking, developed as an aggressive, combative, all-male activity centered on attack and defense. Both remained so in the West from the time of the Greeks until the beginnings of this century.

The roots of this style and form lie deep in the intellectual economy of pre-literate cultures – in procedures for managing knowledge, that is, for remembering hard-won information essential for continuity and survival. These procedures are 'formulaic in design and, particularly in public life, tend to be agonistic in operation' (Ong 1974: 2). The exclusion of girls from formal education meant that few had the chance to develop the required intellectual tools of public discourse, even if some had possessed the necessary vocal power.

In the nineteenth century many factors converged to provide more ladders on to public speaking platforms for women, including:

(1) Changing roles and aspirations of women in church settings in America, partly in response to republican ideals and frontier conditions. These prepared women for active, vocal participation in the great nineteenth- and twentieth-century reform movements – temperance, abolition and suffrage (Griffith 1984).

(2) Growth of public gatherings outside the church context, including the lyceum and Chautauqua movements. These provided new arenas for women's public speaking, even though frequently limited to traditionally women's subjects and roles (Bode 1956; Gould 1961; Harrison and Detzer 1958; Morrison 1974).

(3) Rapid industrialization and the resultant growth of cities, promoting large-scale social movements, led and followed by women.

Direct witnesses to the public speaking of nineteenth- and twentieth-century women in response to these forces, prior to artificial amplification, provide cause to question the absolute primacy of vocal debility in accounting for women's long silence in public:[1]

> Her voice was deep toned and heavy, and well suited to a public speaker. She sometimes spoke in large houses, and even in the open air; and was distinctly heard by large audiences. . . . In the pulpit her appearance was bold and commanding. She used but few gestures, but her manner was such as to gain the attention of those who heard.
>
> (Said of Salome Lincoln, a female preacher; in Davis 1843: 22)

> I remember being one of five thousand who listened to her in Hyde Park, and I shared the general delight in her musical voice and the force of her logic.
>
> (Said of Eleanor Marx; in Rosebury 1973: 45)

> [Her] voice is of small compass, but before an audience it is so excellently 'pitched' and is used with such clarion-like effect that every word, as it comes in soft, measured cadence, can be heard.
>
> (Said of Mrs. Russell Cooke; in Dolman 1897: 677)

The full complement of enabling and disabling factors for pre-microphone women speakers is summed up in the following description of a talented nineteenth-century orator, Lady Henry Somerset:

> As was to be expected, questions of the heart rather than the intellect, questions of moral and spiritual well-being, have been the most effective in leading women to undertake the work of the platform. But for the temperance movement, it is exceedingly doubtful whether Lady Henry Somerset, for example, would have become one of the most widely known public speakers of her time. Her ladyship first discovered that she possessed the gift of eloquence at temperance meetings held in the neighborhood of her Herefordshire estate, and it was through the British Women's Temperance Association that she soon had opportunities of addressing gatherings that numbered several thousand. . . . Whether she is addressing five hundred or five thousand, Lady Somerset is always audible to everyone of her audience. . . . Endowed by nature with a voice clear and musical, but not at all strong, her Ladyship acquired, by two or three years of constant practice, the art of making herself heard without strain or apparent effort. She would take her maid to a meeting, post her at its farthest point, and by signals learn whether or not she was succeeding in filling the hall with her voice. This is the secret of Lady Somerset's great success on the platform, coupled with a rare faculty for seizing hold of the strongest points in her case and presenting them in vivid and graphic speech.
>
> (Dolman 1897: 679–80)

Many of these women were identified with powerful, influential men. The few who were not were unusually endowed with intellectual and educational resources and with personal dynamism rare in either gender, which helped them overcome the problem which may be more critical than vocal or oratorical ability – legitimation of their right to speak publicly at all.

The anti-slavery platform perhaps provides the best evidence of the importance of such legitimation. In 1898, a professor of public speaking reminisced about his first 'teachers' on the abolition circuit:

> [I] cannot remember a really poor speaker; as Emerson said, 'eloquence was dog-cheap' there. The cause was too real, too vital, too immediately pressing upon heart and conscience, for the speaking to be otherwise than alive. . . . [M]y own teachers were the slave women who came shyly before the audience . . . women who, having once escaped, had, like Harriet Tubman, gone back again and again into the land of bondage to bring away their kindred and friends.
> (Higginson 1898: 188)

There, all questions of vocal and oratorical ability and of propriety were put aside by the public's intense interest in what slave women had to say.

The testimony of women who themselves became skilled in oratory is also instructive. A Mrs. Phillips was described in 1894 as one of England's brightest and most successful political speakers. At first, she says, she had a great prejudice against women on the platform. 'Now I am more than reconciled, and I fully appreciate the value of public speech. I consider that it is the revival of one of the noblest of all arts, and should take a place in education, and in recreation as well, alongside with writing books and reading them.'

Asked her advice for women who wished to follow her example, she said,

> Take trouble. I often say to women who feel it their duty to speak, but find it so difficult: 'Do you take as much trouble in trying to make a speech as you would in learning French verbs or cooking an omelette? Why should you expect to make a speech without taking the trouble and going through the drudgery which would be absolutely essential to excellence in a very much easier department of work?'
> (Woman as . . . , *Review of Reviews*, June 1894: 709)

Mrs. Phillips was herself trained in elocution but recommended study of voice production rather than elocution.[2]

Temperance leader Frances Willard (1839–1898) summed up the situation as she saw it in 1888:

> Formerly the voices of women were held to render them incapable of public speech, but it has been discovered that what these voices lack in sonorosity they supply in clearness, and when women singers outrank all others, and women lecturers are speaking daily to assemblies numbering from one to ten thousand,

this objection vanishes. It is probably no more 'natural' to women to have feeble voices than it is for them to have long hair.

(Willard 1888: 53)

Some sociobiological evidence about the power of female voices

Evidence gathered over the past fifty years on sexual dimorphism indicates that gender alone is often a poor predictor of general physical ability. The difficulty of abstracting gender expectations and social norms from 'scientific' evidence can be seen in a study of men's and women's voices made at Bell Laboratories in the mid-1920s.

The conclusion drawn from a series of experiments comparing voices was that women's were equal to men's in *loudness*, but significantly less *intelligible*:

> The experiments which revealed this information were designed to measure the relative difficulty with which the fundamental sounds were perceived when uttered by male and female speakers. Each speaker uttered a hundred simple English words; and observers recorded the words in the usual manner of an articulation test. . . . The percentage of the various vowel and consonant sounds which were correctly perceived was thus ascertained for each of forty speakers.
>
> At the same time the loudness with which the various sounds were spoken was automatically recorded. . . . [M]easurements . . . showed that on the average a woman's voice is as loud as that of a man although individuals differ widely. . . . In the case of the women the enunciation, or articulation, of the vowels was on the average a few per cent less than for the men, and the consonant articulation was about ten per cent less.

(Steinberg 1927: 153)

The author attributes the greater difficulty in understanding female speech to two factors.

(1) Women's higher fundamental tone (250 cycles per second at the lowest end of the speaking range, on the average) produces only one-half as many audible overtones as a man's voice (125 cycles at the lower end of its range).
(2) 'Auditory masking,' whereby if women's speech (or any high-pitched tone) is *loud*, the higher frequencies are obliterated by the ear itself. (It is not mentioned that a similar masking occurs with low frequencies when they are loud.) The author concludes that 'It thus appears that nature has so designed woman's speech that it is always most effective when it is of soft and well modulated tone.'

(Steinberg 1927: 154)

More recent studies suggest that physique may be far less important than acculturation in producing gender-specific variations in speech. In their study of the factors enabling identification of a speaker as male or female, Sachs *et al.* (1973) made some observations that are relevant here:

> There are . . . some rather puzzling aspects to the actual acoustic disparities that exist between adult male and female speakers. . . . [Reanalysis of previous studies suggests that] acoustic differences are greater than one would expect if the sole determining factor were simply the average anatomical difference that exists between adult men and women. It is possible that adult men and women modify their articulation of the same phonetic elements to produce acoustic signals that correspond to the male-female archetypes. In other words, men tend to talk as though they were bigger, and women as though they were smaller, than they actually may be.
>
> (Sachs *et al.* 1973: 75)

In tests with preadolescent girls and boys, matched by size, listeners were almost always able to correctly identify the speakers by gender.

> If there is no average difference in articulatory mechanism size, the differences . . . observed could arise from differential use of the anatomy. The children could be learning culturally determined patterns that are viewed as appropriate for each sex. Within the limit of his anatomy, a speaker could change the formant pattern by pronouncing vowels with phonetic variations, or by changing the configuration of the lips. Rounding the lips will lengthen the vocal tract, and lower the formants. Spreading the lips will shorten the vocal tract, and raise the formants. The characteristic way some women have of talking and smiling at the same time would have just this effect.
>
> (Sachs *et al.* 1973: 80–81)

The first microphones and amplifiers ('loudspeakers')

Techniques for voice amplification are surely as old as public speaking itself. They include manipulation of physical and acoustic space, such as in the amphitheater, and devices based on the horn, such as the speaking trumpet and the megaphone.

The *microphone* is one of three developments based on the transmission of sound vibrations by electromagnetism. The other two, the telephone and the phonograph, are closely connected in the order and method of their development.

As early as 1856, the principle of the first microphone was articulated, and primitive microphones were, of course, part of the first telephones which appeared in the mid 1870s. But their full development as instruments of public address and for radio occurred during World War I, when their value in detection of enemy bomber-dirigibles and submarines was realized (Watt 1878; Du Moncel 1879; Listening for submarines 1915; Aerial range-finding . . . 1915).

Contemporary estimations of the power and impact of some of the first microphones are instructive in the light of later objections to their use by women.

'[T]he steps of a fly walking on the stand are clearly heard, and give the sensation of a horse's tread; and even a fly's scream, especially at the moment of death, is said . . . to be audible' (Du Moncel 1879, 146). 'It conveys speech or music, or the slightest inflections of accent and *timbre*, with perfect distinctness . . .' (Watt 1878, 39).

Fig 1.1 Collecting book donations to be sent to World War I soldiers. Women speaking loudly in public during World War I seem to have been well accepted when it was in support of the war effort (National Archives)

While the microphone converts soundwaves into electrical signals of corresponding wave form, the *loudspeaker* is based on devices for converting electrical signals back into soundwaves – a microphone in reverse (Tucker 1978, 1265). The acoustical problems of loudspeakers have always been very difficult because of the unpredictable and often uncontrollable effects of the environments in which they are used, such as time lag, wind effects, echos and feedback characteristics in building and outdoor spaces.

[. . .]

Women on early radio

Women's voices amplified by radio caused controversy from the beginning. The intimacy of the medium perhaps proved startling to women and men alike, particularly when women performed as announcers.

Then, as now, the job included extempore speaking as well as reading of program information and news. The announcer is the 'presiding officer,' and it should be recalled that only seventy-five years prior to the beginning of radio broadcasting, in 1848 at the women's rights convention at Seneca Falls, the organizers dared not preside over the meeting themselves, but delegated that honor to their husbands (Griffith 1984, 55).

The transition, from the necessarily exaggerated style of the platform to the one-on-one of radio, was not achieved overnight. Men as well as women announcers were accused of monotony in pitch, of poor diction and grammar, and of being either too *chummy* and offensively cordial or too cold and distant (Mix, August 1924, 334; September 1924, 392).

Women nevertheless came under particularly intense fire. Cheris Kramarae (1984) has documented the story of Mrs. Giles Borrett, the British Broadcasting Corporation's first female announcer at the BBC. Though highly praised for her performance during a three-month 'trial' in 1933, her contract was abruptly terminated. Reasons were never specified exactly, but speculations ranged along a familiar gamut, from allegations of listeners' objections to a woman's voice in the announcer's role to objections that, as a married woman, she was taking a man's job.

Attitudes parallel to those in Britain were prevalent in the United States. NBC's first female announcer was appointed in 1935. She was Elsie Janis, an 'actress, writer, and imitator,' described by *Newsweek* as 'mature but still merry.' The only woman among twenty-six announcers, her employer said that he was not

quite sure what type of program her hoarse voice is best suited for, but he is certain she will read no more Press-Radio news bulletins. Listeners complained that a woman's voice was inappropriate. For any other sort of announcing job, however, Miss Janis is well equipped. 'I can even push all the buttons on the control board,' boasted the 44-year-old ex-vaudevillist.

(Radio announcer . . . 1935: 24)

The radio broadcast debate with Jennie Irene Mix

A debate about women's voices was conducted in the pages of *Radio Broadcast* magazine, a popular journal featuring technical and consumer information for non-specialist radio enthusiasts. Jennie Irene Mix wrote a column called 'The listeners' point of view' from April 1924 until her death in April 1925.

Mix was described as a woman of 'striking personality,' and her column was the 'first attempt to present sound radio program criticism in any magazine.' Her qualifications were impressive. Well trained in music, she was a published critic and a correspondent from major European and American cities to a number of American newspapers. The column included her remarks on programs and personalities and analysis of the 'new world of radio' (The listeners' . . . July 1925).

One topic she took on with gusto was the suitability of women's voices for announcing. The discussion began in June of 1924 and continued even after her death, when the column was written by men. It is clear from her remarks that women performed many roles in early, pre-network radio, including that of announcer.

A reader had written to her on his experience as a dealer in phonograph records; he reported that the public refused to buy recordings of women talking. Manufacturers lost several thousands of dollars, he wrote, before they learned that the public will not pay money to listen to the talking record of a woman's voice. His interpretation was that the voice of a woman when she cannot be seen 'is very undesirable, and to many, both men and women, displeasing.'

Mix responds, 'This is interesting. And when one stops to consider the matter it is impossible to recall a phonograph record of a monologue by a woman. Yet, some of the highest paid women in vaudeville are the women heard only in monologues' (Mix, August 1924, 332).

She invited reader's comments. One station director observed that:

For certain types of radio work I consider that a woman's voice is very essential; but for announcing, a well modulated male voice is the most pleasing to listen to. I have absolutely nothing against a woman's announcing, but really do believe that unless a woman has the qualifications known as 'showman's instinct,' it really does become monotonous. As a general thing, a woman's voice is considerably higher pitched than a man's voice and sometimes becomes distorted.

(Mix, September 1924: 393)

A manager of two New York stations complained about the quality of transmission of the female voice but acknowledged the utility of women announcers who knew their subject:

We use, of course, just as every other station, a great many women speakers on various subjects, but in no case does the female voice transmit as well as that of the man. As a general thing it does not carry the volume of the average male

23

voice. As far as women announcers are concerned, we have never used them with the exception of Miss Bertha Brainard, who occasionally broadcasts theatrical material or announces a play being broadcast directly from the stage. In this case she is used because she knows a great deal about the theater.

(Mix, September 1924: 393)

Another associate of a Pittsburg station writes that,

[A] woman speaker . . . is rarely a success, and . . . I would permit few women lecturers to appear [on radio]. The reason is that their voices do not carry the appeal, and so, whatever the effect desired, it is lost on the radio audience. One of the chief reasons for this is that few women have voices with distinct personality. It is my opinion that women depend upon everything else but the voice for their appeal. Their voices are flat or they are shrill, and they are usually pitched far too high to be modulated correctly.

Another reason is that women on the radio somehow don't seem able to become familiar with their audiences, to have that clubby feeling toward the listeners which is immediately felt and enjoyed.

(Mix, September 1924: 391–2)

William Cunningham, writing in *Colliers* at the same time, called the radio microphone itself the 'veiled lady' – the centerpiece of a padded room, the object of near veneration. 'It's the . . . suggestion of thousands of silent listeners out beyond her somewhere, ready and able to hear the very breath you draw, that chills the feet and shackles the speech of the broadcasting neophyte no matter how facile or voluble he may be from the lecture platform' (Cunningham 1924, 24).

The ideal radio voice, according to Cunningham, was a baritone. Tenors and female singers reproduced less satisfactorily, but so did basses, who could 'run into wolf tones.' Vocal power, he thought, was not the problem. 'The operator on the roof can supply the power. What the operator can't supply is life, color, vivacity and tone. These are the things the microphone demands' (24, 48).

Jennie Irene Mix made her own position clear in a review of the radio broadcasts of the 1924 political conventions:

Speaking before the microphone during those conventions were many men (far too many), all of whom should have proved that they knew something about the use of the voice and about diction when addressing an audience. . . . But the large majority of them pitched their voices too high and adopted a booming aggressive tone . . . [that was] intolerable to hear. . . . Many of them gave the impression that they were talking through whiskers that had been allowed to go uncut since the last election. But the moment someone rose to speak who had even a halfway idea of enunciation, and how to poise the tones, that speaker . . . was as plainly understood as if he had been in the very room where the listeners sat.

Which brings us back to women radio speakers. At these conventions some of them had it all over the men. Occasionally one heard a woman who talked through the top of her head. . . . But there were others who came near to being ideal orators. Voices perfectly poised, flexible in pitch, and faultless diction. . . . These conventions proved conclusively that if a woman knows her business when she tries to speak before the microphone she can create a most favorable impression.

(Mix, September 1924, 394–5)

When Mix died the following April, the subject was initially dropped, to be revived briefly by one of her successors who gave a report of a survey.

Men vs. Women as Announcers.
[F]urther light has been cast upon the subject by a questionnaire conducted by WJZ. A canvass of 5000 listeners resulted in a vote of 100 to 1 in favor of men as announcers. . . .

It is difficult to say why the public should be so unanimous about it. One reason may be that most receiving sets do not reproduce perfectly the higher notes. A man's voice 'takes' better. It has more volume. Then, announcers cover sporting events, shows, concerts, operas and big public meetings. Men are naturally better fitted for the average assignment of the broadcast announcer.

[P]erhaps the best reason suggested for the unpopularity of the woman's voice over the radio is that it usually has too much personality. . . . Only male announcers, and only a few of them, have been able to strike the right key, equally remote from the majesty of Hamlet's father's ghost and the sweetness of a night club hostess.

(Wallace 1926: 44–5)

'Radio for women'

At the same time, 'radio for women' was gaining in popularity, both as a retailing and as a programming strategy. The idea was to interest women in listening to and buying radios (Wood 1924; Radio for women 1925). *Radio Retailing* magazine began a nationwide campaign in 1925. Part of the plan included 'radio teas' to gather groups of women to be addressed by radio. Radio dealers gave demonstrations in homes and stores at the times when special women's programs were on the air. The magazine states that, 'This plan presents a great and important opportunity for the radio industry to accomplish a long-desired aim – to get women equally interested in radio reception as are men.' The programs produced for this campaign included speakers of both sexes, but women speakers were frequently limited to 'women's subjects.'

Women and men alike had to learn to perform effectively on radio. But the statement that the equipment was not suited for women's voices was nearly always coupled with remarks about other personal qualities that were far more important in disqualifying them.

The radio soprano

The soprano did, it seems, present the first radio engineers with difficult technical problems. *Scientific American* addressed the issue in 1928. An elderly gentleman is described, demanding adjustment of his new radio set over which he was hearing 'nothing but screeching sopranos.' A survey is cited, showing 'a general dislike for the radio soprano.' Three reasons are given. Dr. J. C. Steinberg of Bell Laboratories is quoted, stating that, first,

> women are found to talk less distinctly than men. Secondly, the speech characteristics of women, when changed to electrical impulses, do not blend with the electrical characteristics of our present day radio equipment. Thirdly, the demand of the radio public for radio equipment to meet their aural fancy had led to design of equipment that impairs the reproduction of a soprano's voice.
>
> (Rider 1928: 334)[3]

Conclusion

Does the development of voice amplification devices deserve as much credit for promoting women's advancement as Walter Ong suggests? It is certain that these devices helped to complete the transformation of public speech from a formal, combative, argumentative style to a more pacific, intimate and informal mode, better aligned with female conditioning. Nevertheless, it seems clear that even with the microphone on the platform, women have had to continue to struggle for legitimation of their right to speak publicly, particularly when their topics or roles have been in conflict with those of men of influence.

Notes

1 While Ong points out that 'there has been no female William Jennings Bryan or Everett Dirksen,' he acknowledges in a brief note the inhibiting association of women vocal in public with promiscuity (Ong 1974: 8, 12: note 30).
2 *Elocution* was a form of oral reading which developed in the 1870s and 'concentrated on dramatic presentation of the written word, using a spectrum of set-piece poses to emphasize various phrases in a memorized passage.' The elocution movement is considered to be the last attempt of the old-style oratory, as Ong describes it, to hold the stage (*This Fabulous Century* 1970: 147).
3 A tone consists of a fundamental tone plus related higher tones – overtones or harmonics. The quality of any particular tone is the result of the relative intensity and amplitude of the fundamental tone and its associated harmonics. 'Remove all the harmonics and the tone has been changed to a sound devoid of mellowness, sweetness and richness.' In the higher range of a soprano's voice, fewer harmonics are produced, and apparently the higher of these were not faithfully transmitted and reproduced by the equipment of the day. The problem, Rider says, was further exacerbated by the regulation of the time, which limited transmission to 5,000 cycle sidebands. Harmonics of a high C would be over 8,000 cycles per second and would not have been transmitted (Rider 1928, 335).

References

'Aerial range-finding with electrical "ears": a microphone system of detecting invisible airships and determining ranges.' (1915) *Scientific American*, 30 October, 377.

Bode, C. (1956) *The American Lyceum: Town Meeting of the Mind*, New York: Oxford University Press.

Cunningham, W. (1924) 'How the veiled lady scares 'em.' *Colliers, The National Weekly* 7:24 (25 October) 24, 38.

Davis, A. H. (1843) *The Female Preacher or Memoir of Salome Lincoln, Afterwards the Wife of Elder Junia S. Mowry*, Providence: Elder J. S. Mowry.

Dolman, F. (1897) 'Women speakers in England,' *Cosmopolitan* 22:6 (April), 676–80.

Du Moncel, T. A. L. (1879) *The Telephone, the Microphone and the Phonograph*, New York: Harper & Brothers.

'Foreign waves dim message.' (1920) *The New York Times*, 2 May, section 1, 14, col. 3.

Gould, J. E. (1961) *The Chautauqua Movement: An Episode in the Continuing American Revolution*, New York: State University.

Griffith, E. (1984) *In Her Own Right: The Life of Elizabeth Cady Stanton*, New York: Oxford University Press.

Harrison, H. P. and K. Detzer (1958) *Culture Under Canvas: The Story of Tent Chautauqua*, New York: Hastings House.

Higginson, T. W. (1898) 'On the outskirts of public life.' *Atlantic Monthly* February, 188–99.

Kramarae, C. (1984) 'Resistance to women's public speaking.' English version of 'Nachrichten zu sprechen gestatte ich der Frau nicht: Widerstand gegenüber dem öffentlichen Sprechen von Frauen.' In Senta Trömell-Plötz, ed. *Gewalt durch Sprache*. Frankfurt: Fischer Taschenbuch Verlag, 203–28.

'The listeners' point of view' (1925) *Radio Broadcast*, July, 343.

'Listening for submarines' (1915) *The Literary Digest* 51:26 (25 December), 1473–4.

Mix, J. I. (1924) 'The listeners' point of view,' *Radio Broadcast*, August, 332–8; September, 391–7.

Morrison, T. (1974) *Chautauqua: A Center for Education, Religion, and the Arts in America*. Chicago: University of Chicago Press.

'Mrs. Glass's appeal heard on Victory Way' (1919) *The New York Times*, 23 April, 4, col. 4.

Ong, W. J. (1967) *The Presence of the Word: Some Prolegomena for Cultural and Religious History* New Haven: Yale University Press.

Ong, W. J. (1974) 'Agonistic structures in academia: past to present' *Interchange* 5:4, 1–12.

'Radio announcer: The "sweetheart of the AEF" joining NBC,' (1935) *Newsweek*, 12 January, 24.

'Radio for women' (1925) *Literary Digest*, 28 November, 20.

Rider, J. F. (1928) 'Why is radio soprano unpopular?' *Scientific American*, 28 October, 334–7.

Rosebury, A. (1973) 'Eleanor Marx, daughter of Karl Marx: personal reminiscences,' *Monthly Review* 24:8 (January), 29–49.

Sachs, J., P. Lieberman and D. Erickson, (1973) 'Anatomical and cultural determinants of male and female speech', in *Language Attitudes: Current Trends and Prospects*, Washington, DC: George Washington University Press, 74–84.

Steinberg, J. C. (1927) 'Understanding women,' *Bell Laboratories Record* 3:5 (January) 153–4.

This Fabulous Century: 1870–1900 (1970) New York: Time-Life Books.

Tucker, D. G. (1978) 'Electrical communication,' *A History of Technology*, Vol. 7. Trevor I. Williams, ed. Oxford: Clarendon Press, 1220–67.

'Urges note purchases as a thanksgiving,' (1919) *The New York Times*, 26 April, 6, cols 4–5.

Wallace, J. (1926) 'The listeners' point of view,' *Radio Broadcast*, November, 44–5.

Watt, A. (1878) *The Microphone, With Notes on the Telephone and Phonograph*, London: Houlston & Sons.

'Will carry voices to all: sound amplifying devices to enable delegates to hear speakers' (1920) *The New York Times*, 4 June, 2, col. 2.

Willard, F. E. (1888) *Woman in the Pulpit*, Boston: D. Lothrop.

'Women as public speakers: advice to beginners,' by Mrs. Phillips, (1894) *Review of Reviews* 9 (June), 709.

Wood, L. (1924) 'Making radio attractive to women,' *Radio Broadcast*, January, 221–2.

Chapter 2

Olive Shapley

BROADCASTING A LIFE

From: Shapley, O. (1996), *Broadcasting a Life*, London: Scarlett Press, pp. 36–40; 48–54; 124–9; 131

1934–37 – Recruitment to the BBC

[. . .] On my first day in the Manchester studios we had a meeting in the office of the programme director, Archie Harding. His extreme left-wing views had embarrassed the BBC so much that they felt they had no other option than to exile him to the north where he could not 'do so much damage'. He had transformed the BBC North Region with the help of an assortment of talented people, many of whom were to become 'greats' in the field of broadcasting. In the mid 1930s Harding began to experiment with the outrageous idea that 'ordinary' people might have something worth saying on the wireless. He recruited an aspiring poet and writer, D.G. Bridson, and together they began taking the first, tentative steps towards what we now know as the 'documentary'. The first of these programmes was called Harry Hopeful and it began in 1935. Bridson went on to produce a series of innovative industrial features called *Cotton, Steel, Wool* and *Coal*.

When one considers today's technical wizardry the problems of that time seem unbelievable. In 1935 we still had not been given our mobile recording van, which was primitive enough but a boon to us in those early days. Indeed, very little of what was broadcast was recorded at all. This meant that the reality of a situation had to be recreated in the studio, using scripted material, sound effects and trust in good luck. Bridson wanted to get as close to the real thing as possible. To do this he went to people in their homes or workplaces and, after taking notes of the interviews, scripted them. Armed with these scripts, he returned to his subjects with a portable microphone and recorded them reading back their own words. This was by way of a rehearsal. The actual programme was sent out live from the studios in front of an audience which included the relatives and friends of those taking part. Today, as I watch Esther Rantzen or any other television reporter or commentator careering down the Uxbridge Road with microphone in hand, able to record, edit, broadcast, all with the utmost simplicity and sophistication, I cannot help thinking of those early days and the painstaking way we went about achieving our aims.

After that first meeting with Archie Harding I was asked to stay behind. When the room was empty apart from the two of us, he extended his hand and said, 'Welcome, comrade.' I was never a very devout communist, but I could tell that I was among friends. But despite Harding's influence broadcasting at that time was a formal affair. The BBC was a very gentlemanly place. Indeed, there was only one other senior woman on the staff at Manchester. On the first day I said to her, 'I know nothing about broadcasting; you must help me,' and she said, 'The first thing you have to know, dear, is how the gentlemen like their tea.'

In those days every new BBC staff member had to meet Sir John Reith. Reith had been appointed general manager of the British Broadcasting Company in 1922 and was the first director-general of the British Broadcasting Corporation from 1927 to 1938. He therefore directly shaped the way broadcasting developed before the war and indeed the legacy of his high-minded vision of public service broadcasting persists to this day. Staff were summoned by a printed card along the lines of, 'You will wait upon the director-general', with your name and the date and time filled in. I went to London at the appointed time and, very nervous, was ushered into the great man's office, the only room in Broadcasting House, it was said, to have a coal fire. Reith was immensely tall, with a scar right down one side of his face from his severe war injuries. He seemed to uncoil from behind his desk as he stood up to shake my hand. 'Good afternoon, Miss Shape-ly,' he said, in his precise Scottish voice. He was the first, but by no means the last, person to mispronounce my name; 'Miss Shapely' has plagued me throughout my life. The meeting was brief and could hardly be described as a relaxed conversation. Reith's opening remark did not help. Referring to a senior staff member in Manchester, he said, 'Tell me, is . . . still drinking?'

Back at the BBC in Manchester I found the atmosphere more congenial. I worked hard, but occasionally found time in the lunch hour to go with some colleagues to dance at the Ritz Ballroom. I had started ballroom dancing at Oxford, where I broke the rules to go dancing with my boyfriend, Peter. I absolutely loved it and became rather good. Immediately before being accepted by the BBC I had actually started a job teaching at a dancing school in London. Who knows what might have happened with that career if I had not applied for the BBC job!

I took to my new job and its location with alacrity. I was in the north of England at last and enjoyed finding out about its people and customs. I found an honesty and a courage in the people of the towns I visited, which I found attractive and rather touching qualities. In a hat shop shortly after my arrival I watched a customer trying on several hats, while the assistant stood by politely. The customer finally turned round in one hat to the assistant, who said, 'Eh, love, you look *terrible*.'

London was still a very far-away place and in the 1930s the north was made up of many tightly knit communities, many people never venturing much further than Blackpool or Southport, and then only once a year during Wakes Week. Everybody knew everybody else's business and amid the stereotypical 'net curtain twitchers' there was support and help to be got from one's neighbours. My first friend in Manchester was Thomas Matthews, who was a violinist with the Hallé Orchestra. Through him I met his sister, Mamie Rogerson, and her husband, Haydn, a cellist. One evening I rang the Rogersons and was told by the telephonist at the local exchange, 'Oh no, I can't put you through. Mrs Rogerson is spending the evening with Mrs Wadsworth and her Haydn is practising his cello and she doesn't want him disturbing.'

This was a warm and courageous place, but it was also a restricted one. For those who did not conform, life in those towns could be cruel. I felt that I was lucky to be part of a group that stood outside some of the ethics of the society we lived in. I had never totally conformed and there were many like me at the BBC.

Looking back, I think it was in the area of relationships and sex that some of us were rather ahead of our time. Nevertheless, there were definitely different standards for men and women. It was a new idea for a woman to explore her sexuality and one that it was not really wise to advocate publicly, especially if you were one of the women doing it. There was pressure both from society and from family to get married at some point. The raising of a family was the female's raison d'être and sexual activity was the man's pleasure and a woman's duty. Contraception was left to the discretion of the man and, when unwanted pregnancies did occur, it was reasonably easy for a man to avoid any responsibility in the matter. Unmarried mothers were outcasts from society and very often the only help at hand were the horrific backstreet abortionists.

A few weeks after joining the BBC I found that I was pregnant, and knew this meant that I would certainly be fired. The father had a senior position and, unusually, was put in a situation whereby he might lose his own job because of the incident. It was because of this, and not out of sympathy for me, that he eventually gave me the financial help I needed to avoid a scandal.

There was no question of my letting the pregnancy continue. I simply did not feel ready to bear a child, and the stigma of having an illegitimate baby was very great then and did not change until years afterwards. I had also just started a job that I could see I was going to love. So, I decided to seek an abortion. In the end I had to go to three different people. The whole thing was extremely dangerous and very painful. The first man I went to literally told me to sit down on a stool and drop my drawers, and he stuck something up. This did not work at all and in fact I could have died from the injuries. Then I went to a woman, again locally, but still the abortion did not happen. Eventually I went to another, ghastly, woman in Kent who charged the earth. By this time I was pretty far on in the pregnancy and the father had had to give me the money I needed to finish the job. The woman I went to had to flee the country very soon after my visit. Her boyfriend came in and watched the proceedings without so much as a by your leave and afterwards

I was shaking so much that she tied me down to the bed with ropes. I had been delivered of two perfectly formed baby boys, twins.

I was still very ill. In the end a nursing home in Manchester said that they would try to clear up all the terrible mistakes had been made. However, they insisted that my family was told. I summoned the courage to tell my mother and she came up. She was wonderful, absolutely wonderful. She supported me entirely, though it must have been a terrific shock for her.

My new life in Manchester and the BBC resumed and I immersed myself in what looked like being a fascinating career ahead of me. [. . .]

1937–39 – Radio documentaries

The first stage of my early career at the BBC lasted from December 1934 to the end of 1939. For almost three years I stayed in my position as *Children's Hour* organiser, North Region. Then, after a brief spell in the staff training school, I was promoted to assistant producer, North Region.

Despite my self-confessed romantic attitude to my new home, I was certainly not oblivious to the economic and social conditions around me. In the early 1930 the depression was at its height and for many Britons, but particularly those in industrial areas, it was a time of extreme deprivation and suffering. Once I was taken to see a family living in indescribable poverty in a derelict mill, illegally I suppose, the five children sleeping head to foot like sardines in a broken down bed. Nobody could stay politically neutral after seeing things like that. It affected all of us.

Slowly this was being reflected in the programmes that were being made. Our programme ideas, however, could not have advanced much further without some crucial technical developments. In 1937 the Manchester studios were refitted with the latest equipment, including the new and improved dramatic control panel already in use in London. We also acquired our new mobile recording unit. I was fascinated by the possibility of combining these facilities, and began to concentrate my work on making programmes in which recorded actuality was mixed, through the panel, with studio presentation and commentary. Paddy Scannell and David Cardiff have described very clearly the recording innovations:

> The recording van was twenty-seven feet long and weighed, when fully loaded, more than seven tons. Its maximum speed was twenty miles an hour. Inside were two turntables, each operated by a technician. The recording time of each disc was a maximum of four minutes. As one disc came to an end, recording was continued on the other turntable, thus securing uninterrupted continuity of a sort. The new equipment could accommodate up to six discs at a time, with remote control to lower the pick-up head onto the precise groove at which to begin the required recorded insert.

Two recording vans had originally been commissioned by London to collect topical items for inclusion in the news bulletins. But they were unsuited for this and were passed over to the regions. Wales, Scotland and West Region, however, had many hilly and narrow roads which the vans could not negotiate. So by the time one of them arrived in Manchester there was some uncertainty as to whether they had any useful purpose at all. Bridson had used it for *Steel* but only for background effects. (Scannell and Cardiff, 1991, p. 345)

When I had the chance of using this equipment I tried to structure my programmes in a straightforward way, with a narrative commentary introducing and linking the recorded material which formed the substance of the programme. This is how Wilfred Pickles introduced my first 'actuality', as we called it then. It was *£.s.d.: A Study in Shopping*.

> Good evening everybody. Before we get going in this shopping programme there are one or two things I want to tell you about it. Now it's what I call a 'homely' programme. No flourish of trumpets about it, you know, but the sort of programme you'll recognise yourselves in maybe. The records you're going to hear were made at a little town called Sowerby Bridge. Sowerby Brigg I call it, coming from that part of the country myself.

I remember very clearly venturing out for the first time with the enormous recording van to prepare this programme. We caused a sensation when we parked the thing in Sowerby Bridge. I, feeling an utter fool and holding a microphone at the end of a long lead, disappeared into the side door of the Co-operative Stores and recorded a conversation between a shop assistant and a millworker called Joe Lum from down the valley, who wanted to buy what he called 'a pair of booits'. People were not used then to having a microphone thrust in front of them with the instruction to 'be natural – just be natural!' The three of us who were there that day sweated over our little recording but, in a humble way, I think we were making broadcasting history. The programme was, of course, received very calmly at the time except by the head of programmes. Nevertheless, he eventually said, 'All right, go ahead, do some more.' And so for a year or two I lived a strange life, in the cabs of long-distance lorries, down coalmines, in dosshouses, on longboats on the canals. Every so often someone said wistfully, 'You know we gave you this job so you could produce a women's magazine programme,' but nothing could stop me.

By the time I made my last 'documentary' programme during this phase of my career, a year and a half later, I had developed more fully and established my own programme style. For *Canal Journey* I recorded men and women working on the Leeds–Liverpool canal, with the help of a fourteen-year-old, Archie Thompson, whose genuine curiosity inspired very direct questioning. I kept my own linking commentary to a minimum and let the canal people speak for themselves. In my introduction I said:

> On this occasion I went after the human story – as the newspapers say – and tried to get the canal people I met to tell in their own words something of what their life is like. In spite of all the jokes to the contrary they are not a very voluble race and some of them found it hard to believe that anyone could find

the details of their ordinary life interesting and, when they had been reassured on this point, it wasn't very easy for them to put their ideas into words. All the records you'll hear were made without script or rehearsal.

There were some strong dialects. I am not certain whether this should have been a cause for celebration or despair, given our country's confusions and contradictions (still) about dialect and accents. *The Listener* radio critic, though generally complimentary about the programme, was in no doubt; there was too much 'obscure dialect', some participants being 'downright unintelligible', and he was 'prepared to swear that very few Londoners understood more than one word in six' (31 August 1939, p. 446). So much for bringing the voice of the people to the nation!

Despite the apparent problems posed by some 'ordinary' English people in communicating with their fellow countrymen, I believed passionately that broadcasting was at last on the right track. It was very exciting to be part of that change, though at the time, of course, I did not see it in any historical perspective. But Scannell and Cardiff have since commented that I was the first to take the van all over the region to record people talking in their homes, at work and on the streets. They went on to assess my contribution to broadcasting in very flattering terms, suggesting that, singlehanded, I 'brought to maturity the use of recorded actuality as the basis of the radio feature in those last few years before the war' and that my programmes 'broke new grounds for radio both in technique and in their subject matter'. They further commented that 'such reportage, combined with her sympathetic skill as an interviewer (a quite new technique which she had to discover for herself), led one contemporary critic to describe Shapley's programmes as "little masterpieces of understanding and authenticity"' (Scannell and Cardiff, 1991, pp. 345, 347).

Unlike *Canal Journey* there had been no problems of intelligibility in *Broadcasting with the Lid Off*, since the voices we heard were mostly of BBC staff going about their work and they therefore represented a suitably Reithian range of humanity. Not everybody at the BBC relished the exposure at the time, though I think in the end it was generally agreed that our professional integrity had not collapsed around us. I had no doubt that it could only enhance the listeners' legitimate interest in the BBC, and I must admit that I immensely enjoyed conveying the interest and excitement of broadcasting.

Manchester itself played a great part in all our lives at the BBC. Many programmes were hatched in one or another of those dark little basement restaurants where elderly Turks rattled their dominoes and smoked foul-smelling tobacco. The Oyster Bar in Lever Street was where we celebrated; their champagne was incredibly cheap. But Archie Harding also encouraged us to travel. We crossed to Leeds by Nont Sarah's pub in all weathers and struggled over the Buttertubs in snow and ice. We would record a brass band in Barrow-in-Furness in the morning and audition a choir in Newcastle a few hours later, having travelled by way of High Force and Haltwhistle. The whole magnificent north of England was open to us and we took our programmes from every corner of it.

For us, though, the travel was only part of our work, the means to an end. In *Night Journey* I looked at the world of the professionals, the long-distance lorry drivers. It was a fascinating one, which aroused in me great admiration for this section of the workforce, largely unseen and unsung. It was quite an arduous job even reporting on it. One night I rode for ten hours on an eight-ton lorry carrying fourteen tons of chemicals and textiles, while a fine rain fell and I wondered how one would even tackle a car journey on that road. I left no stone unturned in my quest for a full picture. That meant a night in a damp ditch on Shap, with microphone ready to catch the first rumble of the fish lorries as they thundered down from Scotland. The engineer, who was crouched down beside me, asked, 'When's your next programme, Olive?'

'Well,' I said, 'next month we're going down a mine so we can get a microphone to the coal face.'

'Thank God,' he said. 'With any luck, I shall be on holiday.'

In another documentary, *Homeless People*, I tried to convey something of the lives of people who were even more invisible than the lorry drivers. I cast my net very wide: casual wards, night shelters, Salvation Army lodging-houses, hostels, training centres and orphanages. It was a rude awakening for me and, I think, for the listeners, even towards the end of that decade which had seen such poverty and despair. The programme was, of course, mostly very sad, but it by no means painted a depressing picture about human nature; I witnessed great dignity and humanity among both the givers and receivers of help to the homeless. Looking back now on my programme, I see that it both tackled a revolutionary subject for that time and did it in a revolutionary style. Maybe some observers thought that it was not a suitable subject for broadcasting. Documentary producers have always trod a delicate line and it is hard to refute accusations of exploitation and voyeurism. Forty-five years later the television channel, Channel 4, devoted two whole weeks to a season of programmes on homelessness. This interested me, not so much because documentaries are now a major part of broadcasting, but because this topic is still there to be covered and so extensively.

Homeless People was very nearly finished when a newspaper editor in Newcastle told me of a community of French monks settled at Scorton in Yorkshire. Apparently these good people ran a hospital for homeless incurables. He rang them up for me then and there, and it was suggested that I call in that evening on my way back to Manchester. I had a very limited acquaintance with monks and the only thing I could think of was to rub off my lipstick and put on a rather withdrawn look. I need not have worried. When I drove up to the gatehouse, there was an eager young monk hanging out of the window. 'Hello,' he said. 'Wonderful to see you. Now, the first thing you must see is my bedroom!' In his bedroom there was a complete small radio transmitting station; this monk, Brother Clement, was obsessed by radio. Within a few minutes he and I were broadcasting Strauss waltzes to the patients.

It was my programme *Miners' Wives* which created almost the most publicity at the time, and this was no doubt partly because I managed to persuade the BBC to let me take one of the participants abroad, more or less the equivalent of going on Concorde today! First I went and lived for about a week with the Emmerson family in Craghead, a mining village in County Durham. Mr Emmerson was a checkweighman at the local pit. Through the family I got an insight into the life of the whole community, but particularly the problems of the women, who spoke very eloquently for my recordings.

The programme was prepared only six months before war broke out and I thought a European twist would make it more interesting. Our contact in France was an Englishman, in fact the batman in World War One of my BBC colleague Donald Boyd, who had married a Frenchwoman. They lived in Marles-les-Mines, near Béthune, and Mrs Emmerson and I travelled there by train, boat and taxi, and stayed for a week with a family which had three men working in the pits. Mrs Emmerson was naturally apprehensive during our long winter journey, and hated London on the way through. However, as the ancient taxi bumped along the road from Béthune past the familiar-looking pit-head shafts and huge conical slag heaps, her spirits began to rise. When we overtook a group of miners walking along the road in their dark Sunday suits and light caps and mufflers, she turned to me and said, 'You know, lass, they couldn't be anything but miners. I think it's the way they walk.' She settled in to that family, with the help of my rather poor interpreting, as if she had just gone down the road from Craghead. Back in England she spoke in the programme about her impressions of the way of life in the two mining villages.

As is probably clear, I was fascinated by the nuts and bolts of other people's jobs and lives, and one of my programmes looked at twenty-four hours in the life of a big hotel from the staff point of view. *Hotel Splendide* remained discreetly anonymous at the time, but I do remember a very interesting weekend in Scarborough, gathering material for the programme, at the luxurious hotel run by Tom Laughton, the brother of film actor Charles Laughton. Here again, as with my other programmes, the interest of such a setting seemed all too obvious to me, but few broadcasters were yet interested in exploiting all these possibilities. There was certainly more scope for innovation then than now, when we have over seventy years of radio and about forty-five years of television behind us.

[. . .]

1949–53 – *Woman's Hour*

In the autumn of 1946 a new radio programme was launched on the Light Programme in London under the control of Norman Collins, the programme head. It was to be a magazine programme for intelligent women and would deal with 'keeping house, health, children, beauty care and home furnishing' and finish with a short serial reading (Donovan, 1992, p. 289). The 2–3 p.m. timeslot was considered just right, after morning chores and lunch and while doing the washing-up before older children came home from school. This was *Woman's Hour*, which was to become one of the BBC's major success stories and is still going strong.

The complete history of *Woman's Hour*, as devotees will agree, is worthy of its own separate history. Some surprising facts stand out. First, contrary to probable expectations when it started, it has often been at the forefront of changing public perceptions of broadcasting taste. This has meant that at times it has been extremely controversial, in both language and content, some would say subversive. Secondly, its listeners are by no means all women. And thirdly, in 1991 its time change to the mornings provoked a major outcry which has not quite died down.

My own active association with the programme, as presenter and producer, lasted on and off for over twenty years. Since then I have several times had a taste of my own medicine by being interviewed myself. Over all these years people's interest in and attachment to *Woman's Hour* has been brought home to me time and time again by its large correspondence and the questions and discussion about it among the community groups I address. When you are in the studio a great deal of broadcasting seems to be launched into the void and it is sometimes hard to visualise the exact audience. But with *Woman's Hour* I always felt that a large section of the audience was fairly constant, and you knew that they listened yesterday and would probably listen again tomorrow, and might even put pen to paper and write you a letter.

At first the programme had a male presenter. He was soon followed by Joan Griffiths, who in early 1949 was due to leave to go to *Housewives' Choice*. I was offered the position of daily presenter (sometimes called 'commère') and started the job in late February, thus becoming the programme's third presenter in its history. The BBC accommodated the juggling act that this move entailed and paid for my weekly commuting from Manchester for some weeks. When I bought a house in London, Alice and the children joined me.

I presented *Woman's Hour* for the next eighteen months and it was an entirely delightful experience. Though I had to be well prepared for the continuity and other live broadcasting, I found this a less frantic job than that of producer, which I had done so much of in the past. It was the programme's team of producers, by and large, who initiated contacts, made arrangements, scripted, recorded and edited material and put together items for transmission.

Woman's Hour was at that time unique among radio shows. Though it certainly tried to lighten the household chores and give listeners a new interest, albeit an appropriately feminine one, it also tried to open a window on the world outside, in a way which listeners themselves may not have had the time or opportunity to do. So, the programme items were always wide ranging, in both subject matter and format: live discussions and interviews, news digests, straight talks, book reviews and, of course, the daily serial. Inevitably the balance has shifted over the years in tune to the radical changes in women's lives, from predominantly housebound topics to more current affairs and employment-related ones. Today's younger listeners would certainly find much to chuckle over in the early programmes.

As the presenter I was obviously one of the few people in the country who heard the whole programme every day without fail, and people often used to say to me, 'What a lot you must know.' What a lot I *ought* to have known! But although I listened each day across the table from the speakers, and certainly found an enormous amount to interest me, I confess that many ideas went in one ear and out the other. When you are partly responsible for the smooth running of a conveyor belt of items, you can never stand back sufficiently to enjoy anything fully. After all, your job is to make sure the listeners do that.

Our speakers were always interesting, whether or not they were used to public speaking or entertainment of some sort. Some 'pros' could be surprisingly nervous and some novices astonishingly assured. People crumpled scripts so that they sounded like bacon sizzling or a storm at sea, muddled their pages and leant comfortably back in their chairs, to the obvious despair of the programme engineer behind the glass screen. Some were very friendly and some put up a barrier, some were just what you expected them to be, some were very baffling; but they were always fun to meet.

Almost all women liked to look nice when they broadcast; a quick dab of lipstick and comb through the hair seemed to boost people's confidence. Quite often people wore hats in the early days, which was fine by us, and some people kicked off their shoes in the studio. I once discreetly encouraged a woman to take off her new corset between rehearsal and transmission, when I had discovered the cause of her pained expression and delivery. The BBC sent out contracts to contributors beforehand and occasionally people arrived clutching two guineas thinking they paid us for taking part in the programme. We liked to be hospitable, but were careful with the lunchtime sherry when it became clear that by two o'clock some women, who hardly ever drank alcohol, were a bit too relaxed even for *Woman's Hour*.

For our Monday guest slot, later renamed 'Guest of the Week', we invited women who had made a name for themselves in some field or other, and of course forty years ago publicly successful women shone even more brightly in the firmament than they do now because there were even fewer of them. I interviewed Margaret Mead, the American anthropologist, and Mrs Roosevelt appeared in a repeat of my previous interview with her for *Children's Hour*. My former headmistress, Dr Brock, now Dame Dorothy Brock, obliged me yet again by appearing in one of my programmes, and I found myself again wondering rather anxiously whether she thought my splendid education had been put to good use or not. Vera Lynn was one of the nicest people I had ever met; no side, no affectations, just a thoroughly nice person, very ready to chat about her house and her little girl. Dame Edith Evans made an appropriately theatrical impact on the *Woman's Hour* studio. She was by no means a beautiful woman, but was very gracious and no one could take their eyes off her. Guests used to choose a piece of music to follow their talk and she chose a rather sacchariny orchestral piece used in *Daphne Laureola*. As her talk ended the music was faded up, Dame Edith rose from her chair and, with the utmost grace and a mixture of sentimental melancholy and burlesque, began to gyrate slowly round the room. My last glimpse of her was wafting majestically through the studio door to that silly music.

Woman's Hour has never been afraid to tackle difficult topics and I am proud of my own role over the years in helping to push back the frontiers of broadcasting acceptability. Many producers working on the programme have known the rather weary nervousness with which their more challenging suggestions have sometimes been received within the BBC. I used to get stern memos along the lines of, 'If Miss Shapley insists on doing an item on the change of life, we insist on seeing the script first.' We were always very careful to warn listeners about such items, giving their exact duration and advising them to turn down their radio sets if they feared offence. This advice was considered necessary also to protect small children who might be listening with mother after *Listen with Mother*. I used to wonder what the average three-year-old would make of a rather technical talk on venereal disease, but such warnings were taken very seriously. Today's audiences are clearly made of sterner stuff and a good thing it is too.

It was not just medical and sexual topics which were considered daring in the early 1950s. Psychology and human relationships were still largely uncharted territory even in ordinary private conversation, and into this area *Woman's Hour* again leapt fearlessly. I chaired a discussion in 1952 called *Women without Men* between five women, including myself: three 'spinsters', as I called them, a divorcee and myself, a widow. Issues which are commonly explored now on radio and television and in magazines, like women's self-image and role in society, loneliness, deprivation of sex or children, and old age, were ranged over with a good deal of frankness for that time. And, as ever, we found that despite male apprehensions these were definitely not taboo topics for our listeners, who welcomed them.

Not that *Woman's Hour* was all dangerous. I think it was balanced, just as life should be ideally, and sometimes it embraced the fanciful. Looking back I am rather surprised at some of the topics I covered with apparent enthusiasm. I must have got carried away in 1953 by the excitement about the coronation robes of peers and peeresses, which were exhibited before the coronation by Norman Hartnell, the royal dressmaker. Mr Hartnell's newly designed alternative robe for a baroness or viscountess was the first major change in peeresses' robes since the reign of Queen Anne. I found that it was 'charming to look at, could be converted into a useful garment afterwards (or is that the wrong thing to say) and only costs something like £30 or £40'. Of the regalia, I liked best the coronet of a marchioness, consisting of four silver balls and four golden strawberry leaves – 'very pretty indeed'. I also noted with approval Mr Hartnell's little caps with floating veils which could be worn by non-titled guests in the abbey: 'beautiful creations in tulle and net, caught up with sequins and jewelled clips'.

> But the robes themselves are somehow unreal. They're pure story book of course, and also, to me, irresistibly reminiscent of the wet afternoons when you were small and 'dressed up' and acted plays . . . it was hard to realise that men and women were going to wear them solemnly on a proper occasion. But there they were, crimson and gold, velvet and fur, strawberry leaves and ermine tails, all the traditional colours and patterns of pageantry in this island, and it was impossible not to fall a little bit under their spell.

I am sure that the listeners also were spellbound by the coronation robes, given that the whole country was at that time caught up in coronation fever. But beneath

39

such decorous concerns lurked a different Britain, as I discovered in the late 1960s when a woman wrote in about her husband's apparently incurable warts and we asked listeners to send in their suggestions. This item was the unexpected hit of the northern *Woman's Hour* year, and the office felt rather as if it had been transported back to the Middle Ages! Letters came from respectable sounding suburban addresses begging the poor man to put his hands out of the window and make washing motions in the light of the full moon; to let seventeen black snails crawl all over his warts and leave the slime on for three days; to spit on them when he woke up (with 'fasting spit', as several listeners called it); to rub them with the juice of the greater celandine; to take arsenic tablets (which seemed a little drastic); to apply the woolly insides of broad bean pods; to hide a piece of bacon in the ground and not tell anyone where he had hidden it; to become pregnant (not very practical advice to a man); and, of course, to consult his local wart-charmer (we were doubtful if the Yellow Pages could help here).

Listeners were also stirred into action by my newspaper advertisement when preparing the item, *What Size Did You Say, Madam?* This looked at the problems of women and girls with big feet, a topic in which I had an unashamedly personal interest. The letters flowed in, including agonised ones from fathers saying that their family life was dominated by their daughters' large feet. We had clearly touched another nerve. Other *Woman's Hour* crowd pleasers I recall were nits and dental phobia. By contrast my meticulously prepared look at Manchester's religious communities for the *Talkabout* programme was no doubt politely received but produced no ripples.

[...]

On a more personal note, I was also grateful to *Woman's Hour* for at times accommodating without fuss my occasional domestic crises, when children had to be brought in to work. Even around 1950, when they were quite young, I was surprised at my children's respectful response to the tense, purposeful atmosphere of the studio. Supplied with a batch of old BBC scripts, typed on one side only, and a pencil apiece they could be relied upon to draw, in dead silence, trains, cats, 'funny people', houses and, for some reason, dustbins – all my children had a passion for drawing dustbins – while the, to them, interminable voice of *Woman's Hour* flowed on above their heads. As they grew older they started to turn the script papers over, leading at times to a rather alarming broadening of their education; I do remember those change of life scripts!

References

Scannell, P. and Cardiff, D. (1991) A Social History of British Broadcasting, Vol. 1, Oxford: Blackwell.

Chapter 3

Fred Hunter

HILDA MATHESON AND THE BBC, 1926–1940

From: Oldfield, S. (ed.) (1994) *This Working Day World – Women's Lives and Cultures in Britain*, London: Taylor & Francis, pp. 169–74

One of the problems faced in studying the pioneer women in broadcasting is the very ephemeral nature of their product, irretrievably lost in the ether when recording was still virtually unknown. How many people know, for example, that it was a woman who helped develop the concept of 'the scripted talk', which brought to a potential audience of five million British 'listeners-in' the voices of the outstanding writers of the 1930s, as well as commissioning Harold Nicolson to discuss new styles in literature and enabling him to play a record of James Joyce reading from *A Work in Progress*? That woman was Hilda Matheson, who today only appears in books about other people's lives where she features, usually, in a lesbian relationship with someone better known than herself.[1]

Born on 7 June 1888 in Putney where her father was a Presbyterian minister, as a teenager she became fluent in French, German, and Italian when her father's breakdown in health necessitated living abroad. In 1908, with his health restored and living in Oxford, his daughter enrolled in the Society of Oxford Home-Students (now known as St Anne's College), where she studied history. Writing about her time at the college, Matheson recalled that 'we [felt] in the very van of progress. I suspect that each generation of women students has felt very much the same'.[2] Even so, to those Home-Students in the first decade of this century, many of whom, like Matheson, lived at home, 'the University, on the side of its undergraduate activities, seemed to us marvellous and remote [but] one had little dealings with them, whatever one might do unofficially'.[3]

Leaving college in 1911, Matheson's first job was as a part-time secretary to H.A.L. Fisher, the husband of her economic history tutor, at New College, before working under the Keeper of the Ashmolean Museum, David George Hogarth, in whose presence she met T.E. Lawrence ('Lawrence of Arabia'), just after the fall of Damascus, in 1918. During World War One she was employed, as were so many more women, to work in army intelligence at the War Office: 'deep in MI5' as her mother described it in her memoir.[4] Later she was sent to the British Mission in Rome with the task 'of forming a proper office on the model of MI5 in London'.[5] When the war ended, in 1919, Matheson, after initially turning down the offer, became political secretary to the first woman Member of Parliament, the American-born Nancy Astor. This put Matheson centre-stage in the worlds of politics, letters, and society. Her competence and the fact that she 'knew everybody' so impressed John Reith, when she visited him on Lady Astor's behalf in 1926, that he persuaded Lady Astor to release her to work for him at the fledgling British Broadcasting Company. In thanking Lady Astor for the farewell gift of a cheque, Matheson wrote:

> I was already feeling ready to howl with misery at your kindness . . . [and now] . . . your reckless generosity . . . and thoughtfulness in devising that way of making me an independent capitalist . . . I hate going, as I have seldom hated anything, and I have loved all the time I have been with you.[6]

What was it that attracted her away from Lady Astor? Apart from a salary of £900 a year, the offer of a position to influence the way a new medium of communication might be developed was certainly not one she could refuse. Immensely energetic, she 'knew everyone' at a time when Reith, whose primary job was the organization, was out of touch with the literary and educational world. Nominally employed to assist J.C. Stobart administer the BBC's Education Department, but really to launch a new department, Matheson did not believe, like Vita Sackville-West, that 'woman *cannot* combine careers with normal life'.[7] Hilda Matheson was soon embroiled in the debate, sparked by the General Strike in May 1926, about the BBC's role as a news provider. During the strike the BBC had, for the first time, used its own reporters to collect news and attempted to present news bulletins 'detached from both sides of the conflict'.[8] However, the Labour MP Ellen Wilkinson declaimed that *she* felt like 'asking the Postmaster General for my licence fee back',[9] so biased did *she* consider the BBC coverage. Reith supported the government because he believed it was acting in the national interest against disruptive sectional interests.

After 1927, when it became the British Broadcasting Corporation, the BBC was permitted to broadcast its first bulletin at 6.30 p.m. Publishers of evening newspapers had been against earlier bulletins, regarding them as unfair competition. Each year the BBC could also broadcast 400 eye-witness accounts [i.e. news reporting] and running commentaries on sporting events. Yet the BBC still received its bulletins *written* by the Reuters news agency, though they were collated by BBC staff, and it was not until 1929 that Reuters and the Press Association agreed to supply their full wire services to the BBC, for its staff to select and sub-edit for bulletins. Since this meant that the BBC could then begin to write its *own* news bulletins, the immediate consequence was the establishment of a small News

Section, in 1927, under Hilda Matheson as 'Head of Talks'.[10] Thus, by the end of the 1920s, the BBC had won the right to provide the new listening public with news and debate on the major issues of the day. And here Matheson was something of an innovator, securing the co-operation of government departments in providing their information direct to the BBC. Soon the BBC news bulletins were cluttered with these releases, so much so that, by 1931, most of it was relegated to a ten-minute programme on Thursday evenings.

In establishing the BBC's first News Section, Matheson sought advice from the Royal Institute of International Affairs, one of whose founders was Nancy Astor's husband, Waldorf, Viscount Astor, and from Geoffrey Dawson, editor of *The Times*, to help her assess what problems the BBC might face by becoming a major provider of news. On their advice she commissioned a former assistant editor of the *Westminster Gazette*, Philip Macer-Wright, to work in the News Section during the summer of 1928 and then to present his observations and recommendations based on his experiences.[11]

Macer-Wright's eleven-page report, essentially the most important document on news values ever produced for the BBC, was constantly referred to during the ensuing decades as the BBC kept refining its news presentation policy. He described in detail the machinery needed for a fully-fledged news room, and outlined how senior staff would need access to 'accredited experts' on financial, sporting, legal, and scientific matters. Macer-Wright's recommendations not only confirmed existing trends within the News Service, but also stiffened management's resolve to wrest control of the news from the news agencies, who were reluctant to acknowledge a new medium of communication, which they saw as threatening to them and to the newspaper press. Macer-Wright asserted that if the BBC wanted to make the news service attractive to the millions of listeners, it could not afford to ignore the appeal of human interest news, simply and attractively conveyed. Radio news, he said, must have 'news values'[12] and he also wanted bulletins arranged in fixed categories with Home News coming first, followed consecutively by Overseas News and Sports News. He also recommended the presentation of a bulletin especially written for listeners' ears. This was something that Matheson, and the Talks Department, had pioneered and to which she had, personally, devoted much time, training would-be broadcasters how to write for the ear. By comparison, the Reuters bulletins were written in involved, cumbersome, and florid *print* journalese, most of which had to be rewritten to make it suitable for reading aloud on the wireless. One of her colleagues credited Matheson with 'discovering, by trial and error, the "technique" of the spoken word over the air'.[13]

Scannell and Cardiff note that the Talks Department under Matheson, from 1927 to 1932, and her successor Charles Siepmann, from 1932 to 1935,

> was inspired by a common commitment to the importance of radio as a new form of social communication, and a common interest in developing effective methods of communicating via the spoken word. Matheson was a woman of courage, originality and culture, and she brought these qualities to broadcast talks.[14]

Those who worked with her described Matheson as 'enterprising, indefatigable, and liberal-minded [with] a sympathetic personality, capable of winning and holding the loyalty of subordinates'.[15] R.S. Lambert later recalled her as 'toiling single-mindedly, night and day [making] the Talks Department a live, energetic and humane department'[16] of the BBC. In Lambert's view,

> Hilda Matheson's outlook was that of the typical post-War Liberal, with its idealistic internationalism expressed in mistaken devotion to the League of Nations, its sympathy with Socialistic experiment, its cultivation of the innovating schools of poetry and art, its enthusiasm for feminism. She brought to the microphone – often persuading with her sympathetic tongue those who had hitherto been hostile or contemptuous – many of the most important broadcasters of our time . . . Wells, Shaw, Harold Nicolson, Winston Churchill and Lady Astor.[17]

Matheson also introduced Vita Sackville-West to the perils of broadcasting, and the two had an intense personal relationship which lasted from 1928 until early 1931, when Matheson was replaced in Vita's affections by another Oxford graduate, Evelyn Irons, of Somerville College, who was women's page editor of the *Daily Mail*. Vita Sackville-West has vividly described what it was like to broadcast a talk on the wireless when she wrote:

> You are taken into your studio, which is a large and luxuriously appointed room, and there is a desk, heavily padded, and over it hangs a little white box, suspended from two wires from the ceiling. There are lots of menacing notices about: 'DON'T COUGH – you will deafen millions of people', 'DON'T RUSTLE YOUR PAPERS', and 'Don't turn to the announcer and say "was that all right" when you've finished'. One has never talked to so few people and so many: it's very queer.[18]

Matheson even had Vita and her husband, Harold Nicolson, who both preferred sexual relations with people of their own sex, discussing marriage and, as Nicolson remarked to Matheson, 'We won't be able to mention sex. I presume'.[19]

According to Lambert, Matheson was invariably tactful and persuasive in her defence of the line of action she believed to be correct and outstandingly successful in the production of ideas, the planning of programmes, and in contact with speakers; but she made enemies by the very persistence of her memoranda, and by the way she sought to extend the influence of the Talks Department in all directions. Someone who worked closely with her at the BBC, Lionel Fielden, felt that both Reith and Matheson

> were the victims of circumstance. Voices whispered to him that he was being RUN by a gang of REDS; he made dictatorial gestures; you took up a cudgel; he became domineering, you wild; until at last there was nothing for it but your resignation. But the real cause, I feel, lay in the twin spectres of Hate and

Fear, which in 1930, were creeping back on to the world stage. The Blimps were on the war-path and you and your kind were doomed.[20]

For another of her BBC colleagues, Matheson's departure from the BBC was the result of one of the many 'misunderstandings' that chequered the first decade of the BBC's history. But to Reith, who had 'developed a great dislike of Miss Matheson and her works' [his diary contains references to 'the Red Woman'] it came as a relief and 'to my much embarrassment I had to hand over the staff's present to Miss Matheson' when she left the BBC in January 1932.[21]

To the *New Statesman and Nation* her departure from the BBC was a disastrous turning point. Matheson chose to resign because Reith refused to allow Harold Nicolson to praise *Ulysses* in a projected talk. But she realized that Reith wanted a return to less controversial talks and, in a draft resignation letter, she wrote that she 'could not loyally administer a policy which seemed to be turning into a reversal of what I had been instrumental in helping to build up'.[22]

Always Matheson's stalwart supporter, Lady Astor suggested that Matheson be appointed to the BBC Board of Governors![23] However, with Siepmann in charge of Talks, Matheson's ideals still flourished until his departure, in 1935, when there was a definite move away from her, liberal, ideas. But her friends were still aware of her liberal ideas and it was with regret that Matheson turned down an offer from Leonard Woolf, in 1932, to run The Hogarth Press.[24] Matheson had met his wife, Virginia Woolf, through her friendship with Vita Sackville-West.

Throughout the 1930s Matheson continued to combine journalism and publishing, working as radio critic on the Astor-owned *Observer*, and as a weekly columnist in *The Week-End Review*, as well as publishing a book on broadcasting in 1933. The decision, by H.A.L. Fisher, to commission this book for the Home University Library, Lord Reith described as 'monstrous',[25] without realizing that Matheson's first job had been as a part-time secretary to Fisher, in Oxford, when he had originally set up the *Library*. Between 1933 and 1935 Matheson worked for two days a week at a salary of £400 a year at the Royal Institute of International Affairs (Chatham House), a major interest of Lord Astor and Lord Lothian, on the *African Survey* (1938), for which she was awarded the OBE. Its nominal author, Lord Hailey, who was taken ill at a vital stage in the research, commented that 'but for her initiative and determination it might never have seen the light'.[26] Indeed, one obituarist noted that 'she took on a great deal of extra work [as] secretary for the enterprise, brilliantly, in a way that would have been quite beyond most men's powers'.[27] Her friend, Dame Ethel Smyth, commented that her greatest 'fault was her inability to say "No" when asked to do a service', adding that she blended 'intellectual grip with . . . perfect manners of soul'.[28] In her book, *Broadcasting*, Matheson commented on how demanding work was in those early days, when programmes could *not* be pre-recorded and those 'who worked all day in the office may be in the studio all evening directing a programme'.[29]

With the World War Two looming, Matheson again found herself involved in broadcasting pro-British propaganda as Director of the Joint Broadcasting Committee at a salary of £1000 a year, which purported to promote 'international understanding by means of broadcasting'. In July 1939, she wrote to F.W. Ogilvie, the new Director General of the BBC, that the JBC would have greater freedom than the BBC to develop propaganda for the German audience in the critical months of August and September of that year.[30]

With her friend and lover, Dorothy Wellesley, she was also involved in another private publishing venture, designed to counteract German propaganda abroad, called *Britain in Pictures*.[31] But, by the end of October 1940, Hilda Matheson was dead and the BBC eventually took over the running of the Joint Broadcasting Committee in July 1941.[32]

Her early death, at 52, was keenly felt, and Dorothy Wellesley, the seventh Duchess of Wellington, erected a plaque to her memory in the grounds of Penns in the Rocks, at Withyham in Sussex, which reads simply 'Amica Amicorum' – 'friend of friends'.

Notes

1   See Victoria Glendinning (1984), *Vita: The Life of Vita Sackville-West*, Harmondsworth, Penguin Books.
2   R.F. Butler and M.H. Pritchard (Eds) (n.d.), *The Society of Oxford Home-Students: Retrospects and Recollections (1879–1921)*, Oxford, p. 113.
3   *Ibid.*, p. 114.
4   [Mrs Meta Matheson] (1941), *Hilda Matheson*, Letchworth, The Hogarth Press. Internal evidence in the Hogarth Press Archives at the University of Reading suggest this was seen through the press by V. Sackville-West (although she considered the contents not equal to the stature of Hilda Matheson). Contributors included Philip Noel-Baker, MP, and Vernon Bartlett, MP, H.G. Wells, Mrs H.A.L. Fisher, Lady Astor, and others.
5   *Ibid.*, p. 10.
6   Lady Astor Archive, University of Reading, MS 1416/1/2/37.
7   Glendinning, *Vita*, p. 209.
8   Paddy Scannell and David Cardiff (1992), *A Social History of British Broadcasting. Volume One: 1922–1939*, Oxford, Blackwell, p. 33. Unlike other histories of broadcasting, this book redresses the balance in Matheson's favour, although the authors are incorrect in stating that she served for several years as Vita Sackville-West's secretary when she left the BBC.
9   *Ibid.*, p. 31.
10 *Ibid.*, p. 41.
11 *Ibid.*, p. 113. Macer-Wright's report is in the BBC Written Archives Centre (WAC), R28/177/1: 'Suggestions for the improvement of the BBC News Service', 24 September 1928.
12 *Ibid.*, p. 114.
13 [Matheson], p. 36, and Scannell and Cardiff (1992), pp. 161ff.
14 *Ibid.*, p. 153.
15 R.S. Lambert (1940), *Ariel and All His Quality*, London, Gollancz, p. 62.
16 *Ibid.*, p. 63.
17 *Ibid.*, p. 64.
18 Glendinning, *Vita*, p. 193.
19 *Ibid.*, p. 214.
20 [Matheson], p. 36.

21 Lord Reith's MSS *Diary 1930–33*, December 1930 and January 1932, BBC WAC.

22 Matheson to Reith, undated draft letter in Astor Archive, MSS 1416/1/1/962.

23 *Ibid.*, letter to Major W. Elliot, MP, 9 December 1931.

24 Leonard Woolf Papers, University of Sussex, Sx MS 13.

25 Reith, *Diary*, January 1932.

26 [Matheson], p. 45. In his privately-published biography of Matheson, '*Stoker*', *the Life of Hilda Matheson* [1999] Michael Carney is highly critical of Lord Hailey's later editions of this work which completely ignore Matheson's contribution.

27 *The Times*, 7 November 1940.

28 *The Times*, 6 November 1940.

29 Hilda Matheson (1933), *Broadcasting*, London, Home University Library, p. 57. Tim Crook's *Radio Drama: Theory and Practice* [1999] has several complimentary references to Matheson's book.

30 Asa Briggs (1970), *The History of Broadcasting in the United Kingdom, Volume III: The War of Words*, London, Oxford University Press, p. 185.

31 Matheson to Astor, 14 October, 1940, Astor Archive: 'I have been engaged since before the war in propaganda, of various kinds, abroad'.

32 Briggs (1970), p. 344.

Chapter 4

Kate Lacey

FROM *PLAUDEREI* TO PROPAGANDA: ON WOMEN'S RADIO IN GERMANY 1924–35

From: Lacey, K. (1994) 'From *Plauderei* to Propaganda: on Women's Radio in Germany 1924–35', *Media, Culture and Society*, Vol 16, No. 4, London: Sage, pp. 589–607.

Introduction

The years following the First World War in Germany saw the simultaneous emergence of radio as a mass medium and the large-scale emergence of women from the private sphere of the home into the public sphere of politics and waged labour. Indeed, it is women's enfranchisement that signals the advent of mass politics in the twentieth century and the arrival of radio which heralds the modern era of mass communication. Nevertheless, references in the academic literature to the relationship between women and the rise of radio in Germany have been both scant and essentially anecdotal (Dahl 1978: 80).[1] Certainly, the story of separate programmes for women (*Frauenfunk*) is barely told, and such references as there have tended to be dismissive of women's radio as a subject worthy of critical attention (Bessler 1980: 30).

Although the surviving evidence is patchy, it is possible to piece together a useful picture of the early history of women's radio from the early days of broadcasting in the Weimar Republic through to the Nazi period and to reinstate women's programming into the history of the medium (Lacey 1996). Within that history the parallels between women finding their public voice, and radio finding an institutional voice which could imitate private modes of speech, become apparent.

It has long been acknowledged that the central place of the family audience in the minds of programme makers during the pre-war period was a major influence on stylistic and scheduling decisions, and that the conditions of reception in the private sphere have important implications for the modes of public speech (Cardiff 1986; Moores 1988; Scannell and Cardiff 1991: 153–78). What is missing from these accounts, however, is a recognition that the development of a form of talk which is both intimate and public was crucially informed during a period when the definition of the gendered boundaries between the public and the private was in a volatile state of negotiation and renegotiation. Radio was a crucial point of intersection for contesting definitions of the public and the private. It both mediated challenges to the established delineation of the two spheres, and in itself constituted a radical extension of the public sphere and a redefinition of the private. More specifically, in Germany at least, the carefully scripted impression of a friendly fireside chat which came to prominence in the 'golden age' of radio was an approach which was pioneered in the realm of women's programming, where from the outset many items came under the rubric of *Plauderei* (Chitchat). Here, the characteristics of private female discourse – chitchat, gossip and the heart-to-heart – were publicly manifested on the radio of the Weimar Republic and later came to be of strategic importance to the domestic propaganda of the 'Third Reich'.

Public radio and a feminised public

Public broadcasting was launched in Germany in October 1923, and developed into a state-controlled system of one nation-wide and nine regional stations transmitting privately produced programmes, guided by the principle of keeping politics off the air (Sandford 1976: 63–6; Hood 1979/80: 16–18; Lerg 1980; Behrens 1986: 162–203). Radio emerged at the height of the great inflation (the first licence cost 350 million marks), and at a time when nationalism, separatism and political violence were shaking the foundations of a young Republic still struggling for legitimacy.[2] The minister responsible for broadcasting, Hans Bredow, defended the policy of non-political radio in terms of the public interest. He argued that with the republic faltering under internal and external pressures, the public needed distraction from politics and party quarrelling and, more particularly, that with radio being promoted as a domestic medium, women and children needed protection from the intrusion of politics into the home (Bredow 1960: 290). In a world which still defined the political sphere as male, the non-political public was ascribed female characteristics; it meant a withdrawal from the civic stage and a retreat to the autonomous regime of home and family.

Yet precisely because of the post-war turmoil, society had become politicised down to its very roots. To turn a blind eye to politics was to admit its all-pervasiveness. To deprive radio of its political function as a mediator of a plurality of opinion, was to admit the victory of political intolerance. In the attempt not to offend any section of the national public at a time when the sense of nationhood itself was unstable, German radio missed its promise to act as a public forum for the exchange and development of ideas and opinions on the political affairs of the state. The consequences for women's political education were particularly grave, given that they had won the right to vote only in 1918, and given that radio was so well-suited to reaching women in the home.

Women's programming

Radio was one of the new technological appliances which revolutionised women's experience in the home in the early twentieth century, and its persuasive powers were enlisted to attract women to the delights of other consumer goods. Its programmes encouraged housewives to learn the principles of the market and the factory, mothers to listen to the advice of invisible experts, and all women to become dedicated followers of fashion, in everything from pickling to parenting.

Separate programmes for women were introduced as early as the spring of 1924.[3] At this time, speech-based programmes tended to be little more than 'talking newspapers, with the regional stations allocating airtime to the major papers in their area. The women's pages of organs like the *Frankfurter Allgemeine* were consequently translated into regular radio bulletins. Later, as radio freed itself from its parasitic relationship to the press, housewives' unions and commercial advertisers were instrumental in shaping programmes for women, although in some regions, particularly in Hamburg and Berlin, the bourgeois feminist movement was also well-represented, aware that the new medium needed to recognise the special situation of women just beginning to be more prominent and active in the public sphere.

While feminists hoped to mobilise radio for women's political education, more reactionary commentators were drawn to it as some sort of saviour promising to bring the outside world into the home, making the private sphere more attractive at a time when the family seemed to be being undermined by the exodus of women into waged labour, politics and expressions of a freer and more assertive sexuality. Meanwhile, the stations' support for regular features for women derived from the need to anchor the daytime audience in the first experimental moves to construct an audience by a targeted scheduling strategy.

Political discourse during the Weimar Republic was expressed in no small measure in terms of gender issues – the equality of representation and employment opportunities, population policy and sexual relations – in short, issues which contested the apparent fixity of the gendered demarcation between the public and the private spheres. Fears of a breakdown of sexual standards and the family informed the rhetoric of both the moral right and the political left as they attempted to discredit each other's policies for their different ends. For the one side it was a rallying point for the preservation of tradition and patriarchal structures, for the other, it acted as a springboard for demands for social reform (Bridenthal et al 1984: 5–20). Social crises revitalised philosophies of security in which the family was of central concern, and a myth of femininity was revived as a symbol of constancy, stability and permanence. The public discourse around and within radio during the Weimar Republic expressed the tension between these philosophies and the ideology of modernity which was one – on the surface at least – of constant change, dynamism and progress. Radio itself was caught up in these contradictions, both as a site for their expression, and in its own essential structural tension between revolutionary potential and stabilising function.

The focus on programmes explicitly aimed at women highlights radio's recognition and negotiation of its intrusion into the private sphere. A review of the types of women's programmes put out by the regional stations during the Weimar Republic illustrates that there was a variety of responses to the central dilemma that was apparent from the start of public broadcasting, the negotiation of the challenge to the public/private divide.[4]

All the stations spoke to women as housewives and mothers, some, like Munich, almost exclusively so in programmes like *From the Empire of the Kitchen* and *The Practical Woman* (1925), while some, most notably Berlin and Hamburg, spoke to them also as citizens, voters and even as intellects, with series such as *Path-breaking Women* and *Women's Achievements in the Twentieth Century* (1927). Hamburg had introduced a 'college of the airwaves' in 1924, and two years later set up a special school for women which broadcast programmes on the whole range of women's issues (Radel 1928). All the stations spoke to women as consumers, but while Frankfurt, for example, whetted their appetites for new consumer goods in a programme called *Three Minutes for the Woman* (1925),[5] Leipzig encouraged their sense of patriotic duty as cogs in the wheels of the national economy in *Market and Kitchen* (1925). All spoke to women in a middle class voice,[6] although some acknowledged more than others the presence of other constituencies in the audience either by broadcasting during the evening, as Stuttgart and Leipzig did at first, or in adopting an express policy of opening up new avenues of culture and education to women whose circumstances otherwise deprived them of such opportunities, of which Hamburg is the prime example.

One thing all the stations had in common was the conviction that broadcasting could change and improve women's experience in the transitional space between public and private life. Another was that they represented a space for women's voices to be heard regularly on the air.

Women's voices on the air

The various *Frauenfunk* programmes were almost exclusively hosted by women, at a time when women's voices were still struggling to be heard in public and long before the possibility of a woman speaking to and 'for' the nation was seriously considered.[7] While men could present programmes on 'women's issues', women could present little else. In a series entitled *Plaudereien zum Ernsthafteren (Chats on Serious Matters)* broadcast from Berlin in 1926, various men expounded their opinions on such matters of general import as the life and work of Henry Ford, or the state of the national economy, while women were left to tell how they had decorated their homes or taught their daughters to cook.[8] Prejudice against women announcers hid behind technological excuses in Germany long after the shortcomings of the hardware had been resolved. The possibility of voice amplification offered by the invention of the loudspeaker and the microphone were important in giving to some women the confidence speak in public but, as McKay (1988: 187–8) has argued, given the strength of ideological opposition to women having a public voice of their own, the decisive factor in women winning access to channels of public communication was feminism.

Women's radio had experimented with less formal modes of presentation early on. The commercial influence on the early *Frauenfunk* had been one incentive.[9] Advertisers encouraged the makers of women's programmes to introduce natural speech patterns with a spontaneous feel, using dialogue, drama, rhyme and rhythm to catch and hold their audience's attention. But it was the notion of women talking to other women in the home that was paramount in finding a mode of speech, the informal chat, that was familiar and effective. Lectures increasingly gave way to dialogues, discussions and interviews as ways of imparting difficult or controversial material in a more balanced, informative and yet easily digestible form. A frequent, though not exclusive, form of talk on the Weimar *Frauenfunk* was either the apparently informal chitchat, or the staged interview between experts and a 'representative' mother or housewife.

David Cardiff (1986) has pointed out that such familiar formats as the studio interview were once innovative strategies in response to a particular broadcasting problem. The often unruly clash of opinions in radio debates could be tempered and channelled by the mediation of a neutral chairperson, even if in practice the chairperson merely functioned to steer the speakers away from potentially controversial areas. This mode of presentation was popular in the radio production of the late Weimar period as the strict ban on all political material gradually gave way to a limited concept of political balance. Of course, censorship proper followed fast on the heels of the Nazi take-over, but in terms of finding a suitable presentational style, old lessons had to be learned afresh.

From *Plauderei* to propaganda

Radio was regarded by the National Socialists as a comrade in arms, sharing a common history and a common destiny: both had burst on to the public stage in the autumn of 1923, both had reached maturity in the early thirties, and neither could reach its full potential without the other (Dreyer 1934: 101). The sort of influence the Nazi party sought to wield could not be realised by control of printing and press alone; only radio offered the possibility of affecting the nation as a whole, proclaiming a unified message from a totalitarian regime (Welch 1993). Radio was centralised and *gleichgeschaltet* (brought into line with Nazi principles) under the close control of Goebbels' Ministry for Propaganda and Enlightenment, and the provision of millions of cheap 'people's receivers' was made a priority. But radio was of little use in such an ideological crusade if its technological promise were not infused with the spirit of the cause and of the new era.

Flush with success and ambitious for rapid acceptance of the new order, the Nazi programme directors initially swamped the airwaves with bombastic music, live transmissions from Party events, and, most ineffectively, declamatory speeches and dogmatic hyperbole (Grunberger 1976: 401–5; Diller 1980). The German radio was the 'mouthpiece of the *Führer*' whose own voice of course regularly punctuated the airwaves to great effect. But in general, the public platform language of the demagogue did not transmit well on the radio, and listening figures plummeted (Behrens 1986: 208). Before long, the malaise was diagnosed, and the remedy prescribed, namely, a mixture of light music and more intimate studio conversation (Zeman 1973: 60). The traditions of family schedules and gendered audiences, together with the evolution of forms of radio talk like the *Plauderei*, meant there were structures already in place for the propagandists to develop and exploit.

It was an approach which some thought could benefit from the feminine touch. Soon after the take-over of power, the leading radio journal, *Der deutsche Rundfunk*,[10] stressed the part women would have to play in realising the potential to transmit the cultural values of the new regime directly into the homes of German families, acting not only as welcoming hostesses to the invisible 'guest' in the home, but as the amicable and intimate *voice* of radio. In other words, if a more subtle mode of address were to be adopted, one in which the sense of community with the audience was promoted in contrast to the hierarchical structures which had gone before, then the 'natural' coaxing, cajoling, caring skills associated with women should be put to good effect. It was in the realm of presentation where the feminine 'spirit' was called on most explicitly to refresh radio output.

The spirit which had imbued the radio of the Weimar Republic was considered to be the *Erkenntnisgeist* (the intellectual spirit). The public service broadcasting ethos with its emphasis on education and information – or on elites speaking down to the masses – was held to have been a betrayal of radio's true 'maternal' spirit, the *Muttergeist* (Peck 1933/4: 246–7). Radio's location in the home, its intimate address, its sensory appeal, grounded it firmly in the female realm as it was understood in the essentialist philosophy to which National Socialism ascribed (Rosenberg 1933; Rupp 1977). The terms *Erkenntnisgeist* and *Muttergeist* defined the rational, intellectual logical perception process assumed to inhere in the male, and its opposite, the instinctual, intuitive and sympathetic perception displayed in the female. According to this scheme of things, the history of radio had been the history of a development away from intellectualism to maternalism. The gradual move away from the 'talking newspaper', from the dry, academic lecture towards dialogue, drama and human interest that was traceable in the history of radio, was interpreted as evidence for the inevitable victory in all aspects of broadcasting of the *Muttergeist*.

Similarly, for the *Frauenfunk*, the invitation of public and political personalities into the home by the turn of the dial, had opened up the world of politics to women who were 'naturally' alienated by the world of debate, public meetings and lengthy editorials. This was the direction in which radio must continue to progress, in the eyes of the new producers. The perceived contamination of some women's radio in the Weimar period with a misplaced *Erkenntnisgeist* was to be urgently eradicated, Hamburg's high-brow programmes being castigated as the nadir of the pre-Nazi period. This 'essential' character of radio demanded that all aspects of radio, but the *Frauenfunk* in particular, continue to be shaped by the *Muttergeist*.

Women's relationship to radio was deemed to be of central ideological and practical importance on various levels in the 'Third Reich', a relationship which a revamped women's service hoped to bolster and utilise. Plans to establish a national socialist women's radio service had been laid well in advance of the Nazis coming to power (von Bremen, 1933: 19). Generally, the Weimar policy of targeting different interest groups with their own programmes was abandoned in favour of a unified, totalitarian vision of radio but, given the high priority attached to enlisting women in the services of the *Volk*, the *Frauenfunk*, along with children's radio, survived.

The obstinate adherence to 'traditional' women's issues is a useful indication of the ideological premise in the producers' minds. The tenet of complementary but separate spheres for the sexes was a broadly consistent theme in the Nazis' often inconsistent ideological schema. Moreover, women's psychology was held to be less differentiated than men's, so all women, regardless of age or class, financial or familial status, could be served by programmes which centred on the home and family. The only difficulty was in finding a register which would appeal to women across the board. Human interest stories and fictional accounts were thought universally appreciated by women, which accounts for the high proportion of programmes in the *Frauenfunk* which took a dramatic or conversational form, despite the recorded popularity of 'hard' news and political programmes among women at the time (Kuhlmann 1942: 138). While the more progressive radio in the Weimar period had breathed the air of modernity directly into the home, the Nazis seized on the most modern apparatus of communication to advocate a return to a vision of womanhood expressed in terms of nature, spirit, instinct and biology.

The Nazi women's organisations, including the *Deutsches Frauenwerk* (German Women's Bureau), were closely involved in the production of women's programmes around the country and in arranging communal listening. The four main propaganda offensives targeted specifically at women were a Party membership drive, pro-natalist and 'racial hygiene' campaigns, the mobilisation of female labour in the latter stages of the war, and the *Verbrauchslenkung* and *Verbrauchserziehung* campaigns (direction of consumption and education in consumption), in which housewives were bombarded with information about how, as customers and consumers, it lay in their power to have a direct and profound influence on the German economy (Stephenson 1981: 130–43; Stephenson 1983: 117–42; Bock 1984: 178; Rupp 1978: 74–136). The propaganda insisted it was their patriotic duty to ensure they acted in the best interests of the *Volk*, the welfare of which, as always, was to come before that of the individual or even of the family.

A contradiction existed between the eulogising of the family in Nazi propaganda and the undermining of family integrity by the intrusion of the state into the private sphere. Contemporary commentators on radio noted how the new order in German politics had upset the usual rhythm of life for men who now had new responsibilities and orders to answer to, and for many children who were organised in the Hitler Youth and League of German Girls, and who were therefore more than ever in need of a stable home life to compensate for the unpredictability outside. The radio with its regular, predictable schedules which provided a background framework for housewives to work to had a part to play in helping women perform this stabilising role (F.M. 1934/5: 47). Radio stood at the very fulcrum of this contradiction in providing both a stabilising 'familial cement', and in spearheading the destabilising public intrusion of the private home. In offering an intimate authoritarian voice, it was both a substitute for, and a reinforcement of, the patriarchal voice in the home.

Propaganda as *Plauderei*

When one thinks of Nazi propaganda, it is doubtful one thinks of it as a cosy chat. However, that is exactly how much of the propaganda on domestic German radio, particularly that aimed at women (who made up an increasing proportion of the available audience as the years went by) was conducted. Unfortunately, very few scripts from the *Frauenfunk* of the pre-war period survive in the archives, a consequence both of the disruption after the war, and of the lack of prestige attached to these programmes at the time. It is tempting, therefore, to ascribe those scripts which do survive a particular significance. Such is the case with a script, held by the DRA, and analysed below, for a programme broadcast from Königsberg on 15th March 1935, entitled, *Mitarbeiterinnen des Frauenfunks plaudern miteinander: Bunter Nachmittag im Frauenfunk* (*The Women's Radio team chat to each other: A social afternoon in the women's department*).

This 'social afternoon', an instalment of the flagship woman's hour, *Stunde für deutsche Frauen* (*Programme for German Women*), took the form of a round table discussion between the presenters of the Königsberg *Frauenfunk* about their work. It therefore has a twofold relevance to the present discussion, furnishing further information about the workings of the *Frauenfunk* and the biographies of its staff, while exemplifying the studied informality and the methods of propaganda in programmes for women during this period.

This was no free-flowing, open-ended discussion. The twenty minute programme was scripted carefully from beginning to end for maximum propagandistic effect, the multiple corrections and amendments of the editor's blue pencil throughout the typescript pages evidence that this is no simple transcription of an unscripted broadcast. Radio was still a live medium, and pre-censorship of broadcasts was essential in the closely controlled environment of Nazi propaganda.

The first thing worth noting is the labelling of the discussion as *Plauderei*. Women's talk about anything from baby care to employment policy was rarely dignified by the name *Diskussion* or even *Gespräch* (conversation).[11] Public female discourse is never fully accepted as having broken out of the private sphere, and by the same token is signalled as being of inferior significance to other discourses (Spender 1980: 106–37; Spacks 1986: 3–46; Brown 1990: 183–200). And yet, almost coincidentally, women's radio had hit upon a presentational approach ideally suited to the medium, whose listeners experience reception as individuals, and not as members of a mass.

The discussion was led by Frieda Magnus-Unzer who headed the *Frauenfunk* department at Königsberg, with its staff of six, from 1930 to 1937. The programme was faded in, to give the impression that the listener was being allowed access to an internal meeting, to eavesdrop on a private conversation already in progress. In so doing, a tension was set up between the effect created and the reality of all broadcast talk which is, by definition, public discourse. This is the 'double articulation' of broadcast talk, the intercourse in the studio, and the simultaneous communication of that intercourse to the absent listener (Scannell 1991: 1). Throughout the script there are at least two levels of meaning set up by this tension. The address to the listener was made explicit only in the summing up statement at the end of the programme. As the discussion faded in, the listener heard Magnus-Unzer in mid-flow, suggesting that women's and children's radio benefited mutually from their close cooperation within the department. One of the longest-serving members of her staff, Frau Creutzberg, replied:

> Yes, dear Frau Magnus-Unzer, after all, mother and child do belong together, and when we work for our children and families, it is the most natural thing in the world to talk about it. . . . Thank God we have so many listeners, many more than fit into a public hall, although as we sit alone at the microphone, we feel we are speaking individually to each of our sisters. We enter their most intimate environment, their homes. We hope they welcome us into their hearts as we share fondly in their lives and in the life of their families.
>
> (*Mitarbeiterinnen*, 1935: 1)

This first statement illustrates a whole range of presentational strategies, both in form and content. First of all, there is the address to 'dear' Frau Magnus-Unzer to create the impression of spontaneous and amicable discussion between colleagues, an impression without substance, for the rest of her speech is quite obviously addressed to the listeners, who by implication become honorary colleagues in the practice of the *Frauenfunk*. It is for the listeners' sake that Frau Creutzberg reiterates the official ideological position on women, that their place is with the children in the home. Repetition of the central tenets of that ideology lay at the heart of the propaganda aimed at women, to the effect that they seemed to become axiomatic, or rooted in the mythical wisdom of the *völkisch* past.

Much of the ideological propaganda aimed at women in this period was based on already established cultural codes – the ideology of motherhood is a case in point. Other positions, such as the duty towards *Führer* and *Volk*, or the exigencies of racial hygiene, met with a greater degree of resistance. But the efforts to make the new ideas as familiar and axiomatic as the old were relentless (Kershaw 1983: 200). All the output of the *Frauenfunk* was infused with overt reiterations of the ideological positions, to the extent that a cookery programme, for example, gave not only tips for recipes and preparation, but spoke of national duty in buying

German produce, maternal and racial duty in providing nourishing meals for their children as bearers of Germany's future, and the duty of a woman always to be prepared to sacrifice herself to the needs of her family, *Volk* and *Führer*.

The next presentational tactic to emerge is the insistence on the listener's personal responsibility in safeguarding the future of the nation. The effect is heightened by a sense of drama, in that but for the grace of God – and by implication, of Hitler – a whole generation of children would be growing up without the benefit of a mother guided by the benefits of national socialist wisdom brought to her by the Königsberg radio.

One of the most important presentational strategies exemplified in the extract is the assurance given to the listener that she is not alone, but is a part of a much larger listening community, and, more than that, that she is an indispensable part. The tone is entirely reassuring. The activity of listening is legitimised by the notion of a listening community, while the women on the 'other side' in the studio understand and respect the privilege of being invited into the private space of the home. But this understanding implies a mutual responsibility, which brings us to the final strategy employed here, the imperative. Couched in the vocabulary of warmth and sharing, and expressed in terms of confident expectancy, this represents a thinly veiled instruction to put up no resistance to the presence of radio in the home, or the message it conveys.

The chat continues with reminiscences about how each of the contributors, aged between twenty-three and sixty, came to work for the radio. Most made their own approaches to the station, a confession which acts simultaneously as an invitation to the listener to get involved themselves. Each contributor stressed how much pleasure their work brought them, because of their belief in the importance of what they were doing:

Frl. Woop:	I'm often aware that there is still a lot of work to be done in the education of women for our fatherland. I wanted to help.
Fr. Magnus-Unzer:	And so you sent your first piece to the radio?
Frl. Woop:	Yes!
Frau Creutzberg:	Didn't you try to get something published in a newspaper before that, Fräulein Woop?
Frl. Woop:	No, Frau Creutzberg, it didn't even occur to me. I wanted to speak directly to my sisters and feel a bond with them.
Frl. Königsegg:	I understand. When your heart is so full, you try to break down all the barriers.

(Mitarbeiterinnen 1935: 4)

Here the propagandistic aims are made quite explicit. The intention is to educate the listener to serve the National Socialist 'Fatherland', driven not by a political agenda, but by an altruism inherent in the female character. As in so much Nazi propaganda, there is a mystic element to the discourse. This is how Frl. Königsegg herself described her work:

> Women care for the things that are passed down to us. . . . And so our cultural history becomes part of my experience. How I found the way, I do not know. It comes from the inside, and leads in all directions. You don't know why, but you can't help it. It must be the same for you, Frl. Treike. That's why all the practical things you talk about sound so convincing, because it comes from a knowledge about the very essence of our people.
>
> (ibid., 6)

These are not women driven by ambitions for fame, fortune or career. They represent the ideal selflessness and passivity of women so lauded by the Nazi ideologues. There is a deeper, essential force which determines the fate and the very knowledge of these women. The implication is that these women are in tune with the natural way of things which imbues them with a natural and lawful authority; and further, that this sets them apart from and above the artificial morality of the Weimar period. Another feature often evident in the propaganda aimed at women was the prominence of emotional and highly personal language, often coloured by high-flown metaphors and abstractions which mask the banality of much of what is being said. An appeal to the emotions was considered the most suitable approach as women were not expected to respond critically or intellectually.

Part of the claim to naturalness was the retention, or adoption, of the natural speech patterns of the local dialect. Frau Treike, for example, mentioned how she also dreamed and prayed in the colloquial Low German dialect, *plattdeutsch*, suggesting that her radio talk was an intimate experience deserving the honesty of unreconstructed language. This confession 'prompted' the following reply from Fräulein Woop, which again illustrates the constant and arbitrary reintroduction of overt ideological statements:

> Yes, Frau Treike, if one tries to be honest in work and prayer, one avoids hollow phrases, preferring the simple speech of one's homeland. I think, for now, I'll always have something to say. And though many say we women are restricted in the Third Reich, it is only now that we can really make demands, because everybody knows what their duty is and everybody must devote themselves to their family and their people.
>
> (ibid., 6)

This overt denial of the increasing restrictions imposed on women in the 'Third Reich' is fortified by many of the propagandistic strategies, including the prolific flattery of the listener and the glorification of the duties of women as mothers. By concentrating on their duties, achievements and value as mothers, the aim was to distract from the fact that women were now esteemed almost solely in terms of their reproductive function.

The purpose of this *Plauderei* was to act as an advertisement for the range of programmes on offer for women. Each of the contributors took it in turn to explain what they found so satisfying about their work on each of the programmes. It also provided the listener with background information about how the programmes were put together. The following serves as an interesting example, especially as it touches on the question of mode of presentation:

Frl. Creutzberg:	It's a pleasure to work *on Working with young housewives*. These programmes feature members of the housewives' union, a sub-division of the *Deutsches Frauenwerk* [a Nazi organisation for women], and I find that they all have a natural speaking manner. My chats with a business woman and a mother of a large family were very true to life. These two brave women impressed me so much that my own small part seemed quite strange and secondary to me.
Frau Magnus-Unzer:	And yet you felt responsible for them. But the women mastered the situation completely. I notice time and again that the people who fight the daily battle of life have steady nerves even in front of the microphone.
Frau Horst:	Yes, we've all noticed that. And it is for this reason that their voices sound so free and natural.

(ibid., 7)

This is a good example of the strategy of flattering the listener, although in this case it is a fragile line between emphasising the natural flair of ordinary women on the radio and the professional skill of the station's employees, as in the following exchange dealing with the merits and otherwise of reading from a script:

Frl. Woop:	Oh my heart beat so fast when I had my reading test!
Frau Magnus-Unzer:	It was all right in your case. But not everyone can read her own work. Few people recognise it. But a lot depends on the delivery. And it would do many people good to ask a practised female announcer to convey their thoughts to the listener. They'd get more from it that way.

(ibid., 7)

This exchange represents a disarming admission that what the listener assumes to be natural dialogue, is in fact scripted text. And yet no explicit reference is made to the fact that this *Plauderei*, too, is scripted. Perhaps this omission was intended to reinforce the deception of simulated honest discussion, to bolster the listeners' trust in the personalities fronting the *Frauenfunk*, as an investment in faith for the future. It is also a declaration calling for the ultimate identification of presenter and listener, the unity of thought and purpose for which the *Frauenfunk* strove. Magnus-Unzer summed up the *Plauderei* with an appeal to maintain the pressure for an even closer relationship between the *Frauenfunk* and its listeners:

We have over 100 people working for us in women's and children's radio. We get a lot of letters, and the prize competitions are very invigorating and give us lots of ideas, and I hope that our current competition will be just as stimulating for us and our listeners. We've asked all our listeners to listen to all the programmes for women until 31st March and make notes about what they hear. All these notes should then be sent to the station, and the best ones will get prizes. Our conversation today is a part of this task. Write down all your thoughts about our women's radio, all you who are listening today. You are all our colleagues, after all. We six women wanted to involve you more closely in our work with our conversation today, and greet you with our hearts in the hope for inner comradeship. Heil Hitler!

(ibid., 8)

It is seductive language. It appeals to a sense of common cause and sisterhood. It promises empowerment and reward. But there is much that it omits to say. The sisterhood is a select one. It excludes all those women whose work outside the home means they cannot listen to this or the other programmes of the *Frauenfunk*. And if they could hear, and if they could suggest changes to the content of the programmes to meet their needs, they would not win prizes. Nor does the sisterhood include those women in whose hearts the words *Heil Hitler* would inspire fear in place of adulation. The discourse is set up between 'us' and 'you' and becomes what turned out to be a sinister community defined against an unmentioned 'other'.

Conclusion

There is, of course, much more to be said about the issues raised here, and there are absences which need still to be addressed, not least that of the social audience. Further work needs to be done to see if radio practices were similarly influenced by the relationship between women and the public sphere as it surfaced in the discourses in other countries. As it is, the purpose of this article has been fourfold: firstly, to demonstrate that in the crucial first decades of German broadcasting the contested nature of the gendered division between the public and the private spheres provided the framework for the public discourse about the social function of radio; secondly, to show how this discourse fed into women's programming, an area hitherto neglected in the literature on German radio; thirdly, to argue that the development of the now familiar intimate mode of public address was not insignificantly bound up with 'feminine discourse' as it was translated into radio for women; and, finally, to explore how this mode of address was mobilised in the domestic propaganda of the 'Third Reich', enabling the Nazi regime to transmit its political messages directly to a nationwide audience and to drive its message literally home.

Notes

1 Since this article was written a welcome contribution has been made by a group of historians led by Adelheid von Saldern and Inge Marßolek on a project about gender relations in German radio of the 'Third Reich' and the GDR.

2 On the very day public broadcasting began, the army removed elected left-wing officials in Saxony, the government of the recently declared Rhein Republic was announced in Aachen, the state of Bavaria and the cities of Trier, Köln, Düsseldorf and Wiesbaden were threatening to secede, and the Ruhr was still under French occupation. Hitler's abortive Munich *Putsch* followed a few days later, and became the subject of the first news broadcast in Germany.

3 There was an early *Women's Hour* on the London programme from Savoy Hill, but this was discontinued by 1924 and there was no regular service for women in Britain until *Woman's Hour* was reintroduced in 1946.

4 The following is a brief summary of a more detailed review of these programmes, based on a variety of radio journals, company reports and listing magazines (Lacey, 1996: 57–95).

5 This slot, though short, came just before the main news bulletin, giving it one of the largest audiences of any *Frauenfunk* programme, and thus eagerly exploited by firms promoting their latest products. cf. *Senderberichte zum ersten Jahr* (Frankfurt: Südwestfunk, 1925).

6 Workers' radio clubs, which had been set up soon after the first transmissions, campaigned vociferously against the middle class bias of Weimar radio, and published critical articles in their journal, *Der Neue Rundfunk.* (Dahl, 1978).

7 There was considerable controversy surrounding the appointment of the first female announcer in Berlin, Gertrud von Eyseren, in 1932. (eg. *Berliner Zeitung am Mittag*, June 20, 1932; *Deutsche Zeitung*, July 23, 1932)

8 *Drei Jahre Berliner Rundfunkdarbietungen. 1923–6*. DRA.

9 By 1926 certain times of day were designated advert-free zones. In 1932, advertising was further restricted to weekday mornings – when housewives were most likely to be listening. Commercials featured until 1936 when it was decreed that the promotion of private interests was no longer compatible with a public medium designed to promote the interests of the national socialist state.

10 (1933) 'Unsere Meinung: Die am Lautsprecher', *Der Deutsche Rundfunk* 12: p.2.

11 The leading participant in this case, however, does refer to the programme as a *Gespräch* (conversation) in her final speech, which may imply that she was trying to recover a little more than its ascribed status.

References

Behrens, T. (1986) *Die Entstehung der Massenmedien in Deutschland*, Frankfurt a.M.: Peter Lang.

Bessler, H. (1980) *Hörer und Zuschauerforschung* vol.5, H. Bausch (ed.) *Rundfunk in Deutschland*, Frankfurt a.M.: dtv.

Bock, G. (1984) 'Racism and Sexism in Nazi Germany: Motherhood, Compulsory Sterilization, and the State' pp. 271–96, in Bridenthal et al (eds) *When Biology became Destiny: Women in Weimar and Nazi Germany*, New York: Monthly Review Press.

Bredow, H. (1960) *Im Banne der Aetherwellen* vol 2, 2nd edn, Stuttgart: Mundus.

Bremen, G. von (1933) 'Frauenschulung für den Rundfunk' *Die Deutsche Frauenfront* 1: 19.

Bridenthal, R. et al (eds) (1984) *When Biology became Destiny: Women in Weimar and Nazi Germany*, New York: Monthly Review Press.

Brown, M.E. (1990) 'Motley Moments: Soap Opera, Carnival, Gossip and the Power of the Utterance' pp. 183–200 in M.E. Brown (ed.) *Television and Women's Culture: The Politics of the Popular*, London: Sage.

Cardiff, D. (1986) 'The Serious and the Popular: Aspects of the Evolution of Style in the Radio Talk 1928–1939' pp. 228–46 in R. Collins (ed.) *Media, Culture and Society: A Critical Reader*, London: Sage.

Dahl, P. (1978) *Arbeitersender und Volksempfänger: Proletarische Radio-Bewegung und bürgerlicher Rundfunk bis 1945*, Frankfurt a.M.: Syndikat.

Diller, A. (1980) *Rundfunkpolitik im Dritten Reich* vol.2 H. Bausch (ed.) *Rundfunk in Deutschland*, Munich: dtv.

Dreyer, E.A. (1934) *Deutsche Kultur im neuen Reich: Wesen, Aufgabe und Ziel der Reichskulturkammer*, Berlin: [n.pub.].

F.M. (1934/5) 'Die festgelegten Sendungen', *Rufer und Hörer* 47.

Grunberger, R. (1976) *A Social History of the Third Reich*, London: Weidenfeld and Nicholson.

Hitler, A. (1938) *My Struggle*, London: Hurst and Blackett.

Hood, S. (1979/80) 'Brecht on Radio', *Screen* 20: 16–28.

Kershaw I. (1983) 'How Effective was Nazi Propaganda? pp. 180–205 in D. Welch (ed.) *Nazi Propaganda: The Power and the Limitations*, London: Croom Helm.

Kershaw, I. (1991) *Hitler*, London: Longman.

Kessler, H. (1981) *Die Deutsche Frau: NS Frauenpropaganda im Völkischen Beobachter*, Cologne: Pahl-Rugenstein.

Koonz, C. (1988) *Mothers in the Fatherland: Women, the Family and Nazi Politics*, London: Methuen.

Kuhlmann, H. (1942) 'Die Frau und der Rundfunk unter besonderer Berücksichtigung des Frauenfunks' unpublished doctoral thesis, Friedrich Wilhelm University Berlin.

Lacey, K. (1996) *Feminine Frequencies: Gender, German Radio and the Public Sphere 1923–1945*, Ann Arbor: University of Michigan Press.

Lerg, W. B. (1980) *Rundfunk in der Weimarer Republik* vol. 1 H. Bausch (ed.) *Rundfunk in Deutschland*, Munich: dtv.

Magnus-Unzer, F. (n.d.) *Gedächtnisprotokolle*, 1 Deutsches Rundfunkarchiv.

Marßolek, I. and A. von Saldern, (eds) (1999) *Radiozeiten. Herrschaft, Alltag, Gesellschaft (1924–1960)*, Frankfurt: Deutscher Rundfunkarchiv, Bd. 25.

McKay, A. (1988) 'Speaking Up: Voice Amplification and Women's Struggle for Public Expression', in C. Kramarae (ed.) *Technology and Women's Voices: Keeping in Touch*, London: Routledge & Kegan Paul.

'Mitarbeiterinnen des Frauenfunks plaudern miteinander: Bunter Nachmittag im Frauenfunk' (1935) in F. Magnus-Unzer, *Gedächtnisprotokolle* 1 Deutsches Rundfunkarchiv.

Moores, S. (1998) '"The Box on the Dresser" Memories of Early Radio and Everyday Life', *Media Culture and Society*, 10, 23–40.

Peck, L. (1933/4) 'Die Frau und der Rundfunk!' *Rufer und Hörer*, 1: 243–51.

Peck, L. (1934) 'Die Frau und der Rundfunk in Zahlen!' *Rufer und Hörer*, 2: 65–74.

Radel, F. (1928) 'Die Schule der *Frau' Die Norag 3. Jahrbuch 1927: Frauenschaffen der Gegenwart*, Hamburg: Rufu.

Rosenberg, A. (1933) *Der Mythos des 20. Jahrhunderts*, Munich.

Rosenhaft, E. (1992) 'Women, Gender, and the Limits of Political History in the Age of "Mass" Politics' pp. 149–73 in L. E. Jones and J. Retallack (eds) *Elections, Mass Politics, and Social Change in Modern Germany*, Cambridge: Cambridge University Press.

Rupp, L.J. (1977) 'Mother of the Volk: The Image of Women in Nazi Ideology', *Signs*, 3: 362–75.

Rupp, L.J. (1978) *Mobilising Women for War: German and American Propaganda 1939–1945*, Princeton: Princeton University Press.

Sandford, J. (1976) *The Mass Media of the German-speaking Countries*, London: Oswald Wolf.

Scannell, P. (1991) 'Introduction: The Relevance of Talk' pp. 1–13 in *Broadcast Talk*, London: Sage.

Scannell, P. and D. Cardiff (1991) *A Social History of British Broadcasting: Serving the Nation, 1922–39*, Oxford: Blackwell.

Spacks, P.M. (1986) *Gossip*, London: University of Chicago Press.

Spender, D. (1980) *Man Made Language*, London: Routledge and Kegan Paul.

Stephenson, J. (1981) *The Nazi Organisation of Women*, London: Croom Helm.

Stephenson, J. (1983) 'Propaganda, Autarky and the German Housewife', pp. 117–142 in D. Welch (ed.) *Nazi Propaganda: The Power and the Limitations*, London: Croom Helm, 1983.

Welch, D. (1993) 'Manufacturing a Consensus: Nazi Propaganda and the Building of a "National Community"' (*Volksgemeinschaft*), *Contemporary European History*, 2: 1–15

Zeman, Z.A.B. (1973) *Nazi Propaganda*, Oxford: Oxford University Press.

Chapter 5

Sally Feldman

TWIN PEAKS: THE STAYING POWER OF BBC RADIO 4'S *WOMAN'S HOUR*

'I don't want your tears. I want your anger.' That was my rallying cry to the troops the day battle was declared. It was 29 November 1990. Michael Green, then Controller of Radio 4, was about to announce to the world his dramatic new plan for the network. Daytime schedules were to be rearranged. *Woman's Hour* was to lose its sacred two o'clock slot and migrate to the morning to boost the legendary low audience figures – the 'hammock' between *Today*[1] and the lunchtime news. It might also lose its name, so as not to alienate the larger potential male audience.

The production team had gathered to be told the news by the editors. There were eleven or so producers plus the usual indeterminate cluster of trainees and 'attachees' and the eight production assistants, one of whom burst into tears. Hence my stinging command.

I was aware that we were going to need all the steely strength we could muster if we were to save the programme we loved. Clearly, without its name *Woman's Hour* could not retain its character and distinctiveness and would lose its power. Clearly, there were going to be storms ahead.

For the past four years the programme had been led by a triumvirate. Clare Selerie became editor in September 1986. I was made her deputy the same day. We were then in our thirties. Overnight, the average age of the team had dropped ten years. Our first task had been to select the new presenter. The saintly, ultra-professional Sue MacGregor, voice of the programme for 13 years, was off to the *Today* programme. Jenni Murray was her chosen successor. In her early thirties, with two young children and a willingness to speak her mind, she represented a new direction for *Woman's Hour*.

Incredibly, *Woman's Hour* had managed to navigate the late 1960s and 1970s without paying undue attention to the advent of women's liberation or even the introduction of equal pay and equal opportunities legislation in the mid-70s. There was polite acknowledgement, certainly. Major figures like Germaine Greer or Fay Weldon had been interviewed with dispassionate interest. But there was no assumption that this was the programme's agenda and certainly it never claimed any partisanship.

This is partly because the style of Radio 4 at this time was a great deal cooler and more formal than it is today. Presenters didn't talk much about themselves, and objectivity was the norm. Also, to identify with the feminist movement would have been foreign to the majority of producers at the time. The BBC was one of the first organisations, along with teaching and the civil service, to offer career opportunities to women. But it was at a price. In the 1950s it was still expected that a woman would give up work when she got married, and that you had to choose between career and motherhood. That is what the majority of the early *Woman's Hour* producers had had to do so it is understandable that they might feel out of sympathy with a new wave of women who were demanding, and getting, it all.

Many of the colleagues I met when I first joined the programme, like long-serving editor Wynne Knowles, still held this somewhat old-fashioned attitude. Undoubtedly they believed, with some justification, that this refusal to bow to fashion or ideology helped to preserve *Woman's Hour* as a programme for all women regardless of their position on sexual politics.

When Sandra Chalmers became editor in 1982 she brought with her a refreshing warmth and modernity. A single mother herself bringing up two teenagers, she was sympathetic to the needs of producer mothers like myself, but also wished to inject a chattier, friendlier tone. Suspected amongst some of the staff of seeking to dumb-down (though probably no one used the phrase at that time), she was keen to be as inclusive as possible, and certainly not to suggest a more feminist line.

Clare Selerie and I never really planned to make the programme a mouthpiece for feminism or any other ideology, though we were much less afraid than our predecessors to acknowledge this constituency in our audience. What we were after, though, was a better defined editorial policy to distinguish the programme from its numerous competitors. To emphasise the achievements and the views of women we encouraged producers to request women speakers on even the most general topics. The serial was to be a showcase for women writers. Men would be featured only when they had something particular to say to or about women.

The most noticeable change of all, though, was in the style of the presenter. Jenni Murray would talk about her children, cry when a guest cried, burst into an infectious giggle when Maureen Lipman or Thora Hird or Jennifer Saunders said something funny. She sounded warm, angry, sympathetic and on your side.

By the time of the Controller's bombshell announcement, Clare was about to go on maternity leave and I was to be acting editor. Suddenly, rather than being the caretaker, I was in charge of a major redesign. I was given nine months, appropriately, to prepare for the relaunch of the programme – but how could I begin while the question of the name remained undecided?

The next day the announcement was made to the press, and from then on, mayhem broke out. Newspapers were unanimous in their condemnation of the plan and their defence of the programme. For a speech radio programme, we made unprecedented headlines, front pages, leader columns and features.

This was partly because of the programme's status as a national institution. It stood for the staid, the unchanging, the world of decent values and proper indignation. At other times, it was a perfect target for those wishing to attack the middle class values of the BBC, or its rampant feminism, or its tedious traditionalism. Right now, though, it had transformed from target to weapon in the press's favourite field sport: shooting at Auntie. Or, as Ian Hislop put it, 'We love it when the grey suits f..k up.'[2] As part of the general pageantry of those first weeks he'd invited me to a *Private Eye* lunch. And that, more than anything, was a signal that this story was only just beginning.

Another reason the media reaction was so vehement was that practically every commentator was not merely a fan of *Woman's Hour*, but an associate. They flocked to the Christmas support party we organised in a pub round the corner from Broadcasting House. It was called The Cock, and no one managed to refrain from unworthy comments on this theme.

At the same time, Broadcasting House was host to a press party to celebrate the marriage of two long-standing characters from The Archers,[3] Shula and David. The Council Chamber is an illustrious room decorated with large, sombre portraits of past Director Generals. Journalists attending the party were enchanted to notice attached to each portrait a badge declaiming: 'I'm a *Woman's Hour* Man.' We'd had the badges made in haste the previous week, to send to the dozens of male listeners who wrote in support of the programme.

The sustained mutiny was regarded by the press as knockabout fun, a light relief from the dark clouds looming as the Gulf War became more inevitable in the closing weeks of 1990. Within the BBC there was amusement from some, mounting disapproval and exasperation from further up. But for the team working on the threatened programme, this was a matter of extreme gravity. We believed we were fighting to preserve something precious – a cultural force that mattered.

So how had an afternoon speech radio programme attained its iconic position in the first place? *Woman's Hour* burst on to the airwaves on 7 October 1946, on the Light Programme. Its purpose, defined by its creator Norman Collins, was to recreate home life after the ravages of war. The first presenter was a man, Alan Ivieson, who introduced the programme to the strains of *Oranges and Lemons*, the first signature tune:

> Good afternoon – and welcome to our first *Woman's Hour*. It's to be a regular feature in the Light Programme – and I hope you will find time to join us as often as you can. In fact, it's *your* programme – designed for *you*. There will be talks by experts on keeping house, on health, on children, furnishing, beauty care – in fact on everything concerned with your sort of problems in the home. Now with us today, we have first of all Mrs Mary Manton, and you are going to talk about midday meals, aren't you, Mrs Manton?

Indeed, the programme did have a passionate interest in domestic detail, with earnest advice on how to knit your own stair carpet, how to bleach your blackout curtains and how to deslime your flannel. Curiously, though, right from the beginning, it began to reach beyond that modest brief.

In 1946 there was a series in which different women talked about their jobs, and in the same year a campaign began for a weekend repeat of the programme for working women. There was coverage of the Royal Commission on Equal Pay in 1946, a campaign for better wages for home-workers in 1947, and in 1948 a talk about the menopause caused angry memos to fly from on high.

> It is acutely embarrassing to hear about hot flushes, diseases of the ovaries, the possibilities of womb removal and so on being transmitted on 376 kilowatts at two o'clock in the afternoon.
>
> (Assistant Controller: 1948)

Those of us working on the programme in the 1980s inherited a powerful legacy. Despite the changes in the lives of women, the shifting attitudes to work and home, children and careers, romance and independence, the programme never wavered in its primary mission – to put women first. The eclectic mix of items – then as now – reflected the culture of women's magazines: something inspiring, something amusing, some domestic advice, lots of medical items, practical and financial tips, inspirational interviews, the arts and current affairs. And a good story at the end.

It was a comforting and at the same time stimulating cocktail, designed for women who were at home. They were learning how to be housewives, feeding their boom babies dead on two o'clock as dictated by the fashionable childcare guru Truby King whose inflexible routines neatly provided *Woman's Hour* with its captive audience. Right from those very early years, it was a lifeline to millions – a friend, a companion, an adviser.

Woman's Hour was one of the earliest programmes to address its listeners intimately and directly and to respond to their questions and needs. Its reputation for speaking frankly about matters that many shy away from was established by our brave predecessors who, with their six million listeners and a thousand letters a week, knew what women needed and courageously provided it. In 1955 the programme was the first to mention homosexuality, and in 1956 prostitution. As the early editor Janet Quigley put it: '*Woman's Hour* has a policy of bringing hush-hush topics into the open' (Quigley 1956). In 1956, when it first broadcast a talk about cancer, there was a warning that some people might wish to switch off. A similar invitation was issued by the veteran presenter Olive Shapley in 1967, when she warned that some listeners may be shocked by the next item, an interview with two young people who had chosen to live together without getting married.

By the time we had taken over, listeners were no longer invited to switch off when sensitive items were broached. While most expected to be challenged by us there was a section of the Radio 4 audience who seemed to look out for it, always writing in to complain if items like contraception, or sexy bits of the serial, appeared during the school holidays. Mary Hill, who was deputy editor of *Woman's Hour* in the mid-fifties, remembers producing a pioneering piece about a family planning clinic with information about contraception (Feldman 1995). She received two huge stacks of mail, one containing disgusted complaints, the other grateful thanks – a pattern that has never changed.

It is in the area of health and medicine where *Woman's Hour* listeners have most consistently valued the programme's frankness and willingness to address intimate subjects. From the very beginning, producers have regularly received what we all referred to as 'that letter' – the letter which says: 'Three doctors told me I was being hysterical and there was nothing wrong with me. And then I heard about it on your programme.' The 'it' may have changed – depression, anorexia, ME, any number of gynaecological complaints – but the sentiment has been the same. I heard about it on your programme and know I am not alone. Many women have written and still write to the programme thanking it for saving their lives.

As well as offering a forum for its listeners to share their experiences and to make others feel less alone, *Woman's Hour* has always followed current affairs, tracing the progress of women in public life, employment and politics. Margaret Bondfield, the first woman cabinet minister, was an early guest, as was Nancy Astor. Politicians like Shirley Williams, Gillian Shepherd and Harriet Harman have been regular contributors – and naturally the first woman prime minister herself was interviewed several times. Women politicians often remarked on how refreshing it was to be able to conduct civilised discussion across parties on subjects of mutual interest. In addition, a whole catalogue of celebrity guests from every walk of life have offered inspiration, role models, fantasy. The programme has been host to countless actresses, novelists, designers, artists, poets, business women, cooks, athletes, explorers, world leaders, academics and musicians.

So it was not merely a radio programme that Michael Green was threatening, but a national institution, a symbol of stability in a changing world, a constant even for those who chose to ridicule or attack it. It was, above all, a brand name. And that was how it survived.

It seems incredible, in the decade of focus groups and marketing strategies, that the notion of brand identity in the early 1990s was alien to BBC radio. One of my first reactions when the bombshell hit had been to write a paper on the value of the WH brand. After some discussion it was accepted that perhaps Radio 4 might benefit from the wisdom of the advertising world. Two agencies were consulted. The Controller selected Lowe Bell, the BBC agency. *Woman's Hour* chose Maggie Taylor, who as Cowan, Kemsley, Taylor had recently set up a breakaway partnership from Saatchi and Saatchi. We briefed Maggie not to question the proposed time change, merely the brand name. She put on an extraordinary performance in the presence of the Controller, the editors and a couple of BBC executives. Pacing the floor with barely controlled energy, she cited brand names she had boosted: British Airways, Guinness, Lucozade, Babycham. *Woman's Hour*, to her, was another strong name which carried more power than meaning. She mentioned a few tactics we might like to consider if the time were changed, just to keep the excellent brand name 'top of the mind'. To do anything else, she opined, would be poor business.

The result, a week later, was climb-down. The Controller confessed he had had a terrible Christmas, 'having my head bashed at parties for trying to kill the nation's most hallowed radio treasure' (Feldman 1991a). He still felt uncomfortable about the name, but Maggie Taylor had convinced him it was 'a useful handle' for guiding the listeners into the new slot. The victory was not without conditions, however. He set me two goals: increasing the male listenership, and maintaining the audience at 500,000 per day (two and a half million per week.) I was asked to write a paper outlining my strategy for achieving these objectives. Amazingly, given the constraints under which programme makers operate today, I was the first editor to be set targets. And I had to hurry. It was now January. Launch day was September.

The strategy paper I presented argued that while the programme would need to match its new morning slot with a busier pace, a more crowded agenda and a less formal feel, it must retain its essential character and appeal. I defined the factors that have always made it unique:

- The female focus. It has always covered areas of special interest to women – from home-making to employment, childbirth to fashion
- It favours women speakers and guests to cover an encyclopaedic range, allowing it to look at the whole world – in a female way.

I dubbed this two-track policy Twin Peaks – both 'women's interests' and 'female perspective'. Exclusively women's items which are closely defined – and a female perspective illuminating a limitless variety of subjects and ideas:

> 'Women's interests' can be defined as any area of life where women's experiences are still separate and different from those of men. Sexual politics constitute one important element – it is part of the programme's mandate to monitor instances of discrimination against women and how that is being combated. This is the lens through which the programme explores life in different countries; different professions; sex and love; psychotherapy or shopping. Whatever affects women distinctly is, for us, women's interests. At the same time we make it our business to address both sexes in areas that have traditionally been regarded as female – parenting rather than mothering; men as well as women talking about cookery, fashion, knitting.
>
> (Feldman 1991b: 5)

The other peak, 'female perspective', accounts for the vast scope of the programme's coverage:

> South Africa; nationalism; the Gulf; nuclear power. *Woman's Hour* debates such matters with female speakers. That is one of the glories of the title. You rarely hear women experts on general subjects elsewhere, because ours is the only programme which positively discriminates in its choice of speakers. This is what gives the programme such a distinctive sound.
>
> (Feldman, 1991b: 6)

To be honest, the changes we wrought were cosmetic rather than fundamental. Reflecting the busier feel of morning routines, more short, snappy pieces were injected to punctuate the longer debates and crafted features, as well as more celebrity guests and audience interaction. The daily serial would continue to be a showcase for women's writing. Two other important elements remained intact. One was the weekly editions broadcast from different regional centres, offering unique coverage of women's lives and interests. The other was international items. Listeners were fascinated by reports from all over the world, and particularly loved details of how women lived and how families operated in different cultures and continents.

What was different, however, was the aggressive self-consciousness with which we trailed and publicised the 'new' *Woman's Hour*. Every hapless celebrity was inveigled to record a *Woman's Hour* tribute. One producer still blushes when she recalls forcing the footballer Gary Lineker to say: 'I scored on *Woman's Hour*.' The trails littered the network for the month running up to the relaunch. Our much-vaunted policy of embracing the male listenership pretty much rested on that – by putting out packages of male voices praising the programme, we were signifying to men that they were welcome.

The relaunch of *Woman's Hour* was the most prominent of a raft of schedule changes on Radio 4 designed to see off a new rival: Radio 5. This was not today's 5Live, a winning combination of news and sport, but an earlier version, a weak hybrid of sport, education, and children's programming. It all helped to keep the spotlight on BBC radio – which was good news for us.

Those early weeks were heady times for the *Woman's Hour* team. Exhausted with early mornings and packed days we may have been, but we were riding high. Audience figures for those first weeks were good and although they had undoubtedly been fuelled by the glare of publicity it was fair to assume that when they settled again they would retain a respectable lift. Possibly that's what happened. But we'll never know. Because, luckily for all of us, this period coincided with another radical change in British radio. Audience figures for BBC radio used to be computed on a different system from those of commercial stations. In late 1991 the two systems were joined to form RAJAR, which estimated audience size and appreciation through new methodology, rendering it impossible to make genuine comparisons with the old system.

This was fortunate for *Woman's Hour*, because according to the new system we were easily past the 500,000 per day figure – averaging nearly 700,000 in the first six months and with a high audience appreciation, though not one that could accurately be linked with the previous method. In addition, it was not clear whether we were meant to be increasing the 10.30am Radio 4 audience (laughably easy to do because it had traditionally bobbed near the bed of the graph) or the existing afternoon *Woman's Hour* audience.

But politics and statistics were both on our side. Having caused all that fuss, the Controller was morally obliged to greet the new schedules, and hence our programme's performance, as a success. Helped by the fudged figures, he did just that. And, miraculously, the male listenership rose from 28 per cent to 33 per cent – I'll never know how. I suppose it could have been those delightful trails. I certainly claimed it was. But probably it had more to do with the passing morning radio trade of truck drivers and travelling salesmen, redundant BBC producers and stay-at-home fathers who were beginning to make up the much-touted changing demographics.

We had been rehabilitated. Indeed, it seemed that we had never been stronger. Clare had returned in time for the historic move, but now working part-time in an inventive new arrangement. The BBC had welcomed into the fold an even stronger partnership than before. We were joint editors, the most senior jobshare in the corporation. No longer rebelling, though, we were once again targets for attack. Inevitably, there was the odd outbreak of criticism of the programme, just as there always had been. A furore erupted when Jenni Murray penned a slightly outspoken think piece for the June 1992 edition of *Options* magazine. She gave the view that marriage was a trap, women shouldn't touch it, it was legalised prostitution. ('I was only quoting Mary Wollestonecraft', she explained plaintively, amid the crossfire.)

Once again, the nation was on fire. The *Daily Mail* sent snoopers with zoom lenses to spy on her family, her kids, her mother. There were questions in the House and calls for her dismissal. We were very chastened. Of course, all this was really business as usual. They loved us when we were fighting a popular cause and loathed us again after we'd won it. Nothing very surprising about that. But I yearned to capture that glory again. The ideal opportunity was the programme's fiftieth anniversary.

Our agreed aims were to extend awareness of the programme right across the country, welcoming listeners from all areas and backgrounds. Emphasising the future rather than dwelling on the past, we wanted to give the audience extra value as a reward for fifty years of loyalty. A schedule of outside broadcasts all over the country included literary discussions and quizzes, as well as a Leap Day all-male balloon debate. At the heart of the year's celebrations was an ambitious initiative, Best of Health! Supported by the Department of Health, it centred round a specially adapted double decker bus which toured the country dispensing advice and offering space to local health groups and campaigns. The programme traced its progress and broadcast live from a series of locations.

In addition to this massive public awareness exercise, the daily programme threw up more and more birthday stunts. We asked listeners to vote for the top fifty *Woman's Hour* men; we created a chart of the top twenty best songs for women. We launched a set of commemorative playing cards celebrating our favourite women. One of the highlights of the year was Jenni Murray's *The Woman's Hour*, a history of fifty years of British women, informed and illustrated by extracts from the programme's archives (Murray 1996). The press coverage was gratifying, with regional coverage all through the year and a blitz of national newspaper articles during the week of the anniversary itself. The *Radio Times*[4] devoted a special issue to us, featuring a naked Helen Mirren on the cover (which caused more anguished debate within the ranks).

Five hundred women from every field – doctors and lawyers, agony aunts and politicians, novelists and actresses, explorers and sportswomen, fashion designers, cooks and captains of industry – attended a glittering celebration at the Victoria and Albert Museum. Champagne flowed as guests paraded before the *Woman's Hour* quilt – an eighty-patch memorial created by listeners in celebration of seventy-five years of women's suffrage. After a two-year national tour, the quilt had been donated to the Museum, and hung that evening as a tribute to the programme and to the women it celebrated.

Clare Selerie and I have moved on now, as have many of the producers who made our working lives so stimulating. Jenni Murray and Martha Kearney are presenting the programme with a younger team, headed by editor Ruth Gardiner, who balances the demands of the job with her two young children. She seems puzzled that listeners are so exasperated at the outspoken nature of the programme. That for every daring discussion, there are two piles of letters: from the disgusted and the grateful.

She, like all of us, is carrying on the candle of a great institution, where all the ghosts of the past are hovering above, smiling ironically and urging her to be just as annoying as all her predecessors. Ruth has, after all, a duty to bring hush-hush topics into the open, and to make everyone who tunes in feel that they have joined a club and found a friend.

Notes

1 *Today* is BBC Radio 4's flagship news and current affairs breakfast programme.
2 Feldman, S., 1990, private conversation with Ian Hislop, editor of the weekly satirical magazine *Private Eye*, whose legendary lunches are much gossiped about in media circles.
3 *The Archers* – the long-running daily soap opera on Radio 4, concerning a farming community.
4 *Radio Times* – weekly listings magazine published by the BBC. The *Woman's Hour* cover edition was 5–11 October 1996.

References

BBC (1948) Internal Memo, Assistant Controller, Talks.
Feldman, S. (1991a), private conversation with Michael Green, Controller Radio 4.
Feldman, S. (1991b) Strategy Paper.
Feldman, S. (1995), private conversation with Mary Hill.
Murray, J. (1996) *The Woman's Hour*, London: BBC Books.
Quigley, J. (1956) Internal BBC memo.
Shapley, O. (1967) *Woman's Hour:* broadcast 28 January 1967.

Chapter 6

Sheridan Nye, Nicola Godwin and Belinda Hollows

TWISTING THE DIALS: LESBIANS ON BRITISH RADIO

From: Gibbs, L. (ed.) (1994) *Daring to Dissent – Lesbian Culture from Margin to Mainstream.* London: Cassell, pp. 147–67.

Why radio?

Radio may lack the glamour of film or television, but it is undoubtedly an essential part of everyday life for millions of people. As an instant, easily accessible means of *communication* it has no equal and here lies its potential for lesbians – both as listeners and as programme-makers.

It would be pre-emptive to construct a theory of a 'lesbian radio genre', as lesbians have hardly developed a large enough body of material from which significant patterns could usefully emerge. Lesbians are rarely heard on radio, and those who are heard are often lone voices from within the heterosexual mainstream. Without the benefit (or hindrance) of a sense of history of our involvement in radio, each lesbian's contribution has tended to be an isolated event, passing by largely unnoticed by wider lesbian culture.

However, what has also been overlooked is the enthusiasm and sheer numbers of lesbian radio listeners who regularly tune in to a variety of programmes, and who are not hearing much that reflects their own lifestyles, concerns and cultures. Data reflecting lesbians' consumer tastes is hard to come by in relation to *any* product, let alone the media, and to estimate the time lesbians spend listening to radio is notoriously difficult.

[. . .]

It is difficult to confirm the extent to which radio is a popular accompaniment to our own daily routines without adequate research material on lesbians' lifestyles.

A clue may be found in the findings of a survey recently completed by One in Ten radio production group. Preliminary results show that around 60 per cent of lesbians questioned (all over 25 years old) listen regularly to BBC Radio 4.[1]

Before considering how lesbian programme makers could tap into this potential audience it is worth taking a look at lesbians' relationship with radio over the past forty years or so.

Lesbians in radio history

[. . .]

Ironically, the BBC's reverence for 'high culture', which continued long after Reith's retirement, ensured that radio drama would often set out to challenge its audience, both aesthetically and intellectually. This occasionally involved challenging pre-conceptions and prejudices as well, and consequently fictional lesbians were featuring on British radio long before lesbianism was considered to be in any way an 'acceptable' lifestyle. In the 1950s several such programmes were broadcast, including *Corrick's House*, a play about a teacher/schoolgirl relationship, and a reading of Sappho's poetry on the Third Programme. In 1952 even *The Archers* explored the lesbian relationship theme (an affair between Christine Archer and an older woman).

Unfortunately, radio's transient nature means that, once broadcast, lesbian material is unlikely to pass into lesbian folklore. Radio listening is often a matter of a 'chance hearing' and individual radio programmes rarely get much in the way of pre-publicity, whereas books and videos can be reviewed, reread and passed around among friends. Sadly, there are no records of most early lesbian material as only a percentage of radio broadcasts are ever selected for preservation in archives.

Some of the earliest references to lesbianism were almost certainly made on *Woman's Hour* (The first radio feature about *male* homosexuality was broadcast on the programme sometime in the late 1940s, although no record is available). From its launch in 1946 *Woman's Hour* continued the BBC tradition of daytime radio as a 'companion' for the housewife. Anne Karpf describes early programmes as seeming sometimes 'like a soothing lozenge'.[2] In fact, the programme's producers were keen to broaden this role at least as early as 1957; in the foreword to *The Woman's Hour Book*, the programme editor, Joanna Scott-Moncrieff, claims: 'With the passing of the years the number of minutes from Woman's Hour devoted entirely to practical, domestic matters has gradually been reduced.'[3] The menopause and wages for home makers were among the subjects aired on the earliest programmes.

There was no assumption that the housewife's lot was a blissfully happy one, either. In 1952, among talks on 'The Christian ideal of marriage' and 'Spotlight on a well-dressed woman', Moya Woodside questioned young women's idealistic expectations of their husbands in 'The ideals and realities of marriage'. In a frank admission of women's dissatisfaction with their lot, Scott-Moncrieff set out the aims of the programme:

to lift the load of loneliness borne by women facing misfortune and to help them realise in time of trouble that they are not alone, that others are having to keep a home running, despite the despair and discouragement of unalterable circumstances.[4]

BBC records may not tell us enough about lesbianism on early broadcasts of *Woman's Hour*, but one particular lesbian was appearing on the programme throughout the 1950s and 1960s, as well as on other popular radio series such as *My Word!*, *Any Questions?* and *In Town Tonight*. Nancy Spain was a flamboyant society lesbian, writer, journalist and broadcaster. Although not 'out' in the 1990s sense (she never referred to her lesbianism on air or in any of her newspaper articles), it was widely known that she shared a house with her long-term lover, the editor of *She* magazine, Joan Werner-Laurie. Spain openly refers to 'Jonnie' as 'my partner' in her 1961 autobiography *A Funny Thing Happened on the Way*.[5]

As a popular gossip columnist she was often found at the social gatherings of the rich and famous, invariably wearing men's trousers and shirt or a suit. She was close friends with Noel Coward, Ginette Spanier and Marlene Dietrich and was admirably suited for her speciality on *Woman's Hour* – the celebrity interview. Her former producer, Sally Thomson, says: 'She loved celebrities . . . She'd treat them like equals . . . and she'd persuade them to give some little nugget which hadn't been given to anyone else.'[6]

At the height of her fame Spain allowed the tabloid press to speculate on a possible marriage between herself and fellow broadcaster Gilbert Harding, although it seems unlikely that this was ever more than a private joke between them.[7] By the 1960s she was finding the transition from radio to television uncomfortable and her fame declined. Tragically, shortly after confiding to a friend that she thought she would probably die in an air crash, both she and Jonnie were killed while travelling on a chartered flight to the Ascot races in 1964.

One of the most popular radio plays to feature a lesbian couple as central characters was broadcast in April 1975 as part of Radio 4's 'Monday Play' series. Although a simple portrayal of a relationship, *Now She Laughs, Now She Cries* challenged contemporary mores by presenting lesbians in a positive and realistic light, while exploring negative social attitudes. The BBC, overly anxious not to offend its regular audience, broadcast an announcement before the play warning of its unsuitability for 'family listening'. As it turned out the response was pronounced and enthusiastic and the author, Jill Hyem, received hundreds of letters from delighted lesbians who felt they had been accurately represented for the first time. Ironically several listeners wrote to the *Radio Times* to complain that the warning itself was offensive and unnecessary, including a vicar who condemned the caveat and declared: 'this was the best play about love I have ever heard'.[8]

While the portrayal of lesbians in drama can present a rare opportunity for the lesbian listener/viewer to experience complex, well-rounded characterizations within mainstream culture, the temptation to succumb to stereotyping as a form of shorthand has overwhelmed many writers and producers. The caricature butch and unhappy lesbian in film has been well documented,[9] but stereotyping on radio is not such an easy option. In their survey of lesbian and gay portrayal on television and radio,[10] Lorraine Trenchard and Mark Finch comment: 'Lesbian and gay stereotyping seems dependent on a *visual* checklist – the overtly masculine or the limp-wristed' (emphasis added). Their survey showed that, of 688 hours of British radio monitored during the week 12–18 August 1985, only 0.32 per cent mentioned either lesbians or gay men. Lesbians were mentioned only once during the monitoring period – an insulting remark made during a drama, *Bilgewater*, serialized on *Woman's Hour*.

Portrayal of lesbians in drama is always controversial because its unavoidable by-product is a contribution to mainstream society's perception of lesbians. In the United States the portrayal of a bisexual, ice-pick-wielding murderer in the film *Basic Instinct* attracted condemnation from the Gay and Lesbian Alliance Against Defamation (GLAD). Claiming the film would create an unflattering image of lesbians and bisexual women as homicidal maniacs, GLAD expressed a very real fear of the effects of negative 'PR'.

In contrast, coverage of lesbian issues within radio news and current affairs is sporadic, but often surprisingly fair. In part this demonstrates the advantage radio can offer as a *live* medium for lesbians to express their views directly to the public. Access to live broadcasting is far easier on radio than on television, particularly on local radio where the 'phone-in' discussion programme is a cheap and popular format; as dependably 'controversial' subject-matter, lesbians are often invited to face inquisition by the curious public. The publishing and social group Sappho appeared on numerous such programmes during the 1970s and 1980s, discussing subjects ranging from artificial insemination and lesbian motherhood to general equality issues. Jackie Forster, a Sappho founder member, claims she was usually treated fairly in the debates and often felt that the presenters were 'on our side'.

The passage of Clause 28[11] through Parliament in 1988 caused a flurry of interest in lesbian and gay issues, particularly on BBC radio. On *Woman's Hour* Ann Taylor brought a rational perspective to the issue of gay sex education in schools, contrasting the views of Conservative MP David Wiltshire on 'pretend' families with the contented family life of a lesbian couple and their five-year-old child. *Third Ear* on Radio 3 examined the threat of 'backdoor censorship' posed by the clause, and *File on Four* investigated the potential increase in incidences of 'gay bashing'. All these programmes betrayed an undercurrent of liberalism in allowing both sides of the debate to air their views, while focusing on the negative effects of the clause. Phone-ins on Radio London's *Robbie Vincent* show and Radio 4's *Call Nick Ross* opened the floor to gay men, lesbians and homophobes alike.

Obviously, access to radio is not always enough to guarantee a fair hearing. In 1972 Sappho complained to *Woman's Hour* after one of its members, a lesbian mother, was invited on the programme only to find that her co-guest was a psychiatrist. At the time it was considered appropriate in the media to 'qualify' the opinions of lesbians and gay men with comment from the medical profession. Sappho were among the first to challenge this and was rewarded by *Woman's Hour* capitulation when the group refused to appear on any future programme if a psychiatrist was also invited.

Undoubtedly there have been occasions over the years when newsworthy lesbians have not been represented at all. In April 1993 the lesbian and gay 'March on Washington' was reported neither on BBC radio nor on television despite being the largest civil rights march ever held in the United States, and despite wide coverage in the British press and on satellite television. It is possible that the complaints which followed, made by various lesbian and gay organizations including Outrage and the BBC's own lesbian and gay group, affected the BBC's coverage of the serial-killer story which dominated newspaper headlines during June 1993. In something of a departure for the BBC, both television and radio broadcast interviews with community activists and gay men in pubs and clubs during the hunt for the killer of five gay men in London.

While this may be an indication of a new willingness to listen to the gay community, *Woman's Hour* is probably the only programme to have addressed lesbian representation head-on by allocating a producer with particular responsibility for lesbian issues. This clearly had some bearing on a discussion in 1993 on the Child Support Act which featured lesbian mothers as participants. In March of the same year a feature on lesbian crime fiction included readings by some prominent authors, including Mary Wings.

Women make up just over half of Radio 4's weekly audience of nine million, and *Woman's Hour* itself commands a daily audience of 600,000, so the programme's reputation of being almost a part of the national fabric is hardly surprising. This explains the outrage felt by the tabloid press at *Woman's Hour's* positive attitude towards lesbians. In an article in the *Daily Mail* headlined 'BBC Lesbians' Hour'[12] a former presenter, Jean Metcalfe, described the programme as having 'an obsession with being politically correct'. She continued, 'there's so much militancy at the BBC. They keep going on and on about feminism and gay issues'. The current programme editor Sally Feldman responded, 'We have always evoked criticism from one corner or another. It is an established tradition of *Woman's Hour* to go ahead and talk frankly about any subject. We have a duty to do that.'

A national radio station that has frequently covered lesbian and gay issues, often with little or no comment from the press, is Radio 5. Launched in August 1990 as a repository for the sport, youth and schools programming previously broadcast on Radios 3 and 4, Radio 5 has struggled with its ungainly remit to establish a coherent identity, and was recently described by one journalist as a: 'jerry-built shambles'[13]. However, the influence of gay-positive producers at the station has inspired confidence in gay programming for teenagers, and Radio 5 has included young lesbian and gay participants in several of its programmes, including a *Guardian* award-winning feature on safe sex. Caroline Raphael, editor of youth programmes on Radio 5, chose to appoint some of her producers from theatrical rather than broadcasting backgrounds in the interests of encouraging originality in her section. As a consequence new people were brought in who were either gay themselves or who were used to working on gay and lesbian productions.

In 1991 one such producer, Anne Edyvean, directed a dramatization by Sarah Daniels of Nancy Garden's novel *Annie on My Mind* (Virago Upstart series, 1988), which told the tale of schoolgirl love in the face of condemnation at home and school. Although not sexually explicit, the novel was notable for alluding to teenage lesbian sex while managing to avoid moral condemnation by the tabloid press. Says Anne Edyvean, the producer, 'I don't really know why the tabloids didn't pick up on us. In fact we got good reviews in both the *Daily Telegraph* and the *Times Educational Supplement*.'

While local authorities dared not be seen 'promoting' homosexuality, fearing the uncertain consequences of contravening Clause 28, Radio 5 fulfilled a valuable role in bringing lesbian and gay life to Britain's teenagers. This makes the announcement that the station is to close in April 1994, to make way for 24-hour news and sport, all the more tragic.[14]

Radio: up for grabs in the 1990s?

Both the commercial and public-service sectors of the radio industry have experienced radical change over the last decade. Some of these changes, while doing little for job security in the industry, do offer possibilities for new and exciting programming as competition between rival broadcasters hots up.

[. . .]

In their drive to deliver maximum audiences to advertisers, ILR may leave lesbian, gay and progressive women's programming out in the cold. This is often proving to be the case as many stations are choosing to concentrate on local news and events, these being cheaper to produce than speech-based features.

An exception that proves the rule is the 1992 Sony award-winner for best new station, Wear FM. Commended by the judges for its 'verve, style and wit' the Humberside station includes a regular lesbian and gay programme, *Gay 2 Gay*. If *Gay 2 Gay* sometimes sounds like a camp version of Radio 1's *Steve Wright Show*, with the 'Gay 2 Gay Gang' providing a backdrop of frivolous gay banter, the host, Michael Lumsdon, is unrepentant: '*Gay 2 Gay* is definitely not a political programme ramming gay rights down people's throats. I think you can get the message across in a less confrontational way through entertainment.'[15]

[. . .]

In his 1992 policy document *Extending Choice*, Director General, John Birt sets out the BBC's objectives for radio: 'to assign priority to those networks and services which are truly distinctive and unlikely ever to be matched in the commercial marketplace.'[16] Significantly for potential lesbian programme makers, under the heading 'A clear public purpose for the BBC' another stated aim is 'to take risks with innovative programming'.[17] In the summer of 1992 BBC Network Radio pre-empted an expected statutory requirement for radio by announcing it would be working towards a voluntary target of 10 per cent independent production by 1996. These two factors, 'distinctive' programming and the opening up of production to outsiders with the necessary skills and ideas have already resulted in more out lesbians on BBC radio.

The first independent production on Radio 4 was also BBC Radio's first lesbian and gay programme. *A Sunday Outing*[18] was a two-hour live magazine programme broadcast of St Valentine's Day 1993 from Broadcasting House in London and the Flamingo Club in Blackpool Produced by Outcast Media Productions (an offshoot of an informal networking group for lesbians and gay men working in the media called 'First Tuesday'). *A Sunday Outing* was promoted as 'taking the lesbian and gay community into the heart of the establishment', but was allocated a Sunday afternoon slot where, by Radio 4's own admission, there were 'no listeners left to lose'. Under pressure to address straight Radio 4 listeners as well as a general lesbian and gay audience, Outcast stuck to familiar themes – coming out, homosexuality and religion, the existence or otherwise of the gay community – interspersed with vaudeville cabaret. In the event the programme suffered somewhat from its own self-consciousness as the first gay and lesbian enterprise on national radio. Described by the *Independent* as a 'tranquil affair' the programme failed to generate much enthusiasm among gay or straight listeners although it was a success in technical terms considering the ambitious scale of the event.

Despite *A Sunday Outing*'s lukewarm reception BBC Radio, encouraged by the lack of any serious backlash against its first lesbian and gay production, went on to commission two other gay magazine programmes. *Loud and Proud* was a series of six half-hour shows on Radio 1, 'for young lesbians gay men and their friends' Broadcast during August and September 1993, and made by Outspoken Production Company from Manchester the series used an eclectic mix of news, opinion, music and celebrities to attract both gay and straight listeners. Under John Birt's *Extending Choice* regime Radio 1 has to distinguish itself from commercial stations which also rely predominantly on pop music. *Loud and Proud* fitted the bill by virtue of its lesbian and gay remit and its even balance of music and speech-based features. In contrast with *A Sunday Outing*, *Loud and Proud* managed to breathe new life into well-worn subjects by the inspired use of celebrities to present features, including Terry Christian on homophobia, Neneh Cherry on bisexuality and Margi Clarke on sex.

Although lesbians and gay men appeared on the programme, there were objections that the presenter of the first national radio lesbian and gay series was a straight woman. Club DJ Paulette is a popular performer in gay clubs in Manchester and London and was invited to anchor the programme by Outspoken. *Loud and Proud* producer Mark Ovenden explained in the *Pink Paper*: 'We asked Paulette to do the show because she epitomises everything about the way we want to make lesbian and gay issues more acceptable to the straight community.'[19] While this stance against ghettoization may have been successful in not alienating straight listeners, it raises the question of how 'acceptable' lesbians can be – or would ever wish to be.

While both *A Sunday Outing* and *Loud and Proud* sought to fit in with the established order, another BBC lesbian and gay magazine series, *Gay and Lesbian London*, has been spared scrutiny and allowed simply to reflect the interests of London's gay and lesbian community. *Gay and Lesbian London*, on the Corporation's local station, Greater London Radio, is a weekly hour of news and pop music similar to *Loud and Proud* but with more emphasis on news and events. As a community access (rather than independent) production, all staff and presenters are volunteers and the programme is put together on a less-than-generous weekly budget of £90. The BBC recently showed its commitment to the show by moving it to GLR's FM frequency. (GLR's medium-wave frequency is likely to be reallocated by the Radio Authority to ILR in the near future.) Roving reporter Rebecca Sandles believes the project is benefiting from the way lesbians and gay men are 'taken more seriously these days'.

Gay and Lesbian London's success highlights how lesbians and gay men living in innercities form *geographical* audiences sharing common interests and so are ideally suited to local radio 'special interest' programming. The *commercial viability* of this gay, urban audience was demonstrated recently by the success of *G-Spot* on Brighton Festival Radio. The two-hour weekly magazine programme comfortably financed itself with on-air adverts made by the G-Spot production self for various local lesbian and gay businesses.

[. . .]

Community radio has spawned Britain's longest running gay radio programme, *G.A.Y.*, broadcast on the west London station Spectrum 558.[20] *G.A.Y.* started in August 1992 and is one of a number of programme 'strands' on Spectrum, most of which target London's ethnic communities. Effervescent club DJ Jeremy Joseph hosts and produces the programme, blending the latest in club-music with celebrity interviews (Debbie Harry and Jason Donovan have both been guests), phone-ins and discussions. Interestingly, response to the phone-ins suggests the audience is probably made up of equal numbers of men and women – nearly as many lesbians as gay men phone in to the programme to express their points of view during discussion slots. Although this could mean simply that lesbians are more inclined to phone in to radio programmes, it may be that club culture can reach across gender boundaries in a way that more serious, issue-based programming can not.

Despite its community-service remit Spectrum is an unashamedly commercial enterprise. By the end of its first six months of broadcasting *G.A.Y.* had conclusively demonstrated its commercial viability by virtue of the enthusiastic response of London's lesbians and gay men and by the amount of advertising time bought up by lesbian and gay businesses. Joseph's reward was an increase in air time from one hour a week to ten, and the programme now broadcasts five two-hour programmes every week.[21]

The way forward?

In short, radio is a relatively cheap and accessible medium, ripe for exploitation by lesbian programme makers. But before we can take full advantage we need both to overcome our commercially ill-defined status and to convince programme commissioners of the size and enthusiasm of the lesbian audience.

Past performance shows lesbians' access to radio is sporadic at best and largely subject to the editorial whims of established programmes like *Woman's Hour*. Blending in with mainstream programming may be what most lesbians want from radio, but the One in Ten survey shows that most of the lesbians who regularly listen to Radio 4 are unhappy with its coverage of lesbian and gay issues.

Radio 4 drama producer Sue Wilson is optimistic that the only thing standing in the way of greater lesbian input to BBC radio drama is the willingness of lesbian writers to submit suitable material:

> I think even less interest is taken in lesbian issues than in gay men's, and I think that's regrettable. But, to be honest I can't even say I've had bad lesbian plays submitted to me because I've never even had one. I'd very much like to see more lesbians sending in their material.[22]

So far lesbians have had most success achieving *regular* air time when working with gay men. The successes and failures of these projects have thrown up two points. First, the tastes of lesbians and gay men, while not mutually exclusive, will not always coincide. As BBC Radio and *A Sunday Outing* producer Nicola Meyrick describes it: 'Lesbians and gay men share a common repression, but do not always share common interests.' Second, keeping a balance of these disparate interests within programmes can be difficult, particularly when so few lesbian performers feel they can safely be 'out' without jeopardizing their careers. Meyrick believes lesbians who choose to be out in their professional lives: 'risk being type-cast as some sort of arbiter of lesbian experience',[23] and may lose out on mainstream opportunities.

[. . .]

A short-term but successful women's radio station broadcast on a festival radio licence in March 1992. Timed to coincide with International Women's Week, Fem FM grew out of the ideas and enthusiasm of two women from Bristol commercial radio, Caroline Mitchell and Trish Caverly. Although Fem FM broadcast no explicitly lesbian-targeted programmes, lesbian perspectives tended to pop up quite naturally in coverage of the arts, entertainment and health, and several lesbian technicians and presenters were involved. The project worked well as a collaboration between straight and gay women, and between professionals and women new to broadcasting. All programmes were produced locally and roughly equal amounts of air time were given over to music, presented by local women DJs, and speech. Undoubtedly Fem FM would never have got off the ground without the inspiration and fund-raising skills of Mitchell and Caverly, who secured £20,000 sponsorship from sources as diverse as Avon County Council and Aer Lingus.

Women involved in Fem FM testify to the easy-going atmosphere at the station. Most decisions were made only after collective discussion and 'goodwill was Fem FM's most valuable resource'.[24] Several women have since got together to launch another station, this time as part of the Women in Music festival in London in March 1994. Brazen Radio aims to be London's first women's station and to 'give London a taste of what women can do'.[25] The Brazen production group already has in place a provisional programming schedule which includes a Saturday night magazine-style programme for lesbians. Brazen's Vicky Carter says: 'We want a lesbian programme which reflects lesbian interests, but we don't want to pigeon-hole people. We want lesbians to contribute across the board to different areas of the station.'[26]

[. . .]

Establishing commercial confidence is not the only obstacle to lesbian exposure on radio and it would be naive not to acknowledge how mainstream radio places restrictions on programme makers. Both the BBC and commercial sector are subject to guidelines on political impartiality, taste and decency, enforced ultimately by the government. Commercial values in themselves can amount to a form of self-censorship, given that all forms of commercial media are obliged to avoid offending the advertisers who fund them. Perhaps even more significantly the personal beliefs and values of station controllers and commissioners often determine the tone of programmes – in 1983 a BBC producer came close to losing her job for daring to combine the subjects of lesbianism and religion in a feature she made for a Radio 4 religious series.

A radical way of avoiding commercial restrictions and mainstream pressures is to take control of *distribution*. Fruit FM is the provisional title of a pirate radio station planned by three young lesbians in Hackney, London for launch in 1994. Describing their programming as, 'a mix of radical music, features, weird jingles, improper poetry and bad language' and with material '*chosen* by lesbians, but not necessarily by or about lesbians,'[27] Fruit FM challenges the view that the only way into the media is via mainstream acceptance.

Queertalk is another example of the do-it-yourself spirit. Produced with the help of the Local Radio Workshop in 1993, a series of 30-minute tapes were distributed to gay bars and cafés in London. Each tape contained a slightly uneven blend of irreverent humour, news and features. Lesbian involvement in the project was minimal and the material itself contained little of direct relevance to lesbians.

Despite some of the difficulties outlined above there are many ways lesbians can exploit radio's potential. Only rudimentary training is needed and radio offers a whole range of opportunities for creative and political expression, from drama and music to news and current affairs. Several colleges and organizations provide courses for women who wish to learn radio production skills.

It has been said that a basic requirement of a democratic media system should be: 'that it represents all significant interests in society. It should facilitate their participation in the common domain, enable them to contribute to public debate and have an input in the framing of public policy.'[28] According to these standards lesbians are entitled to a channel of communication through which to address one another and society as a whole. Until lesbians take more responsibility for radio output we will twist the dials in vain in our effort to find a voice which speaks appropriately and independently about our culture and experience.

Notes

1 The results of this survey were not fully collated at the time of writing.
2 Anne Karpf, *Radio Times*, in K. Davis *et al.* (eds), *Out of Focus*. The Women's Press, London, 1987, p. 175.
3 Joanna Scott-Moncrieff and M. Hart, *The Woman's Hour Book*. The Windmill Press, London, 1957.
4 *Ibid.*
5 Nancy Spain, *A Funny Thing Happened on the Way*. Hutchinson, London, 1964.
6 *Radio Lives*, broadcast on BBC Radio 4, 17 June 1993.
7 Biography of Nancy Spain by Rose Collis, Cassell, London, (1995).
8 Jill Hyem, personal notes.
9 Caroline Sheldon, 'Lesbians in film', in K. Davis *et al.* (eds), *Out of Focus*. The Women's Press, London, 1987.
10 Lorraine Trenchard and Mark Finch, Gays and Broadcasting Project, *Are We Being Served?* Hall-Carpenter Archive and London Media Project, 1985.
11 This clause of the 1988 Local Government Act prohibits the 'promotion' of homosexuality by schools and local authorities.
12 Rebecca Hardy, *Daily Mail*, 9 February 1993.
13 John Dugdale, 'Breaking up is hard to do', *Guardian*, 26 April 1993.
14 Maggie Brown, 'BBC plans to move Radio 5 down-market', *Independent*, 7 October 1993.
15 In interview with authors.
16 *Extending Choice: BBC's Role in the New Broadcasting Age*. BBC, London, 1992, p. 45.
17 *Ibid.*, p. 22.
18 *A Sunday Outing*, Outcast Media Productions, produced by Nicola Meyrick, 14 February 1993.
19 Trish Lesslie, 'Fleshed out radio', *Pink Paper*, 13 August 1993.
20 *G.A.Y.* broadcasts from 1 a.m. to 3 a.m. Monday to Friday on Spectrum 558am in London.
21 A lesbian presenter, Dawn Thorp, has recently been drafted in to present the Wednesday night show.
22 Sue Wilson in interview with authors.
23 Nicola Meyrich in interview with authors.
24 Vicky Carter, Fem FM, interviewed by authors.
25 Press release issued by Brazen Radio, 1993.
26 Sara Dunn interview with author.
27 Fruit FM in interview with authors.
28 James Curran, 'Rethinking the media as a public sphere', in *Communication and Citizenship*. Routledge, London, 1991.

Chapter 7

Women's Airwaves Collective

WOMEN'S AIRWAVES SURVEY

From: Local Radio Workshop (1983) *Nothing Local about it, London's Local Radio*, London: Comedia, 131–41.

Men's voices

The most striking indication of sexism on local radio was the predomination of male voices. In the week that we monitored the majority of presenters and guests on all three stations were men. On LBC's Jellybone, a two hour programme for young people (Saturday 2 May), the presenter was male, the young people's panel was exclusively male, the Agony Uncle (sic) was male and the three guests were male. Not surprisingly, all of the phone-in contributors were male: any young woman listening for the first time might have assumed that it was a programme for boys. On BBC Radio London's Rush Hour (Wednesday 29 April), one of the two presenters was a woman but of 23 voiced items only 5 of the voices were female, of the 8 reporters/interviewers only one was a woman and of the 8 interviewees only two were women. On Capital (Friday I May) all but one of the programmes were presented by men and all of the guests and presenters of items in the morning DJ show were men. The programme plans of the commercial stations provide evidence of in-built sexism. For example, although LBC claimed that they would 'encourage the expression of every shade of opinion' and give 'a fair hearing to all strata of society', they nevertheless anticipated that the only programmes to be presented by women would be 'light' ones and their use of language indicates an assumption that all their listeners would be male.

Women's Voices

Women's voices could be heard in the morning phone-in shows on BBC Radio London and LBC but very often the format of these shows mitigated against women callers and was exploited by the male presenters who seemed to use their position to patronise and make women appear stupid. They frequently interrupted women, interpreted and redefined what women were saying and were sometimes blatantly obstructive as on Radio London (Wednesday 29 April):

woman caller:	I want to talk about this Conservative council and the money they're wasting – the GLC. Cutler says you have to waste money to make money. £3½ million spent on painting the East London line and then all torn down for structural repairs.
man presenter:	(silence)
woman caller:	Are you there?
man presenter:	Yes, I'm waiting for you to explain more you see because I don't really know what you're talking about.
woman caller:	They painted the East London line up . . .
man presenter:	Right, and now it's had to be painted again.
woman caller:	They're pulling it all to bits . . .
man presenter:	Really . . . You asked Mr Cutler specifically did you why the East London line had been painted and after it had been freshly painted, structural work had been carried out?
woman caller:	No I didn't ask him.
man presenter:	Who did?
woman caller:	Well I can't mention names.
man presenter:	Well if you believe what somebody else has told you . . .

Women were speaking from their own experiences, trying to express themselves as well as they could within the limitations of the phone-in format; the short amount of time allocated to each call and the way that time was paced by the presenter's interruptions made it difficult for women to explain their views. The presenter's attitude was often dismissive instead of helpful (LBC Tuesday 28 May):

man presenter:	I don't believe you about social workers and teachers . . . Let's not get exaggerated, we're already building up some kind of myth about what social workers do. I need to be convinced that what happens happens as simply as what you told me . . . Let's not get carried away and come to the conclusion that it is the fault of the media that this happens or that happens. Thank you.

The woman was given no chance to reply. She was accused of being 'emotional' about the subject. When the presenter said he was not 'convinced' the implication was that she had to be wrong.

85

Although it is claimed that phone-ins give listeners a chance to air their views, we were left with the impression that they give the presenter the opportunity to voice *his* opinion. When women called in he effectively silenced them or trivialised their views by implying that his own were more important and obviously so. Women often sounded hesitant and apologetic (LBC Monday 27):

woman caller: You were speaking to a gentleman earlier concerning jobs availability, as I gather, I may be wrong. You seem to be implying that if one is out of work one should try to take any job that is available – am I right in thinking that?

man presenter: Yes, that's one way of putting it. What I was arguing was . . . (he explained his philosophy).

woman caller: But isn't that dictating a lot of jobs, isn't that taking someone else's job? Because practically everyone is trained or adapted to a certain job. What happens . . .

man presenter: Well, you're obviously not going to get a job for which you're not trained . . . Obviously I'm not suggesting that plumbers should take the jobs of bricklayers if they can't get a job as a plumber because they couldn't do that unless they were qualified as a bricklayer.

woman caller: Exactly.

man presenter: Yes well that's common sense of course – I'm not talking about that.

woman caller: What are you suggesting then that they should do? In other words . . .

man presenter: I'm suggesting that if there is a job available and they find they are capable of it then they should apply for it whether it's a plumbing job or not. That's all. Thank you . . .

The presenter used his position to have the last word, leaving the listener with his opinion – women's opinions were often lost in this way.

The few women presenters on local radio that week were frequently subjected to sexist comments from male presenters: 'You looked smashing on telly last night' (BBC Radio London news Tuesday 28 April). The attention of the listeners and that of the woman was diverted from the woman's task as a broadcaster to her sexual 'attractions', thus belittling her. An example from an afternoon DJ show on BBC Radio London (Thursday 30 April):

man presenter: But right now, looking as beautiful as ever, it's . . . Oh aren't you nice ha ha. Hello. Well, old flatterer that I am, yes indeed, I've forgotten what you're going to talk about today. Er yes of course, fruit and veg time isn't it?

woman presenter: That's right, yes. We've had lots of nasty weather . . .

man presenter: Let's just talk about you and forget the fruit and veg.

woman presenter: I'm sure no one's interested in me.

man presenter:	Yes they are, yes. Alright, we'd better talk about fruit and veg.
woman presenter:	'Cos it's quite sad really, we've had some quite nasty frosty weather all over the country . . . It's destroyed all the blossom on the English cherry trees and pear trees, so of course . . .
man presenter:	Has it interfered with your *pears* then?
woman presenter:	Yes it might do later on in the year. These things show later on in the year. We shall have to see, won't we?
man presenter:	Your *pears* show later on in the year do they?
woman presenter:	Yes they do.
man presenter:	Yes, because of the cold weather is it?

Here the man was wielding his most obvious weapon – sexual innuendo – to assert his power over the woman.

A woman guest on LBC's morning magazine programme (Wednesday 29 April) was similarly insulted and objectified, and her role in the programme trivialised. The introduction set the tone of the 'interview':

I kept fairly quiet about our next item on AM this morning because I didn't want (the other presenter) to get too excited. He knows we were expecting a guest (whoaa, gre-er, whoaa noises in the background). Alright, control yourself. But I don't think it had sunk in that not only does the young lady lay claim to the title of Miss Austria but she's also reigning Miss Europe.

Throughout the interview the woman was treated as a sexual object available to men and further objectified by being referred to by the men in the studio as 'her' and 'she':

presenter 1: I'd like to ask you a personal question, how old are you?
presenter 2: I'd like to ask her a question too, what's she doing tonight, ha ha.

Women presenters and guests were often relegated to the 'light' slots in programmes, as the subjects of 'humour' at the end of a show, or providing a break in a DJ show, dealing mostly with trivia. When it came to more serious subjects, these were not only presented by men but were also presented as being of no interest or relevance to women. On the evening phone-in show on LBC (Monday 27 April) the male presenter and male guest talked about levels of unemployment benefits. From the male guest:

' . . . as against the amount that *he* would get if *he* were working'
' . . . the employer doesn't have to pay the employee so much for *his* take home pay'
'People are maintained at levels very close in fact to average earnings if they've got a wife and two children'
'They're not just things that benefit the average man . . . '

The underlying assumptions were that everyone in the job market is male and that all of the listeners were male, for the presenter made no attempt to include women either. The news provided further evidence of 'serious' subjects being the domain of men. In six consecutive news items on Capital (ie. five bulletins from IRN and one First Report) all the main newsreaders were men. Of 14 items reported, only one came from a woman journalist. Of 10 interviewees, only one was a woman.

Lads together

On occasions when there was more than one man in the studio, the conversation reflected their alliance as men based on a patronising attitude to women. For example, the conversation between two male presenters in the presence of the woman producer of a mid-morning DJ show on Capital (Friday 1 May):

'I don't want to spread salacious gossip but I think she's wonderful.'
'Yes I think she's wonderful as well.'

On LBC's Jellybone (Saturday 2 May) when the invited panel of boys in the studio failed to say anything about young people's sexuality the male presenter and so-called Agony Uncle commented:

'Their bodies are going to change and they're going to end up like the rest of us chasing women for fifty years.'
'Whoaa, it'll be alright in the end, lads.'

On Capital's First Report (Friday 1 May) a lengthy item about how an air hostess had repaired a film projector using one of her stockings was reported in a leering and suggestive manner. The woman was referred to by her first name and the wording was sensationalist: 'Off came one of . . .'s stockings' rather than 'she used one of her stockings.' When the man who was reading the item stumbled over the words, the following exchange took place between him and the other male presenter:

presenter 1: The thought of that made my concentration go awry.
presenter 2: Why doesn't that happen to me? I was in an aeroplane the other day and the projector broke down and the stewardess went up and just hit it. I made no attempt to take her stockings off.
presenter 1: I can never read stories about ladies' stockings . . . etc, etc.

Women listeners

When it was assumed that the audience was mostly female, as with the afternoon DJ shows on BBC Radio London and Capital, the implied relationship between the presenter and listener seemed to be based on the assumption that a woman needs a man around the house while her husband is at work: 'D'you know girls I feel like stepping out of your radios this afternoon and giving you a great big hug and a kiss' (BBC Radio London Friday 30 April); 'The Everlies, just for you. Bye lovey' (Capital Friday 30 April). The familiarity is quite spurious, besides being insulting to heterosexual and lesbian women alike. The music played was mostly on the theme of love and romance. 'He's my guy', 'You're nobody till somebody loves you', 'The most beautiful girl in the world', 'This little girl is mine' etc. It seems that these stations think that women have no interest in 'difficult listening' or in subjects other than love and romance.

At lunchtimes, when the DJ could assume that people at work might be listening, we got an indication of the value that they attach to women's paid and unpaid work: 'Five and a half minutes away from one o'clock – if they let you out at one, ahh, not long to go, men' (Capital Friday 1 May). In the afternoon, a man spoke to the DJ on the phone (Capital Friday 1 May):

male caller: I'm at work . . . She's at home doing the ha ha housework.
presenter: She's no fool.

The implication here is that the man is doing 'proper' work and the woman is having an easy time of it.

Exclusion of women

Women were excluded through the use of language of male presenters, guests and reporters. The words 'ambulancemen', 'spokesman' (referring to a woman) and 'pressmen' were used on LEC between 9 and 10am on Wednesday 29 April, implying that all ambulance staff and journalists are male and that a spokeswoman was a man. Women were also misrepresented by male defined language when referred to as 'girls' as in 'career girls' (LBC Tuesday 28 April) and 'The French girl', referring to a woman tennis player (LBC Monday 27 April); the equivalent term 'boy' would not be used so freely. On LBC's Nightline (Monday 27 April) the male adviser implied that all surgeons and doctors were male (surgeon: 'his assumption . . .'; doctor: 'his time . . .').

The content of items specifically about women were often misrepresentative in their portrayal of women's lives and views. Outdated and chauvinistic views were expressed which perpetuated the image of a woman as a willing, unpaid labourer in the home or which trivialised her role in paid work as in an item on LBC about an employment agency's survey about what 'career girls' were wearing:

'"The clothes for Miss Smith in 1981 are neat and designed more for comfort than wolf whistles" the survey says, "She wears nail varnish . . . make up . . . a bra".' This survey was reported without any comment about its superficial nature. Two further items from LBC indicated that women rather than men are assigned to domestic chores: Jellybone (Saturday 2 May) reported the 'Persil Clean Team' award – 'it's not just about clean kit, that's just who had the most diligent Mum';

Sight Unseen (Sunday 3 May) chose a newspaper story about a six year old girl shopping and 'doing what Mummy did'.

Most news, current affairs and information subjects were covered with no attempt to include a woman's perspective. In a discussion about video and education on LBC (Tuesday 28 April), at no point did the guest or the presenter consider, for instance, the possibility of using video in schools as a means of combatting the sexism perpetrated on television. In some discussions it seemed that the existence of feminist politics had been forgotten. An LBC interview (Monday 27 April) conducted with a spokeswoman from the National Council for the Single Woman and her Dependants covered the ground that a woman might sacrifice her career to look after a dependant relative but did not question the basis of this – ie. why is it that women, not men, undertake this role?

Capital Radio's Teach Yourself You (Monday 27 April) was on the subject of 'getting away from it all'. Near the beginning of the programme, a well known television personality said that his idea of getting away from it all was to spend a couple of hours with his 3 year old child in the park. The male presenter said:

> If you're a young mother you're probably astonished that supervising a lively 3 year old might be a way to relax. But . . . in a recent survey people were asked what they thought of as their greatest treat. Most of them mentioned holidays in the sun and meals out, but a surprisingly large proportion of the men said they'd like to spend more time with their children. Their wives (sic) took a very different view. Their idea of a treat was to get away from the kids and this makes the point that there's no universal recipe for successful escapism.

The last comment on the programme was from a housewife who said ruefully that holidays were too much of a strain. However, the bulk of the programme was devoted to discussing the problems that businessmen have in relaxing on holiday. The fact that housewives clearly have a different attitude to holidays, ie. they don't stop organising and doing domestic work while 'on holiday', was marginalised in the most blatant way by the presenter's glib dismissal at the start of the programme and the throwing in of a housewife's opinion, evidently for joke value, right at the end.

On LBC's Nightline (Monday 27 April) the male problems adviser counselled women without considering any of the alternatives developed by the women's movement. For example, he advised women to go to the Marriage Guidance Council rather than suggesting that they go to a women's centre or some other feminist group; he encouraged an older woman to marry a man for companionship rather than suggesting alternative ways of living and finding friendship.

The discussion on teenage sex on LBC's Jellybone (Saturday 2 May) seemed to be based on the assumption that heterosexuality is the desired norm. Earlier in the week (Monday 27 April) a report on LBC identified homosexuality as a problem: 'It can't be as perfect as they expect . . . they begin to think they're no good at it, or they're homosexual or they're impotent or something like that . . .' The lesbian relationship of a woman sports personality was described in news items from IRN as a 'romance', a 'love affair'. Because there is so rarely any mention of lesbianism on the radio, and therefore no context in which to place it, this 'story' was likely to suggest that lesbianism is an aberration to be regretted. On LBC's morning phone-in (Monday 27 April) the guest was euphemistically described as 'flamboyant' by the presenter although neither the guest nor the listeners were frightened to discuss homosexuality.

Although advertisements are not specifically a part of the commercial stations' programme output, they do form a part of the programming flow. Many of the advertisements broadcast in the week we monitored contained sexist language and assumptions (Daily Express Photoworld, Allied Carpets, Sketchley . . .) and their inclusion between other items which were insulting to women had the effect of reinforcing the negative attitudes to women often expressed in the stations' own material. The speed with which items follow one another on LBC meant that advertisements sometimes became part of programmes as on the morning phone-in (Tuesday 28 April): '. . . thank you very much indeed, it's 14 minutes to eleven', 'When's dinner Mum?' (first words of fish advertisement).

Listening to their programmes, we got no indication that any of the stations were aware of the activities of the women's liberation movement in London. The news and magazine programmes contained no items that might be of interest to feminists, apart from the Sutcliffe trial, and this was treated as an opportunity for sensationalist reporting, rather than the serious consideration of violence against women. What's On items did not mention any social or political events for women. The two occasions on which there was any discussion of feminism on BBC Radio London were both in the context of Christianity: an interview with a Roman Catholic feminist (Sunday 3 May) and an interview with an Anglican feminist (Wednesday 29 April). In both interviews the women argued strongly and successfully for a challenge to the male structures of the church; to limit discussion of feminism, however, to issues around the Christian church is to mislead listeners about the concerns of the women's liberation movement. The last word should go to Penelope Keith, interviewed on the morning phone-in show on BBC Radio London, after some provocation from the presenter: 'If a man speaks his mind he's called frank – or George, or Ted – but he's called open and what a good, open straight talking guy but if a woman does she's called a bitch . . .'

Summary of findings

1 There were very few women presenters and reporters and those few were assigned to the 'lighter' areas of programming.
2 The portrayal of women's lives and views was misleading; there was no serious attempt made to consider subjects from a woman's perspective; feminist ideas and practices were virtually ignored; the women's liberation movement in London was totally ignored.
3 The language used by male broadcasters was alienating to women and served to perpetuate and reinforce sexist attitudes.

4 The behaviour of male presenters towards women listeners, phone-in contributors, presenters, producers, guests and interviewees was offensive and degrading.

We defined overt sexism as the belittling of women by treating them as sex objects and not taking their opinions seriously. Given the number of incidents of overt sexism, we concluded that London local radio stations at best have no interest in challenging the sexist attitudes of their male broadcasters, and at worst organise their broadcasting on the assumption that women are inferior to men.

Recommendations from Women's Airwaves

The following recommendations do not constitute a strategy for achieving non-sexist local radio that is sympathetic to women. A blueprint for local radio as we would like it should not be read from them. Rather, we see them as minimal changes that are essential if London local radio is to be less offensive and more interesting to women.

There should be more women reporters and presenters on all three stations. Women should not be restricted to 'light' subjects (eg. the arts, shopping news, celebrities' weddings, horoscopes etc.) The distinction between 'light' and 'heavy' (eg. politics, business etc) perpetuates a vicious circle of assumptions about women: light topics belong to the female sphere and the female sphere is light and by implication unimportant. More women reporters and presenters would necessitate more women editors and producers, employed specifically for their interest in treating women as intelligent, and women's issues as important. This is not to say that we consider, for instance, celebrities' weddings as serious; but marriage, one of the central institutions of our society, is clearly amenable to thought-provoking treatment on radio. The 'light'/'heavy' distinction that would thus begin to be broken down is one that is represented in other ways besides sexism; changes in the employment of women of the kind suggested above would therefore have wide implications.

The three stations should be aware of the existence of feminism and recognise the necessity for women's points of view to be heard. For instance, why interview a man on the subject of female offenders and shoplifting? More women should be interviewed in general. All 'information-giving' programmes (news, magazines etc) should include reporting on women's campaigns and issues. What's On items should include social events for women in London, many of which are organised by women in the women's liberation movement. There are thousands of women's organisations in London which the listener never hears about. There should be an hour-long weekly programme at peak listening time on all three stations, produced and presented by women who are receptive to feminist ideas, giving London women an opportunity to air their opinions. Women in London who are producing radio programmes, but are not employed by stations, should be guaranteed regular access to airtime.

All scriptwriters, reporters and presenters should be made aware of sexist language. The use of non-sexist language should be an integral part of radio practice, and sexist comments and remarks made by guests, phone callers and interviewees should be challenged. We recommend that 'The Handbook of Non-Sexist Writing for Writers, Editors and Speakers' by Casey Miller and Kate Swift be required reading.

We think that the reliance of all the stations on DJs, the main perpetrators of overt sexism, should be reconsidered. We do not think that the employment of women DJs is a solution. It should, however, be possible to devise programmes in which music is played, and interviews, discussions and telephone conversations conducted, without the presenter being projected as supremely socially successful and the authority on what constitutes having a good time; and if male, as the answer to every woman's dreams. Without the position of DJs on local radio being changed, the other recommendations would be less effective.

Chapter 8

Caroline Mitchell

SISTERS ARE DOING IT ... FROM FEM FM TO VIVA! A HISTORY OF CONTEMPORARY WOMEN'S RADIO STATIONS IN THE UK

With powerful voices, women can organise, train, take collective action and ultimately build communities and a society based on self-determination.

(Stuart and Bery 1996: 211)

A unique experience – a knowledge that things can be done, can be different, doors can be opened. There are alternatives and women have a collective power that is inspiring ... When people come together united by a compelling idea and working in a spirit of co-operation and mutual trust, they can do anything.

(Mitchell and Caverly 1993: 10)

Introduction

In this chapter I will draw out a critical history and definition of women's radio stations in the UK and discuss how such stations may forge a gendered space, in a radio environment dominated by male broadcasters.[1]

In March 1992 Fem FM, the first women's radio station in Britain, broadcast in Bristol under a short-term licence. Since then six other women's radio stations: Elle FM in Merseyside, Radio Venus in Bradford, 107 The Bridge on Wearside Celebration Radio, Brazen Radio and Viva! in London have broadcast. Apart from the notable exception of Viva! radio, a full-time but short lived commercial enterprise, all were short-term community radio stations[2] where community based outreach and training was behind much of the involvement of women and the programming of the stations.

Most of the projects and radio stations I refer to challenge mainstream representations of women. Harnessing female flair, creativity, wit, energy and bravado they provide a platform for new voices and perspectives and facilitate access to skills, training and airtime so that under-represented women can, through their own stories, become the subject, not the object of the media. I describe how UK women's radio stations were developed from, and influenced by, feminist radio activity in the 1970s and 1980s and explore the current social and cultural context in which women are getting involved in women's stations.

Women's radio activism in the UK in the 1970s and 1980s

In the late 1970s the BBC had expanded to include local radio and the first local commercial stations were established. In this burgeoning radio landscape male presenters dominated the national and local airwaves and much of local radio output was aimed at 'Doreen' the housewife (Baehr and Ryan 1984). Apart from Annie Nightingale on Radio 1, there were virtually no female DJs or daytime presenters and very few women worked in radio news-rooms or in senior editorial and management positions. Women were also poorly represented in pirate (unlicensed), hospital or student radio.

It was in response to this under-representation that in 1979 a radio collective called Women's Radio Workshop, later renamed Women's Airwaves (WAW), was established in London at a socialist feminist conference (Valentine 1980). WAW offered training and support for women working in radio and carried out research to support its campaigns to increase representation of feminist issues on air. In a content analysis of a week of London's local radio, co-ordinated by the activist radio group Local Radio Workshop, WAW concluded first there were very few women presenters and reporters on London's local radio. The few that there were, were assigned to 'lighter areas' of programming. Secondly that there was no serious attempt to represent issues from a woman's perspective, let alone a feminist perspective (Local Radio Workshop 1983).

WAW was also a programme-making group, (funded through local arts funding and the Equal Opportunities Commission). Members made programmes with a feminist content and explored issues like violence against women, women and work, feminist music, young black women, housing, and lesbian lifestyles: issues that are considered to be relatively mainstream now. WAW's philosophy was to gain access to mass audiences on established local stations like Capital Radio and BBC Radio London. The group was however split between members who wanted to make programmes aimed at mainstream local radio stations and those who supported the concept that women would be better represented through being involved in community stations. Some women in WAW, therefore, aligned with Local Radio Workshop who saw community radio as part of the UK Conservative party's campaign to deregulate radio. Later Women's Airwaves changed its name to Women's Radio Group (WRG) and broadened its remit. Currently WRG's activities include training women for both mainstream and community radio. In 1994 the group took part in Celebration Radio and members of WRG were part of Viva! Radio (see below).

The Black Women's Radio Group (BWRG) was established around the same time as Women's Airwaves. This group came together to share experience about sound recording and to compile information about activities in the Black community in London. BWRG also took part in the Local Radio Workshop research. They found that there was a lack of peak time coverage of Black issues, a lack of knowledge and respect for cultural difference and that there were few Black reporters and producers working in London's local radio (Local Radio Workshop 1983).

Fiske argues that people with less economic power may choose to use low tech and sometimes illegal means to communicate (Fiske 1994). Amongst the many pirates that emerged on London's airwaves in the early 1980s 'Our Radio' (1982–3) saw itself as an 'open access pirate' with a number of different individuals and small groups contributing to programme making. One of these groups produced *Gaywaves,* a programme whose producers 'planned' to include lesbian contributions but in practice was made by and for gay men (Hooligan 1987). The *Women on the Waves* programme included music and political features, for instance about Greenham Women's Peace Camp. Our Radio broadcast illegally for just over a year, but closed down due to external pressures, including Home Office raids and internal pressures such as disorganisation and a lack of money (Barbrook 1995).

A more successful example of women's piracy is the Leeds pirate station, Dream FM. The ten female DJs (there are also 30 men) programmed the station for a day in 1993. 'We're not DJs in the dreadful sense of the word . . . We're northern lassies, play club music and behave like normal people: we're not as separated from people's lives as a radio station normally is' (Karpf, 1993).

Women also made a mark on some alternative initiatives within more mainstream local radio. Cardiff Broadcasting Company went on air in 1980 and was the first commercial radio station to be partly owned by a community trust. The Equal Opportunities Commission[3] funded a women's radio producer to work on a series of health programmes from a woman's perspective. The project also established guidelines for promoting women's issues in commercial radio and for redressing some of the inequalities in employment and representations of gender on the radio (Baehr and Ryan 1984).

The BBC *nearly* made history by almost turning Radio London – one of its ailing 'local' stations – into a women's station for London: 'a station run mostly by women, fronted by women – not a feminist station (though that would form part of the output) – appealing to a mix of ages, incomes and ethnic groups' (Karpf 1985: 14). But the BBC got cold feet and opted for a more conservative format. It was left to the community radio sector to experiment with women's radio.

'Short term bursts of inspiration' – women's community radio

In the late 1980s ten new 'incremental' licences were awarded by the IBA[4] to stations with community remits (Crisell 1997). These stations had what I would call 'islands' of women's activity. Here and there, there were a few women presenters and women's programmes, for instance the *Woman to Woman* magazine programme on For The People (FTP) in Bristol. Whilst having aims and charters that supported equal opportunities, community radio stations often reflected the gender stereotyping of mainstream radio stations in staff and volunteer roles. A Europe-wide survey (Lewis 1994) found that men outnumbered women volunteers in all work areas apart from administration and finance. Where there were full-time paid staff only 22 per cent were women. Of the stations awarded incremental licences in 1986 the majority of paid workers and volunteers were male, specialist women's programmes were moreover often axed if the stations had to make financial cuts or were bought out by commercial operators.

In the 1990s, UK broadcasting legislation and policy still failed to distinguish between commercial and community radio structures (Shingler and Wieringa 1998). There were few full-time community stations that operated under a community charter. Aspirant community radio groups can take advantage of a Radio Authority licence for short periods of broadcasting each year called a Restricted Service Licence (RSL). These permit groups to learn about all aspects of setting up, financing and programming a community station and can serve as a tool for experimenting with new formats and target audiences. Women who had been involved in community stations or active in feminist initiatives saw the chance to set up short-term stations, run by women and aimed primarily at women. All these RSLs showcased women's radio.

Rather than providing a description of each RSL, station by station, what follows is a thematic exploration of women's RSLs that emerged in the 1990s exploring how they addressed their audiences, how the stations were set up and structured and how they organised their programmes. A more detailed discussion about how women's radio can be defined in theory and praxis and in particular its role as a feminist radio training tool can be found in Part 2 Chapter 15.

> . . . the Fem experience . . . showed how rigid structures in broadcasting can be abandoned without losing style and professionalism. It unearthed hidden talent. It took risks and got away with it.
>
> (Mitchell and Caverly 1993: 10)

The concept of a women's RSL was pioneered by Fem FM in Bristol and launched on International Women's Day, 1992 (Mitchell and Caverly 1993). As the first women's station in the UK it has been acknowledged as being an inspiration and structural role model for most of the women's stations that followed (although each had important local strengths and differences).

Table 8.1 UK women's restricted service licences 1992–2000

Station name	Area	Date	Main characteristics	Funding/sponsors
Fem Fm	Bristol	March 1992 (8 days)	First women's station in UK. 250 volunteers Women only training in programme making and engineering	Gulbenkian Foundation Local City Council grant Sponsors: Aer Lingus Co-op Retail Society Celebrity and local fundraisers
Brazen Radio	London	March 1994 (2 weeks)	First women's station for London. 500 women trained	Sponsors: Virgin, Revox, Co-operative Bank Celebrity Donation: Emma Thompson
Celebration Radio	London	April 1994 (7 days)	Managed by Women's Radio Group. Testing format for Viva!	London Arts Board grant Local Leisure Services Women's Radio Group
Elle FM	Merseyside	Various – 1995–present (4 weeks)	Women's training Representative of Black and ethnic minority groups in area	Local council grants European funding Local sponsors Ariel Trust
Venus FM	Bradford	Various – 1995–present	Part of mixed gender station: Bradford Community Broadcasting (BCB)	Local council, arts and education grants. European funding
107 The Bridge	Washington, Tyne and Wear	March 2000 (6 days)	Partnership between University and Bridge women's education and training group	Local and millennium arts grants European Social Fund Local partners

The name Fem FM had been chosen carefully, to be deliberately ambiguous and open to interpretation:

> It could be the abbreviation for feminist, feminine or female . . . also it worked well on air and sounded good in the jingles . . . We didn't want to alienate people by being considered 'too feminist' . . . On air though there were so many versions of women's lives in the programmes, including feminist views. Part of the success of the station is that it really did represent the hundreds of women who had got involved in one way or another.
>
> (Mitchell 1993)

Most of the stations had feminist aims even if participants were careful not to label them as such. What united all these stations is a practice of women led, community-based training, resulting in individuals and specific groups of women setting up a station and making programmes: promoting women positively through and on the radio. In the case of stations like Venus FM it enabled women who may not have felt attracted to their local community radio station before, to participate.[5]

Elle FM's co-ordinator Ami Yesufu's response to a local newspaper's survey about the station (sensationally represented in the headline 'Sexism row over all women radio plan' [Stocks 1995]) encapsulates the dilemma for women in the nineties about feminist labels and separatist initiatives:

> People are bound to call it sexist – what can you say? You just can't win. If this is such an enlightened day and age then why is most of the media run by white middle class males? OK, there are more and more women researchers, reporters and technicians but the people making all the decisions are men. Elle FM is not going to be a feminist station – I am not setting out to burn my bra on air. We are doing it because there is an identified need.
>
> (Stocks 1995: 13)

Venus FM's co-ordinator Mary Dowson was also sensitive about using the 'f' word in relation to women's RSLs:

> I think it's a feminist statement – a feminist project – but then I don't mind calling myself a feminist . . . I wouldn't necessarily use the word in publicity. Or talking to groups because of what's happened to the word feminist . . . They are happy with calling it women's radio but not feminist . . . they may shy away from the f word because of the ridicule it has attracted and would see it as being a middle class station.
>
> (Mitchell 1998)

Women's stations had to respond to accusations of sexism. Although the butt of many jokes, *Men's Hour* was a serious programme on Fem FM – a space for alternative views about male lives and sexuality. Brazen took the idea further with *Men's Minute* (well they say length isn't important . . .). For the stations it was also a useful rejoinder when countering accusations of sexism – a reminder of *Woman's Hour* and the paucity of daily space that women had secured for themselves on BBC Radio 4.

Hundreds of women gained access to radio airtime and training as a result of the women's RSLs of the 1990s. Many women have been able to use contacts and experience from the stations to get on in the radio world.

Fig. 8.1 UK womens radio stations: publicity leaflets and programme guides

In 1992 Fem FM put women's radio on the national and international agenda.[6] The station has since been used as an inspirational model of women's radio for stations that have emerged since 1992 and some mainstream stations have arranged women's programming on International Women's Day each year.

Female producers and audiences – 'but men can listen too'

Your mother, your sister, your daughter, your lover, your friend – we're everywoman – Fem FM.

(Fem FM station jingle)

In today's media climate commercial and even public service radio stations are required to target channels and programming at specific audiences and the first questions that women setting up stations are asked are: Who are you aiming at? Do you want men to listen too? Unlike commercial radio stations that are usually fairly narrowly targeted at an age group or musical style, most of the women's RSLs followed a traditional public service ethos of catering for all. Most said that their core audience was women of all ages, musical tastes, sexual orientations and ethnicities – Fem FM's main jingle was 'we're everywoman'. However implicit in all the programming was the notion of addressing the needs of women who were not catered for in mainstream radio. The Venus slogan: 'Real Women Real Radio'[7] sums this up and in its mission statement Brazen felt it was also aiming at people dissatisfied with the quality of radio as a whole. They aimed at: '(W)omen of all ages but ultimately to attract a wider audience of committed radio listeners hungry for quality and innovation (Brazen Radio 1994).

Two stations talked about their audiences as women's magazines: Elle FM 'as more *Marie Claire* than *Woman's Weekly*' (Stocks 1995: 13) and Fem FM's post-station audience research found that when women were asked to define the station in terms of a magazine there was equal weighting to *Cosmopolitan* and *Spare Rib* (Mitchell and Caverly 1993: 10). If this is a useful way of categorising consumption then we might deduce that these stations were mainly reaching educated women (*Marie Clare*) in the 30–40 age group (*Marie Clare*, *Cosmopolitan* and *Spare Rib*) who had feminist tendencies (*Spare Rib*, *Marie Clare*) and a penchant for fun and sex (*Cosmopolitan*)! However in practice the programming reflects a much wider age and interest range and a more complex representation of different women's lives. (See table 8.2).

Stations used community development and networking methods as well as more traditional publicity and marketing campaigns to promote themselves and achieve as big an impact as possible as stations that were on air for a short time. Fem FM held volunteer recruitment meetings in four community centres in different parts of the city and ran training courses in youth clubs and adult education centres. Brazen Radio had ways of employing its volunteers creatively:

I was impressed to see how organised Brazen was with groups already being formed and newsletters keeping you updated on their progress. Since then I have become more actively involved and am now part of the programming group, helping out with jingles, contacts and anything else I can! . . . More recently I dressed up in a 'Radio Bra' at the Exploding cinema which has to be definitely on of my all time most memorable Brazen experiences!

(Marden 1994)

Most women involved in the RSLs were anxious not to alienate men. I would argue that this is indicative of an awareness of how men consume media (*Woman's Hour* has a significant male audience [see Feldman in this volume] and men read women's magazines [Hermes1995]) rather than an outright rejection of radical/separatist feminism. Indeed the separatist nature of the programme making and organisation of the stations seemed to be celebrated, as testified by two Fem FM volunteers:

> Very enjoyable – the best thing I've done in broadcasting (probably as there were no male managers)
>
> (Mitchell and Caverly 1993: 9)

> I had never worked in an all women environment before. I found it to be very special, everything got done.
>
> (Mitchell and Caverly 1993: 10)

Gendered structures and programming

Fem FM, Brazen and Elle FM were set up from scratch. There were no paid workers: and everything from establishing technical resources, studios and transmission facilities, finding a base for the stations, fundraising, promotions and publicity, outreach and training were done by volunteers. The Bridge, Celebration and Venus had some paid workers and the use of studios and resources from partner organisations. All the stations were non-commercial in terms of profit distributing although some carried local commercials and sponsored programming. Funding for the stations came from a wide variety of sources: the Gulbenkian Foundation funded training for Fem FM and most stations had grant aid from their local authority or local arts, community and education sources. (See Table 8.1)

Fem FM and Brazen had over 200 volunteers each and like any voluntary organisation communication between people in the lead up time to the station going on air was crucial. Fem FM had a 'functional hierarchy' with two station co-ordinators and a series of volunteer co-ordinators and programme editors who met regularly in the year running up to the station launch. (Mitchell and Caverly 1993:2) All the stations had one or two women in a leadership role who had taken the station from idea to reality.

All the women's stations had a remarkably similar format of programming: presenter-led programmes at breakfast, lunch and drive time (often two women presented these programmes) with women's specialist interest in the daytime and arts and music throughout the evening. All the stations apart from Celebration had a 60:40 or 70:30 music speech mix (Celebration had magazine programmes with some music content throughout the week with some specialist music programmes at the weekend). The weekend schedules were more diverse with an eclectic mix of specialist programmes. The 'everywoman' audience was addressed through programmes made by the groups they were catering for. Most stations had programmes made by young women and women from minority ethnic groups

Table 8.2 UK women's restricted service licences: programming

Station name	Music format	Speech format	DJs	Women's interest	Information/ Education	Arts/ Entertainment	Other
Fem FM	60% music Eclectic/world/ dance/specialist music Female artists	40% speech live and pre recorded on magazines documentary	Over 50 local and national DJs: Queen B, Rankin Miss P, Angie D	*Girls Express*, *Rang Tarang* – Asian Women *Intermix*-international	*Up Front* – Community groups Local news	*Artery* – Women's Comedy Women's Writing	*Men's Hour*
Brazen Radio	Playlist chosen by women. Specialist sessions Live concerts and women's work premiered	Various magazines with live and pre-rec. speech items	Sarah HB DJ Ritu Tasha and the Killer Pussies, Sue 'C' Janey Lee Grace	*Bus pass posse* – older women *The Big 'O'* – Lesbian *Sisters against symmetry* – disabled women	*Women in the media*. *Get thee to a nunnery* Environmental affairs	*Hoover my love rug* – comedy *Telling Tales* – female authors *Dalston Days* – soap	*Men's Minute* *Kids Audio* *Cartoons* Link to women and music festival
Celebration Radio	Music as part of speech magazine programmes	Celebrity interviews Male and female presenters	Occasional DJ lead programmes	Various	Political and current affairs programming and interviews	*Artbeat*	*Celebration Playtime* children's programme
Elle FM	Wide mix of music	Magazine and specialist programmes	Local DJs	Various Young Somali Women	*Visions of Black* – history and culture *Health and Self*	*Her Waves*: plays. *Kulture Word* – arts/poetry	Links to Black History Month Festival events
Venus FM	Specialist music and music in magazine programmes	Magazine and specialist programming	Local DJs History of women in pop music	Asian Women, *Sportstalk, Girlzone* – local schools	Local news and politics *Moving on Up!* Training/jobs opportunities.	*Under cover Handbags* – Comedy	*Now and then* – Oral history
107 The Bridge	Mixed pop music chosen by women	Magazines and live discussion	Trainee local presenters	Global women Daily youth programme	Local/ current affairs. Sports	Daily soap Creative writing	Link with local commercial radio station

including immigrant communities (for instance Asian women in Bristol and Bradford and Somali women in Liverpool), many of whom had been on training courses arranged by the station. However specialist programmes were not the only platform for these women who also contributed to general and music programming (see below).

Lesbian women involved with Brazen made their own programme, *The Big 'O'*, although the organising group was keen that there should be lesbian influence right across the station (see Nye et al 1994). At Fem FM lesbians were consulted about how they wished to be represented, there being no obvious group who wanted to produce a specialist programme. In their history of lesbian radio in the UK (see Chapter 6), Nye, Godwin and Hollows commented on the partnership between straight and gay women at the station:

> Although Fem FM broadcast no explicitly lesbian targeted programmes, lesbian perspectives tended to pop up quite naturally in coverage of the arts, entertainment and health, and several lesbian technicians and presenters were involved. The project worked well as a collaboration between straight and gay women, and between professionals and women new to broadcasting.
>
> (Nye, Godwin and Hollows 1994: 163)

Although not at the time an explicit policy, this also worked in other areas, for instance, at Fem FM women who identified themselves as Asian were presenters and producers of daily programmes like *Fem AM* or *Artery*.

Another major characteristic of the women's station was how embedded the programmes were in the culture of local women. Elle FM for instance had programmes about local health, employment, arts and cultural initiatives:

> All other radio stations in Liverpool cover male things – so everyone knows what's going on generally but they don't know what's happening specifically for women . . . like health, new initiatives, schemes for women, funding opportunities for women, things for single parents, male and female.
>
> (Mitchell 1995)

A major achievement of all the stations was to give a platform for female DJs, helping women to break into this area of work:

> I think Brazen speaks for itself, a station like this deserves the most credit and I hope it will make people aware of how much talent there is out there being overlooked just because there is no outlet for them to use . . . It has also helped women in the music industry to get together and work together instead of competing and working against each other, a much healthier and far more productive avenue!
>
> (Marden 1994)

Presenters came with experience from pirate and hospital radio, club DJ-ing, courses and that traditional space for honing DJ–skills: their own bedrooms. A simple headcount using the programme schedules shows that Fem FM and Brazen had at least 50 DJs each, and for many this was their first broadcast.

It is possibly easier to characterise the programming on women's RSLs in terms of what it was not. None of the stations had solo male DJs, continuous chart music or endless advertising dominating the schedule. However leaving it at that would be denigrating the creativity and talent unearthed by these stations. The overall sound was energetic and refreshing: enthusiastic female presenters, plenty of humour, cheeky jingles, eclectic music, personal stories and testaments. This is summed up by one listener to Fem FM at the end of the station's run:

> It's Monday morning, Fem is off the air, on Radio 4 they're talking about dead male authors, with reverence, on Radio 1 there's the normal diet of pap music. Where is the radio station relevant to my life?
>
> (Mitchell and Caverly 1993: 9)

Fem FM was a 'one-off' in Bristol and it is telling that the organisers felt that it was too expensive and energy consuming to repeat the project.

After their broadcast the Brazen group intended to apply for one of the full-time London licences offered by the Radio Authority. Although they got some financial backing and did market research, the £3 million couldn't be raised in time for the Radio Authority deadline. Maud Hand, the driving force behind the bid, concluded:

> All the goodwill we got from the Brazen Radio RSL was tremendously empowering but goodwill is not enough in the market place. Even in non-profit making operations work must be quantified. Women don't measure or value their time and energy enough.
>
> (Mitchell 1999)

Elle FM and Venus FM still broadcast and are part of the growing community radio movement campaigning for licences that exist separately from the commercial radio sector.[8]

The rise and fall of Viva! Radio

> It is not a feminist issue, but a question of style and approach which is not currently available. (Katy Turner, Viva! Radio)
>
> (Sullivan 1994: 31)

> It didn't fail because it was meant for women, it failed because it was bad. (Carmen Callil, publisher)
>
> (Bathurst 1996: 8)

The story of Viva! the first full-time commercial station in the UK aimed at women, starts with another women's RSL in London: Celebration Radio. Labelled 'a voice for women in London' this was directed by the Women's Radio Group (WRG) and went on air for a week in April 1994. Celebration had a similar mix of programming genres to the other women's RSLs – music, drama, arts, news, comedy and features. Unlike other women's stations Celebration had male presenters, interviewees and contributors. It had less DJ-led specialist music programmes and a high proportion of personality presenters and celebrity guests compared to 'ordinary women' in its output. In fact rather than aiming at 'everywoman' it deliberately targeted an older audience of mainly professional working women. It was a way of testing out several programme formats for a full-time medium wave licence for London. The director of WRG, Julie Hill went on to become head of presentation for Viva! and was on the board of management presented in their application.

The Viva! Group was awarded the licence in June 1994 and went on air from July 1995 until November 1996. Its development was headed by a powerful and experienced group of women including the PR guru Lynne Franks, TV executive Linda Agran and sales and marketing director for London Jazz Radio, Katy Turner. Turner became seriously ill just before the station went on air and BBC producer Chrissie Burns stepped in as station controller. The Viva! board had representatives from Golden Rose Communications (the owner of JFM radio, the jazz-based music station) and was completely financed by them. JFM provided sales, promotions, accounting and engineering services for Viva! In fact Franks said it was the men in these positions who pulled Viva!'s strings (Hellen 1995; Bathhurst 1996).

The station application was based on three main themes: music policy, speech programming (50 per cent of each) and its general stance of supporting women – it promoted equal opportunities through programming, family friendly campaigns and radio training. The music promised to be at 'the more sophisticated end of the vocal spectrum' (Viva! application, 1994:18), dubbed 'wall to wall Streisand' by radio critic Anne Karpf (1994). The station's speech was based on a magazine format, covering news, current affairs and family issues 'from a feminine perspective' (Viva! application 1994:18). There were warnings early on that the budget was not enough to support this high level of speech.

The programming was mainly produced by female presenters and reporters but unlike the RSLs, prominent positions were given to men, for instance co-hosting the breakfast programme. Viva!'s audience research focus groups amongst 25 to 49 year-olds found that women would listen to Viva! provided that it wasn't overtly feminist or anti-men, that it was entertaining as well as informative and that it had male as well as female presenters. The station's target audience was defined by Lynne Franks as:

> . . . aged between 25 and 45, probably working, possibly a mother – 'the professional woman of today juggling her social life, her family and her career'.
> (Wroe and Brooks 1995: 10)

A radio station run by women attracted a lot of publicity.[9] It had many professional media women involved and a budget of one million pounds, the publicity for the launch of the station was enormous. However this seemed to be the only successful phase of Viva's short life. Incredibly the first three voices heard on air were male and programmes were criticised for being 'boring and banal' (Carter 1996: 20). In the first year the station achieved only just over a quarter of the expected target of 400,000 listeners. Barely a year after its launch, Viva! was bought out by Mohamed el Fayed and changed its name to Liberty. The format changed to appeal to less of a niche audience and the doyen of UK housewife radio, Simon Bates, was brought in as a presenter.

So why did Viva! fail? It seems that a potent mixture of problems contributed to its downfall and seemingly to the failure of women's radio as a commercial format. The station had considerable technical problems from the start: transmitter problems combined with the un-sexy medium wave frequency meant that listeners (including the all-important advertisers) complained that they couldn't hear the station in several parts of London. Viva! was also under-funded. Summers (1995) commented that Viva! effectively produced 12 hours of speech a day with fewer staff than BBC *Woman's Hour* had for five hours of programming to produce each week. Programme funding became an ongoing problem because very little advertising was coming in to the station.

Other important factors in Viva!'s failure were the programming, music choice and performance of presenting staff. The reviews (in papers that the target audience might read) were scathing:

> Twenty-five years of throwing their weight about amongst the suits have left the backers of this station barely in touch with their own gender and hardly professional enough to work in student radio . . . hours of aimless chat interspersed with middle-of-the road seventies male pop is not programming for women.
>
> (Grant 1995: 9)

Arguably the most interesting discussion to be had about Viva! is as a cultural phenomenon: how Viva! management, its programme makers and advertisers negotiated their way around the kind of women they were aiming the station at. Competing discourses of feminism and femininity surrounded the station. The formal marketing campaign,[10] interviews about the station by people such as a Lynne Franks, the programme content, music policy and the expectations of advertisers about the station's audience all differed in terms of their definitions of the female audience. Labelling Viva as 'women's station' would situate Viva! outside the mainstream of commercial radio. Were advertisers still expecting to be delivered audiences of the traditional 'Doreen'[11] (with limited career aspirations and her mind focused on the weekly shopping basket) or an up-market Radio 4 type audience? Lynne Franks saw the station as a tool for consciousness raising, other presenters used it both as a celebrity gossip shop and as a serious news and social organ. The format must have been confusing to listeners whether they wanted challenging or comforting programming. Both sets of listeners may have been alienated – the former finding the format patchy and patronising – the latter finding it was done more professionally in one of the other nineteen London stations.[12]

Future sounds of women's radio?

As we start the new millennium there are examples of pirate stations that have some radical women's programming: Brighton's Radio 4 Ⓐ subverts the BBC Radio 4 schedule and includes a *Woman's Hour*, 'brought to you by HAG – the Hellraising Anarchist Girls' (Lowe and Zobel 1999). Student radio has been seen as a test bed for future radio. A skim through the schedules available on the Internet reveals women presenting a whole range of programmes including confident 'girly shows' (where often 'girly' signifies lots of confidence and a little smut). The new sector of Internet Radio (as a separate broadcaster rather than purely re broadcasting existing services) is still being defined. Tacchi notes that the Internet will be looked at 'as a space where they might legitimately set up the kind of radio service that otherwise seems impossible' (Tacchi 1999:8).

Conclusion

Women's radio stations in the form of RSLs have increased the audibility and skills of women in community radio and despite the short-term nature of these stations and some backlash against women-only formats they are still regularly organised across the UK.[13] While the UK Radio Authority refuses to recognise or award full-time licences to community based stations it will be difficult for women to make permanent waves and truly exploit their creativity on air.

In appealing to 'everywoman' women's community RSLs acknowledge multiple representations of women in their programming. However such eclectic programming which allows for women to tune in and out of shows (and have a role in producing them) is anathema to commercial radio's need for large, faithful audiences. The women's market is too broad for niche commercial radio and arguably radio advertising cannot draw in enough revenue to fund a speech-based radio station in the same way that a women's TV channel might.[14]

A final irony. Next time you go shopping pop into any large branch of British Home Stores. You might hear 'FEM FM', part of BHS Radio, aimed at female shoppers. Two 'easy listening' DJs, one male, one female, keep 'thirty something, family oriented fashion moderate' women informed and entertained (RBS 1998: 2). So Fem has become FEM and 'retail radio' is the ultimate in niche radio for women.

Notes

1 This study is based on ethnographic research in the area of women's community radio, interviews with and observations of women in London, Bristol, Bradford and Merseyside about their involvement in women's radio stations.

2 'Women's community radio' recognises community radio as a sector distinct from the BBC and commercial radio (Lewis and Booth 1989). It is important to be aware that the term 'community' has in the past been used in the UK context (particularly within government/regulatory circles) to mean 'small-scale commercial' radio.

3 EOC was created in 1975 to monitor and enforce the Sex Discrimination and Equal Pay Acts. It is a national, government funded, statutory organisation that funds and carries out research into equal opportunities and monitors and supports cases of discrimination.

4 The IBA (Independent Broadcasting Authority) granted commercial radio and TV licences until the 1990 Broadcasting Act created a separate body for radio – The Radio Authority.

5 In this case in a mixed gender community station, Bradford Community Broadcasting.

6 News items about the station were broadcast on both Sky satellite news and BBC Radio 4 national news on 8/3/92 as well as items in national newspapers.

7 Radio Venus acknowledges that this jingle line was first used by 2 SER Australia.

8 A campaign for community radio as a separate public service sector of radio is spearheaded by the Community Media Association, (see contacts section).

9 The station was marketed as the first women's station in the UK, ignoring Fem FM's achievement here.

10 Two posters around London included the captions: Man in kitchen: How do you like your eggs? Woman: unfertilised. Question: What's the best way to balance your budget? Answer: With a credit card in each hand.

11 Doreen was the name of the woman at home at whom DJs ostensibly aimed their programmes (Baehr and Ryan 1984).

12 I am indebted here to BA Media student Lucy Kearney's work on this area as part of her final year dissertation.

13 The most recent RSL run by women was 107 the Bridge which broadcast in Washington, Tyne and Wear in March 2000 from the Bridge women's training and education centre. The station was part of a European Social Fund training scheme and was funded through the EU, the University of Sunderland, Northern Arts and Millennium Arts Funding.

14 America has a women's cable channel called 'Lifetime' (dubbed 'Wifetime' by critics because of its 'soft tone'). It remains to be seen how a cable channel like 'Oxygen' (led by Oprah Winfrey and funded by major investors) survives in the marketplace. It aims '. . . to understand women bone-deep and tell the world what we learn . . . we'd like women to rewrite the world's script to reflect their values and goals' (Willis 2000).

References

Baehr, H. and Ryan, M. (1984) *Shut up and Listen! Women and Local Radio*, London: Comedia.

Barbrook, R. (1985) 'Community Radio in Britain: Reach out and touch everyone', in Radical Science *Making Waves – The Politics of Communication*, 16, 53–77.

Bathurst, B. (1996) 'Viva l'indifference', *The Observer* review, May 1996: 8, London.

Carter, M. (1996) 'Can Liberty set Viva free?' The *Independent*, section 2, 7 May 1996, London.

Crisell, A. (1997) *An Introductory History of British Broadcasting*, London: Routledge.

Fiske, J. (1994) *Media Matters: Everyday Culture and Political Change*, Minneapolis: University of Minnesota Press.

Grant, L. (1995) 'Who stole all the women's input?' *Guardian*, July 4 1995.

Hellen, N. (1995) 'Viva! goes macho as men move in to lure more female listeners', *Sunday Times*, 20 August 1995, London.

Hermes, J. (1995) *Reading Women's Magazines*, Cambridge: Polity Press.

Hooligan Press (1987) *Radio is my Bomb*, Bristol: Hooligan Press.

Karpf, A. (1985) 'Not airwaving but drowning', *New Statesman*, 1 March 1985.

Karpf, A. (1993) 'Making Waves – Will women win the bid for London's new 24-hour radio station?' *Guardian*, 8 June 1993.

Karpf, A. (1994) 'Making Airwaves', *Guardian*, 17 October 1994.

Kearney, L. (1997) 'Is Doreen dead? Attitudes to women in radio and on the radio', Unpublished dissertation presented for the degree of BA (Hons.) in Media Studies. UK: University of Sunderland.

Lewis, P. (1994) *Community Radio-Employment Trends and Training Needs. Report of Transnational Survey*, Sheffield: AMARC Europe.

Lewis, P. and Booth, J. (1989) *The Invisible Medium – Public, Commercial and Community Radio*, London: Macmillan.

Local Radio Workshop (1983) 'Women's voices', in *Nothing Local About it, London's Local Radio*, London: Comedia.

Lowe, G. and Zobel, G. (1999) 'Anarchy ahoy!' *The Big Issue*. October 18–24: 22–3, London.

Marden N. (1994) 'My Brazen Experience' press release, Brazen Radio, 2 March 1994.

Mitchell, C. Interview with Trish Caverly, Fem FM co-ordinator, 1993.

Mitchell, C. Interview with Ami Yesufu, Elle FM co-ordinator, 1995.

Mitchell, C. Interview with Mary Dowson, Venus FM co-ordinator, 1998.

Mitchell, C. Interview with Maud Hand, Brazen Radio co-ordinator, 1999.

Mitchell, C. and Caverly, T. (1993), *Fem FM 101-First in Women's Radio*, University of Sunderland.

Nye, S., Godwin, N. and Hollows, B. (1994) 'Twisting the Dials: Lesbians on British Radio', in L. Gibbs, *Daring to Dissent, Lesbian Culture from Margin to Mainstream*, London: Cassell.

RBS (1998) 'BHS Radio – The Next Step', RBS internal document, London.

Shingler, M. and Wieringa, C. (1998) *On Air, Methods and Meanings of Radio*, London: Arnold.

Stocks, C. (1995) 'Sexism row looms over all-women radio plan' Liverpool: *Daily Post* Newspaper.

Stuart, S. and Bery, R. (1996) 'Powerful grass-roots women communicators: participatory video in Bangladesh', in Servaes, J., Jacobson, T. L. and White S.A. *Participatory Communication for Social Change*, London: Sage.

Sullivan, J. (1994) 'Can programmers target women better?', *Music and Media*, vol. 11, issue 42, p. 1.

Summers, S. (1995) 'Vivant feminae! Vivat Viva!' *The Independent on Sunday Magazine*, 25 June 1995: 30–31.

Tacchi, J. (1999) 'The need for radio theory in the digital age', Paper delivered at Radiocracy: Radio, Democracy and Development Conference, Cardiff University. November 26–8, 1999.

Valentine, P. (1980) 'Making radio waves', *Time Out*, 24 February 1980: 17.

Viva! (1994) An application to the Radio Authority for a Greater London Licence, London: Radio Authority.

Willis, J. (2000) 'Take a deep breath, Oxygen is here', *Guardian*, 31 January 2000, London.

Wroe, M. and Brooks, R. (1995) 'Rough ride on the radio waves', *The Observer*, 2 July 1995: 10, London.

Part 2

Radio texts and audiences and the rise of feminist radio

Women and radio: research contexts and themes

Most of the themes and interests that have emerged from the study of women and radio mirror the development and rise of feminist Media and Cultural Studies. These include the study of histories, texts, representations, production, institutions and audiences (active and passive), all contextualised with an inherent critique of a male dominated radio industry.

The development of theory and research in the area of women and radio is somewhat fragmented, eclectic even, but some patterns have emerged since early pieces of research which were usually done under the umbrella of Communication Studies. The dominant themes are as follows:

- *Female audiences*: Audience studies that reveal how women make sense of radio, how they use the medium as part of their every day lives and how they negotiate identities through the medium.
- *Studies of gendered radio texts, practices and discourses*: These include analyses of the 'female listener/male producer' binary and DJs and 'housewife radio'.
- *Women's radio formats and the rise of women's radio stations*: the production of 'women's radio' – mainstream formats and alternative/feminist programming and the distinctive nature of women's stations.

Gendered listeners, texts and practices

Chapter 9 is included in this volume for both its historical and theoretical importance. Shaun Moores' ethnographic study of domestic early radio use in the 1920s and 1930s documents women's early exclusion from radio listening. It reveals how radio changed from being used as a 'boy's toy' to catering for the needs of families; in particular women as they went about their daily domestic routine.

Moores notes that early radio sets were given pride of place in the front or best room in the house and listening was necessarily contained within that room. From the late sixties however radio sets were portable, even ubiquitous: programming and listening could be fitted in while working, or playing inside and outside the home.

However most programmers were fixated by the notion that women belonged inside the home in the private space. Radio is not alone in aiming at female consumers but the 'housewife' audience[1] has been a particular target group for daytime radio and the men who present programmes. In Chapter 10 Barnard discusses a number of key pieces of critical writing about the relationship between male disc jockeys and their perceived constructions of a female audience (Ross 1977; Hobson, 1980; Karpf 1980; Baehr and Ryan, 1984; Coward, 1984). The debate is focused on the way that radio practitioners have produced daytime music radio that patronises and provides a narrowly-defined set of women's interests, the relationships between DJs and women through programmes such as 'Our Tune' and the reasons why women seemed to be excluded from the job of presenter.

Some of the answers to questions raised by Barnard are answered by Gill's important research (Chapter 11), this provides us with a framework to understand how radio stations explain and justify their failure to employ women as DJs. In his discussion of radio as 'a set of social practices' Tim Wall (1999: 3) notes 'The meaning-making of staff about their practices and their professionalism is just as much a product of the radio station as the programmes they produce' (1999: 6). Gill's article presents a methodology – Critical Discourse Analysis – with which we can analyse how power co-constitutes the language of 'flexible sexism' of DJs and programme controllers (Gill 1993: 328).

In an example of a piece of research into the way female listeners responded to Radio 1's Tony Blackburn show, Dorothy Hobson (1980) suggested that music radio functioned as a reminder of what they did before they married. Barnard notes that 'this assumes a passivity, even a helplessness, which is perhaps questionable, but fantasy and memory are potent qualities that underlie much of the appeal of music radio in particular.' (Barnard 2000: 103). Jo Tacchi is interested in the different ways that men and women actively listen to and use the radio. In Chapter 12 her detailed study reveals how they choose different spaces and ways of listening to explore fantasy and reinforce their identities through the everyday soundscapes provided by the medium.

Women's radio in theory and praxis

> Assigning a more powerful role to the women as audience member . . . tends to obscure a perhaps even more important aspect of broadcasting's social address, actively competing for control over voices and venues, vying for the right to speak and be heard by the public at large.
>
> (Hilmes 1997: 131)

The final three chapters in this section demonstrate how women in the Irish Republic, Scotland and England have set up their own radio stations – the ultimate active audience. This space for alternative, and sometimes subversive, women's voices has been set up predominantly outside the mainstream radio industry. In Chapter 13, Margaretta D'Arcy's unique ethnography tells the story of Radio Pirate Woman, a station broadcasting from her kitchen in Galway, West of Ireland. She uses radio as an extension of the old Irish custom of rambling (i.e. visiting houses for chat, 'craic agus ceol' [good conversation and music] and politics). The soundscape woven by the women on this radio station is radically different to the 'pop and prattle' promulgated by mainstream radio. The station uses the airwaves to subvert, create and campaign and is active at both parochial and global levels.

Another example of small-scale woman's radio making waves is discussed in Chapter 14. Karen Qureshi also uses ethnographic techniques to explore how young Scottish Pakistani women negotiate their identity though broadcasting their own programme on a short term radio station in Edinburgh.

In Chapter 15 I map out a definition of 'women's radio space' discussing women's radio stations as a generic form and a discourse outside the area of programmes and stations defined by male DJs and managers. I conclude that women's community stations are continuing to negotiate an alternative space despite being marginalised by a deregulated commercial radio industry.

Note

1 Nowadays the term 'housewife' is still used by many presenters and managers to describe day-time listeners. Some organisations like RAJAR, the radio industry audience research organisation, puts the title housewives in quotation marks. The term 'main shopper' is also in use.

References

Baehr, H., & Ryan, M. (1984) *Shut Up and Listen! Women and Local Radio*, London: Comedia.

Barnard, S. (1989) *On the Radio: Music Radio in Britain*, Milton Keynes: Open University Press.

Barnard, S. (2000) *Studying Radio*, London: Arnold.

Coward, R. (1984) *Female Desire: Women's Sexuality Today*, St Albans: Paladin.

Gill, R. (1993) 'Ideology, gender and popular radio: A discourse analytic approach', *Innovation*, 6(3), 332–9.

Hilmes, M. (1997) *Radio Voices: American Broadcasting, 1922–1952*, Minneapolis: University of Minnesota Press.

Karpf, A. (1980) 'Women and radio', *Women's Studies International Quarterly*, 3, 41–54.

Hobson, D. (1980) 'Housewives and the mass media', in S. Hall, D. Hobson, A. Lowe, and P. Willis (eds), *Culture, Media, Language*, pp. 105–14, London: Hutchinson.

Wall, T. (1999) 'The illusive object: General theories of radio communication', paper presented to 'Radiocracy – Radio, Democracy and Development' conference, Cardiff University, November 1999.

Further reading

Dyson, F. (1994) 'The genealogy of the radio voice', in D. Augaitis and D. Lander, (eds) *Radio Rethink: art sound and transmission*, Canada: Walter Phillips Gallery 167–86.

Ross, M. (1977) 'Radio', in J. King and Stott, M. (eds) *Is This your Life? Images of women in the media*, London: Virago.

Shingler, M. and Wieringa, C. (1998) *On Air: Methods and Meanings of Radio*, London: Arnold. (*For a discussion of Dyson and Valentine and Damian's research about the 'ideal' broadcasting voice.*)

Shaun Moores

FROM 'UNRULY GUEST' TO 'GOOD COMPANION': THE GENDERED MEANINGS OF EARLY RADIO IN THE HOME

A reworked and edited version of Moores, S. (1988) '"The Box on the Dresser": Memories of Early Radio and Everyday Life', *Media, Culture and Society*, Vol. 10, No. 1, pp. 23–40.

There is now a growing body of feminist scholarship on the gendered meanings of objects in material culture (see Kirkham 1996) – and, more specifically, on the significance of domestic leisure and labour technologies like the video recorder (Gray 1992) and the microwave oven (Cockburn and Ormrod 1993). The research findings which are presented in this chapter complement that work by focusing on the 'hidden history' of early radio in the home during the 1920s and 1930s. Through an analysis of oral history interviews with elderly people living in a town in the North of England, and by drawing on documentary sources from the period, I am concerned here to try to chart the formation of broadcasting's relationship with the household. To borrow a phrase from Lesley Johnson (1981), early radio was involved in 'capturing time and space' in everyday life. Its position in the private sphere, both as a technological object and as a provider of programme services, went through a transformation over these two decades. From being an 'unruly guest' in the living room, the radio became – symbolically at least – a 'good companion' to household members, and my research demonstrates how this process had an important gender dimension. At the moment of its arrival in the home, masculine discourses constituted the radio set primarily as a site of technical experimentation and adventure. Only later did women start to incorporate the wireless into their day-to-day routines, as changes were made to the design of the listening apparatus and as broadcasters began to address their audience as 'the family'.

Broadcasting enters the living room

If broadcasting was to capture a place in the spatial and temporal order of daily life, then the 'domestication' of this new media technology was less than immediate. At the point of its entry into the living room in the 1920s, radio is remembered by my interviewees as the cause of some considerable disturbance to household routines. According to their reports, broadcasting's initial appearance in the home was marked by deep social divisions between family members. In that phase of its development, audiences for radio tended to reflect the technological novelty of the medium. Consumers concerned themselves above all with the means of reception as opposed to programme contents – and the interview material suggests it was mainly young men, caught up in the play of experimentation, who were listening to broadcast transmissions. There are many recollections of male relatives or neighbours constructing their own radio receivers:

> Uncle Bill made our first set from a kit. Oh, he had diagrams and goodness-knows-what . . . he used to get the components and piece them together. Uncle Bill was a bit of a one for hobbies.

Question: Your brother was interested in making radios from kits?

> Oh yes, he loved anything like that. He started building these wireless sets and he had to send away for the blueprints . . . I've known him to be working on a wireless for hours and hours, he'd be telling me to clear off when I went to see how he was getting on.
>
> As I remember, it was the young inquisitive fellas who took it up first. They'd all be messing around with these bits and pieces, just like the kids round 'ere are today with their cars, always pulling the guts out of the engine and shoving other bits back – and just like they run round for an engine part these days, so they always used to be on the look out for extra little things to improve the radio sets. It was what they'd call today 'a craze', d'you get my drift?
>
> The other day, I was watching a programme about . . . Alexander Bell, and it made me think of our old wireless set. It reminded me of when my father used to be experimenting with these radios, trying to hear a voice come through. Our first set was made from a kit . . . most people had the kits.

These 'do-it-yourself' sets were popular early receivers, and articles devoted to the construction and operation of such gadgets were published in specialist periodicals. No doubt the preference for kits was partly a consequence of their relatively low cost. A home-built receiver could be bought at a vastly cheaper price than the already manufactured sets which were on sale in shops. Even so, an elementary wireless kit – purchased for around three pounds in 1923 – would still have been an expensive commodity for working-class listeners like those featured in my data, forcing enthusiasts to acquire pieces separately and assemble their radios bit by bit. For example, a woman recalls saving money to buy the components for her husband: 'When it was his birthday or when Christmas came, I used to give him parts for his wireless, d'you see? I'd put fourpence away every week to save up and get him the bits he was after.'

The technical limitations of early radio sets made good reception a rare event: 'All you could hear was the sea, you know, like the sound of waves – but oh, there'd be such a hullabaloo if you could hear one voice, just one voice.' As Mark Pegg (1983: 40) has pointed out, this was 'a time when the technical problems of listening were of paramount importance, whilst programme policy or content were secondary considerations'. Indeed, he noted that three-quarters of listeners' letters sent to the BBC in the 1920s were concerned with the difficulties of getting a clear signal. Only a small minority of correspondents remarked upon the quality of programming. Radio discourses were very much in a formative stage and programme output often referred to its own mode of production. Up until 1926, for instance, technical language had a strong presence in BBC entertainment – characters appeared on air with names like 'Atmos P. Herics' and 'Oscar the Oscillator'.

So when broadcasting arrived in the private sphere, it did so in the shape of a 'miraculous toy' – a novel gadget which husbands, fathers, brothers and uncles might play with. However, early radio sets and their accessories were miracles which provided an obtrusive new addition to domestic furnishings. Paddy Scannell and David Cardiff (1991: 356) have written that, at the birth of broadcasting, 'receiving equipment looked more like something out of contemporary science fiction than a simple household object.' To pick up a signal successfully, several of the original receivers required a long aerial extension which had to be stretched to an outside mast. The following memories give an idea of just how unsightly this arrangement must have been. One speaker remembers that 'all down the backs there'd be poles . . . they'd use clothes props and brooms and things like that, nail 'em together – as long as it was high up, you'd get a better sound.' A second interviewee says: 'Oh, it was something out of the ordinary in them days, having this box in the living room . . . there was a square piece of wood and on it was all these wires.' 'You had', she continues, 'to have a big pole at the bottom of the yard with a wire coming right in . . . all along the living room wall.' Evidently, the wireless did not always live up to its name.

A particular sort of set, which was powered by heavy wet-celled 'accumulators', constituted a double hazard – to the furniture it rested on and to the family member who took the batteries to be recharged, usually at the local bicycle shop:

I remember once when a battery leaked. It was on the dresser, and it leaked all over the carpet and left a big white patch. My mother was furious.

We used to have the radio on the sideboard in the living room. My mother used to be going mad . . . in case it took the polish off . . . my mother didn't like it on there, she was always polishing and that . . . I don't think she was as interested in the radio as my dad.

I remember when I had to take those batteries to be recharged. I was only a young girl. I used to take this glass-looking battery to the cycle shop. My mother used to tell me to keep it away from my clothes because there was acid in them, and I used to walk up the street very gingerly with it.

You had to be careful how you carried 'em. If you dropped one, you'd run like hell.

Corrosive acid, coupled with the ungainly mechanical appearance of the original sets, meant that radio's location in some households remained uncertain. Here, for example, is a description which illustrates precisely this 'transitional' stage in the domestic history of broadcasting: 'We used to put it away in either the cupboard or the pantry when we weren't using it. We only brought it out when we wanted it on. It wasn't like television, stood in the corner, it was brought out.'

It is also important to bear in mind that, for the majority of people who came into contact with radio in the 1920s, listening to the wireless was not a shared cultural experience. Initially, because many of the sets lacked speakers to amplify incoming messages, broadcasts were commonly heard over headphones. The apparatus prescribed individual reception and its single listener typically seems to have been male. In fact, on occasion, wives and daughters could be actively excluded from or silenced by radio consumption practices – leading women to feel frustrated with the situation:

> Only one of us could listen-in and that was my husband. The rest of us were sat like mummies. We used to row over it when we were courting. I used to say, 'I'm not coming down to your house just to sit around like a stupid fool.' He always had these earphones on, messing with the wire, trying to get different stations. He'd be saying, 'I've got another one,' but of course we could never hear it – you could never get those earphones off his head.
>
> I had to sit with my arms folded while he was fiddling with his crystal. If you even moved, he'd be going 'shush shush', you know. You couldn't even go and peel potatoes, because he used to say he could hear the sound of the droppings in the sink above what was coming through the headphones.

Question: Did the set have headphones?

Oh yes, only one person could listen at a time.

Question: Who had first choice?

My father, of course. I remember he used to listen to the news with the earphones on. I don't think we ever heard the news, my father always got the earphones. Well, he was in charge, you see – what he said went.

> My father, he was a bit short tempered – and he'd be saying, 'Would you bloody well shut up', threatening us if we opened our mouths. Oh God, we daren't move when my father had that wireless on. None of us dared move a muscle.

There is clearly a comparison to be drawn between these accounts of radio in everyday life during the 1920s and the ethnographic research on family TV viewing which was carried out by David Morley (1992). In analysing the operation of power in domestic cultures, Morley argued that the contemporary remote control device used to switch channels is appropriated by men as a sign of patriarchal authority, referring to the object as a twentieth-century descendant of the 'medieval mace'. Perhaps the earphones worn by early radio enthusiasts might then be read as a kind of 'crown', with similar connotations of power and control.

At any rate, the oral history interviews which I recorded all point to the conclusion that – at this stage in broadcasting's development – radio had quite different meanings across gender divisions and those varied interpretations were a focus of friction in households. For men, radio was a 'craze' or a 'toy', yet women perceived it as an ugly box and an imposed silence. The masculine pleasures of reception were grounded in the technical apparatus itself, in the whole adventure of 'listening-in'. In contrast, women were often literally excluded from listening – but their social relationship to the wireless was about to go through a transformation which would symbolically reposition them at the heart of the intended audience, and this transformation proved pivotal to radio's capturing of time and space in the home. I will now identify three interconnected shifts that took place during the 1930s in the years leading up to the Second World War. Firstly, the mechanical operation and aesthetic style of the radio set changed dramatically, turning it into a source of shared entertainment and a fashionable piece of living room furniture. Secondly, there was the introduction of broadcast discourses which addressed the 'family audience', while specifically seeking to 'interpellate' mothers as the feminine monitors of domestic life. Finally, broadcasters began to order their programme output into fixed schedules that revolved around the rhythm of daily routines and especially the imagined activities of the housewife.

Capturing time and space in everyday life

By 1932, sets run off mains electricity were already being sold in greater numbers than the early contraptions described above. Although not all households would have had access to an electricity supply, radio manufacturers encouraged consumers to get 'mains minded' (see Scannell and Cardiff 1991). The pre-manufactured mains set, which remained expensive at five or six guineas for even the cheapest of models, was nevertheless dropping in price – and this newer wireless equipment arrived in the domestic sphere at a moment when many homes were becoming more comfortable places to live in. A crucial advance in the technical apparatus was the ability these machines had to separate one incoming signal from another and to amplify sound through a small loudspeaker. So basic problems with interference on reception decreased as a result of improved tuning, while listeners were no longer reliant on headphones to hear broadcast material. The days of the boffin, experimenting with set construction, were coming to an end. Programme content was fast gaining in importance for audiences, over and above the actual means of communication and the pleasures of technological 'tinkering'.

Even before this change, there is evidence in the oral history data I gathered that some consumers had started to modify their kit-built gadgets for group listening of a primitive sort. Consider these two stories which were told to me by interviewees:

There was a basin my brother would put on the living room table, and then he'd get the earphones. There'd be my other brothers and my sister crowding round this basin and listening to the sound coming out.

Question: Sorry . . . what exactly was this basin doing?

Well, my brother used to put the earphones in the basin and the sound was amplified by it. I can vividly remember the family crowding round and listening with their ears all close up to this basin on the table. The sound must only have been very faint, but it meant that more than one person could listen at a time.

I'd put the earphones on, and then anything my wife wanted to listen to, I'd turn one earphone outwards and she used to lean her head against mine – put her ear to it. Then we both used to listen together.

Soon after, though, such bodily contortions could be avoided altogether – as an amplification system enabled household members to sit back and concentrate on the programmes being transmitted. The style of wirelesses altered during this period, with radio becoming a far less obtrusive part of the furniture – blending in with the fixtures and fittings of the living room. Pegg (1983: 56) explained how manufacturers 'decided to give designers their head . . . exploiting the flexibility of . . . materials like Bakelite'. In advertisements, Murphy claimed its sets possessed 'a quiet dignified style in harmony with any furniture'. Meanwhile, rival company Pye was proudly announcing in its publicity material that 'the survival of the experimental era in the outward appearance of radio belongs to a chapter. . . closed by the introduction of the Pye "Cambridge Radio".' 'Realistic entertainment and artistic beauty,' it boasted, 'have long since overshadowed the miracle of radio in the minds of listeners.' Similarly, a BBC *Radio Times* editorial from 1931 heralded the changes by stating how 'the novelty of 1922 has become . . . day-to-day routine' – and shortly afterwards, broadcasting critic Filson Young (1933) was able to call the medium 'that inexhaustible familiar'. The wireless phenomenon was passing from the miraculous to the taken-for-granted.

Its shifting cultural status and domestic significance are well demonstrated in this particular memory, in which a mains set was purchased by a man as a special present for his spouse back in the late 1930s: 'I can remember it now, a black Ebonite affair. That cost me four guineas. I carried it all the way home for her from the wireless shop.' In the interview extract below, a married couple give detailed descriptions of the position occupied by the object in their parents' houses shortly before the war:

Husband: There was the fireplace, and next to the fireplace was my father's chair, and behind that there was a bit of a recess near the chimney breast. Aye, that's right. On the other side, there was a cupboard next to the window and near to this cupboard was another recess, and in that recess there was a shelf with glassware and ornaments on – you know, pots and china and that. Well, just underneath, there was a ledge for the wireless to go on.

Wife: Now I remember our living room was different to yours. We had a cupboard next to the window, and where we used to keep the coal, that was next to it. Then there was a door next to the coal place which led to the hallway and right opposite there was the door leading to the kitchen. We had a trolley in the corner next to that door, and the wireless was on top of there . . . Well, it was a fixture, wasn't it?

Here, the accepted place of radio in the 'micro-geography' of the home is carefully remembered.

Radio's evolving discourses came to be targeted at a family audience – either at the household group as a whole or, in particular scheduled slots, at selected family members. Broadcasting thought of itself as 'one of the family', with the task of supplying a kind of 'cosy companionship'. This role was perhaps best symbolised by a programme like *Children's Hour*, in which radio 'aunts' and 'uncles' kept the youngsters amused while Mum prepared the evening meal. Wireless presenters here played the part of extended kin, lending a hand with childcare at a busy time of the day. More generally, the 1930s saw the development of what are now very familiar evening entertainment formats. Quiz shows, serials and variety performances were essential in constructing the shared 'pleasures of the hearth' (Frith 1983).

Indeed, the image of the fireside was commonplace in broadcasting literature of the period. A winter issue of the *Radio Times* in 1935 declared: 'To close the door behind you, with the curtains drawn against the rain, and the fire glowing in the hearth – that is one of the real pleasures of life.' 'And it is when you are settled by your own fireside', continued the copy, 'that you most appreciate the entertainment that broadcasting can bring.' The hearth and the wireless were represented together as a focus of interior space and family pleasure. Of course, what the *Radio Times* offered was an idealised picture of the household in harmony – and actual living rooms were presumably less cosy, more conflict-ridden places – yet its preferred image was still a remarkable move away from the earlier significance of radio as a 'toy for the boys'.

Previously excluded from the audience, housewives and mothers were in many ways central to broadcasting's new 'hailing' of the family. Daytime radio features addressed the woman as monitor of the private sphere, issuing her with information on childcare techniques or advice on home management. In a survey carried out in the late 1930s, *Broadcasting in Everyday Life*, Hilda Jennings and Winnifred Gill (1939: 17) wrote about the reception of these programmes:

Doctors' talks on Friday mornings were said to be helpful practically, especially by mothers of small children, many of whom . . . have become more open minded and ready to seek advice as a result of the teaching of Mothercraft in the infant welfare centres. Some women said they found talks on laundry work and other branches of household management useful . . . Their whole attitude to housekeeping and motherhood is undergoing modification in the direction of increased knowledge, control and dignity.

Health of family members was equated in these discourses with the general 'health of the nation'. The welfare of individual bodies and that of the whole 'social body' were quite explicitly connected. So, for instance, in 1931 *The Listener* magazine stated that: 'Our bad food habits are responsible for impairing our national capacity for work and output . . . The loss of the nation's time through sickness disablement in industry now averages no less than a fortnight per head per year.' A pamphlet for mothers, *Choosing the Right Food*, was published by the BBC – in which doctors advised on the planning of a well balanced diet from basic foodstuffs. The Minister of Health delivered a radio talk entitled 'Motherhood and a Fitter Nation', encouraging women to forge closer links with the doctor, the clinic and the hospital – whilst in 1934, a series of lectures was transmitted on topics like 'Strong Bones and Good Muscles', 'Teeth and Their Troubles' and 'Colds, Tonsils and Adenoids'.

Up to now, I have focused on radio's capturing of space in the home and on the ways in which broadcasters addressed audiences located in household settings, but it was only with the allied capture of family time that the domestication of the technology – its integration into day-to-day life – was completed. Back in the experimental era of broadcasting, there had been a deliberate avoidance of continuity and regularity in the organisation of programming. Periods of silence were left in the gaps between individual programmes and the same feature might return at a different moment each week. The purpose of these disruptions was to encourage selective and attentive consumption, rather than allowing listeners to slip into regular patterns of everyday use. However, with the increasing success of foreign competitors like Radio Luxembourg in delivering popular forms of output at times which viewers could rely upon, there was a gradual move by the BBC during the 1930s towards more predictable scheduling that 'chimed in' with existing domestic rituals. Radio in Britain began to fit itself into the repetitive rhythm of quotidian culture. ·

It was the imagined daily routine of the mother which provided a basis for the broadcasters' new programming plans. Her supposed round of household activities was adopted as a general guide to the changing shape of audiences throughout the day, as schedulers tried to take account of when different people would be listening. Below, one of my interviewees recalls precisely how the resulting schedules eventually came to be interwoven with mundane practices of housework and child rearing. He also indicates overlaps with the man's work and leisure, with the youngsters' school and bedtimes, and with the whole family's mealtime and evening relaxation:

I remember *Housewives' Choice* for women who were at home in the morning. It started about nine o'clock, and housewives used to write off and ask for a record. Oh, and *Listen with Mother* at lunchtime, for women with young children at home. There was a children's programme on late afternoon for when the older ones came in from school, and then there was the news on at the same time every night – I always used to listen to that when I came in from work, during the evening meal. Then later, there'd be music or shows or stories – maybe a quiz – and I used to have favourite programmes on different nights of the week. I remember there used to be a programme called *Monday Night at Seven* . . . of course, with everyone being in early evening, they used to put things on that kids could listen to as well . . . something for all the family.

Johnson (1981) argued that early Australian radio promoted itself as the constant companion of housewives, and the BBC developed similar scheduling strategies. Still, it is important to highlight instances in which women did not – or were unable to – accept the 'friendly' offer of company. For example, when asked whether she had listened during the day, a woman replies: 'I never had time. There were too many jobs to do, what with baking and washing and all that.' In this case, part of the problem seems to have been the positioning of the set. Her recollection is that 'the radio was in the parlour, whereas I'd be in the back most of the time.' Keeping the wireless in the front room of the house appears to have signified a 'Sunday best' attitude to broadcasting, as compared with the usual placing of the object in the rear living room, where it offered a background accompaniment to routine tasks.

A crucial point in the schedules was the transition from daytime broadcasting to evening listening, often the moment of the family meal. On this matter, Pegg (1983: 143) referred to the words of another social survey from the late 1930s entitled *The People's Food*, which noted that 'the hour of the tea-time meal is even more important to wireless broadcasters than breakfast and lunch.' The authors of the report warned: 'a programme of special interest to housewives will not secure its maximum listening public if it clashes with the preparation of tea or the washing up.' Subsequent evening entertainment slowly started to fall into regular nightly and weekly patterns, but repetitive scheduling was not fully established until the 1940s. In fact, of the programmes named above in the interview extract, only *Monday Night at Seven* does not date from the Second World War or later. There is evidently a compression of 'linear time' in the speaker's account, with the rhythms of 'cyclical time' having left a much stronger trace in the memory.

References

Cockburn, C. and Ormrod, S. (1993) *Gender and Technology in the Making*, London: Sage.
Frith, S.(1983) 'The Pleasures of the Hearth: The Making of BBC Light Entertainment', pp. 101–23, in Formations Collective (ed.) *Formations of Pleasure*, London: Routledge and Kegan Paul.
Gray, A. (1992) *Video Playtime: The Gendering of a Leisure Technology*, London: Routledge.

Jennings, H. and Gill, W. (1939) *Broadcasting in Everyday Life: A Survey of the Social Effects of the Coming of Broadcasting*, London: BBC.

Johnson, L. (1981) 'Radio and Everyday Life: The Early Years of Broadcasting in Australia, 1922–1945', *Media, Culture and Society*, 3(2): 167–78.

Kirkham, P. (ed.) (1996) *The Gendered Object*, Manchester: Manchester University Press.

Morley, D. (1992) *Television, Audiences and Cultural Studies*, London: Routledge.

Pegg, M. (1983) *Broadcasting and Society, 1918–1939*, London: Croom Helm.

Scannell, P. and Cardiff, D. (1991) *A Social History of British Broadcasting, 1922–1939: Serving the Nation*, Oxford: Blackwell.

Young, F. (1933) *Shall I Listen? Studies in the Adventure and Technique of Broadcasting*, London: Constable.

Chapter 10

Stephen Barnard

MOTHER'S LITTLE HELPER: PROGRAMMES, PERSONALITIES AND THE WORKING DAY

From: Barnard, S. (1989) *On the Radio: Music Radio in Britain,* Milton Keynes: Open University Press, pp. 141–50.

[. . .]

Housewives' choice?

The housewife is of course particularly central to BBC radio mythology. The idea of a diligent, houseproud, housebound wife running a household and taking on the day-to-day responsibility of bringing up children dates in BBC terms from the immediate post-war period and was for many years encapsulated in the Light Programme's *Housewives Choice,* heard on every working day (including Saturday mornings) between 9 a.m. (later 8.30 a.m.) and 9.55 a.m. Sandwiched neatly between taking the children to school and going shopping, when housework activities were confined to the kitchen (washing up after breakfast) and the living room where the radio was commonly housed (polishing the furniture), the programme was very much a product of post-war thinking, designed as a kind of recognition of or even reward to the female populace for giving up their wartime occupations in the munitions factories and service industries and returning to an almost wholly domestic role. The post-war years saw considerable development of women's media in general, with the same network also starting a daily *Woman's Hour* and the launching of a number of new women's magazines – *Housewife, Women's Mirror* – giving a similar mixture of consumer advice (deemed important in a time of austerity, when rationing necessitated economical use of resources), romantic fiction, practical features such as recipes or cleaning suggestions, human-interest articles and advice on personal matters. They reinforced the notion that housework was 'women's work' by offering endless suggestions as to how to lighten the housework load and cope with the attendant pressures. Above all, such magazines offered their readers reassurance that their renewed peacetime role as housewife and mother was both necessary and valued; rebellion against these 'norms' (i.e. refusing to accept a subordinate role to the man, either within or outside the family) was characterized as undermining the fabric of family life.[1]

The characteristics of housework in modern industrialized society are defined in Ann Oakley's study, *Housewife*, as:

(1) its exclusive allocation to women rather than adults of both sexes; (2) its association with economic dependence, i.e. with the dependent role of the woman in modern marriage; (3) its status as non-work – or its opposition to 'real', i.e. economically productive work, and (4) its primacy to women, that is, its priority over other roles.[2]

One of the most consistent features in popular culture's portrayal of, and catering for, the housewife is the manner in which each of these points is transformed into a positive aspect, delighting in the exclusivity of the role and emphasizing the importance of the woman in the context of the family – as the one who binds family relationships together, who keeps the family afloat in a practical and emotional sense. The importance of housework is never belittled, but rather revered and exclusified: for men to undertake domestic chores is an incursion into female territory, and one of the clichés of housewifery is that men are hopeless at house-work. The most highly circulated women's magazines, even in the modestly liberated 1980s, still follow this line: their ideological strength comes from the fact that they are edited and written largely *by* women, that they do not have the air of a dispensed sexism.

Analogies between women's periodicals and programmes on radio aimed at women are instructive, up to a point. Commercially, the impetus is the same, to provide entertainment of a kind assumed to be of most interest to the home-tied woman and thereby create an editorial environment in which advertisers will want to promote products of traditional bearing on the female purse. When Capital Radio altered its programming in 1983 with a view to mining more finely the housewife audience in which its advertisers professed most interest, it hired the editor of *Honey*, Jo Sandilands, for the purpose. Editorially, there are obvious parallels between radio and traditional women's magazine journalism: mid-morning programmes in local radio are traditionally the home of the 'guest expert' – someone brought in to the studio once a week to give advice on a specific household topic, often keep-fit on a Monday ('to get us all in trim for the week ahead'), consumer matters on a Thursday ('to give a helping hand *vis-à-vis* the weekend shopping') and more practical matters (do-it-yourself, gardening) on a Friday, 'with a weekend of leisure in mind'.[3] The expert is usually someone representing local officialdom, for example the director of the local Citizens Advice Bureau, the chairman of the local gardening club, a local GP, officials from the local inland revenue office or small claims court. Then there is the radio agony column, a vein of programming first tapped by Capital in the mid-1970s in the form of an evening phone-in but now a regular feature of daytime programmes throughout local radio; most of radio's agony aunts and uncles are in fact writers on emotional or sexual topics (Claire Rayner, Anna Raeburn, Philip Hodson) who first made their name in magazine journalism. Phone-ins in general are little more than letters pages of the air, beloved of local radio because they combine cheapness of programme matter – the only cost incurred is use of the telephone facility, callers usually bearing the cost of the calls themselves – with the appearance of giving listeners 'access' to the airwaves.

However, daytime radio departs from the women's magazine approach in two ways. First, radio offers more than just a commentary on or a practical guide to domestic tasks: looking beyond the factual content of daytime radio, it is the message inherent in the entertainment provided – the seemingly inconsequential chat, the lyrics of the records played, the requests and dedications honoured, the relationship of the (male) presenter to the audience – that betrays radio's true perception of and attitude towards the female listener. Second, and related to this, radio is overwhelmingly a male domain, in which women have traditionally found difficulty in winning acceptance either as producers or as presenters and in which marketing principles – identifying a market for a product (in this case a radio programme) and fashioning that product to meet the perceived 'needs' of that market – remain prevalent even at supposedly 'public service' stations. The 'market' for daytime (post-9 a.m.) radio that stations have identified to their satisfaction is the woman at home, but is this traditional perception in fact correct?

The evidence of BBC and IBA research is that 'housewives' (using Ann Oakley's definition of a housewife as, effectively, a female houseworker) no longer (if they ever did) constitute a huge proportion of the daytime radio audience. During the hours of 9 a.m. to 12.30 p.m., 66 per cent of the audience is estimated to be female, 44 per cent male (IBA).[4] The BBC's *Daily Life in the 1980s* shows that 21 per cent of the female population with access to a radio set is listening at 10 a.m., 16 per cent at midday; comparative figures for male listening are 16 per cent at 10 a.m. and 19 per cent at midday.[5] While there is a clear female bias earlier in the morning, it is hardly enough to justify gender-specific programming. But much more pernicious than the simple attempt to translate a female bias in listenership into 'female programming' is the tendency to stereotype that listenership as housewives alone – and, worse, the tendency to stereotype housewives as passive home-makers with limited imaginations:

We [Essex Radio] call our average listener Doreen. She lives in Basildon. Doreen isn't stupid but she's only listening with half an ear, and doesn't necessarily understand 'long words'. That doesn't mean that we treat her like a fool but that we make certain she understands first time, because when listening to radio you can't re-read what's just been said as you can in a newspaper. Her husband Bill is treated in the same way.[6]

In programme plans submitted to the IBA prior to the awarding of the London ILR franchises in 1973, Capital Radio pontificated with breathtakingly pompous certainty on women's interests and emotional 'needs':

> In constructing programmes to appeal to women (and to a large extent women as housewives) two things have been borne in mind. The first is that there is a very wide area of overlap between programmes that might be called 'general interest' and subjects that are also of deep interest to *some* men, but not of automatic interest to *all* men. . . . Lively programming in these areas ought to mean that not only would the housewife not turn off the programme – assuming she could rid her hands of flour quickly enough – but that a man punching the buttons of his car radio might find his attention caught. . . . The second thing is that there are certain fundamentals that women enjoy. Women are sentimental, or they care deeply about emotions. . . . They are escapists, or they are not sufficiently cold-blooded to enjoy drama which, if taken seriously, would represent alarm and despondency.[7]

This was, in Anne Karpf's words, 'a masterpiece of doublethink. It categorizes and stereotypes women in the crudest and most traditional way . . . but at the same time attempts to soften its impact with approvingly unctuous and apparently flattering alternative explanations'.[8] Such stereotypes have been forcefully challenged in a study by Helen Baehr and Michele Ryan, *Shut Up and Listen!*, which confronts the issue of the treatment of women in and by ILR by reference to the latter's experiences as a producer with CBC in Cardiff in 1981–2. They point out the lack of real research into 'the needs and interests of women listeners' and comment on the

> remarkably universal profile of 'the housewife' in the minds and hearts of ILR programme makers [from which] a very specific picture of the housewife can be built up: she is young, or at any rate 'young at heart'; she is married; she is part of the nuclear family, with husband (out at work) and children (in school); she does not work outside the home; she does all the housework; she is satisfied at being at home; she is generally content.[9]

Quoting figures documented by the Equal Opportunities Commission, they show that these kinds of perceptions have no real basis in fact. Britain's workforce comprises 15.6 million men and 10.4 million women; only 5 per cent of households follow the so-called average family pattern of a husband at work, a wife at home and two children; 62 per cent of married women are either working or actively looking for employment.[10] What Baehr and Ryan do not explain, however, is quite why ILR management teams should persist with the stereotype: can it be put down simply to the prejudice of male management, is it simple ignorance of the changing socio-economic fabric of Britain, or a pandering to the stereotypes beloved of the advertising world on which ILR depends for its commercial survival? It is clear that, for the radio stations, maintaining such a limited perception of the daytime audience is a matter not just of tradition or convenience but of deliberate policy. This, for example, is an ILR programme controller writing in the IBA's official quarterly, *Independent Broadcasting*, in 1984:

> When I joined Mercia Sound in Coventry, prior to going on air in 1980, I discussed the format of my programme – which was 9.30 a.m. until 1 p.m. – with my Programme Controller. He gave me a clear, if broad, outline of what he wanted and left me to it. From our discussions, I gathered he wanted to go for the housewives. And so we did. But people kept saying, 'there's 20 per cent unemployment in Coventry – shouldn't you be catering for the male listener at that time of day?' The Head of Music at the time was at the end of his tether with me, because I would insist on playing Mario Lanza or Mantovani next to Slade or Shakin' Stevens. But I remained totally sexist in a pro-female way, and it worked. The increase in the JICRAR [Joint Industry Committee for Radio Audience Research] figure was quite appreciable. We aimed for a particular segment of the audience, our assessment of the potential was apparently right, and we got results.[11]

The assumption that particular artists have automatic feminine appeal, that it is actually possible to be both 'totally sexist' and pro-female, that 'results' matter more than devising ways to meet the needs of the whole listening community, all indicate the nature, if not the origins, of ILR's housewife preoccupation.

Such attitudes are not, of course, confined to ILR: Britain's version of commercial radio was constructed in the light of BBC experience. I have commented elsewhere on how Radio 1 placed its faith in a mass audience of housewives during its early years, and that tendency has persisted. Speaking in 1977, Derek Chinnery described the average female listener to the network as 'this dreaded housewife figure who I think of as someone who, perhaps last year or two years ago, was a secretary working for a firm, who is now married and has a child. She wants music that will keep her happy and on the move'.[12] At that time, David Hamilton, presenter of the mid-afternoon show, still felt able to reprimand a listener who had written in to complain that his 'keep young and beautiful' spot (featuring beauty tips sent in by listeners) was patronizing and sexist with the remark that it was 'only a bit of fun'; he described his own image of his typical listener as 'a housewife, young or young at heart. She's probably on her own virtually all day. She's bored with the routine of housework and with her own company and for her I'm the slightly cheeky romantic visitor'.[13]

The preoccupation remains – Johnny Beerling referred in a 1986 interview to Simon Bates (Radio 1's 9 a.m. to 11.30 a.m. presenter) 'targeting to people listening in their own houses – that has to be generically housewives'.[14] This is despite the fact that Radio 1's image of its housewife listeners has modified over the years, there being no way that Bates for one would revert to the recipe features that Jimmy Young made his trademark between 1967 and 1973, or to features like the 'tiny tots spot' (a children's record played 'to give you mums a moment to put your feet up') which Young's mid-morning successor, Tony Blackburn, made a particularly patronizing part of his programme. Similarly the current occupant of the mid-afternoon programme, Steve Wright, would regard it as an offence to his professional standing to have to present such overtly sexist features as Hamilton's beauty tips or his predecessor Terry Wogan's 'fight the flab' exercise spot. Indeed, Radio 2 – home of Wogan, Young and Hamilton since the mid- to late 1970s – has fostered and perpetuated many of the traditional sexist perceptions in a much more overt manner. But we are to some extent talking of generational differences here: Radio 2 speaks to an audience both older in profile than Radio 1 and conservative in more than just the musical sense. It is characteristic of the Jimmy Young approach to women's programmes to emphasize domesticity in a material sense – the concentration on consumer affairs, the questioning of political guests on economic matters as they affect 'the family budget' (and Jimmy Young is Margaret Thatcher's favourite interviewer precisely because of this bias) – while the Radio 1 approach is more openly acknowledging of the fact that women have sexual lives, sexual banter and innuendo (and an apparent obsession with the sexual lives of the famous) being one of the chief characteristics of the Steve Wright show in particular. What has changed is simply the degree of permissiveness within daytime radio: Radio 1 attempts to speak to a supposedly more 'liberated' female, but the underlying attitudes remain. Looking at the style of presentation adopted, the speech content, the music chosen and the manner of its programming, daytime pop radio (including much of ILR) perpetuates a superficially more contemporary version of the old stereotype – woman as not only inherently domestic but romantically inclined to the point of obsessiveness.

Women's programming?

Rosalind Coward, in an essay in *Female Desire: Women's Sexuality Today*, has identified 'sexual desire, attraction and love' as the chief themes not only of the music featured in daytime radio but of the major part of disc jockey chatter.[15] She shows how the features of a typical daytime show – the dedications of records to loved ones, slots like Capital's 'top six' feature in which listeners ring in with their personal selection of favourite records, even the horoscopes that only half-jokingly promise romantic encounters – are all geared to the romantic lives of women; both the music played and its framing by the presenter encourages listeners towards an appreciation of popular music for its *emotional* value, that is to associate the popular records of today and yesterday either with specific memories of particular emotional moments (a first kiss, a blind date, a summer romance) or with a more generalized nostalgia for a pre-nuptial past. 'Daytime radio', she writes, 'works to validate the choices which women have made. The phase of their lives when they went to parties, experienced their carnival of emotions, is treated nostalgically as part of a comfortable personal history . . . [it] tells women who are isolated and at home, and possibly very fed up, that the choices which they made were OK'. Dorothy Hobson, in a study of women's uses of daytime radio, similarly suggests that it 'can be seen . . .

as providing women with a musical reminder of their leisure activities before they married' and also as a 'substitute for the real world of music and discos which they have lost'.[16] What daytime radio attempts to offer to women is escapism, but not just the mundane escape from tedium or the rut of housework: at its most effective, it also *engages* the listener in a manner which critics of the assumed blandness (i.e. *lack* of engagement) of radio programming often fail to fully appreciate. Contemporary radio does not *simply* act as a barrier against boredom or as a setter of time boundaries for the day, it also peddles fantasy of a deliberately modest, yet still powerful kind. A very subtle form of oppression is at work here.

Simon Bates's Radio 1 show provides excellent examples of the tendencies identified by Coward and Hobson, particularly the constant assumption that nostalgia – the rooting of musical meaning in memory or evocative value, not in straight musical appreciation – is an intrinsically 'feminine' concern. Bates has a daily spot called 'Our Tune', for which listeners are invited to pick a record associated with particularly strong memories of an event, person or time: according to a feature in the *Sun*, 'up to 500 letters pour in each week from listeners revealing a secret sadness they haven't shared with their nearest and dearest'.[17] A piece of lush orchestral music played gently under Bates's voice sets the tone for a story of personal upset or tragedy – a child born to a father shortly to die of cancer, a marriage that both sets of parents said would never work and didn't – that acts as a prelude to the song in question. It is sentimental theatre, deftly done, and can be undeniably moving at times, but it is of course deeply manipulative: the stories (or rather, Bates's telling of them – he rarely quotes direct from the letters) evoke sympathy or even empathy while providing reassurance. They suggest to the listener that she is not alone, or that her own situation may not be so bad after all. Above all, Bates offers a kind of temporary *resolution* to what are often fairly universal and time-honoured situations: a listener's letter is rarely featured which does not carry some implicit moral or message, even if the ending is a sad one. 'Our Tune' is admittedly a very special example of the kind of emotional stage management that is endemic to daytime radio, but in essence it is no more than an extended dedication spot, in which the customary baring of feelings for lovers, family or friends takes on an almost confessional aspect.

Another regular feature of the Bates programme is the 'golden hour' of oldies, divided into two 30-minute sections covering a selected year. The fact that virtually the only extended slot for oldies on Radio 1 should be within a show targeted primarily at housewives is revealing. Bates's technique is to frame records from the year in question with the headline news of the time, cleverly juxtaposing the world-shattering with the parochial, 'silly season' news stories with brief accounts of political upheavals or distant wars and a flurry of statistics on prices, tax fates, television ownership or cinema-going. Although Bates – a Radio 2 newsreader-cum-continuity announcer before he became a Radio 1 presenter – has perfected a cool, measured, even faintly ironic delivery, the effect of this constant juxtaposition is to reduce every event referred to down to the same level of nostalgic, romanticized trivia, a uniting of personal and public history under the same cosy umbrella. It *packages* the past in a manageable, undemanding way.

Bates is a self-confessed populist, and his programme betrays an alarming tendency not so much to talk down to his (apparently) mainly female audience as to assume of them a limited range of expectations and interests. His stock-in-trade is gossip about show business personalities, usually from the pop, film or television worlds, studiously gleaned from the pages of the tabloid press or from his own 'researches'; he features pre-recorded interviews (often 'exclusives', extensively trailed in the *Radio Times* and in other Radio 1 programmes) which gently probe the life-styles of the stars in the manner of a Sunday supplement article, but one continually senses that he imposes deliberate constraints on his questioning in deference to his audience; that he can be an intelligent and incisive commentator on events is evident from his occasional programme-making for Radio 4, notably compiling and presenting *Pick of the Week*. Certainly he and his producer generally avoid the worst excesses of *outright* sexism that characterize the programmes of many of his competitors on other stations. Elsewhere, indeed, mid-morning presenters parade their populism by taking ostentatious delight in patronizing their listeners and, occasionally, their guests. A woman ringing in to take part in a phone-in competition is sent up unmercifully because the milkman happens to call for his money at the same time ('you mean you're paying *him*, darling?'); another competition contestant is 'reassured', after telling the presenter that she is 'only a housewife', that 'housewives do a marvellous job – tell your husband I said that and perhaps he'll drop you an extra quid in the housekeeping'; a woman from the Citizens Advice Bureau (invited on to a programme to discuss returning defective goods) is asked if she has done her ironing yet 'because there's lovely weather forecast and you don't want to be stuck behind an ironing board all weekend, do you?'[18] Then there is the self-parodic figure of Tony Blackburn, who has 'progressed' from preaching to women listeners to his 9 a.m. to 12 midday Radio 1 show about the perils of adultery and how divorce actions hit the husband hardest, to running a daily morning programme on BBC Radio London in which women are invited to indulge in sexual flirtation with him over the air. ('Have I got a 12-incher for you today, ladies . . . how about if I call round and kiss you in all those important places?'[19] Blackburn's portrayal of sexual excess as harmless macho fun needs little comment: it is precisely the 'page-three broadcasting' of which Radio Clyde boss Jimmy Gordon warned in 1984, writ large.[20]

Jockeying for position: the male preserve

Dorothy Hobson describes Blackburn (in his mid-1970s guise) as representing 'an extreme form of the reinforcement of the dominant ideology of domesticity of the housebound listeners of Radio 1'.[21] What the presenter says, the tone of voice he adopts, the attitude he strikes all articulate that ideology in subtle ways, 'he' being the operative pronoun. While women are coming to play a more active role in radio presentation, particularly at local level, the mid-morning show remains an almost exclusively male preserve throughout national and local radio. The low ratio of women on the presentation side of radio is itself a reflection of the prevailing daytime radio perception of the woman as housewife, and the usual reason forwarded by station executives as to why women do not occupy the mid-morning slots is that such an apparent contradiction of that perception might alienate the listening audience. 'If a girl in some studio in London starts talking about getting your washing and ironing done, you're going to resent it', Doreen Davies, Executive Producer at Radio 1 until her retirement in 1987, has said: 'It just sounds personal to another woman. It's different if Tony Blackburn says it; that's just light-hearted'.[22]

But why should *any* presenter, male or female, necessarily have to talk about housework anyway? The fear of station managers is possibly not so much the question of causing resentment as the implicit calling into question of the listener's own role as a domestic labourer: the conventional ILR perception of the woman-as-housewife is reinforced by the advertisements themselves, which invariably feature women as housewives and/or mothers while depicting men in positions of authority. The voiceover in radio advertising is itself an almost wholly male domain, because male voices are traditionally seen by agencies and their clients as carrying authority and influence. There is an unspoken fear, too, that the placing of a woman in radio prime time might *create* expectations among the female audience. This is precisely the argument *for* more women at prime time put forward by a number of the women who are already established (albeit in non-prime-time shows, like Radio 1's Anne Nightingale and Janice Long) as radio voices: one clear way to get more female voices heard on radio, to encourage new talent to come forward, is to provide role models. Of course, there is something backhanded about this, echoes of the woman having to prove herself in what is accepted to be a man's world, to be accepted in effect as an honorary male. An alternative way forward is mapped out in the pages of *Shut Up and Listen!*, where Baehr and Ryan suggest that it is the very nature of 'women's programming' in radio (patriarchal, imposed, limiting and limited) that requires changing by pressure from women listeners themselves.[23]

Sexism within radio runs deep. Senior male staff even refer to their stations in 'feminine' terms: 'Capital is the woman who is ageing, used to be beautiful and has to wear heavy make-up to cover the cracks', Tom Hunter, head of publicity at LBC in London, has opined in the pages of *Broadcast*, 'whereas LBC is the undiscovered beauty who has been living at home with her mother'.[24] Would-be women presenters have to counter a number of ingrained and rarely questioned prejudices: the belief among programme controllers that a woman would limit herself to talking about traditional women's concerns, the belief that high voices do not carry authority (Nightingale and Long, it is pointed out, have deep, husky voices), the feeling that women are somehow not assertive or ambitious enough to take the top spots in radio, the feeling that those women who are ambitious and assertive will be detected as such by the audience and disliked as the 'pushy woman' of male myth. Speaking at the Radio Festival in 1984, Red Rose Radio's managing director, Keith Macklin, came up with a further variation (and prompted a furious reaction from women in the audience) when he suggested that women presenters 'always sound as if they're metaphorically putting on make-up'. Though

Baehr and Ryan found some general enthusiasm among programme controllers for recruiting more women, the common argument was that women simply do not see radio as a potential career and, unless some kind of tokenism is operated, men will invariably be granted the plum jobs because of greater radio experience. Meanwhile, IBA-sponsored research into public attitudes to women on radio is not encouraging: among the findings of a 1984 study into listener's perceptions of presenters in general was the belief that 'few women are as well equipped as men to handle humour in public . . . comparatively few female voices are conducive to relaxed listening', though reactions to established women presenters in two of the areas covered by the survey (County Sound in Guildford, Piccadilly in Manchester) was positive.[25]

In Baehr and Ryan's book, the Controller of Invicta Radio, Michael Bukht (who had the same position at Capital in its early years before taking up a position with the National Broadcasting School), suggests that women are more capable of handling the 'meaningful speech' element of ILR content than music-based shows. Accepting that Bukht's definition of 'capability' means the skill with which women presenters can replicate the customary tone of voice or the cultivated macho presence of male music presenters, he has a point: the very presence of a female voice on daytime radio does alter the nature of the rapport with women listeners, as it draws on an essentially asexual intimacy rather than exploiting the sexual potential (albeit entirely in fantasy) of the relationship between the male presenter and his female flock – a relationship Doreen Davies likens to 'having a male friend in the house while the husband's away without the obvious repercussions'.[26] Davies also suggests that prejudice against women within music radio may also be a reflection of that against women in the music industry itself, where it is only in recent years that women have come to be accepted in a major way as musicians in their own right rather than simply as singers or as glamorous figureheads, and where women have traditionally played an important backroom role (as press officers and personal assistants) yet have been largely excluded from positions of influence in management and A & R. Perhaps more significantly, if music radio is, as Baehr and Ryan describe ILR, 'a medium dominated by male producers and female consumers', then traditionally the same has been true of pop music production itself. Indeed, the traditional contemptuousness shown not only by producers but by media commentators and critics towards the tastes of female record buyers in their teens mirrors and *anticipates* that of radio gatekeepers towards women in general and housewives in particular.

Notes

1 For an analysis of women's magazines in Britain before, during and after the Second World War, see Joy Leman, 'The advice of a real friend: codes of intimacy and oppression in women's magazines 1937–1955', in Helen Baehr (ed.) *Women and Media*, Women's Studies International Quarterly, 3(5), Oxford, Pergamon Press.
2 Ann Oakley, *Housewife*, Harmondsworth, Pelican, 1976, p. 1.
3 Comments heard on Bill Young's mid-morning show on Chiltern Radio, August 1984.

4 Information presented by David Vick at 1985 Music Radio Conference, 1 March 1985.

5 BBC, *Daily Life in the 1980s*.

6 Quoted in Helen Baehr and Michele Ryan, *Shut Up and Listen! Women and Local Radio: A View from the Inside*, London, Comedia, 1984, p. 37.

7 Capital Radio programme plans (extract), reprinted in the Local Radio Workshop, *Nothing Local about It: London's Local Radio*, London, Comedia, 1983.

8 Anne Karpf, 'Women and radio', contained in Helen Baehr (ed.) *Women and Media*, Women's Studies International Quarterly, 3(5), Oxford, Pergamon Press, 1980.

9 Baehr and Ryan, p. 37.

10 *Ibid*.

11 Dave Jamieson, at that time Head of Presentation at Radio Viking on Humberside, writing in *Independent Broadcasting*, winter 1984.

12 Derek Chinnery, interviewed in *Melody Maker*, 15 July 1976.

13 Quoted in Mileva Ross, *Is This Your Life? Images of Women in the Media*, London, Virago, 1977.

14 Johnny Beerling, quoted in 'Pleasing all the people' *Observer*, 19 January 1986.

15 Rosalind Coward, 'Our song', *Female Desire: Women's Sexuality Today*, St Albans, Paladin, 1984, p. 145.

16 Dorothy Hobson, 'Housewives and the mass media', in Stuart Hall *et al.* (eds.) *Culture, Media, Language*, London, Hutchinson, 1980, p. 109.

17 *Sun*, 31 July 1985.

18 Comments heard on mid-morning shows on Chiltern Radio, BBC Radio London and Essex Radio during August 1984.

19 For profiles of Tony Blackburn and accounts of his Radio London show, see Conor Gleason, 'In a blue funk with Blackburn', *Media Week*, 15 March 1985, and Jane Butterworth, 'Black chat', *Ms London*, 22 July 1985.

20 Jimmy Gordon's address to the 1984 Radio Festival, UMIST, Manchester, 3 July 1984.

21 Hobson, p. 108.

22 Karpf op cit.

23 Baehr and Ryan, Ch. 7 *passim*.

24 Quoted in Terence Kelly, 'LBC: undiscovered "beauty" of the air', *Broadcast*, 31 October 1986.

25 'A qualitative research appraisal of the role of the presenter on radio', *IBA Radio Research*, January 1984.

26 Quoted in Karpf, p. 46.

Chapter 11

Rosalind Gill

JUSTIFYING INJUSTICE: BROADCASTERS' ACCOUNTS OF INEQUALITY IN RADIO

From: Gill, R. (1993), in: Burman, E. and Parker, I. (eds) *Discourse Analytic Research: Readings and Repertoires of Texts in Action*, London: Routledge, pp. 75–93.

What I want to do in this chapter is to use the discourse analytic approach developed by Potter and Wetherell (1987) to examine broadcasters' accounts for the lack of women disc jockeys (DJs) at the radio stations where they work. It forms part of a wider project concerned with the ideological features of DJs' on-air talk and how this is understood or 'read' by radio listeners, and the ways in which DJs construct their role and their audience.

One of the most striking features of popular radio in contemporary Britain is the lack of female DJs – at least during the day. When radio stations do employ women as presenters they tend to be on in the evenings when audiences have historically and consistently been at their lowest. BBC Radio One is a good example of this: during weekday daytime programming, women are conspicuous by their absence[1] whilst a small handful have been allocated night-time or weekend slots. Such inequalities in the number and status of women DJs have been well-documented (Baehr and Ryan, 1984; Karpf, 1980, 1987).

What has been less well researched, however, is how these inequalities are understood and made sense of by people working within radio. The aim of this chapter is to examine the accounts put forward by five male DJs and programme controllers (PCs) to explain the lack of female DJs both at their own stations and more generally. In this way we should learn something about how this inequality is perpetuated.

The approach used in this chapter is one which draws, with certain reservations (see Gill, 1991) on Potter and Wetherell's formulation of discourse analysis (Potter and Wetherell, 1987; Potter *et al.*, 1990; Edwards and Potter, 1992). This work acknowledges theoretical debts to a variety of different approaches: linguistic philosophy and speech-act theory (Austin, 1962; Searle, 1969; Wittgenstein, 1953, 1980); semiology and post-structuralism (Barthes, 1964, 1972, 1977; Derrida, 1978; de Saussure, 1974); ethnomethodology and conversation analysis (Garfinkel, 1967; Heritage, 1984; Wieder, 1974); and recent studies of rhetoric (Billig, 1987; Simons, 1989). From this disparate collection of work a coherent approach to language and discourse has been fashioned, which has been articulated primarily in relation to the sociology of scientific knowledge, and social psychology.

Analysing broadcasters' accounts

The analysis which follows uses a discourse analytic approach to study the accounts of five broadcasters from two independent local radio (ILR) stations for the lack of female DJs. In terms of female DJs neither station was atypical; one had no female DJs at all, whilst the other employed one female whose phone-in show was broadcast twice a week between 11.00 p.m. and 1.00 am. (For reasons of clarity I will treat these two stations as if they were one, which I shall call Radio Matchdale.) Two of the five broadcasters were DJs, two were programme controllers (PCs) and the fifth was both a DJ and a deputy PC. The interviews were conducted by a female interviewer and covered a range of topics including how the broadcaster saw his role and responsibilities, what he saw as the function of the station, his view of the audience, how much autonomy he felt he had, as well as questions about the lack of women DJs.[2]

What I am interested in are what Wetherell *et al.* (1987) have called the 'practical ideologies' through which gender inequalities in the employment of DJs are understood. The transcripts were analysed to find the broad types of accounts being offered by the broadcasters for the lack of women DJs. Five different types were identified, each organized around a particular claim, such as 'women don't apply' or 'the audience prefers male DJs'. What I want to stress is that these were not alternative accounts which were espoused by individual broadcasters. Rather, the DJs and PCs *all* drew on and combined different and contradictory accounts for the lack of women DJs. The analysis is divided into four sections, which deal with four of the five accounts, and examine some of the warrants which were put forward to support each broad account. The aim is not to provide an exhaustive analysis but simply to give a sense of how discourse analysis can be used to analyse this sort of material.

Accounting for inequality: (1) 'Women just don't apply'

The first and most prevalent type of account offered for the lack of female DJs was organized around the claim that women do not 'apply' to become radio presenters. Four out of the five broadcasters drew on this idea. ((.) indicates a pause in speech.)

Extract one (Goodman)
Int: Why do you think there are so few female DJs?
DJ: (laughs) probably because they don't apply. It's, it's that literally is it.

Extract two (Dale)
DJ: It's a more popular sort of occupation to men. We get a lot of tapes from people who want to be DJs and they're all from men.

Extract three (Chapman)
PC: It's a question that. I get tapes from hopefuls on my desk every day of the week and none of them are ever women.

Extract four (Lightfoot)
PC: I get all the applications to come in here (.) We get about 400 a year (.) We've had none from women in the last year. Not one to be a presenter.

One of the most interesting features of these interviews is that for each of the broad explanations put forward to explain the lack of women DJs, such as the one above that women do not apply, the broadcasters spontaneously offered further accounts, often constructed around little narratives or stories. These can be understood as ways of *warranting* their explanations which make them sound more plausible. In the case of the claim that no women apply to become DJs, four different types of supporting account can be identified – that women are not interested in becoming DJs, that 'education and social process' does not prepare them for it, that they opt instead for jobs in journalism or television, and that they are put off DJing because 'it's a man's world'. Here I will examine two of these.

Accounting for women' s non-application: 'There aren't many . . . who are interested in doing it'

In the following extract the PC, Chapman, has just been explaining how Radio Matchdale recruits its staff.

Extract five (Chapman)
PC: and it's where people come from (.) so in hospital radio there aren't many women DJs (.) there aren't many women DJs in pubs (.) there aren't many female DJs (.) especially teenage age which is when we're looking to bring people like (.) who are interested in doing it.

What Chapman is doing here is accounting for the lack of women DJs at Radio Matchdale by reference to the lack of women DJs in the station's traditional recruiting ground – hospital radio and pubs. But he does not stop there: he offers an explanation for this – 'there aren't many women [.] who are interested in doing it'. In making this psychologistic claim, Chapman does two things. First, and most straightforwardly, he denies that there is any *real* or *genuine* motivation on women's part to become DJs. It would be interesting to discover just how common is this pattern of accounting. I want to suggest that the idea that oppressed groups do not 'really' want to change their position, is one frequently drawn on by members of dominant groups in order to justify their actions or inaction.

Second, this assertion serves to deflect criticism or charges of sexism from radio stations in general and from Radio Matchdale in particular. It gives the impression that radio stations would be happy to take on women as DJs but that they are faced with a wall of disinterest from women. The idea that radio stations are battling against women's lack of interest in DJing, and are even putting in extra effort to find female presenters is reinforced by Chapman's comment a few moments later: 'so we have to look hard'. That Chapman is looking hard for female DJs establishes his 'good faith', his lack of sexism, and responsibility for the lack of female DJs is placed firmly on women's shoulders.

The idea that women are not interested in becoming DJs is also drawn on by Goodman.

Extract six (Goodman)

DJ: I'm sure there's a helluva lot of them out there that would be really er good communicators but have never even given a thought of doing it (.) Maybe they're doing a job that either pays more money or is more interesting to them.

This is an explanation which rests upon an implicit view of society as characterized by social mobility. It suggests that women *could* become DJs but have *chosen* to do other work. The salary and satisfaction of a radio presenter is downgraded. In fact, women's non-application is made to appear eminently sensible and rational when contrasted with the likelihood that they are doing better paid or more interesting jobs. Again, the picture presented of women doing other highly paid and satisfying work serves to undermine the notion that women *really* wish to become radio presenters.

Accounting for women's non-application: 'It's a man's world'

A different explanation for women's claimed non-application is put forward by the PC named Lightfoot.

Extract seven (Lightfoot)

PC: It's also very much a man's world so they're picked on if they are here (.) you know a woman has got to assert herself pretty definitely if she's working in radio.

It is clear that the phrase 'it's a man's world' is being used to refer to much more than the simple numerical superiority of males at the radio station, since it is used to explain the 'fact' that women are 'picked on'. What's interesting, however, is the fact that it is *not formulated as sexism*. To be 'picked on' is to be subjected to nasty and unjust behaviour, but it is the behaviour of *individuals* – something that can be highlighted by trying to imagine a formulation in which a *radio station* was deemed to 'pick on' women. The choice of this construction serves further to play down any notion of structural inequality or institutional practices.

It is significant that for the first time a feature of life within the radio station is introduced to account for women's non-application. But finally, the problem is not one for the men at the radio station, nor for the radio station as a whole to deal with, but rather it is up to each individual woman to 'assert herself pretty definitely if she's working on radio'.

Accounting for inequality: (2) audience objections: 'It's a bit strange to have a woman talking to you'

A second type of explanation for the lack of female DJs focused on the audience's expected or apparently 'proven' negative reaction to female presenters.

Extract eight (Dale)

DJ: Research has proven (.) and this is not mine but it's echoed by many surveys throughout the years (.) that people prefer to listen to a man's voice on the radio rather than a woman's voice. Women like to hear men on the radio because they're used to it (.) and it's a bit strange to have a woman talking to you. And men like hearing men on the radio (.) perhaps because they're just chauvinistic. Whatever the reasons, research has borne out this fact you know that people like to have men on the radio (.) and we just go along with the consensus of opinion. We do have women – Marie does an admirable job on the phone-in. We've got a lot of women newscasters so you know there's certainly no prejudice.

The first thing to note about this extract is that it came from Dale, (see page 139) arguing that the lack of female DJs can be explained by the fact that no women apply. Here, he constructs a different explanation for the small number of female DJs. Suddenly, the lack of female presenters looks less like the result of a lack of applications from women, and more like a deliberate policy not to employ women – because of audiences' alleged preference for men. In both formulations, it should be noted, the radio station is depicted as blameless – in the first because it is women themselves who are choosing not to apply and in the second because the radio station is merely serving its audience by giving it the presenters it wants.

Several authors have pointed out that accounts which merely appear to be describing the world are more persuasive than accounts which seem to be motivated by particular interests or psychological dispositions of the speaker (Smith, 1978; Potter and Wetherell, 1988; Edwards and Potter, 1992). Thus, one of the problems for a speaker is to accomplish the 'out-thereness' (Potter and Wetherell, 1988) of their claims. One way this is achieved by Dale in this extract is through the discursive work being done by 'research' and 'surveys'.

Audience objections: research, surveys and more research

These terms give authority to Dale's claims. In the first sentence alone Dale talks about 'research' and 'surveys' implying that these are separate rather than different words for the same thing: not only has research shown it, Dale argues, but it has also been echoed by 'many surveys'. The use of these terms and their associated vocabularies such as 'proven' lend credence and a sense of objectivity to Dale's claims.

The terms also serve to distance Dale personally from the claim that listeners would prefer to listen to a man. It is constructed not as an aspect of his own beliefs, not an opinion, but rather something 'out there' which 'research' and 'surveys' have 'proven'. Dale's *own* role, as someone involved in the recruitment and appointment of staff, in mediating between research findings and appointment policy, is completely glossed over in his talk. The research findings which 'prove' that listeners prefer male presenters and the lack of female DJs are presented as related together in a way which is totally independent of human action.

Audience objections: a 'new sexism'?

One of the most interesting features of this extract is the striking parallel with what has become known as 'new racist' discourse (Barker, 1981). This type of discourse is characterized by the tendency to justify racist acts or legislation in non-racial terms, often drawing on other values such as equality and fairness (Billig, 1988). It is also marked by denials of prejudice, frequently accompanied by the claim that it is the liberal anti-racists who are the *real* racists (Barker, 1981; Billig, 1988). Perhaps the most straightforward type of denial takes the form of the 'disclaimer' (Hewitt and Stokes, 1975). Typically, a statement such as 'I'm not being racist' is followed by a 'but' which precedes the expression of something which could easily be heard as racist.

The widespread existence of denials of prejudice has led to some discussion of the possibility that there exists a 'cultural norm against prejudice' (Barker, 1981: Van Dijk, 1984; Reeves, 1983; Billig, 1988).

Racism is generally taken to be the prototypical example of prejudice, and indeed 'prejudice' is often used as if it were synonymous with racism. Yet, if we look back at extract eight we see that there are significant similarities with the 'new racist' discourse. The most obvious of these is the disclaimer – 'We've got a lot of women newscasters so you know (.) there's certainly no prejudice.' It does not take the classic form discussed by Hewitt and Stokes (1975) – it is retrospective rather than prospective – but the work it is doing in the extract in attempting to disclaim a prejudiced identity is the same as that identified by researchers studying racist talk. In the extract here, the disclaimer is reinforced by the contrasts which are established between men who demand male presenters because they are chauvinist and the women who do so from force of habit and the radio station where 'there's certainly no prejudice'. It is worth noting Dale's use of the notion of 'chauvinism' and contrasting it with the term 'picked on' discussed in the consideration of extract seven. It is an interesting indication of the fact that broadcasters do have access to the notion of chauvinism, which, although not politicized in the same way as 'sexism', does at least have the merit of suggesting a *pattern* to discrimination. The broadcasters use this notion only to do particular work: *not* as a characterization of the radio station's behaviour, but rather an attitude with which Radio Matchdale can be contrasted favourably.

A further notable similarity with 'new racist' discourse is to be found in Dale's claim that 'we just go along with the consensus where Dale presents himself as a mere *victim* of *other people's* prejudice. This 'I'm not prejudiced myself but the audience wouldn't like it' type of accounting bears such a similarity to new racist talk that it suggests that the existence of a 'new sexism' might be worth investigating.

Accounting for inequality: (3) gender differences: 'Those things are not as advanced . . . as far as women are concerned as with men'

A third type of explanation for the small number of female DJs focused on women's putative lack of the *qualities* and *skills* necessary to be a DJ. The following extract from Chapman is an example of this kind of account. We will examine it in some detail.

The interviewer's question is a response to Chapman's claim (see the first section of this chapter) that none of the tapes he receives from applicants are from women.

Extract nine (Chapman)
Int: Do you think there are a set of reasons why women are put off from entering the DJ world?
PC: (. . .)Presenters have to have a number of skills. They've got to have . . . they've got to be very very dextrous (.) they've got to be very familiar with technical equipment (.) they've got to have a personality they are used to expressing and they've got to have a good knowledge of music as well as having a good personality (.) and those things are *not* as advanced in my view as far as women are concerned as with men. Um (.) um (.) I've got to be able to sit somebody in a radio studio and they've got to understand what they're doing kind of thing as well as being a good broadcaster and women (.) in their whole background are not brought up in that kind of environment.

Two aspects of this extract are immediately striking. First that Chapman does not appear to be answering the question he was asked. Instead of explaining why he thinks women are put off from *applying* for DJ jobs, he appears to be providing a justification for *not employing* women: 'I've got to be able to sit somebody in a radio studio . . . .' In this respect his answer is defensive. The second is that his opening words are extremely formal. One important effect of Chapman's use of the passive form and of his use of a list construction (however stumbled over) of attributes needed for radio presentation is to give the impression that certain impersonal, objective and, crucially, non-gendered, criteria are applied to the selection and appointment of DJs. What Chapman is suggesting is simply that women fail to meet these (necessary) standards.

It is worth looking at this point at the *nature* of the skills and qualities which are formulated by Chapman as necessary for DJs. What is striking about the list is both its inexplicitness *and* the fact that the skills mentioned do not seem to be tied to stereotypes about gender. DJs have got to be 'very very dextrous', 'very familiar with technical equipment', have 'a personality they are used to expressing' and 'a good knowledge of music'. With the possible exception of 'familiarity with technical equipment', none of these qualities seems to fit more readily with stereotypes of masculinity than femininity. Indeed, if anything, the qualities appear to match more closely stereotypes of women: it is women, who, according to stereotype, are dextrous and good at expressing themselves. The significance of this can be highlighted by rereading the extract, substituting 'men' for 'women'.

The point is, then, that the force of the passage derives from the list itself rather than from the specific items which comprise it. The only arguably stereo-typical item is 'familiar with technical equipment' which is interesting both for its vagueness and for the fact that it suggests that potential DJs should *already* be working technical equipment. Again, this supports the impression that Chapman is accounting for not employing women rather than for why women do not apply.

As with other explanations, Chapman spontaneously offered reasons to account for why women lacked the skills and qualities necessary for a DJ. I will examine just one of these.

Explaining gender difference: 'Education and social process'

For Chapman there seems to be nothing mysterious about why women fail to live up to the selection criteria for DJs. He accounts for it with reference to 'lay sociological explanations' (Potter and Wetherell, 1988).

> *PC:* Those things in education and social process are *not* as advanced in my view as far as women are concerned as with men (. . .) and women (.) in their whole background are not brought up in that kind of environment.

Although the language is vague, it is clear that an explanation is being constructed around notions of the contrasting socialization and education of women and men. I am not here concerned with the 'truth' or adequacy of such an explanation but rather with what its articulation achieves for Chapman.

One of the functions of the use of this lay sociological theory for Chapman is to provide a mitigation for women's failure to meet the appointment standards for DJs. In a society where at least one strong ideological current emphasizes meritocracy and individual success, failure can easily appear as blameworthy. In this extract the lay sociological theory provides a mitigation by offering reasons or causes for women's putative failure – 'education and social process' – which make it understandable and thus less potentially blameworthy. The notions of 'education' and 'social process' are ideal for doing this kind of work since they are both extremely vague and suggest no particular agency on women's parts. Yet it should be remembered that women's 'failure' is as much Chapman's construction as the mitigation for this failure. If he characterizes women as lacking the skills and qualities to become DJs, why should he also provide a mitigation for them?

Potter and Wetherell (1988) discovered similar simultaneous constructions of blame and mitigations in Pakeha (White New Zealanders') discourse about people from the Pacific Islands living in New Zealand, and have suggested why this pattern should occur. They argue that one of the problems for speakers of producing negative claims about a group of people is that it can easily be heard as prejudice, something (as discussed in the second section of this chapter) the speaker may be anxious to avoid. One of the ways in which the hearability of this can be reduced is 'to reduce the force of the blamings being made' (Potter and Wetherell, 1988: 64). And in turn one of the ways that this can be accomplished is by the use of a mitigation. In the current example, Chapman could easily be heard as an out-and-out sexist, arguing quite simply that women are not as good as men. By providing a mitigation Chapman reduces the availability of this charge.

A second related function of Chapman's use of lay sociological theory is to emphasize the 'out-thereness' of his characterization of women. That is, his spontaneous production of an account for women s 'failure' actually *reinforces* the idea that it is because women fail to meet the selection standards that there are so few women DJs. Just as the terms 'research' and 'surveys' give the impression of facticity to claims so the sociological notions suggest that Chapman is merely describing the world as it is. Chapman's independence from the object of discussion is reinforced by the regretful tone of his next remark:

Extract ten (Chapman)
Int: Well I think that in the last say ten twenty years things have changed (.) have
PC: Yes they've changed. But they haven't changed enough.

The implication is that the world is not the way he would like it to be, but that is the way it is – regardless of his motivation.

(A contrasting explanation focusing on 'natural' gender differences and aptitudes was put forward by the DJ, Goodman. I have discussed this elsewhere (Gill, 1991).)

Accounting for inequality: (4) women 's voices: too 'shrill', too 'dusky' and just plain 'wrong'

The fourth type of account put forward by the broadcasters to explain the lack of women DJs centred on women's voices. In making these claims the broadcasters placed themselves within a long tradition in British broadcasting. Women's exclusion from particular types of employment within the media on the basis that their voices are 'unsuitable' is now well-documented (Ross, 1977; Karpf, 1980; Kramarae, 1989).

As recently as the 1970s similar reasons were being offered by the BBC for their refusal to employ women as newsreaders. Mileva Ross showed how the most pervasive arguments were that women s voices were 'too high' or 'lacked authority'. In the words of Jim Black, then editor of Radio Four:

> If a woman could read the news as well as a man then she could do it. But a newsreader needs to have reliability, consistency and authority. A woman may have one or two of these things but not all three. If a woman were to read the news no one would take it seriously.

(quoted in Ross, 1977)

As Ross wryly comments, did he expect us to fall about laughing or just to disbelieve it? His colleague Robin Scott was of a similar opinion. He said it was 'unnatural' for women to read the news: 'There's always bad news about and it's much easier for a man to deal with that kind of material' (quoted in Ross, 1977).

The concerted efforts of the feminist campaigning group, Women In Media, led to a small handful of women being appointed as newsreaders by 1975. Jim Black spoke of 'an awful lot of special training' which had 'come to fruition' leaving two female newsreaders to take their place alongside their fifteen male colleagues. Black commented: 'I think we have got the right mix now. I don't want Radio Four to sound all-female . . . If you have two on it sounds a lot' (quoted in Ross, 1977).

All the DJs and PCs interviewed in this research found women's voices worthy of comment. Although one remark by Toller seems to be a positive one – he says that he does not think the Radio Two presenter Gloria Hunniford has a shrill voice – the mere fact that he felt it worthy of comment is significant. There were no comparable remarks about men's voices. Next, we examine the rather more lengthy comments of Goodman when asked to elaborate upon his claim that women's voices are 'not right'.

Extract eleven (Goodman)

DJ: As I said to you before (.) people are sensitive to voice (.) they pick up a lot in a voice. They can see it as exuding friendliness, sarcasm, angriness or whatever and if it happens to be (.) and if a woman's voice sounds grating or high (.) shrill, then that will switch them off. If it sounds dusky and sexy (1.0) unfortunately that switches them on (.) now Marie has got a dusky, sexy, deep voice perfect for it (.) she's actually nothing like that when you meet her (.) she's a very sweet lady but she's not like that but people are conned totally by the voice.

The extract is similar to that discussed in the second section of this chapter in that Goodman is involved in justifying not employing women as DJs by reference to what listeners like or dislike. However, whereas on p. 141 the listeners' resistance to female DJs was characterized 'chauvinist' or merely habitual, and the DJ presented himself as regretfully just 'going along with the consensus', here listeners' putative reservations about (some) female voices are characterized as perfectly reasonable. What could be heard as prejudice is recast as 'sensitivity'. Listeners' sensitivity, unlike their chauvinism, is not to be regretted. The radio station merely translates this sensitivity into appointment decisions.

One of the ways in which listeners' sensitivity to women's voices is brought off as reasonable by Goodman is through the subtle linking of notions of sensitivity to particular emotional or motivational states (angriness, friendliness, sarcasm) and sensitivity to particular vocal pitches. Goodman starts by asserting that people see voices as 'exuding friendliness, sarcasm, angriness or whatever' and goes on 'and if a woman's voice sounds grating or high (.) shrill then that will switch them off'. The 'reasonableness' of this second phrase is effectively achieved by its ostensible connection to the first. For whilst sensitivity to friendliness or sarcasm seems admirable, 'sensitivity' to pitch may betoken prejudice.

It is worth briefly considering the way that pairs of words are used to characterize women's voices. The first thing to note is that the notion of what is 'shrill' or 'dusky' is not unproblematic: these are not neutral words to describe pitch – whatever a neutral word may be. Indeed, Goodman starts by characterizing some women's voices as 'high' but then substitutes a word which has far more richly negative connotations – shrill. To object to (or be 'sensitive' to) 'high' voices could be heard as blameworthy, but to object to 'shrill' voices seems perfectly reasonable – it is a word which contains an evaluation (cf. Wowk, 1984).

Second, we should note the way the second word in each pair is used to add to and to describe the first – giving the impression that, for example, dusky *is* sexy. I want to argue that it is not insignificant that the two examples used seem to fit almost perfectly with two commonly used stereotypes of women – the 'nag' and the 'femme fatale'. This is not to imply, however, that these stereotypes are somehow static and non-changing.

What Goodman seems to be doing is presenting a 'no-win' situation for women. If they sound 'grating and shrill' then that 'switches listeners off'. This phrase has a fascinating double meaning. Goodman may mean simply that shrill or grating female voices displease people, turn them off. But his phrase also serves to remove all agency and responsibility for switching the radio off from listeners, and places it instead on women's voices. In this way people's sensitivity comes to seem perfectly reasonable; it is women's voices in themselves that do the switching off, and are therefore blameworthy.

If a woman sounds 'dusky and sexy' 'that switches them on'. One might imagine that this is exactly what the radio station would want, but Goodman treats it ambivalently describing it as 'unfortunate', but also describing Marie's 'dusky sexy deep' voice as 'perfect for it'. This becomes explicable if we understand the 'it' for which Marie is apparently 'perfect' as her own show (which is broadcast between 11 p.m. and 1 a.m.) rather than more prime-time radio presentation. It also illuminates a further nuance of meaning for the word 'dusky' – suggesting appropriateness for nighttime broadcasting. More generally, it seems that Goodman's ambivalence about 'switching them on' is due to its sexual connotations. This would denote a level of sexual assertiveness deemed unacceptable in a woman.

Goodman's remarks about Marie are also interesting for three other reasons. At one level they serve simply as a reminder (in what may be for the speaker a critical interpretative context) that the radio station *does have* a female presenter (albeit only one who is relegated to the wee small hours). By explicitly praising Marie's presentation style, Goodman reduces the hearability of sexism. This also accounts for his ambivalence: for he is both justifying the non-employment of women as DJs and attending to the possibility that he may be heard as sexist.

Second, the passage is interesting because it supports the idea raised earlier that 'dusky' and 'sexy' are tied to the notion of the 'femme fatale'. What Goodman seems to be saying is that she *sounds* dusky and sexy, but *actually* she is not – she is no 'femme fatale'.

Finally, the passage is significant because it reasserts the importance of voice – 'people are conned by the voice totally'. However, it does so in such a way as to undermine completely Goodman's earlier claim that people are 'sensitive to voices' and can 'pick up a lot in a voice'. For listeners so easily 'conned' the notion of 'sensitivity' as a justification for not employing women who apply begins to look a little thin.

It is tempting to suggest that the only way a woman can succeed is by sounding like a man. And indeed, this is what Goodman seems to have concluded.

Extract twelve (Goodman)
DJ: They they build a mental picture so it's really your voice (.) if your voice is right. For some women that can be hard because their voice is naturally higher.

If we leave aside the considerable debate over the supposed differences in the pitch of male and female voices (see, for example, Spender, 1985) what is clear from this short extract is that the male voice is being used as the norm against which other voices are judged for their appropriateness. Implicit in the extract is the idea that a low, male voice is somehow naturally right for DJs. This extract is a very good example of what has been called the 'male as norm' phenomenon (Spender, 1985; Griffin, 1985) and it is against the background of this norm that becoming a DJ can be judged 'hard' for 'some women'. Significantly, although the male voice is presented as the 'natural' 'right' voice for a DJ it is presented as non-gendered.

Discussion

This chapter has examined some of the practical ideologies through which the lack of female DJs is explained and justified. What I have tried to show is that far from the broadcasters each espousing a particular attitude or advancing a specific explanation to account for the lack of women DJs, each had available a *whole range* of ways of accounting, which they drew on selectively in the interviews.

Overall, I pointed to a pervasive variability in broadcasters' accounts which would be overlooked or suppressed by more traditional, social psychological approaches. The accounts constructed by broadcasters were flexible, inconsistent and sometimes contradictory. The claim by the DJs and PCs that no women apply, within moments of explanations by those same broadcasters about why those women who do apply are not suitable for DJing, is simply the most dramatic example of this, and poses severe problems for attitude theories and all other approaches which work with a realist view of language. Rather than seeing such assertions as unproblematic statements of fact, discourse analysis argues that they are better understood in terms of their discursive functions.

The chapter also looked in detail at the construction of particular accounts, examining how broadcasters attempted to accomplish them as factual or 'out-there' and discussing the way the accounts offered seemed to make the lack of women flow apparently self-evidently from the explanations. Specifically, all the accounts put forward by broadcasters to explain the lack of women DJs constructed the reasons as lying *in women themselves* or in *the wants of the audience*. The role of the radio station was made invisible in these accounts, and discussions of employment practices and institutional sexism were conspicuous by their absence. In this way broadcasters were able to present themselves as non-sexist, whilst they simultaneously justified the lack of women at the radio station.

None of the DJs or PCs said at any point that they did not think that women should be employed as DJs. On the contrary, they were keen to point out their lack of sexism ('there's certainly no prejudice') and that they were 'looking hard' for female presenters. However, what they produced were accounts which justified the exclusion of women. In providing these accounts for why there are so few female DJs now, the broadcasters also provided justifications for the continued absence of women in the future. The ideological effects of these discourses is to perpetuate inequality within radio stations.

One potential disadvantage with this kind of discourse analytic approach is that it does not produce the broad empirical generalizations which are developed in more traditional sociological and social psychological work. Thus, the analysis here cannot be understood as identifying a universal process underlying gender discrimination in employment or even sexism in radio stations. What it does is examine the explanations put forward by a particular group of white, male broadcasters in a particular social and historical context, in the course of interviews with a white, middle-class and almost-certainly-feminist (from the broadcasters' perspective) woman. For discourse analysis, the failure to theorize universal processes is not a weakness but an inevitable consequence of the fact that explanations are always constructed out of particular interpretative resources and designed for specific occasions (Wetherell and Potter, 1988). Thus, we might expect to see different accounts put forward to explain the lack of women DJs if the broadcasters had been talking amongst themselves or had been interviewed by a male. This does not invalidate the research but merely serves to emphasize discourse analysts' point about the constructive, action-orientated nature of language.

A further disadvantage for people thinking about doing discourse analytic work is the sheer effort involved. Discourse analysis is extremely labour-intensive, and the time taken up conducting interviews and transcribing them can be considerable. In order to produce this analysis, for example, I produced five transcripts which totalled 114 pages of typed A4 script. Added to this is the length of time it takes to learn and develop the skill of analysis. As Wetherell and Potter (1988) have argued, discourse analysis is a craft skill, and it is possible to work with an analytic schema for several days only to find that it cannot be validated by the available materials.

However, against this, discourse analysis has considerable value. It offers both a practical and theoretically coherent way of analysing a whole variety of talk and texts, taking them seriously in their own right (not as vehicles for some underlying psychological reality) and treating them in their full specificity.

Discourse analysis also constitutes a *systematic* approach to the evaluation of texts whose findings are open to evaluation. Reports of discourse analytic work include either full transcripts or samples of the analytic materials used so that readers are able to assess the success of the interpretations, and indeed, offer alternatives (Wetherell and Potter, 1988).

Finally, and most importantly, discourse analysis offers a new way of understanding ideology. It sees ideological discourse not as a fixed subset of all discourse which works in standard recurrent ways and is defined by its content or style, but rather as a *way of accounting* It highlights the fact that what is ideological cannot be straightforwardly read off: propositions do not come with their ideological significance 'inscribed on their backs' and nor is the operation of ideology limited to discourse which naturalizes, reifles or legitimizes – or any of the other familiar modes (Thompson, 1988). Discourse analysis suggests that what is ideological is an *analytic question*. In the present analysis I hope to have shown that even as broadcasters declared their desire to see more women DJs, they produced discourse which was ideological – because the accounts they produced served to justify and perpetuate inequality within radio stations.[3]

Notes

1 Except in the new 'weathergirl' (sic) role in which female news or weather readers or production assistants are used by male DJs to feed them witty one-liners and create an impression of relaxed banter.
2 I would like to thank Sue Reilly for her help in carrying out these interviews.
3 I would like to thank Michael Billig, Jonathan Potter and Andy Pratt for their comments on an earlier draft of this chapter.

References

Austin, J.L. (1962) *How to do Things with Words*, Oxford: Clarendon Press.
Baehr, H. and Ryan, M. (1984) *Shut Up and Listen: Women and Local Radio: A View from the Inside*, London: Comedia.

Barker, M. (1981) *The New Racism*, London: Junction Books.

Barthes, R. (1964) *Elements of Semiology*, New York: Hill & Wang.

—— (1972) *Mythologies*, London: Paladin.

—— (1977) *Image-Music-Text*, London: Fontana.

Billig, M. (1987) *Arguing and Thinking: A Rhetorical Approach to Social Psychology*, Cambridge: Cambridge University Press.

—— (1988) 'The notion of "prejudice": some rhetorical and ideological aspects', *Text 8*: 91–110.

Coward, R. (1984) *Female Desire: Women's Sexuality Today*, London: Paladin.

Derrida, J. (1978) *Writing and Difference*, London: Routledge & Kegan Paul.

De Saussure, F. (1974) *Courses in General Linguistics*, London: Fontana.

Edwards, D. and Potter, J. (1992) *Discursive Psychology*, London: Sage.

Garfinkel, H. (1967) *Studies in Ethnomethodology*, Englewood Cliffs, NJ: Prentice Hall.

Gill, R. (1991) 'Ideology and popular radio: a discourse analytic examination of disc jockeys' talk', unpublished PhD thesis, Loughborough University.

Griffin, C. (1985) *Typical Girls: Young Women from School to the Job Market*, London: Routledge & Kegan Paul.

Heritage, J. (1984) *Garfinkel and Ethnomethodology*, Cambridge: Polity Press.

Hewitt, J.P. and Stokes, R. (1975) 'Disclaimers', *American Sociological Review* 40: 1–11.

Karpf, A. (1980) 'Women and Radio', *Women's Studies International Quarterly* 3: 41–54.

—— (1987) 'Radio Times; private women and public men', in K. Davies, J. Dickey and T. Stratford (eds) *Out of Focus: Writings on Women and the Media*, London: The Women's Press.

Kramarae, C. (1989) *Technology and Women's Voices*, London: Sage.

Potter, J. and Wetherell, M. (1987) *Discourse and Social Psychology: Beyond Attitudes and Behaviour*, London: Sage.

—— (1988) 'Accomplishing attitudes: fact and evaluation in racist discourse', *Text* 8: 51–68.

Potter, J., Wetherell, M., Gill, R. and Edwards, D. (1990) 'Discourse analysis: noun, verb or social practice', *Philosophical Psychology* 3: 205–17.

Reeves, W. (1983) *British Racial Discourse: A Study of British Political Discourse about Race and Race-related Matters*, Cambridge: Cambridge University Press.

Ross, M. (1977) 'Radio', in M. Stott and J. King (eds) *Is This your Life? Images of Women in the Mass Media*, London: Virago.

Searle, J.R. (1969) *Speech Acts*, Cambridge: Cambridge University Press.

Simons, H. (1989) *Rhetoric in the Human Sciences*, London: Sage.

Smith, D. (1978) 'K is mentally ill: the anatomy of a factual account', *Sociology* 12: 23–53.

Spender, D. (1985) *Man Made Language*, London: Routledge.

Thompson, J. (1984) *Studies in the Theory of Ideology*, Cambridge: Polity.

Van Dijk, T. (1984) *Prejudice in Discourse: An Analysis of Ethnic Prejudices in Cognition and Conversation*, Amsterdam: John Benjamins.

Wetherell, M. and Potter, J. (1988) 'Discourse analysis and the identification of interpretative repertoires', in C. Antaki (ed.) *Analysing Everyday Explanation: A Casebook of Methods*, London: Sage.

Wetherell, M., Stiven, H. and Potter, J. (1987) 'Unequal egalitarianism: a preliminary study of discourses concerning gender and employment opportunities', *British Journal of Social Psychology* 26: 59–71.

Wieder, L. (1974) 'Telling the code', in R. Turner (ed.) *Ethnomethodology*, Harmondsworth: Penguin.

Wittgenstein, L. (1953) *Philosophical Investigations*, Oxford: Blackwell.

—— (1980) *Remarks on the Philosophy of Psychology*, Oxford: Blackwell.

Wowk, M. (1984) 'Blame allocation, sex and gender in a murder investigation', in *Women's Studies International Forum* 7: 75–82.

Chapter 12

Jo Tacchi

GENDER, FANTASY AND RADIO CONSUMPTION: AN ETHNOGRAPHIC CASE STUDY

Introduction

A study of gender and radio consumption starts from the premise that such consumption is indeed gendered. The research that underpins this chapter[1] did not start out with an intention to specifically investigate gender differences, yet information generated can be used to explore such differences. In particular the research can be seen to demonstrate that one of the generally understood, and apparently universal ideas about gendered media consumption – that is the link between women's media consumption and fantasy – might usefully be reframed. Here I demonstrate that, whilst it is possible to see a clear link between women's radio consumption and fantasy, radio consumption by men can also been seen as demonstrating such a link.

It is important to establish early on in the chapter what I mean by 'fantasy'. The work on women and radio by Hobson (1980) contributed to the view of women radio listeners as 'isolated', seeking the company of male disc jockeys about whom they had sexual fantasies. In turn the DJs play on this perception of lonely housewives and take on the role of sexual fantasy-figure. In the music radio industry, there has been a long-standing notion of a stereotypical female listener, who invites the male presenter into her home, as 'romantic visitors descending on a bored housewife' (Baehr and Ryan 1984: 8). Such relationships appear to be tacitly accepted while at the same time criticised despite the lack of research to investigate this perceived relationship on a deeper level. The notion of fantasy as it is experienced through media consumption is often assumed to be a female trait. According to my findings fantasy is also present in male media consumption, albeit in a different form.

Elsewhere (Tacchi 1998), I explored the radio listening of one of my female respondents who displayed the obvious, almost stereotypical qualities and behaviours of the female listener having an affair with her radio station. This woman was a member of her local station's listener panel and was described to me by the consultant who ran the panel as a typical 'anorak' or radio station 'groupie'. On closer inspection of her relationship with the station it was clear, however, that she was using the radio in a qualitatively different way, for different purposes. She in fact was using radio to reinforce and maintain her own identity as an individual who is serious about music. This she opposed to her understanding of how her family and the radio station staff see her.

In order to define what I mean by 'fantasy' I draw on two authors that have addressed fantasy and media consumption. Radway's (1987) study of romance readers in an American town will be discussed along with the criticism and differently defined pleasurable media consumption that Ang (1996) locates. Radway separates fantasy from real life and concludes that it creates false models of reality that are harmful to women because they then fail to take actions in real life to redress what she sees as gender imbalance (a feminist issue). Ang prefers to see fantasy as a reality in itself – a dimension of our psychical reality where excesses can be played out. Relative to these two positions I use the term fantasy to describe imaginative and routine aspects of daily life and identity creation and maintenance – I see fantasy as 'embedded' in everyday life, an aspect of reality and a contributor to our perception of our worlds. Furthermore, it is shown to be employed by men and women.

After briefly outlining the methods used in this study of radio consumption I present case studies of four individuals. Two are husband and wife, two are *former* husband and wife. Both couples talk about their radio tastes and consumption as opposed to their partner or former partner. The first couple uses this to demonstrate the success of their relationship and how they overcome their differences in order to achieve complementarity. The second couple demonstrates how talking about their radio tastes and habits can serve to illustrate underlying problems in their relationship, which ultimately led to its failure. They provide examples of how we might begin to understand the relationships and significance of gender and media consumption, or as Ang and Hermes put it, gender *in* media consumption (1996). I conclude that the men in this chapter use radio sound differently from the women, but in both cases there is an element of mediated fantasy involved.

Methods

This chapter draws on ethnographic fieldwork, part of a three-year study of radio consumption in a city in the South West of England. The study explored the role of radio in domestic life and relationships. As a social anthropologist I wanted to understand what it was about radio that made it so pervasive, so much a part of domestic everyday life. The study took an ethnographic approach using in-depth interviews, participant observation, observation at local listener panels and focus groups. Some respondents completed diaries of their listening and viewing.

A major problem facing an anthropologist interested in carrying out ethnographic research on radio listening is how to carry out participant observation. I sought other ways of getting to know my respondents beyond the in-depth interview technique carried out by 'reception ethnographers' in the field of media and cultural studies (Moores 1993). To this end I attended a single parent social club for twelve months. There I got to know people in a social setting and took part in leisure activities with them before interviewing them about their radio listening. In addition I attended two local radio listener panels over a period of two years enabling again a more extended and holistic relationship to develop with those that I went on to interview. Of the couples that I discuss in this chapter, I met Sue through one of the listener panels, and Bob through the single parent club. They in turn introduced me to their husband and ex-wife.

Sue and Roy[2]

Sue is fifty-two years old and lives in a three-bedroom house in a semi-rural area a few miles from the city. She lives there with her husband and her son when he is not at university. She is a part-time manager of some retirement flats. I first met Sue at a listener panel meeting for her local Classic Gold station. She has been listening to Classic Gold for a few years now and likes the music it plays (chart hits from the 1950s, 1960s and 1970s), 'you can listen when you're doing other things because its quite bouncy and cheerful, it sort of helps the work along.' She will sing along to this music station when in the car, and sing and dance along at home. She listens mainly to the set in the kitchen whilst doing other things, either in the kitchen, or elsewhere in the house with the volume turned up. Until breakfast she listens to BBC Radio 4[3] with her husband, one of the few times they listen together.

They listen first to the set in the bedroom, then in the kitchen. Apart from at this time of day, the set in the kitchen will change stations, depending on who is in there or who got there first. When at home, Sue spends most of her time in the lounge or kitchen. She spends the evenings in the lounge once she has finished preparing dinner. At this time she is likely to watch television. She enjoys watching soap operas like *Neighbours*[4] and *EastEnders*,[5] drama, news and some documentaries. She is unlikely to watch television during the day but may look through the television guide to see what is on that evening, 'We always have the *Radio Times*. I wouldn't think it was a house if we didn't have the *Radio Times* in it.'

Roy, her husband of nearly thirty years, has different tastes in radio and television. As Sue told me, 'we tend to compartmentalise our lives, for a lot of time I'm in here [lounge], my husband is in his den . . . very rare that we watch together.' Roy's den is a small room with a television, radio, desk, books, magazines, and comfortable chair. The den embarrasses Sue, she thinks it is 'awful' because it is untidy and smoky. She will keep the door closed when her friends visit, while Roy's friends are generally 'very envious'. I asked Sue if she thought they ever watched the same programme without realising it, Roy in his den and Sue in the lounge,

Sue:	That has happened, yes
Researcher:	So you don't necessary discuss what you're going to watch
Sue:	No because we don't need to . . . I mean we have supper at nine so he comes in here at nine and even if he starts watching the same as me he'll want a smoke at about quarter to ten so he goes back in there . . . when there's three of us in the house and the majority wants to watch something then that's in here and the minority goes in there
Researcher:	Seems like a sensible arrangement
Sue:	Well it is, but everybody thinks we're really weird.

Roy is fifty seven and works for a local utility company. He listens to BBC Radio 4, and occasionally to BBC Radio 3[6] and Classic FM.[7] He listens a lot during the day in his van, and sometimes when working outside he leaves the van door open and turns up the volume. He likes news, plays, documentaries, anything he considers 'stimulating', 'I'm not interested in being amused all that much, I can do that myself, but stimulation is a different subject altogether'. Roy will not listen to Sue's choices which he calls 'light and fluffy'. He feels she uses it as 'wallpaper', and does not see the point. If he is not interested in what is on the radio he says he will switch it off. On television he will look for 'stimulation, education and information' watching mainly BBC2 and Channel 4 and no soap operas. He uses the newspaper to find out what is on television and radio. He fails to see the point in buying a listing magazine such as *Radio Times*, which in his opinion has nothing to do with television and radio programmes but is 'all advertising, just another form of advertising'. His idea of relaxation and indulgence is to spend time in the garage, listening to the radio and polishing his motorcycles.

Sue and Roy consume different media in a shared but 'compartmentalised' space. When I have spoken to Sue and Roy together, their different tastes and interests have struck me, yet I have been equally struck by their total acceptance of this in each other. There is not a suggestion of resignation by them, rather there is a developed form of complementarity. The lounge where they come together at meal times is predominantly considered Sue's space and her media choices dominate. The other area where they both listen to the radio is the kitchen. Here they have worked out a way of avoiding conflict. As Roy said,

Roy:	we should have a pre-set tuner button so she can ding that one and I can ding that one, because that would in fact be the case
Researcher:	What if you're both in the kitchen?
Roy:	I'll duck that one . . . its never possible, it wouldn't be a very good idea, we worked that one out very early in life, we don't even get up together. For the same reason . . . I like to go in my own little limbo and that's the way I like to stay.

Ironically, Sue used to listen mainly to BBC Radio 4 until Roy discovered Classic Gold,

> it was Roy that actually found it, he said, 'hey, here's one that plays your sort of music' and then I found it, but it was him, so now when he says, 'oh not that again' I say 'well it was you that found it in the first place, it's your fault'

Sue and Roy may appear to have little in common upon which to base a lasting relationship. They do, however, have an enduring happy relationship. Over the years they have worked out how to incorporate their different tastes into their shared lives. Indeed, their ability to live with and accommodate their conflicting tastes appears to be part of the reason that their relationship is successful.

Bob and Faye

Bob is forty-six, works as a financial advisor for a firm of accountants and lives in a modern three-bedroom house. His ex-wife Faye is forty. She is studying literature and lives in a fourth-floor council flat two miles from Bob. They have a ten-year-old daughter, Suzie, who lives with Faye during the week and with Bob at weekends and holidays. Bob also has Suzie regularly on a Monday evening when they attend the single parent club. Bob has one radio in his kitchen diner and one in his bedroom. Often, when he is at home, they will both be on in case he needs to move around the house. The sound from these radios can be heard throughout the house if the volume is adequate. Bob listens exclusively to BBC Radio 4. It is usually on when he is at home, and when in the car. If Suzie is with him, he will listen to the radio whilst she is in the lounge watching television or a video. When Bob has the radio on, he says he is paying attention,

> I would pick up an awful lot of information from the right sort of programme, if there was a science programme on that interests me I'll pick up an awful lot of that, if there's a play or a story on that interests me I'll get the whole of it without doubt, no question about that . . . even if I'm doing something else at the time, I will get the whole thing that's on the radio.

Bob hardly ever watches television, and BBC Radio 4 is hardly ever absent from his life when he is alone, or in the company of his daughter.

Faye, on the other hand, describes herself as an 'intermittent' radio listener, according to her mood,

Faye: Basically, when I'm feeling down I don't listen to Radio 4.
Researcher: So, you find it depresses you, or, if you're already depressed, you find it depressing?
Faye: I feel alienated from it if I'm depressed, its um, I don't know if its a social class thing or what it is, Radio 4 definitely has that feeling

about it doesn't it, . . . and yet, when I'm feeling good *Woman's Hour*[8] feels like family. That's the thing. There's certain things I like to listen to, especially *Woman's Hour*, I feel part of it.

Researcher: So if you're confident in yourself then you can be part of it?

Faye: Yes.

Researcher: And if you're full of self-doubt?

Faye: Then I want to put a music tape on, I won't put the radio on I'll put a music tape on.

Faye describes a 'love-hate' relationship with Radio 4, partly because of Bob's affinity with it. Faye's listening is also affected by the seasons; in the summer she rarely listens, but in the winter she feels 'closed in, claustrophobic, I sit down and listen to the radio cause you're not out and about'. She sometimes listens to a music station to accompany an activity like decorating. In the evenings she will usually watch television rather than listen to the radio, or play her own music tapes.

Before meeting Bob, Faye used to listen to BBC Radio 1.[9] Bob introduced her to BBC Radio 4 about 20 years ago and then 'took over', so that while they were together his listening tastes dominated. Like Bob, her father was also a 'radio fanatic'; she remembers asking him, when she was very little, 'not to change from the Third Programme to the Home Service because I wanted to hear music, but I was fed the Home Service'.[10]

It is clearly not necessary in a successful relationship to share radio listening yet when forced to do so or when prevented from choosing one's own sound environment problems can arise. Faye recognises its role in her failed marriage:

Faye: When I was living with Bob I was forced to listen to the radio and told to shut up.

Researcher: It sounds like he has Radio 4 on whenever he's at home.

Faye: Yea, he's the kind of person that listens to PM [afternoon news programme] and it comes on again, the same thing, and he still listens.

Researcher: The same news story?

Faye: It's chopped up isn't it for people to switch off and on, but he listens because there might be something in between, and '*shhhh*, didn't hear that, *shhhh, shhhh*'.

Researcher: Now of course he listens to it on his own most of the time I guess.

Faye: Yea, he probably inflicts it on Suzie [10 year old daughter] as well, I wouldn't be surprised . . . he pushes her off into the front room . . .

Researcher: She watches TV and he listens to the radio in the kitchen?

Faye: I think that's awful . . . but I mean, I do do it a bit, but I think I have to share whatever she's listening to because it's a point of communication isn't it, otherwise they're not communicating . . .

Researcher: So did that cause friction between you when he wanted to listen and you wanted to talk or something?

Faye: Well, I remember, in the end I thought the best thing was just not to talk, so we stopped, it caused internal problems for me but, I got used to it, it was just, the radio was in the kitchen . . . it was when he wanted to sit down and listen to it in the front room as well that it got a bit irritating, and that Robert Robinson thing, I used to think, if this is my life listening to Robert Robinson[11] on a Saturday night – is this the climax of my week? And I used to get very depressed . . . [laughter] . . . no, its awful really, and I didn't like being told that I would like something, that was the thing, that was the thing . . .

For Faye, Bob's need for radio was a snub to her and to their relationship,

It's like, 'go away, you're not important, the radio's more important to me' I mean, that's how I heard it . . . you can use it as a tool in an argument and a power thing . . . accentuate the tension between you.

It is interesting to observe how the infliction of a soundscape[12] on an unwilling partner, or conversely, criticism of a preferred soundscape and its restriction, is seen by Faye as a contributor to the failure of her marriage,

Faye: I can remember Bob used to be very angry with me about liking pop music. He would say, 'well that's crap' and I would say 'well yes, but I enjoy it, maybe I'm just not cultured enough for you' . . . and yet he seems to go to [single parent club] and dance to crap, *ha, ha* . . . You know, its OK in that context . . .
Researcher: So you were not able to put your music on?
Faye: I used to put my music on when he wasn't there . . . I used to think, oh yea, great, I can put my music on, I don't get so excited about putting it on any more . . . I can have it when I like and I quite often choose not to, and I'll put Radio 4 on, I mean, he introduced me to Radio 4 . . . but he also encouraged this love–hate relationship with it I'm sure . . . because it is that really . . . he used to like *Woman's Hour* . . .

There does seem to be a need amongst the couples that I draw on in this chapter, to share at least some aspects of media consumption. Sue and Roy both listen to BBC Radio 4's *Today* news programme while getting up and eating breakfast, and will come together again in the evening around 6pm, and again at 9pm, when radio and television consumption will be shared, despite Roy's vehement criticism of Sue's media choices.

Even Faye, despite her remembered unpleasant experience of having Bob's radio choices inflicted upon her, will attempt to interest her current boyfriend in her own radio preferences,

Faye: I've introduced Barry to thingy, the political thing, *Week Ending* [political satire] . . . and I said, 'come on we've got to listen to

this, it comes on at such and such time', fiddled around with the
aerial, sat down and listened to it, and then after, there was
something on gay men after that, new men or something . . .

Researcher: *Locker Room?* [magazine programme for men]

Faye: Yea, and I thought, right you ought to listen to this, and I could
tell he didn't like it, but uh, he was listening under protest. And I
thought 'I think I'll leave this to *Week Ending*', so we listen to that
together.

These remarks prompted Faye to remember her 'terrible' evenings spent with
Bob and Robert Robinson; she is determined not to inflict her tastes on Barry,
but is pleased that they can both listen to *Week Ending*. Faye sees her relationship
with Barry as full of potential for sharing interests; a more well-balanced
relationship, where one partner will not impose their needs on the other, against
his or her will.

Relationships, fantasy and romance

Radway (1987) studied romance reading amongst a group of women in an affluent
Midwestern town in America. Radway admits in her introduction to an 'excessive
preoccupation with gender and to the use of a rather rigid notion of patriarchy'
(1987:9). However, the study holds some indications of how romance and fantasy
are seen by academia, and by 'ordinary' people, as gendered concepts.

The women of her study insisted that,

[T]heir reading was a way of temporarily refusing the demands associated with
their social role as wives and mothers. As they observed, it functioned as a
'declaration of independence', as a way of securing privacy while at the same
time providing companionship and conversation.

(Radway 1987: 9)

Radway sees the women as wanting to maintain a distance between their 'ordinary'
lives and their 'fantasies' and to some extent equates fantasy with 'escape'.

Radway's respondents 'fervently' insisted that 'romance reading creates a feeling
of hope, provides emotional sustenance and produces a fully visceral sense of well-
being' (ibid.: 12). Radway tried to understand how, despite what she saw as their
own dissatisfaction with traditionally structured heterosexual relationships, and
their sometimes exhausting role of nurturance, women could experience such
pleasure through the heroine's re-creation of a similarly structured arrangement
between a man and a woman. She does not construct any grand conclusions and
sees her research as inadequate as a means of understanding the effect of romance
reading on the women's lives more widely, or through time. As Radway states 'we
simply do not know what practical effects the repetitive reading of romances has
on the way woman behave, after they have closed their books and returned to

their normal, ordinary round of daily activities' (ibid.: 217). Yet there is a strong suggestion in Radway's work that romance reading reinforces women's oppressed state in traditional, heterosexual, American marriage.

Radway's work separates fantasy from everyday life as though they exist totally in different spheres. Romances embody fantasy yet she does not see this as embedded in 'ordinary' life, but separate from it. The women claimed that their marriages were happy, which Radway says she does not doubt, and yet the picture she paints is of wholly inadequate relationships which make the women search for compensation in the pages of romantic fiction.

Ang (1996: chapters 5 and 6) seeks to understand the *pleasures* inherent in such media consumption and explores what she sees as our need, as women, for 'melo-dramatic heroines'. Ang suggests, in criticism of Radway's 'rationalist proposal', that it is precisely the 'actualization of romantic feelings' that is at stake in romance reading, that the 'tenacity of the desire to feel romantically' (1996: 107) is sig-nificant. Fantasy is thus linked not only to the concept of 'escapism' but also to our need for romance. In both works it is a thoroughly gendered concept. But whereas Radway sees such media consumption as 'disabling' in that it allows women to accept and do nothing about their unequal 'real' lives, Ang sees it as demonstrating a 'determination':

> It is this enduring emotional quest that, I would suggest, should be taken seriously as a psychical strategy by which women empower themselves in every-day life, leaving apart what its ideological consequences in social reality are.
>
> (Ang 1996: 107)

I would go further than this to suggest that such consumption practices and associated fantasy is a part of our social reality, and is experienced by both women and men. Not an escape from social reality, but an enhancer of and contributor to the same.

Faye has a working notion of a well-balanced relationship, the kind that Giddens (1992), in optimistic vein, sees as emerging in present day lives. According to Giddens we are undergoing a democratisation of personal life and relationships which women will benefit from. *Confluent love* 'presumes equality in emotional give and take, the more so the more any particular love tie approximates closely to the prototype of the pure relationship' (Giddens 1992: 62). This transformation of intimacy is clearly seen by Giddens as a progressive movement towards emotional and sexual democracy. However, as he himself points out, the pure relationship is a 'prototype', an ideal. Here I think we may have an important clue to under-standing domestic emotional 'realities'. When Faye tries to get Barry to listen to and share a radio programme about 'new men', she has in mind an ideal notion, and something she feels will contribute to her idealised relationship. Despite his dislike of the programme she is not put off, her ideal is not significantly damaged, and she is happy that they can share another programme on a regular basis.

We all work with ideals that inform our actions and perceptions. Our imagination works to help to form a part of our reality. If we look at Giddens' argument in a slightly different way we can see that the sorts of prototypical notions he discusses, like romantic love and the pure relationship, exist in more than one realm. It is the sum and/or interaction of these different parts that make up what we might call affective realities, or affective economies, in domestic lives (Tacchi 1997). It may be that such ideals provide us with the will to always strive for something, even though we may never achieve it. The we can see that Faye's working notion of a well-balanced relationship is an ideal that she words towards and strives for.

I have found that men are more likely to rationalise their listening, while women more frequently talk about their radio listening in relation to their emotional life, how they feel or have felt, in romantic terms. This is so even when the listening habits of my informants did not match the more stereotypical consumption habits described by Roy, Sue, Bob and Faye. For example, Roger and Julie were another married couple that I talked to. Whilst Julie does not engage in 'inane' listening (she listens to Radio 4), Roger uses radio as background sound (listening to a local commercial music radio station). Nevertheless, Julie talked about radio much more in terms of how it made her feel, or helped her emotionally than Roger who rationalised his listening (he could get traffic reports on this station).[13] Both those that we might (somewhat superficially) name 'rationalist', and those we might name 'romantic', use radio sound as an aid to the affective dimension of their everyday living, and both incorporate fantasy.

Bob and Roy are in effect fantasising – through their use of radio sound – about not fantasising. Bob denies his use of radio sound as an emotionally comforting thing through describing its functionality. He will only listen if it is interesting or educational, and he 'swallows news all the time'. Faye could not understand this 'obsession' with news or why he would want to listen to a whole news programme when items get repeated. Having heard them once she felt he could have turned off and could not see the 'functionality' in continuing to listen. On the other hand, Faye readily talked about her emotions in relation to radio and how her radio listening affected and was affected by her emotional states. Bob would not engage in conversation with me about this, even when I had known him for ten months and had regularly talked to him about radio and many other things. Ten months after his first interview I re-interviewed him and tried to get him to talk about how he *felt* about radio, how it fitted into his emotional life:

Researcher: Do you think it's something to do with needing company, radio – to not have silence?

Bob: No it's more than that because I am often specifically listening to it and it will modify my behaviour. I will wait for something to finish before I go out. Or if I go upstairs, I'll blast it on really loud so I don't lose it while I'm going upstairs, even though I might have a radio on in the bedroom . . . I might think 'I don't wanna miss any of that' so I'll turn it on loud, so no, its more than that, I'm actually listening to what's there.

Researcher: But is it that you need some sort of distraction from . . .

Bob: No, if it's just a distraction I don't think I would turn it up loud to walk upstairs to avoid the possibility of missing something significant . . .

Researcher: You talked about listening to *The Archers* even though you're not a fan, but if it's on you'll listen.

Bob: Sometimes yeah, sometimes I get interested in the story line, I mean I've been listening to it a lot lately. I go through phases with *The Archers.*

Researcher: What's that sort of listening about, where you'll leave it on even if you're not too interested?

Bob: There's just the possibility that something might come on that interests me.

Bob insists that he listens because there is something interesting to listen to, or there may be something interesting coming up. For him this is something 'more' than using radio for company. Bob always presented himself as in control of his life, and applied scientific, rational principles to problems that he might encounter from time to time. Yet it is Bob who can be seen as more emotionally dependent on radio sound. Faye talks more easily about how radio makes her feel, and about how it can alter or be used to match her mood yet it is Bob who appears to be more dependent on radio in his everyday life.

Conclusion

These two informants illustrate a pattern, often observed, albeit in more subtle forms, of a male functionalist routine as contrasted to a female romantic routine. If we move beyond the accounts of informants like Bob and Faye, and observe them in their social and domestic lives more broadly, we can see that Bob is in some ways much more emotionally dependent and less 'objective' in his listening than Faye. She is able to see more clearly how radio sound fits in with her life, life changes, seasonal variation, and emotional states.

Despite his rationalist explanations, radio appears to provide Bob with contact with an other world, a world that is rational and functional, predictable, informative, and intellectually stimulating. Radio creates a different world for Faye – either emotionally supportive, or, emotionally unsettling. Radio constitutes a part of Bob's routine reality. Faye saw this as obsessive, a slight on their relationship and her. His routine continues without her, emphasising the importance of the soundscape that radio helps him create. Bearing in mind the importance of the world that Radio 4 creates for Bob, and Faye's some time alienation to it, it is not surprising that she saw his listening in negative ways. Through the use of radio sound he surrounded himself with a rationalised yet affectively supportive soundscape, which helped him to avoid looking at aspects of his everyday life which were difficult to think about in terms other than emotional. That is, his intimate relationship with another person.

Faye observed Bob's intimacy with radio and saw it as a rebuff to her and their non-intimate relationship. This can be seen as an example, following Giddens, of a male inability to deal with intimate aspects of relationships, whilst women are 'burdened' with them. Yet in some cases such complementarity in relationships works well, as Sue and Roy demonstrate. It also emphasises that, although radio sound is naturalised in the home, and perhaps because of this, it holds the potential to comment on self and social relations in a profound way.

For Bob, routinised radio listening and the soundscapes it creates in his home help him to maintain an affective equilibrium: in his relationships and in his view of self in relation to others. His radio listening provides a means to avoid dealing with affective aspects of everyday life. He can anchor his affective self through the world created by the radio sound. He is no less dependent – and perhaps more so – than Faye, on fantasy, as a part of the way that his domestic reality is created.

Roy rejects Sue's use of radio as 'wallpaper', which he associates with her gender. He rationalises and legitimates his own consumption as 'educational, interesting and informative' and therefore, functional, practical and wholly rational. He cannot understand Sue's use, which is irrational to his way of thinking. On my third visit to their home to collect diaries of listening we had the following conversation:

Roy:	There was a friend of mine, we occasionally have little heart-to-hearts, like I'm the old man and he sort of bounces ideas off me; and he had the same observation of his wife as I have of mine: television, and radio is there as a distraction, it's soporific if you like, whereas he was interested in television and radio for the things that he was interested in or would educate him or what, but as far as churning out wallpaper, no, no . . .
Sue:	Yes because men aren't interested in the everyday little dramas of life which is what soaps are, they're not interested in that sort of thing whereas women are . . .
Researcher:	Men do watch things like *Coronation Street* and *Eastenders*[14] don't they, and a lot of men seem to listen to *The Archers*,[15] did I ask you if you listen to that Roy?
Roy:	Definitely definitely not! I have no agricultural background whatsoever.
Researcher:	You don't need to have do you, its a soap isn't it?
Sue:	I used to listen but . . .
Roy:	No I find it, again you see this is where we contradict each other, I find things like *The Archers*, I mean if you really want to go back *Mother Dale's Diary* was another one, so totally unrealistic, I mean they live in a world which I have no idea about at all and which, as far as I was concerned was fantasy, their so called problems, I mean good god! They haven't got any, you know . . .
Sue:	You can remember when Grace Archer got burnt in the stables?
Roy:	Course I can.

Sue:	Was that the night ITV started?
Roy:	It was the night ITV started.
Sue:	Yes it was, they put a really sort of big thing on *The Archers*, that was Phil's first wife, she died in the stables, oh it was big drama wasn't it?
Roy:	Yes, she went in to rescue Midnight.
Sue:	The horse . . .
Roy:	I used to listen to it because I was waiting for the damn news to come on and this was in the middle of it, that was probably one of the reasons why, no, I only listened to *The Archers* like racing, every now and again, it would be accidental. I mean now, if *The Archers* is on, I hit that off button dead on first time, I can't stand it, I wouldn't have it on.
Researcher:	It's quite nice listening to it like on a Sunday morning when you're having a bath, it's like something to do.
Sue:	Yes.
Roy:	What a depressing little life you must lead!

Roy maintained that he would not waste time listening to, or watching, something that was not informative or educational. Yet he remembers the name of the horse that Grace Archer tried to rescue, in an episode of *The Archers* that was broadcast over 40 years ago. Sue explains the gendered difference in media consumption as reflecting different interests – women are interested in 'the everyday little dramas of life'. Through the diary Roy kept for me it becomes apparent that he does listen to radio and watch TV programmes for reasons other than pure education and information. For example, whilst in the garage cleaning his motorcycle one lunch time, he recorded that he listened to a serial and the news on Radio 4, commenting that he did so as it 'distracts from cleaning tedium'. The evening before he had watched a film in his den whilst reading the paper recording that he did not find it very interesting or enjoyable and paid it little attention as it was 'not so interesting to stop reading paper'.

His actual listening and viewing is not quite as clearly informative and educational as he might like to think. His diary reveals a less discerning listener and viewer than he suggests in his own interpretation of his listening and viewing practices. Sue accepts his criticism of her 'wallpaper' listening and viewing, understanding this as due to her gender. They, to some extent, fantasise their characters in relation to each other. Their talk about media consumption reinforces an idealised or fantasised rational man and, in contrast, 'irrational' woman.

There *is* a big difference between their listening and viewing demonstrating the accuracy of Roy's statement that 'we're totally different, we're totally different in attitudes, we're totally different in everything; it's amazing how we're still together'. Not only are they still together, they are happy: theirs is a successful relationship. The exaggerated differences between them can be seen to take place as much in fantasy, as in practice. Rather, it would be more accurate to state that fantasy *is* practice – it is a part of our everyday lives and we (women and men) use mediated fantasy to explore, establish and maintain our selves as gendered individuals.

Acknowledgement

Thanks are due to my research respondents and to the ESRC who funded my research. Thanks also to Danny Miller, Caroline Mitchell, Deborah Nagle-Burks and Paul Fitzgerald who all commented upon a draft of this chapter.

Notes

1 This research was carried out in the Department of Anthropology at University College London under the supervision of Professor Daniel Miller.

2 Names and identities have been altered to protect the confidentiality of my research respondents.

3 BBC Radio 4 is a news and current affairs station, which also provides documentaries, plays, poetry, and other programmes which are 'thought-provoking' and 'opinion-forming' (BBC booklet, 'Facts and Figures 1995/96')

4 Popular Australian soap opera shown on British TV.

5 Long-running British TV soap opera.

6 Radio 3 is the BBC's classical music station (BBC booklet, 'Facts and Figures 1995/96')

7 Classic FM is a national commercial station providing classical music, in a way that is deemed to be more accessible and populist than BBC Radio 3 (see Radio Authority Pocket Guide)

8 *Woman's Hour* is a one hour long magazine programme broadcast every weekday on Radio 4. It deals with issues from a female perspective.

9 BBC Radio 1 plays contemporary pop music and aims to attract a young audience of mainly 15 to 25 year olds.

10 The Third programme changed its name to Radio 3, and the Home Service to Radio 4 in 1967.

11 Presenter of a long running end of the week show on Radio 4.

12 I use the term soundscape to indicate more than simply the sounds of a radio station in the home. Radio sound contributes to a domestic soundscape, but radio sound itself is meaning laden and these meanings contribute to a 'textured soundscape' (see Tacchi 1997, 1998). The term soundscape is fairly commonly used in discussions of music and more general sounds. Its definition (although not its invention) as the sonic environment consisting of both natural and manmade sounds, is generally attributed to R. Murray Schafer (1977, 1994).

13 Audience research carried out to support the application for a commercial licence in London found similar gendered differences. Men say they use radio for utilitarian purposes (information etc.) women relate their radio use to their emotions (Viva! Application to the Radio Authority for a Greater London Licence. June 1994, p37).

14 Two long-running TV soap operas.

15 *The Archers* is a radio soap that is broadcast each week day. In addition, all of the week's episodes are broadcast together in an omnibus edition on Sunday mornings.

References

Ang, I. (1996) *Living Room Wars: Rethinking Media Audiences for a Postmodern World*, London: Routledge.

Ang, I. and Hermes J. (1996) 'Gender and/in Media Consumption', in J. Curran and M. Gurevitch (eds) *Mass Media and Society* (second edition), London: Arnold.

Baehr, H. and Ryan M. (1984) *Shut up and Listen! Women and Local Radio: A View from the Inside*, London: Comedia.

Giddens, A. (1992) *The Transformation of Intimacy: Sexuality, Love and Eroticism in Modern Societies*, Cambridge: Polity Press.

Hobson, D. (1980) 'Housewives and the Mass Media', in S. Hall, D. Hobson, A. Lowe and P. Willis (eds) *Culture, Media, Language*, London: Routledge.

Moores, S. (1993) *Interpreting Audiences: The Ethnography of Media Consumption*, London: Sage.

Radway, J.A. (1987) *Reading the Romance: Women, Patriarchy, and Popular Literature*, London: Verso.

Schafer, R.M. (1994) *The Soundscape: Our Sonic Environment and the Tuning of the World*, Rochester: Destiny Books.

—— (1977) *The Tuning of the World*, NY: Knopf.

Tacchi, J. (1997) 'Radio Sound as Material Culture in the Home', unpublished PhD Thesis. University College London.

—— (1998) 'Radio Texture: Between Self and Others', in D. Miller (ed.) *Material Cultures: Why Some Things Matter*, London: UCL Press/University of Chicago Press.

Chapter 13

Margaretta D'Arcy

GALWAY'S PIRATE WOMEN

From: D'Arcy, M. (1996) *Galway's Pirate Women, A Global Trawl*, Galway: Women's Pirate Press, pp. 4–5, 7–11, 23–29, 68–71, 83–84.

Let each woman speak freely

1987: Galway City, Ireland, had its first low-powered neighbourhood women's non-licensed autonomous radio station. Women's Scéal Radio (Scéal = gossip, stories), 'Free the Air Waves: Free Women'. To begin with, it broadcast for a week in the February of '87, twice daily, 11a.m. to noon and again from midnight onwards.

Its aims:

A. To honour and celebrate women's oral language, because it is women who pass on the spoken word to the children. Without the spoken word there can be no written word. Women are the prime source amid custodians of language.

B. To recognise that the three ages of women are a continuity, pre-menstruation, menstruation and post-menstruation. No one of them is more valuable than the others.

C. To let each woman speak freely without being controlled by another woman.

D. To speak freely on all subjects in the spirit of Article 19 of the UN Charter of Human Rights (Freedom of Speech, Freedom of Expression, Freedom to Impart Information). This meant defiance of the Irish censorship regulations, i.e: Section 31 of the Broadcasting Act, the prohibition of information on abortion, and the banning of certain books and magazines dealing with sexuality.

E. To promote the concept that a woman has as much right in her own space to have her voice heard via a low-powered radio transmitter as she has to listen to the voice of someone else on a radio receiver.

[. . .]

WOMEN'S SCÉAL RADIO

FREE THE AIRWAVES

Tune in to
F.M. (MhZ) 106

FM 104 | 106 | 108 M"Z

PHONE—IN 65430

Twice daily
Sun Feb 14th - Sun March 6th
11AM – NOON
MIDNIGHT ONWARDS

MAKING LINKS— LINKING WAVES

Sun Feb. 14th - Sun March 6th 3pm - 8pm. daily at 10 St . Bridget's Place Lower, Woodquay, Galway.

FILM/VIDEO FESTIVAL
The Cinema of Women has kindly lent us six new international feminist video-films, including: **'Leila and the Wolves'**, the first Lebanese feature made by a woman, drawing on her Arab heritage. **'Donna'**, the story of an independent radio station in Rome, run by housewives for housewives, and bombed by the fascists in 1979. Also, thirty-odd videos; ranging from the songs of *Marlene Dietrich, Agnes Bernelle, Mary Coughlan* to contemporary social themes -PTA, Strip-searching, Emigration, South Africa, Central America, and women's issues: self-help, abortion, the value of women's work etc.

CHOOSE YOUR VIDEO AND TIME OF VIEWING.
These films are a unique experience which should not be missed.
TWO PRACTICAL WEEKEND WORKSHOPS ON USING VIDEO AND RADIO. Feb 13/14, and 20/21.
March 1st-6th: OPERA AGUS OBAIR * Who Owns Ireland, Who Owns You?** A combination of professional classical, jazz, & Irish traditional musicians and performers will be creating this new Irish feminist musical work:
Breda Lewis, *banjo, mandoline, songwriter & singer.*
Maria Lamburn, *composer, saxophone, viola & keyboard.*
Sarah Homer, *clarinet.*
Sue Shattock, *singer & performer.*
Margaretta D'Arcy, *playwright & performer.*
The weekend 5/6 March will be open to all women who wish to participate in part 1 of **OPERA AGUS OBAIR.**

Contributions and help needed for radio programmes:
Phone Margaretta at 65430, or call at house.

ALL WOMEN WELCOME.

GALWAY WOMEN'S ENTERTAINMENT
GALWAY WOMEN'S SCÉAL RADIO, VIDEO & MUSIC FESTIVAL
*closed on Thursday March 3rd, 3pm-8pm.

FREE WOMEN! FREE THE AIR-WAVES!

TUNE IN TO

GALWAY WOMEN'S SCEAL RADIO

(FM 106: Within approx 2-mile radius of Woodquay)

EVERY SUNDAY 12.00 MIDNIGHT
EVERY TUESDAY MORNING 11.00 A.M.
EVERY TUESDAY 12.00 MIDNIGHT

The only women's radio-station run by women for women

THE UNCENSORED RADIO
THE FREEDOM OF SPEECH RADIO
THE NON-COMMERCIAL RADIO

Every woman is welcome to
Participate / Contribute / Chat / Ideas / Poems / Stories / Songs / Music

WANTED

COMEDY ACTS / REPRESENTATIVES / DJs
MAKE YOUR OWN TAPES / PROGRAMMES

HAVE COURAGE! HAVE A GO!

Write to:
MARGARETTA D'ARCY, 10 ST. BRIDGET'S PLACE LOWER, WOODQUAY
or call or phone
(091) 65430 an hour before we record
This station is YOURS: it's for YOU to keep it on the air!

Free Air-Waves: Free Women
International Women's Radio Festival

Starting: Thursday 7 March '91
for two weeks until 22 March

TO DENY KNOWLEDGE IS TO DENY FREEDOM!

Tune in to Radio Pirate-Woman
FM 102 FM 102 FM 102mzh

RADIUS TWO MILES (NOT RENMORE AREA)
Twice daily: 11 a.m. - for 2 hours (approx.)
Midnight - for 2 hours (approx.)

Women's voices will be heard on our airwaves from the four corners of Ireland (north, south, east, west, & the islands), from the Southern Hemisphere, Latin America, Africa. Wilmette Brown (black) and Selma James (white), from the International Wages for Housework Campaign, will be on the air for international dialogue - on why we women, unwaged and low-waged, are still clearing up the garbage of the world!

Hey Pirate Woman, what-u-cookin today?
I'm airin subversion the radio way!
Excuse me, Galway women, play a pirate today
Join the craic on the free air way!

Raising Children is not counted or paid as Woman's Work:
KILLING CHILDREN IS PAID WORK FOR THE MILITARY

RADIO PIRATE-WOMAN
10 ST. BRIDGET'S PLACE LOWER
WOODQUAY, GALWAY
Phone 091-65430

Freedom of Information
Freedom of Speech, Freedom of Expression
Article 19 of the UN Charter of Human Rights

TO DENY FREEDOM IS TO DENY POWER!

Figure 13.1 Radio Pirate Woman and Women's Scéal Radio: Fliers

A leap into the unknown

Surveys had shown that most daytime radio listeners are women. If we women listen so much why can we not own and run our own station? It is not as though women do not know how to use complicated technology, being perfectly capable of controlling washing-machines, cookers, micro-ovens, electric irons. What was the taboo against women operating a transmitter? GWE obtained a small transmitter, I put an aerial on my roof, a couple of microphones and a mixer were donated, and I already had a music-centre. I looked up the newspaper and found a free airwave, FM 104 to begin with; and there was Women's Scéal Radio, up in the sky.

None of us had had any experience of broadcasting, let alone running a radio station.

We had decided that unless we went on air cold we never would have the courage to go on at all. A leap into the unknown. Organising the radio as part of a wider festival meant that radio, instead of being an isolated medium sufficient to itself, became part of the whole creative experience and also part of the improvisational nature of our work. Inside my house, a terrace-house with one room down and two up, the downstairs was the performing space and the upstairs the radio.

Our research into women's relationship to the 'Arts' had shown us that the unwaged, the unemployed, single mothers, widows solely on pension and older women generally felt excluded – by lack of money, by extended family responsibilities or just because they were women of spirit, from those communal artistic activities which needed constant rehearsal-times or a consistent commitment to regular attendance. We were, at this stage, more interested in encouraging women onto the radio than in building up a listenership, so we did not plan programmes, and any woman who wanted to could drop in for a cup of tea. If she then wished to be part of the radio, she could be. In fact, we brought back the old rural tradition of 'visiting'.

[. . .]

The live GWE Festival was running from Monday to Sunday, which meant that the women participating in the evening entertainment would go straight up to the radio-room at midnight. We already had a nucleus of about twenty musicians, singers, poets, etc., who had been coming regularly. They were all keen to take part in the radio experiment.

During the week we had Breda Lewis and friends, traditional musicians, and Rose Brock from South Africa with rhythm and dancing. We showed four videos, two of women performers and one the Galway premiere of my own *Circus Exposé of the new Cultural Church*. Marilyn Hyndman from Belfast presented her Channel 4 video 'Under the Health Service'. We finished with a grand finale, alternative health, aromatherapy, and a 'Mussels and Muscles Wine Party' (to say thank you to everyone who had helped, including several men. The name of this party tickled the fancy of the popular press). Loads of poets turned up, a young anarcho-feminist writer from Manchester, and Sarah Hipperson from Greenham Common who stayed with us for the weekend participating in all the events and the broadcasts. The men were allowed to have the Sunday midnight broadcast to themselves.

(Sunday night taught us a lesson, by the way: it is not a good idea to hand over women's airwaves to men. One of them decided to give a rambling lecture on the Spanish civil war. Another interrupted him with a lengthy account of his cruel experience in a mental hospital, which would have been genuinely moving if a drunken fiddler had not collapsed in the middle of it across the music-centre, clutching the wires as he fell, nearly wrecking our whole station. We heard the crash downstairs and hurried up to find the two boyos still in full flood waving their microphones around the place, ignoring all but their own words.)

By and large the week fulfilled everything we had hoped for.

The first morning, the Monday, we had all been extremely nervous, and never did an hour seem so long. Mary McGing, a Sinn Féin candidate in the European election, recently released from gaol after a two-year sentence on a kidnapping charge, spoke about her experiences as a civil engineer – very unusual for a woman in Ireland. Margaret Sweeney, the first Travelling woman to stand in a national election, spoke about her problems with the jealousy of the main parties and their dirty tricks and bribery.

Because we had no monitor on our home-made transmitter and could only check the quality of our sound by listening to a not-very-reliable radio in the next room, we had runners coming in from different parts of the town to tell us how much (if anything) they could hear. We all saw it as a piece of slapstick theatre or an early movie showing the first car on the road with a man running in front carrying a red flag. It certainly freed us from the awe of radio as a Sacred Voice out of the beyond, unmarred by human fallibility; and it did create the atmosphere we wanted, a neighbourhood centre where anyone could come in to give any question, criticism or assistance, as for example an urgent message to switch on the microphone, or not to shout too much, or to speak up. It became a real party on the air. A very shy elderly neighbour, who had sworn she would never go near the radio, to my astonishment entered breathlessly one morning (during a broadcast by Sarah the aromatherapist) to give a long list of all her aches and pains and could she please have a massage?

Sarah Hipperson from Greenham, who is a strong Catholic, debated religion and nuclear weapons with Deirdre Manifold, one of Galway's home-grown polemicists, noted for her global theory of an antichrist as personified by Karl Marx and the Freemasons, a subject on which she has written several books. (In the end we pointed out to Deirdre that she was an unwitting throwback to an ancient Gnostic 'heresy' identifying God with the Devil – our assessment of her, not hers: she strongly denied it! But we did come to a consensus with her on the horrors of nuclear war.)

By the end of the week we had become so wrapped up in our debates and polemics that we almost forgot we were on the air. The midnight broadcasts turned out to be open-ended celebrations with women turning up all the way through to take part and enjoy themselves – a botanist came and gave us a fascinating feminist analysis of how the kernel of the hazelnut is just like a vagina, which is why the tree has always been magical and sacred to women.

We did have one angry woman ringing up to say she preferred to read a Harold Robbins novel rather than listen to our rubbish.

A member of Galway's other (male, commercial) pirate-radio stopped me in the street and told me he had never enjoyed himself so much as when he had tuned in to one of our midnight broadcasts. He said, if we would just 'cool down the feminism' and play more music, we were onto a sure winner.

Everyone was impressed with the quality of the sound, amazed that it came from so small a transmitter.

Our energies were kept up by the sheer uncertainty of the business, the fact that we never knew what was going to happen next. I should add that Galway is very much an 'oral' town; the texture of spontaneous speech is very rich. It is also a bilingual town; both Irish and English can be heard. Bursting into song or reciting a poem in the middle of a serious conversation is as natural as breathing.

At the end of the week I had to go to England to serve a gaol sentence for non-violent direct action at Greenham Common. I handed over the transmitter to one of the first of our Scéal Radio women, Janet Watts. She hoped to be able to continue broadcasting from her flat.

Culinary

[. . .] The world of radio is a bit like serving hot dinners. Every cook is different and so is every recipe, but you cannot have a hot meal without some sort of heat-source – even if it is only an open fire – and you cannot have a radio without a transmitter and a rudimentary understanding of how it works. (Live theatre, at its most basic level, does not require technology, only a 'story' and performers – in other words, food that has to be prepared but does not have to be cooked.)

So, to run a radio you first have to get a cooker. In our case, my third son Jake made the initial contact for me. One of his friends had a friend who was working with a group of young black men in Brixton, London. They wanted to start a black pirate radio and he was helping them to build small-powered transmitters, using a handbook called *Radio is my Bomb*, written by an old Welsh anarchist who believed passionately that the radio is based on our right as human beings to communicate without commercial exploitation. His giving of his book was a kind of unwritten contract of good faith. Richard, the 'friend of a friend', was delighted to hear that we in Galway wanted to set up a women's radio. He made us the transmitter (I paid him a small sum, £50, for the components). He brought it over to Ireland. He set it up for us and showed us how to use it.

The 'us', to begin with, was myself and Janet Watts. She was a single mother, just returned from America, so she knew about independent radios. She lived in a block of flats in Rahoon, an estate on the edge of Galway which is used by the corporation as a clearing-house, or dump, for people on the housing-list. She was one of a large Galway family and she roped in her brothers to help put up our aerial. They fetched a friend called Niall Hughes from the fringes of the local music-scene. He had also been in America, involved with a radio station in San Francisico.

I had another contact, members of the North of Ireland Video Association (part of the Just Books anarchist collective), Dave and Marilyn Hyndman and Gerard MacLaughlin. Marilyn was interested in setting up a women's pirate radio for International Women's Day in Belfast. Richard had brought over a second transmitter; I carried it to the North and received in return a small mixer and a batch of fliers which they printed for us there.

We now had our cooker: what were the ingredients of the meal, who were the cooks, and who was going to eat it?

We finally evolved a sort of do-it-yourself Kitchen of the Air, where you brought your own food and cooked it yourself; Australians would call it an 'outback barbie'. (Not long ago, when I was in Australia, my second son Adam and our daughter-in-law Debra gave a barbie for me to taste the national lifestyle: the guests arrived with their own steaks, chops, peppers and so forth, and queued up to use the barbecue. We all shared the food, everyone free to enjoy themselves and no martyred women-of-the-house slaving over kitchen sink or stove.) I need to dwell a little on this image of radio-as-kitchen; it liberates the subject from male-dominated laboratory/garage/workbench language and earths it in the centre of our domestic lives. Before the 20th century there were communal bakehouses for the urban working class. Neighbours would fetch their Sunday joints down the street to be popped into the oven together. Nowadays there are all sorts of eccentric cafes and restaurants in every city, odd unexpected little places into which you stumble to find an unaccountably varied clientele and a highly individual management which seems to get more satisfaction from a diversity of diners than from making money. (Our radio is that type of kitchen: other independent stations are more like those workers'-co-operative eating-houses where the tone is set by a 'collective'.)

Of course smart-alec business-people have tried artificially to create such an atmosphere, while causing the customers to pay through the nose for it. An artist friend of mine, for instance, was once hired as a waiter deliberately to insult the customers. The ruder he could be, the more the trendy aficionados came back to spend more money. In Sydney there is a restaurant in a four-star hotel where as soon as you sit down the waiter throws his tray onto the table, grabs your plates, hurls them to the floor and jumps on them, at the same time flinging the knives and forks around. In radio terms this is the American shock-jock style. But Radio Pirate-Woman could never have attracted that kind of fashionable clientele, avid for a phoney breaking of taboos.

We were breaking REAL taboos.

First: by ignoring the censorship. The political climate at that time was one of increased demonisation of 'subversives'. Government policy insisted that Sinn Féin be totally isolated and boycotted. Not only did the Broadcasting Act exclude its members from the airwaves, but local politicians were forbidden by their parties to sit on committees with elected Sinn Féin councillors. For giving airtime to Mary McGing, we were effectively smeared as a 'provo-front' by every mainstream party in Galway.

Second: by getting women on the air in informal groups, just as they came, and not being frightened of making fools of ourselves.

Third, by not caring whether anyone listened to us or not.

[. . .]

1988: Galway Women's Entertainment Spring Festival: we decided to extend the operations of the radio for three weeks altogether, twice a day at 11a.m. and midnight. And then, after that, to carry on broadcasting three days a week twice a day. We were slowly building up our confidence and our contacts, and getting women artists to make tapes of their own work and send them if they were unable to come in person. Also we acquired tapes of women's music of a sort normally played at women's clubs and events but never played on radio programmes. We fitted a 'tap' to the telephone, enabling us to broadcast phone-calls.

Before we did this, we carried out a survey (based on 100 houses in our immediate area), which proved there was a real need for us. The area was a largely working-class neighbourhood with a strong extended-family structure. Ninety-eight of the respondents said they wanted a women's radio, they wanted to 'hear about everything' (provided they did not have to express an opinion themselves). Only four of them said they would be willing actually to participate on the radio. In general, they did not feel confident to speak in public until they had first listened and found what it was all about.

Then we made another survey, in a different part of town, targeting 30-plus women of a more yuppy type. They weren't interested in having a women's radio: they were perfectly satisfied with the existing radio stations, so obviously censorship did not bother them. The more educated you are, in Ireland, the more access you have to censored information such as abortion clinics, banned books, etc. They also were totally against the IRA in the North and supported the government absolutely in banning Sinn Fein from the airwaves.

These two surveys show very clearly the difference between the two cultures.

We decided that our priorities were now to get women on the air; to make them feel at ease and not to bother with the technology or programme-continuity; whatever we'd be talking about, we'd break off and welcome a newcomer in, and let it flow from there. If we were playing a tape and someone came in, we'd stop the tape and talk; 'live' was more important than 'tape' and listeners had to adjust to the hands-on spontaneity or else switch off . . .

Personalities

We had women musicians.

Breda Lewis, traditional musician and songwriter whom I met when I went to one of her twice-weekly sessions in the Crane Bar – we made tapes with her for the radio.

Maria Lamburn from England, who brought other musicians to our Spring Festival. The contacts were continued through tapes of their music. I had met her while working at the Queen Elizabeth Hall on an updated version of the Eisler/Brecht cantata, *The Mother*. She came to Galway with Sarah Homer (a musician from the National Theatre, London) and Sue Shattock.

Camilla Cancantata, who had come with a group of women to busk in Galway. She took one of my fliers about the radio and they all turned up the next morning. They came onto the radio with a flourish, playing all along the street, up the stairs into the little bedroom where the transmitter was located. Camilla too continued to send us tapes.

Doreen Phelan, bodhran-player and Shen healer, of Galway. She introduced me to Ray, who had been busking in the town with her dulcimer. Doreen was always one of the 'barometers' whom I would meet in the street to tell me that 'the sap was rising'. We'd go off and have a coffee and the foliage would begin to burgeon.

Agnes Bernelle, of course, sending tapes of her songs from Dublin

Clea and McLeod sent a tape: Scots-Canadian, radical feminists, jazz-players and songwriters. I first came across them when they were playing at an International Wages for Housework conference in London. They heard of my radio through Selma James of IWfH.

Because we were a women-only radio, and because it was (and still is) very difficult for new women musicians to have their tapes heard, in particular lesbian women with an overt message, we received a lot of support from lesbians even though we were not a lesbian-separatist outfit.

We had poets.

Bernadette Matthews, Ann Rodgers and Joyce Ray Mahér, who all lived in Galway. I met Bernadette at an Equal Employment meeting; Ann, after she had received a flier from Bernadette Divilly; Joyce, an American, at a planning meeting for International Women's Day – she was expecting her first baby and was happily married at that time.

Máire Bradshaw (from Cork): she responded to one of our mailouts.

Caítlin Matthews, who had reviewed my book *Awkward Corners*, and had been very taken with an essay there about Greenham Common. She sent us her tapes from London: she is a devotee of the Goddess and uses Celtic mythology for her songs (which she accompanies on the harp). As well as being a Priestess of Isis she is also a devout Catholic. She got her women contacts to send us tapes of poetry.

Rosemarie Rowley, based in Dublin (I met her at a poverty conference): she sent her poetry in book form and on tape.

Anna Taylor, from Huddersfield, Yorkshire, sent tapes, after I had travelled at her invitation to address a series of 'Troops Out' meetings in the north of England.

Máirín McLoughlin, from Connemara: Irish-language poet.

Dachine Rainer, an American anarchist poet, who had been shunned by the literary establishment because of her support for Ezra Pound.

Our midnight broadcasts were mainly music and poetry: one of our public described her feelings about listening to them – 'It was as though I had found a magic world'. This remark came back to me when Sheila McCrann brought a friend of hers in to visit me, and the friend asked did I really run a women's radio? because her mother had told her of hearing a kind of fairy music late at night: she had thought that the mother, an insomniac, had in fact been asleep and dreaming. But the mother insisted – 'No, no!', she wasn't dreaming, she had heard it. I realised she had been listening to our tapes of Chinese music. We had a good collection of such 'exotics', tapes from China and Central America, and Inuit music from Canada.

We were told that a good number of men listened as well.

Our morning programmes were entirely different.

They were about the chat and gossip of the town. At eleven o'clock the radio would start and women would come in from different parts of Galway, most of them from corporation housing estates, bringing their own recent experiences.

Janet introduced Sybilla (Billie) Snake to the radio. Billie was living in Rahoon with Janet's brother Fergus. They had two small children. Both of them were members of the new Unemployed Centre and were trying to get the centre to set up a food co-op. There was already a cafe there, workshops and classes, and a co-op pub next door. In the end a big row blew up over this co-op: Billie and Fergus were thrown out of the centre and retaliated by mounting a picket-line: Women's Scéal Radio covered the story and supported their stance. This made us so unpopular with the centre that its management refused to allow us to distribute our leaflets on the premises. The real issue in this row was 'who makes the decisions, the members or the management?' To begin with, all the members were unemployed; it was a genuine grassroots organisation. The centre then started to get funding from the Trades Council and other established bodies, and as a result developed a management-committee structure with paid employees who were not elected by the members. The members had no say of any sort in these appointments.

Ann Rodgers, in Castlepark, had experienced the way politicians had taken over the local Residents' Association for their own electoral purposes and then used it as a species of Ku-Klux-Klan outfit against the Travelling community encamped in neighbouring Hillside.

Margaret Sweeney was able to tell us the Travellers' experience from the inside, and how the Travellers' attempts at self-organising were manipulated by certain priests and nuns with money from the Social Services. She was a member of the recently-formed Travellers' Committee in Roscommon, where she found the shots were being called once again by the clergy and the settled community. Settled people on the committee kept on deploring the fact that Travellers had 'no interest in it', but made no arrangements to provide expenses for them to get there. Margaret and her husband Joe also campaigned for Travellers' halting-sites, which had been promised by Galway Corporation but not built.

Eilis de Burca brought her gossip from another housing estate, on the city's west side, of women trapped inside the hire-purchase system and their consequent intimidation; as well as of marriage breakdowns and the authoritarian unfeeling attitude of the church toward women who embarked upon 'second relationships' – the priests would forbid them to receive Communion.

Another of our regular contributors was embattled with the corporation over its failure to undertake repairs on the Rahoon flats: as a protest she withheld her rent. They in turn were bringing her to court to evict her. She had been raped when she was younger, and so joined the Rape Crisis Centre as a volunteer. She felt that her ordeal should be used to help other women. The Rape Crisis Centre was trying to get funding support from the business community and the corporation. She was not the kind of person whom they wanted as a visible presence in their organisation; she 'damaged the image'. The most they let her do was go out on a flag-day to collect money. Like the Unemployment Centre, the Rape Crisis Centre had started from grass roots and was rapidly becoming 'professionally-minded', hiring women with degrees. The criterion was not so much experience as having the bit-of-paper.

Joyce: her marriage broke up and she found herself homeless. She opened our eyes to the reality of Bethlehem House, a hostel run by the Catholic Church, where she and all the other homeless young women there had to be out-of-doors from 8am to 8pm with nowhere to go except pubs and cafes.

Mary Sheehan: she lived just up the road. I met her at a women's conference called to organise lobbying of politicians in an election. She was recently widowed. Even though she and I were poles apart on such issues as contraception, divorce, abortion, lesbianism, etc., we found each other's company very stimulating: we are both great arguers. Mary is one of the world's natural broadcasters; she can talk about anything under the sun. She always came to the radio prepared with some biting comment on local incidents revealing a whole perspective of civic injustice and maladministration. She was very active in a number of social clubs, such as the Ladies' Flower Group and the Young-at-Heart.

Sheila McCrann, a friend of Breda Lewis. In the 1970s she had set up a self-awareness group out in Spiddal where she lived, along the coast of Galway Bay, some eight miles from the city. She was a pioneer in the cause of Battered Wives and had worked in one of the first refuges in Dublin. She naturally thought her help and knowledge would be welcome when a refuge was established in Galway and she did find a temporary paid job there for a while. The newly-formed Social Services council decided to make the temporary job permanent. She applied for it but was rejected. She felt she was frozen out because of her personal life: she lived in partnership with an ex-priest from America, was not legally married and had children. The chairperson of the Social Services council was the Bishop of Galway (Eamonn Casey who later became an unmarried daddy himself). Sheila now runs a successful cultural/language school for foreign visitors.

Poking our noses

So all in all we were a busy little radio, poking our noses into everything. We did effect some change. Mary Sheehan came in one morning to tell us about a visit to an old people's home, where the men were allowed to walk in the gardens, but the women weren't. We rang the supervisor and asked why: he said the women had never said they wanted to go out. We asked, were they ever asked if they wanted to go out? He said, no. The women in fact believed they were forbidden to go out. So he promised to change it: and he did.

Billie came in one morning. She expressed herself shocked at what she had found on her cereal packet: an Irish cereal company was promoting American Star Wars toys. We wrote off to the company, complaining that it was in violation of Ireland's neutrality and was allowing itself to be used by the Reagan-era American military/industrial propaganda. The company removed the promotion.

Every morning I used to cut out items from the day's newspaper to have ready just in case no women turned up. All our programmes were unplanned and all the subjects I've mentioned arose spontaneously. One of these was the forthcoming execution in South Africa of Theresa Ramashamola, a young woman who had been found guilty, along with five men, of being present in a crowd when someone was killed (a 'necklace burning'). Mary Sheehan was deeply affected and insisted we did something. She went home and wrote a mantra. By this time other women had arrived. Janet's mother found an air to the words of the mantra. Maria Lamburn organised us into a percussion group and a vocal chorus. We went out the next day into the middle of the town and for three hours we sang and played the mantra over and over again. Maria had structured it in such a way that the air could be carried through while passers-by were able to join in, beating drums and singing. We collected hundreds of signatures in support of Theresa and sent them to the South African Embassy in London. In the end there was a reprieve for all of the accused, and we rejoiced that we had been able to contribute to it.

At that event we met Gabrielle McMorrow, a very active shop-steward in one of the big Galway department stores. Her union, IDATU, had a vigorous policy against apartheid and strong connections with the Third World. She became a contributor to the radio on trade union affairs, particularly working conditions in the retail trade and the increasing use of part-time workers there.

We didn't deal only with social problems. Doreen made a tape of her pilgrimage up Croagh Patrick. Margaret Sweeney went down to interview a group of 'mature women' who, every day of the year, winter or summer, sun, rain, snow or sleet, go for a sea-bathe after Mass. They came back to the radio and talked about the spiritual dimension of swimming. Mary and I made a tape on a Young-at-Heart outing to Bunratty Castle. I made tapes at the county agricultural show and the Corrandulla pony show. I broadcast a story which I had made up for Doreen's daughter – it was later published by Attic Press in their series of 'feminised' fairytales. I wrote another story which I gave as a present to John Arden (in recognition of his support and helpfulness toward the radio, mainly his typing skills). He inserted it into his prize-winning book *Cogs Tyrannic*. Joyce wrote stories for the radio. Just Books of Belfast, which at that time was being run as a collective by women, made a tape for me, as also did the Spellbound feminist press in Dublin. Two young women, disc-jockeys, came and ran their own programme for a time, independent of our normal broadcasts.

My neighbour Nellie Casserly had a job, teaching young Travellers to sew, in the Fairgreen Training Centre. They used to take in orders to make banners and buntings. She was very supportive of the radio. Margaret Sweeney's teenage daughter Madeleine thought it would be a good idea to broadcast a country-and-western programme for the centre and play requests. Nellie got permission for the radio to be on in the workroom. Madeleine and a friend of hers acted as DJs.

The Woodquay Residents' Association used the radio. The Abbey Youth Group (who were trying to get a social centre going in a disused police station) used the radio. Doreen persuaded her mother and her mother's friend to come down and have a good old natter with Mary Sheehan about Galway and Connemara 'in the old days'. These chatty mornings proved very popular with my neighbours who had felt nervous about the radio because they feared it would all be 'feminist stuff'.

[. . .]

Mary Duffy

How I became involved in Radio Pirate-Woman and what happened next

I am writing this up in Nimmo's wine-bar at 5.16 pm on 11th of August 1995. Earlier last week I was looking through my diaries. I wrote 6 of them between 1 January 1993 to 21 June 1995, each of them about 100 pages long.

Anyway, the first mention of Radio Pirate-Woman was on 4 March 1993. I was being upset and hurt about how badly an ex had treated me. Whilst listening to the radio I heard a song, 'I am not in the wrong, the only wrongs I have committed have not been playing by the rules', an Age of Intolerance – I realised then that this is why I had been treated so badly, I refused to be a smiling trendy or to make myself corpulent to please him, and I also refused to be his mirror (reflecting his ego), somehow I just couldn't see the point in it. To think like this in Ireland means that one can never have a boyfriend (well, an Irish one, anyway).

On March 6 I brought kids that I was babysitting into town to get ice-cream. The Reclaim the Night march was on so we had to investigate. I met Margaretta there, she had a tape-recorder and taped the conversation she had with me and the kids. It was fun to hear us on radio that night. A whole lot more fun than a commercial radio station, where one gets forced to listen to ads for things one doesn't want, where one only hears mainstream chart music and where the DJs have the IQ of a peanut and never tell you what's really going on.

Margaretta asked me if I'd like to do videoing of the morning shows which take place in her house on St Bridget's Place Lower. I said, 'Yeah, fine!', et voilà! I am in the middle of it, and videoing a women's-only space. I'd been reading Dale Spender who had done research into exactly how talkative are the female sex. She planted tape-recorders in rooms where 'conversations' between men and women were taking place, and later checked them to study the characteristics of women's talk and how much of it is done in proportion to men. She got a PhD for this study on women and language so it is a genuine study and not just pronouncements ex-nihilo: the results are that women are not the talkative sex. Women never got beyond talking 30% of the time, and if they ever got even near that 30%, they were seen as talking too much. Men performed 98% of the interruptions (to send the conversation on another tack), phrased as 'What you mean is – ?', etc. They also like to dominate the content, direction, tone and emphasis of a conversation. They also love to treat your contribution as if it were never spoken, and then three minutes later the men will take up the idea and pass it off as their own – and expect an applause of sorts for it.

Virginia Woolf says that 'women are expected to be mirrors reflecting men at twice their natural size' and if one like me decides that she'd rather see and do than reflect, the trouble begins.

I went to university in Galway to get away from dreary Longford and a household where slaving for a pittance was valued over having and enjoying a life. I hated the idea that my middle-class acquaintances at school were automatically entitled to a whole lot more privileges than me by virtue of their parents having better jobs. It just didn't seem fair to me that my parents would work harder than, say, a school-teacher and only get one-third the wage, and why were people so silent about such an obvious injustice? The poorer we are, the harder we are forced to work. But then this is Ireland and if people realised truly what was going on, there'd be Exclusion Orders against gombeen men (and landlords). I did not meet many like-minded people in the university, most of them seemed to be more interested in careers, husband-hunting, and strutting about with the much-touted 'attitude' (which seems to be something that sells rather a lot of coffee). And nobody was interested in discussing the true causes of things and their consequences, or changing anything. Luckily, though, not everyone here is like that so I could stick it out long enough to get a degree.

On a year that I took off college to heal a broken heart and meet real people and do something useful I got involved in Radio Pirate-Woman. I read a book of plays that Margaretta and her husband John wrote together, and the preface by Margaretta said that the aims were 'recognition of women's invisible work, women's power subverting the military/industrial complex, spectators' power to subvert the power of the actor, where all activate and none are passive, everyone becoming their own scriptwriter, director, performer.' This sounds great to me, because for so long as I can remember, people had told me that I was 'to be seen and not heard', and in college not seen and not heard unless I could comply to the rules of conduct, speak important-sounding vacuities with a ridiculous Dublin 4 or pseudo-English (more prestigious but a mouthful) accent and not mention the war against the under-privileged. Also the radio station and plays are about something and have content rather than just a style, a whole lot more noble than the self-reflexive posturing of Martin Amis and his post-modernist triumph of clever-clever impenetrable-style-over-content buddies. Radio Pirate-Woman, rather than being a sedentary self-reflexive thing, is something which calls for a change in Irish society, which I for one think is long overdue.

'Ireland is the sow that eats its own farrow' – James Joyce. I agree.

A part of the active attempt to change society is the affiliation of Radio Pirate-Woman (Women in Media & Entertainment) to the Western Women's Link and more importantly the International Wages for Housework Campaign. On

26 October 1993 I read out a speech that Margaretta wrote about our efforts in Ireland to get women's unwaged work recognised – in a committee room in the House of Commons . . .

[. . .]

Sheila McCrann

From the start the most obvious thing about Radio Pirate-Woman was that all women were welcome. Over the years, visiting Margaretta D'Arcy's house at St Bridget's Place Lower in Galway, I have met a wonderful group of women from totally diverse backgrounds. I feel it says a lot, that Travellers, single mothers, academics, Catholic grandmothers, students, ultra-right Catholics, black feminists, lesbians, actors, poets, musicians, business-women, have visited the house and had the freedom to speak or perform on the radio.

The other aspect is the challenge. For some of us women who called to the house, actually speaking on the radio was immensely difficult. It was also very interesting to find that the least likely women adapted easily to the airwaves. After about six years, I still experience a lot of shyness and insecurity about speaking on the radio but I really appreciate how patient Margaretta has been, allowing each of us to take it at our own pace. We had an awful lot of fun, probably more before or after the broadcast, when everyone is more relaxed. We've seen that radio is more straightforward than we imagined, not such a mystery. We've enjoyed many zany outings, gatherings, dinners, parties and street-theatre to celebrate St Brigid's Day, Awards to Wise Women, the end of the broadcasts, etc.

Radio Pirate-Woman (read Margaretta D'Arcy) continues to be a challenge. I'm amazed how difficult such small things can be, such as standing on a street corner to protest, going out on the street to celebrate, sticking out, standing up to be counted. It has been a good experience seeing how women together, apart from initial fears and embarrassment, really begin to enjoy themselves and experience the power of union.

[. . .]

Margaret Sweeney

In 1988 there was a vicious attack by 300 settled people against the Travellers' Camp where I lived with my five children and my husband in a caravan, on Circular Road near the Rahoon flats in Galway. I thought we were all going to be burnt alive. That was when I found my voice. The local and national media arrived in force and I was interviewed.

That is when I realised the power in me to speak up.

From that day to this I have never shut up, or allowed myself to be silenced in my pursuit of justice and an end to the discrimination that permits inhuman conditions and lets a government treat a section of its citizens as my people, the

Travellers, are treated. We have apartheid in this country. It is slowly being recognised but it is not yet ended.

I was the first Traveller in the West of Ireland to stand for the Dail in national elections. Because of that, for the first time in my life I was treated as a human being, having been featured on TV: 'Hanley's People' and 'Saturday Live'. That made me realise the power of the media in changing people's attitudes toward Travellers. I speak and write anywhere I have the opportunity, no matter how large or small an audience.

I am a recognised unofficial leader of Travellers in Galway, even though I am not paid.

I feel that Radio Pirate-Woman is the kind of radio station where I can drop in any time I want, and bring with me my daughters and nieces. I feel it is as much *my* radio as anyone else's. Travelling women should be encouraged onto the radio as much as possible: we are the ones who could be natural broadcasters, as for years we were given no real education and had to educate ourselves through talking with one another, sitting by the fire, begging at house – which was one of the main channels of communication with the settled women. When Travelling women went round the houses, it was women who opened the door to them and had the chance to unburden themselves of their problems with a Traveller, who became a therapist and a psychologist as she listened to them.

Through Radio Pirate-Woman I became involved with WIME and became a delegate to the National Women's Council of Ireland. I am now a committee member of the Travellers' Support Group in Galway.

[. . .]

Chapter 14

Karen Qureshi

LIMITED TALK

Four young women, casually dressed in jeans and sweaters purposefully set about last minute preparations for their broadcast slot. Posters advertising 'Bollywood' blockbusters and others featuring the actors and actresses who star in these films hang on the rough plastered walls which form the small and decrepit basement room which serves as a studio. The news which is being relayed from *Sunrise* radio in Southall is drawing to a close as the women take up their positions at the control panel and microphones ready to begin their broadcast.

The scene I describe above was the setting for a temporary 'Asian' radio station based in Edinburgh. This was an enterprise initiated by an English/Indian DJ, long settled in the city, who, with limited financial backing from a handful of local Pakistani and Indian business men, succeeded in obtaining a number of Restricted Service Licences.[1] Applying for these licenses under various names enabled the station to be broadcast intermittently over a period of months. The presence of local 'Asian' radio was made known to the city's modest South Asian population through word of mouth and it is unlikely that many of Edinburgh's other inhabitants were aware of its existence.

Several women, both young and middle-aged, were among the presenters who took part in this project. My main focus here,[2] however, is on a particular group of young Scottish/Pakistani Moslem women, and my concern is with how these women's participation related to their efforts to create a public space for themselves and negotiate their own definition of gendered identity

It is noted elsewhere that British 'Asian' women develop supportive friendship networks (Werbner 1988) and come together in groups actively creating a cultural space for themselves (Brah 1996). Brah (1996: 82) states that these 'female cultures . . . are a means of negotiating and/or combating hierarchies of power in the household and in the wider community.' A group of young Scottish/Pakistani women friends in Edinburgh set up a women's group in the city aimed at fulfilling the social and cultural needs of second generation women like themselves.[3] They felt that these were being neglected within the wider Pakistani 'community'[4] (see also Qureshi and Moores 1999). The eight founding members were all in their early to mid twenties when the group was established. Some of them are married and most have completed further or higher education and are in employment. In the three years since the group began they have organised a variety of social functions and educational and informative workshops for young women focusing on concerns from 'health and beauty' to 'women's safety'. They have gained recognition from other groups and organisations in the city including Lothian and Borders police with whom they recently co-organised a workshop on personal safety.

As well as actively attempting to construct a public space for themselves where they can make their voice heard, they are, as a group of friends, involved in a collective process of working on/working out an acceptable self definition of Scottish/Pakistani/Muslim feminine identity. One of the group's stated aims is to counter the negative stereotypes bound up in dominant discourses which position Muslim women and/or women of South Asian descent as passive and oppressed. Haleema and Nousheen, two of the group's core members, express this intention here:

Haleema: I wanted to show through (the group) that . . . we're happy to be Asian.
It's not like something that's forced on you, it's like you're happy to be Asian. We enjoy wearing Asian clothes, we enjoy Asian weddings you know.
Nousheen: The Asian part of our lives is a happy part of our lives.
Haleema: Yeah it enriches our lives, it's not something that is forced on us . . .

When they were invited by the DJ referred to above to present a weekly programme they enthusiastically accepted the opportunity. The women set out to produce a magazine-style programme where, in addition to playing popular Asian music and having regular light-hearted slots dedicated to horoscopes and joke telling, they would introduce and discuss various issues which they thought would be relevant and of interest to young women like themselves. Rather than simply express their own opinions their intention was to offer information and a chance for open debate around topics. The group had hoped that people would participate in on-air discussions by phoning in with contributions. However, as it turned out callers preferred not to speak live on the radio and wanted the presenters to relay their comments to the listeners.

While the group received a little technical training their initial presentation was 'amateurish'. Drawing upon the skills they had developed in study and work environments, however, they put considerable effort and time into the preparation of their broadcasts, meeting to talk through and plan the programmes' content and format and organise the necessary research, sometimes using the Internet to gather information. Over the duration that their programme ran the topics they discussed included 'women's safety', 'post-natal depression', 'women back to work' as well as regular items relating to health, diet and 'beauty'. On several occasions they had invited guests in the studio who had some form of expertise pertaining to the subject under discussion.

It is possible to interpret the group's radio programme and radio talk as an attempt to question and resist the discourses which work to position second generation Scottish/Pakistani Muslim women. The very fact of these young women's presence on radio, and indeed, that of other young women who took part in presenting programmes, subverts the private/public dichotomy embedded in 'traditional' discourses relating to 'Asian' and Muslim feminine identity. Furthermore, the agency evident in their efforts to produce informed and, as became apparent in some cases, controversial programmes problematises dominant western notions of 'Asian' and/or Muslim women as passive. The topics they chose to present for discussion, and, as I will go on to illustrate, their responses to listeners' contributions, attest to their challenge to both these forces which work to subject them.

Mitchell (1998: 83) observes that '(h)ow much freedom women have on air is related to institutional constraints and audience expectations that surround their space'. The freedom of these and other women presenters was restricted in ways which meant that the potential for a public challenge to both 'traditional' patriarchal and dominant western discourses was limited and, indeed, finally curtailed. Central to many South Asian families is the cultural concept of izzat (family honour and respect)[5] which is highly dependent on the perceived behaviour of female family members and is vulnerable to 'community' gossip. Bound up with izzat and articulated in such gossip is a discourse pertaining to a 'traditional' ideal of femininity which incorporates modesty in dress and demeanour; respect for, and dependency on male and elder family members; and chastity outside of marriage. It also locates women predominantly within the domestic sphere and posits them as skilled in domestic labour, pious and proficient in 'cultural tradition'.

In the following two extracts from their broadcast talk during one of the group's early programmes where the topic under discussion was 'the role of Asian women in today's society', they and one of their female listeners can be seen to draw upon religious discourse to resist 'traditional' patriarchal discourse.[6]

Fatima: Hi, we've just had a caller who's actually quoted from the Hadith (Islamic religious text) and she is saying – this is for all the men out there – 'the best among you are those who are kindest to your wives.' What do you think of that then eh? . . .

Salma: Okay we've just got another call from a guy called Saib. He says that 'girls should not go to college as they get funny ideas.' But the prophet Muhammad, Sal Allah Alaih Waslam (may God's peace be upon him), said the search for knowledge is the duty of every Muslim – male and female.

However, in the same broadcast about 'the role of Asian women in today's society', Nousheen relayed comments from a female family therapist who had phoned in to say that she thought that 'Asian' parents should not put so much pressure on their daughters because, in her experience, it led to emotional breakdown. Nousheen distanced the group from this woman's sentiments by concluding: 'I'll just reiterate that was Margaret Robertson's point of view and not anybody in the . . . group'. This manoeuvring reflected the women's concern to protect themselves and their families from possible criticism of members of the audience. Although some of the group who are married enjoy a high degree of independence in established equitable relationships with their husbands, and are no longer concerned about the impact of gossip on them personally, the danger that their public talk carries of causing harm to their parents' izzat prompted them to exert self control. The following extract from one of my subsequent discussions with the group, where they are talking about how they decided against a particular topic, illustrates their concerns:

Halleema: I think you (to Nousheen) said why don't we discuss it but once you (to Fatima) explained then we understood that you were right 'cause you know the problems that we would have. You know it made sense because you know you realise what the community is like.

K.Q: Is that because of a fear of a reaction against your programme?

Fatima: Yeah yeah and against individuals as well.

Nousheen: Against the group.

Haleema: I think with me it's that I always worry about what we say because I just think what ever I say reflects on my family, it's my parents. I think more about my parents when I say anything. I'm not really bothered about what people think about me but it's more they'll be saying 'that's L's daughter, L's daughter was saying that'.

The behaviour of young women who presented other programmes on the radio was criticised, in my company, by a Pakistani man because they were laughing and acting as if 'they were at a disco or something'. Shabana, whose responsibility it was to manage and train the presenters, told me that on one occasion when some young women were presenting a programme men had phoned in and asked them intimate questions about their clothing. The implication here is that because the young women in question were participating in a public context and exhibiting enjoyment in what they were doing, they were perceived by some people as indecent and therefore vulnerable to sexual pestering. Concern about negative reactions within the community prevented some young women who would otherwise have liked to participate from doing so, and one young women that I knew of withdrew because of other people's responses.

Despite the group's self-censorship in the content and presentation of their on-air discussions they were subjected to further reprimand and disapproval of the station's management. They were chastised, for example, for referring to the 'bikini line' within the context of a 'health and beauty' slot concerned with hair removal, and the appropriateness of their choice of discussion topics was often questioned as Nousheen describes here:

One of the directors – they've got this lady that does shows and she's like, kind of seems to supervise the shows now – she was like not very happy that we were doing that topic . . . because it was a very sensitive topic and a lot of people might be offended by it and I mean that was just post-natal depression.

Shabana, the woman responsible for managing the programmes and presenters, had worked professionally in radio broadcasting in England and Wales on programmes aimed at British 'Asian' audiences. She has a different class background from the majority of the Pakistani families in Edinburgh. Later, during an interview with her I asked if there had been any occasions when presenters wanted to talk about things that she had thought they should not and she replied:

There were some things for instance some to the girls – there were some girls who eh thought they were quite sort of liberated and this and that (laugh) and it was fine but I just think there is an appropriate time for certain things. Like they would quite happily – em it's certain attitudes to things – like post-natal depression and stuff. I'd say without a doubt that within the Asian culture something like post-natal depression is kind of non-existent in a way. People do not accept the fact that there is such a thing . . . so you have to be very careful in the types of subjects aren't going to embarrass grandma sitting there or if auntie's sitting there or dad's sitting there.

The members of the group realised that post-natal depression was not recognised by the larger Asian community but they viewed the fact that their programme would have a mixed audience as an opportunity to try to effect some change in this direction. Haleema told me:

Maybe because people who listen to our show won't just be women our age, you know a lot of families will have it on and maybe older people will hear it and be a bit more sympathetic if somebody that has just had a baby is maybe acting a bit strange.

The radio station organisers were keen for listeners to write to the Radio Authority to lobby for a permanent license to be awarded for an 'Asian' station in the central belt of Scotland. Shabana's priorities in her role as manager were to encourage audience support and not to alienate listeners or advertising sponsors by allowing talk which might cause offence. However, it is possible that the patronising tone evident in her explanation reflects her different position as a Pakistani woman from a privileged class background. She is likely to take for granted a relatively 'liberated' experience as a woman and so may not identify with the young women's attempt to breakdown such prejudices.

Eventually the group were asked to accept either a change in the timing of their broadcast from a weekday evening to a Saturday afternoon or to confine the content of their programme to music and 'light-weight' talk. Because the alternative timing was inconvenient for them and because they thought that the principal audience they had hoped to reach would not tune in on a Saturday afternoon they reluctantly took up the latter option for a while. The women felt stifled and frustrated, and that the time and energy they were investing as a group and as individuals could be better spent. Shortly afterwards they decided to withdraw completely. As efforts to obtain a permanent license (have so far) failed the opportunity for them to present any type of programme was ultimately removed anyway. The group, however, continues to be active in other contexts in trying to negotiate a public space and voice for themselves and other women, and to work on/work out their own definitions and ways of being Scottish/Pakistani/Muslim women in Scotland's capital at the turn of the millennium.

Notes

1 Restricted service licences are awarded by the UK Radio Authority for up to 28 days a year to stations who want to cover small scale events, test out a new radio format or act as a training tool.
2 This short paper is based on some of the data generated from my on-going ethnographic research which is looking at the processes of culture and identity as they are played out in the lives of second generation Pakistani Scots in Edinburgh. The names of all the women participants have been changed.
3 The intention of the founding members was that the group would be open to all 'Scottish ethnic women'. In practice, however, it is mainly Scottish Pakistani women who are members.
4 While space prevents any detailed discussion of the homogenising, essentialist and/or reifying capacity of terms such as 'Asian', 'traditional', 'cultural tradition' and 'community', by placing my use of them within inverted commas I wish to signal their problematic nature. See Baumann (1996) for an examination of the difficulties surrounding the concept of 'community'.
5 See Gillespie (1995: 33) for a useful explanation of the meaning of izzat to South Asian families.
6 The use of Islamic religious teaching by young British Muslims to challenge and question elements of the parental generation's interpretation of 'cultural tradition' has been noted elsewhere. See, for example, Ali (1992) and Jacobson (1998).

References

Ali, Y. (1992) 'Muslim women and the politics of ethnicity and culture in Northern England', pp. 101–23, in G. Sahgal and N. Yuval-Davies (eds) *Refusing holy orders: women and fundamentalism in Britain*, London: Virago Press.
Baumann, G. (1996) *Contesting culture: discourses of identity in multi-ethnic London*, Cambridge: Cambridge University Press.
Brah, A. (1996) *Cartographies of diaspora: contesting identities*, London: Routledge.
Gillespie, M. (1995) *Television, ethnicity and cultural change*, London: Routledge.
Jacobson, J. (1998) *Islam in transition: religion and identity among British Pakistan youth*, London: Routledge.
Mitchell, C. (1998) 'Women's (community) radio as a feminist public sphere', *Javnost: The Public*, Vol. 5: 2. pp. 73–85.

Qureshi, K. and Moores, S. (1999) 'Identity remix: tradition and translation in the lives of young Pakistani Scots', *European Journal of Cultural Studies.* Vol. 2: 3 pp. 311–30.

Werbner, P. (1988) 'Taking and giving: working women and female bonds in a Pakistani immigrant neighbourhood', pp. 177–202, in S. Westwood and P. Bhachu (eds) *Enterprising women: ethnicity, economy and gender relations*, London: Routledge.

Chapter 15

Caroline Mitchell

ON AIR/OFF AIR: DEFINING WOMEN'S RADIO SPACE IN EUROPEAN WOMEN'S COMMUNITY RADIO

From Jankowski, N. and Prehn, O. (eds) (forthcoming), *Community Electronic Media in the Information Age: Perspectives, Findings and Policy*, New Jersey: Hampton Press

Introduction

[. . .] Feminist media academics have emphasised the importance of alternative sites of media practice. These sites promote feminist ideas, practices and content and counteract what Tuchman (1979) calls the 'symbolic annihilation' of women by the mass media, caused by under or misrepresentation. Feminist-oriented research into alternative media practice (Bredin 1991; Steiner 1992; Jallov 1992, 1996; Riaño 1994) has explored and theorised some of the ways that women have intervened to challenge mainstream media representations of themselves.

Jankowski (1991) underlines the need for more research in defining the theory of alternative media. Bredin's review of work on feminist intervention into cultural production, which includes radio stations and programmes, notes the lack of documentation and analysis 'of their politics and practices' (Bredin 1991: 36). Her work on women in community radio in Canada constitutes one of the few contributions to the theory and praxis of women's radio.

The central theme of this chapter is to consider how inequality may be countered by alternative practice. It explores how a number of women's stations and radio training projects in Europe forge a gendered space within this practice. Finally, it will to contribute to a theory and praxis of alternative media as a development tool for women's participation in the public arena or in social space.

[. . .]

Feminist research into the processes of cultural production

In defining women's cultural production it is important to discuss the distinction between women's production and feminist production. Bredin (1991) outlines a number of different levels and definitions of feminist cultural production. It should be *by* women, but the fact that women are involved does not mean that it will be feminist. Feminist production should be about the politicization of culture in resistance to patriarchal oppression. A recognition of cultural factors surrounding different groups of women (e.g., race, class and sexual orientation) is integral to a neo-Marxist feminist ideal of eliminating oppression. A key question in defining feminist radio praxis is the manner in which women negotiate how their lives are defined on and by the radio.

Bredin argues that feminist production should demystify the role of producer so that the boundaries between producers and consumers of culture are broken down: 'A work is never inherently feminist but depends on a feminist consciousness shared by both producer and consumer' (Bredin 1991: 36). Coward (1987) considers how feminism has redefined women's interests in terms of being involved in production, by, for example, setting up women's production companies, or as women producers (Coward 1987). The establishment of UK women's radio stations in the early 1990s can be seen in the context of other feminist media enterprises in the 1970s and 1980s, for instance *Virago Press*, *Spare Rib* magazine and the independent television production company *Broadside*. Women's community radio stations are also clearly targeted at female audiences but usually at a local level and with a volunteer base. What might the characteristics be of a 'gendered structure of media production' (van Zoonen 1994: 49) at the local level? How 'alternative' in content and process can women's production be when it is in competition with so many other more mainstream representations? What contribution might women's community radio have to an alternative public sphere or 'space'?

Representation of women's issues and feminist content

In terms of constructing a 'public identity' for the women's movement, the relationship between the media and the feminist movement has been both complex and problematic. In a survey of local radio in London, 'Women's Airwaves'[1] concluded that 'feminist ideas and practices . . . and . . . the women's liberation movement in London were totally ignored' (Local Radio Workshop 1983: 140). Van Zoonen (1992: 453) notes that 'feminism has not gained access to the media on its own terms'. She found that mainstream media's construction of the women's movement in The Netherlands in the late 1960s and early 1970s showed that certain discourses of feminism were acceptable. The discourse of equal opportunities was acceptable, but political feminism was not. Mainstream media perceived a gap between the interests of 'ordinary women' and activists and the movement was 'anti-men'. She notes that even in this framework there was some room for divergent views (van Zoonen 1992: 474). She acknowledges that the women's movement and definitions of feminism in the 1990s are more diverse. These conclusions might be usefully applied to discussing radio representations of feminism, particularly where women are active producers of radio.

Feminist interpretations of Habermas

Many feminist academics (for example, Fraser 1985, McLaughlin 1993, 1995) question the usefulness of the concept of the public sphere as developed by Habermas (1974, 1989). Feminist readings of Habermas reveal that 'the key axis of exclusion from the liberal public sphere was gender' (McLaughlin 1993: 604). A feminist critique is partly based on the binary opposition inherent in Habermas where men are associated with the public and women with the private sphere.

The mass media are integral to any discussion of the public sphere. An awareness of the nature of media ownership and how control over the means of production structures access and representation is crucial. Community stations fit Wasco and Mosco's progressive vision of democratic communication that includes participatory and alternative media forms and media strategies committed to social change (in Dahlgren 1995: 13). McLaughlin argues that feminists have not paid enough attention to the media in their discussions of Habermas. She suggests that media should be placed in the foreground in a feminist theory of the public sphere and that feminist media studies should attend to the public sphere. Women's interests can be transformed through forms of resistance, including setting up oppositional discourses. Women's stations can be seen as examples of 'new media developments and alternative forms of media and participation in order to develop new forms of public life' (McLaughlin 1993: 616). In her interesting feminist revision of a theory of the public sphere, Lara identifies the need for 'feminist models of recognition . . . as long as groups needing to be heard or accepted do not first conquer channels of communication to call attention to the way they have been treated, nothing will change.' (Lara 1998: 151)

Benhabib (1995) supports the discursive model of public space as compatible with feminist ideals. She promotes the idea of bringing areas previously considered to be of only private interest in the traditional women's sphere (e.g., housework, reproduction, child care) into the public discursive arena and argues that through 'discourses of power and their implicit agendas' they will be demystified. An extension of this is that practical discourse has to be 'feminized' (Benhabib 1995: 95). Lara (1998: 76) identifies the importance of the 'invaluable discovery of one's own narrative voice', narratives which 'can be seen as instruments and expressions of learning' (Lara 1998: 103). Can women in community stations who are involved in such discourses at a very practical and everyday level, play a role in this process by defining 'feminized' modes of training, production and programming?

[. . .]

Lacey (1996: 223) views radio as 'bridging the divide' between public and private and 'redefining the boundaries between them.' Although she primarily talks about early German radio, it is still a useful way for considering the role of radio in contemporary women's lives. It recognises the negotiation that continually goes on within the public, private social and cultural spaces of women's lives. The institutional and ideological context in which women's radio is situated is crucial to how women can use the space discursively.

Whilst the concepts of public and private spheres (and recent feminist revisions of this area) are useful for theorising popular culture and gender, feminist post structuralist analysis of how women are both excluded yet at the same time gain access may account for how the dominated within society can act to subvert the acts of the dominant.[2] If one considers radio as a *disembodied* space (where the woman's *voice* could be said to supersede the body),[3] this opens up subversive options. Using Butler's notion of 'performativity' where identity is enacted and continuously re-enacted (Butler 1990), can community stations provide a space that enables women to produce programming and meanings that transcend some of the more limiting mediated constructions of their lives?

Women's radio stations as sites for representation and production

[. . .]

Community radio as a site for women's cultural production necessitates an understanding of the nature of both women's alternative media (WAM) and community radio (CR). They share many characteristics, and have experienced the same kinds of pressures (from inside and outside the movements) for change over the last three decades. Steiner (1992) [. . .] highlights some of the problems associated with WAM projects in the 1970s and 1980s; for instance, the difficulties projects have during the transition from a short term project to a more sustainable long term enterprise. She says the main aim of WAM is to 'express and celebrate' the views of a wide range of women while using media as a tool to help the women's movement achieve its aims. WAM are usually small-scale enterprises, addressing geographical or communities of interest. Most WAM products are made by women, often working collectively; they aim where possible to involve women in the production process, including provision of training to undertake specialist roles. There may be some involvement of men. There tends to be a feminist ethic, often valued above a professional ethic. If necessary, work will be done by voluntary or low paid labour. Most activities are non-profit oriented.

Research into how women's community stations in the 1990s have developed their practices and programming is important in terms of updating the history of feminist alternative media and contributing to a deeper understanding of feminist cultural production.

Women's community radio stations and alternative media practice

Whilst having aims and charters that support equal opportunities, community radio stations often seem to reflect the gender stereotyping of mainstream radio stations in staff and volunteer roles. A pan-European survey found that men out-numbered women volunteers in all work areas apart from administration and finance. Where there were full-time paid staff, only 22 per cent were women (Lewis 1994). Community radio as a site for alternative practice and the place of women's radio therein has been documented by Jallov (1992, 1996). She defines the different 'forms' of women's radio, characterising women's radio production as taking place at several different levels:

> (I)n an all women's radio station, in an autonomous collective in a mixed station, in a women's group who are not totally autonomous in a mixed station, . . . an individual women making a women's show, . . . an individual woman working in a mainstream setting with a gender conscious perspective.
>
> (Jallov 1996: 16)

Women's radio stations and programming within community radio have existed since 1969 when WBAI in New York introduced feminist programming – including taped consciousness-raising sessions (Steiner 1992). Other forms of early programmes and stations included Radio Donna in Italy (see Karpf 1980), Radi-Orakel in Norway, (Jallov 1992) and Radio Pirate Woman in Ireland (D'Arcy 1996). In addition there are specialist news agencies that provide news and features with a women's and feminist agenda. These include 'Women on the Line' in Australia, Women's News gathering Service in the USA (Werden 1996), Feminist International Radio Endeavour, Costa Rica (Suarez Toro 1996) and Women's Feature Service, India (Anand 1996).

Bredin (1991) finds that most urban community stations in Canada have feminist programming of some kind (between 1.5 and 8.5 hours a week) and notes that cities with most active women's movements and other feminist media forms (e.g., a women's press) have the most radio programming. She is, however, critical of the impact of this programming and of the participation of women in programming roles in the stations (particularly minority ethnic women and lesbians). She suggests that action is needed: 'something more than complacent lip service to community radio as a "participatory medium" and "open forum" is required' (Bredin 1991: 39). She concludes that 'despite its current limitations, feminist community radio is actively engaged in the politization of culture and the affirmation of marginal experience that characterises women's resistance to oppression everywhere' (Bredin 1991: 40).

Woman's community radio praxis: towards a model of feminist radio practice[4]

Five examples of women working in community radio settings in the UK and the Irish Republic can be used to develop a model of feminist radio practice in community stations and training projects.[5] *Fem FM* was the first women's station in the Britain,[6] *Radio Venus* is part of Bradford Community Broadcasting, and the *Women on Wearside* group broadcasts in the North East of England setting up a station called 107-the Bridge – all have used the Restricted Service Licence[7] as a way of broadcasting. *Radio Pirate Woman* is an unlicenced radio station and *Women On Air* is a radio training, research and policy project. Both are based in Galway in the west of Ireland but have no other connection.

[. . .]

I would like to try to draw out some defining characteristics of feminist radio practice from the Irish and British examples.

Women-centred training, community outreach and programme development

[. . .]

Fem FM, Radio Venus and Women on Wearside had a multi-level, holistic approach to training, integrating training and programme making, and employing community development methods to reach women who might not have been aware of community radio. An essential approach was to make courses, and the whole idea of radio, accessible and welcoming to women. The demystification of technology related to programme making and confidence building were core aims of all courses. Development of a feminist ethic of communication in the context of women's radio included strategies developed by the women's movement. Parallels might be drawn between a holistic approach to training and feminist consciousness raising. For instance, they shared the objectives of instilling confidence and re-skilling women, raising awareness of women's oppression; working collectively, developing women's creativity and networking. Part of the contemporary ethos of community development and education work (stemming in part from development education) is the idea of sustainable resourcing of community projects – that is in terms of leaving people with skills and knowledge as well as financial resources. The idea of 'capacity building' amongst community representatives can be applied to women in community radio.

[. . .]

At Radio Pirate Woman formal radio training is eschewed. Information about broadcasts is publicised around the small city of Galway via posters and word of mouth. D'Arcy notes that working class women surveyed in Galway were nervous about speaking out on air: 'they didn't feel confident to speak in public until they had at first listened and found out what it was all about' (D'Arcy 1996: 24).

[. . .]

Specific and specialist programming, community development and training initiatives have facilitated the participation of a wide range of women in radio stations. Influenced by good practice in community development and adult education, the initiatives included those based partly outside the station to encompass places where women normally meet (e.g., near local facilities) and were timed to be convenient for women with children with funded childcare. The courses were flexible and 'student centred', often combining confidence building, creativity and aspects of women's studies with practical radio skills and programme making. New technology training aimed at women in different age groups – in computer skills generally and digital editing and mixing specifically – is particularly important. Training trainers and working in partnership with specialist organisations like women's centres and minority ethnic groups helps to make women's radio sustainable. (For further discussion of women's training and adult education see Günnell *et al.*: 1999). I argue that training and community-based programme making is just one aspect of changing the roles and representations of women in radio. Community radio RSLs play a very important part in giving women vital experience and confidence so that they can work in different radio settings on an equal basis with men.

[. . .]

The importance of collective action

Women in the women's stations communicated a feeling of empowerment through making and hearing back a representation of themselves and their lives as confident women. There was a sense of strength in collective action – strengthening women's voices. So in programme making there is still some sense of women taking on equal roles, sharing voluntary labour. However, even where work was voluntary I would argue that there was more awareness than in the 1970s and 1980s (see Steiner 1992) of people's strengths and weaknesses and of the need for specific roles and functional hierarchies to 'get the job done'. This was evident at Fem FM where the co-ordinating group of the station effectively consisted of 'heads of department' who effectively managed a group of volunteers. Similarly, each programme producer was responsible for a team of volunteers and reported to a programme editor. The core group of female workers in the WOA central office work closely together, but not collectively. What has remained though is the strong ethos that women's development won't happen without planning, community outreach and training and that the experience women get as volunteers on such projects is invaluable in terms of future confidence, contacts and paid work opportunities.

Programme content based around women's lives vs. 'feminist' concerns

Many programmes broadcast by women's stations put an emphasis on every-day women's lives rather than an overtly political feminist content. Women were sensitive to what others would think of their programmes and what was 'acceptable' and thereby defining their programme content through how others will see them. All the women's stations in the UK were tentative about associating publicly with discourses of feminism. The Radio Venus co-ordinator summed up her position:

I think it's a feminist statement – a feminist project – but then I don't mind calling myself a feminist. I wouldn't necessarily use that word in publicity or talking to groups because of what's happening to the word feminist . . . They may shy away from the 'f' word because of the ridicule it has attracted and would see it as being a middle class station.

Community radio can provide a space for women; its participatory processes may have a transforming function with the potential to enable women to produce programming and meanings transcending some of the more limiting ideological constructions of their lives. I suggest, however, that 'different' and radical discourses of women's radio conflict with the radio discourses that audiences are used to. Radio representations of feminism in its most political and oppositional stance are rare in the UK community radio setting.

Within mixed stations like Radio Venus on BCB there is a mismatch between the amount of feminist radio consciousness raising, training, organization and development work being achieved in the space *off air* in the radio stations and the *on air* radio discourse. Clearly, women are moving out of the domestic space into a new community radio social space 'off air.' But it is hard for women to bring the discourse of their everyday lives into the radio studio and into the 'on air' space. At Radio Venus one woman talked about what happened when they moved from the private talk space outside the studio to what happened when they went on air:[8]

when we were all outside the studio . . . we were talking about huge issues . . . Then as soon as we got into the studio were talking about '5 best blokes' and everything . . . I think it's just this image that we have in 'us heads about what it should be like . . . what is acceptable.

[. . .]

Radio Pirate Woman has no management structure and allows any woman to walk into a studio based in a house and speak into a microphone in order to debate issues without censorship. The station's aim to allow 'each woman to speak freely without being controlled by another woman' (D'Arcy 1996: 5) seems close to the ideal of Habermas' conditions for a public sphere. The station's programming is more like a translation of daily life over the airwaves. There are no set programmes as such: I have observed women walking in off the street and joining in broadcasts, hardly drawing breath before going on air – perhaps continuing a conversation that they had been conducting with a neighbour. D'Arcy likens this to the rural tradition of visiting, highlighting the importance of oral cultural discourse. This form of radio free from any institutional or commercial restrictions may represent the bridge between public and private social space that Lacey (1996) identifies. D'Arcy (1996: 3) says of her perception of women at the microphone: 'Each of us remains private, we are public at the same time.' However, the simplicity of this model may also be its main weakness, as it is potentially subject to the control of one woman (who lives in the house) and as an unlicenced station is vulnerable to closure by the regulatory authorities.

[. . .]

D'Arcy documents how feminists in Galway viewed Radio Pirate Woman, particularly its aim to broadcast all women's views (including traditional Catholic views of some older women) whether they fitted in with the women's movement or not:

I began to feel a certain coolness and stand-off-ishness from certain women
. . . (they said) 'Women's Sceal Radio is *not* a true feminist radio' and someone
like D'Arcy ought not to be giving space to women who were 'turning the clock
back'.

(D'Arcy 1996: 31)

[. . .]

At Fem FM, where women had a high level of structural control, the discursive
space of programming was still designed and made through women negotiating
a version of women's radio that was acceptable to the audience. It was affected by
a complex range of expectations from both producers and consumers which, I
would argue, limits the extent to which the programming discourse can be radically
feminised.

The programming at Radio Pirate Women shows that women's community
radio has the ability to produce 'soundscapes' or narratives based on women's
experiences, embedded in the local and the 'everyday'. This feminist radio praxis
happens when women have control over every aspect of the station, including
choosing the broadcast frequency, programming, scheduling and decision making
about who gets on air. Importantly, mainstream notions of accepted radio discourse
have been completely rejected at this station. The notion of radio programme
discourses, and indeed the whole sense of the radio space/airwaves as being
fundamentally, historically and culturally, 'male' deserves more research.

Developing 'female friendly' radio station structures

Hélène Cixous (Cixous & Clément 1986) argues that there are two generic forms
of economy – a masculine one based on fear of loss of accumulated capital and a
feminine one based on a logic of *giving* without any expectation of reward. In
community radio stations I argue that a male economy exists more in terms of
individuals being unwilling to give up competitively fought for air time or
management positions than in terms of the formal financial structures 'controlled'
by men. The UK competitive system of awarding licences based on financial acumen
rather than community worth can also be read in this way. Women's stations on
the other hand have characteristics of the feminine economy, for instance the
work of volunteers and subsidised training can be seen as 'gifts' – freely given.[9]
Nye, Goodwin and Hollows (1994: 163) quoted a Fem FM participant as saying
'Goodwill was Fem FM's most valuable resource.'

[. . .]

Utreras (in Peruzzo 1996: 172) defines three levels of popular participation – at
the production level, decision making level and at the planning level. Women at
Women on Wearside/107 the Bridge were involved not only in making programmes but in deciding on programme scheduling, sponsorship, station image
and publicity. Course participants learned about and make key practical decisions
– giving them experience in radio management.

[. . .]

One development that might help women overcome the tyranny of the pressure of radio station cultures is to open up and explore the feminine/feminist economic space more fully in both separatist and mixed stations. More sustainable structures can be developed like part-time or shared programming, and more sophisticated station structures that allow for protection of women's rights and status within stations. How much freedom women have on air is related to institutional constraints and audience expectations that surround their space. In mixed stations that depends on how the women's space is valued in the station.

Discussion and conclusions

[. . .]

I have concentrated mainly on factors related to station structures and training and development strategies, and their contribution to women gaining a sense of space, independence and empowerment on and off the air in community stations. How women produce radio must be seen in the context of a complex range of influences: how they have grown up with radio use, role models, how confident they are in broadcasting and the institutional context in which they are producing radio.

Media production at the local level can be structured by gender. Women's radio production is facilitated by women-oriented training and community development strategies. Women's community radio training is based on the premise that women are able to *participate* in programme production and are given access to broadcasting time – space on the airwaves. This participation is achieved through training and confidence building taking place inside and outside the radio stations. Community-based training means that courses and workshops are located where women meet as part of their daily lives. Participation is further facilitated by programme-led training where broadcast technology is demystified through women-only training and confidence building. Targeted training has led to a wide range of women producers in terms of ethnic and class background.

Women's radio broadcasting can be structured through two main models – a women's radio station organising separately and women's radio as part of a mixed station. What is shared with Fem FM, Radio Venus and Women on Wearside is the value of working towards a collective goal and getting broadcasting experience and space on the airwaves. Women involved in these stations were positive about the amount of publicity and audience response that women's radio activities achieved. This added to their image of themselves as confident women; they were pleased with the positive reflections of themselves that they were seeing and hearing on the airwaves.

[. . .] The women's station organised in the separatist model of Fem FM has a function of exciting, enthusing, focusing on and publicising women's radio in a short term burst. Woolf (1993: 175) cited Fem FM as an example of 'power feminism'. Clearly, collective action by women in mixed stations, while 'making waves' when they asserted their rights to resources, left them with a feeling of empowerment and satisfaction at having achieved the space they have. Where community stations compete for scarce resources, the longer, less glamorous slog of women carving out a space within a mixed station may be more sustainable in the long term. Certainly women need to have control over the structures that influence their 'on air' space to match the work that they are doing to gain the space 'off air' in community radio stations.

Community radio is a space where alternative publics can gain access to debate in a media space produced by people who have a local interest in the debate. How politicised or feminist this space can be depends on the ideological discourse of the space and how feminism or women-oriented subjects are understood. Women's perceptions of their own identity in relation to feminism is integral to this and Lacey's (1996) conclusion that women should carve out a separate space as citizens rather than as women is pertinent. Women find the community radio environment more accessible because of its open structures. However, in mixed stations, maintaining that space and translating off air activity into on air programming is often hard fought for and has to be continually asserted.

There are structures and models of long term success that exist within different broadcasting systems. RadiOrakel in Norway, for instance, has survived as a women's station since 1982. It grants men airspace provided that the station as a whole prioritises women in its management and scheduling. Whilst the current RSL system in Britain has allowed a range of women's stations to showcase alternative programs and practices, there is no doubt that the lack of legislation for permanent community stations has hindered the development of women's programming and stations in the long term. Licensed community stations in Ireland have a statutory quota of women on their board of management. The survival of community radio in the commercial media landscape remains an issue and more research is required into the viability of women's stations as permanent entities.

Notes

1 Women's Airwaves was a programme making, training and lobbying organisation based in London (UK) in the early 1980s.
2 This argument is developed more fully by Mitchell and O'Shea (1999).
3 In her seminal article, 'When a woman reads the news' Holland (1997) discusses the tyranny of the visual for the woman news reader on screen and relates this to Mulvey's theory of the male gaze.
4 Some of this model was first developed by Mitchell (2001).
5 Ethnographic research including interviews with women in women's radio stations was carried out by the author between 1992 and 1999.
6 See Mitchell and Caverly (1993) for report on this project.
7 RSL – Restricted Service Licences which can be obtained from the UK Radio Authority for short periods each year.
8 See also Scannell (1996) regarding studios and public talk space.
9 This argument is developed by Mitchell and O'Shea (1999).

References

Anand, A. (1996) 'Starting up, staying there and moving on, the women's feature service', in A. Sreberny-Mohammadi, D. Wynseck, J. McKenna and O. Boyd-Barrett (eds), *Media in global context* pp. 293–305, Leicester: University of Leicester Centre for Mass Communications Research.

D'Arcy, M. (1996) *Galway's pirate women, a global trawl*, Galway: Women's Pirate Press.

Benhabib, S. (1995) 'Models of public space', in C. Calhoun (ed.) *Habermas and the public sphere* pp. 73–98, London: MIT Press.

Bredin, M. (1991) 'Feminist cultural politics: Women in community radio in Canada', *Resources for feminist research*, 20 (1–2), 36–41.

Butler, J. (1990) *Gender trouble – feminism and the subversion of identity*, London: Routledge.

Cixous, H., and Clément, C. (1986) *The newly born woman*, Minneapolis: The University of Minnesota Press.

Coward, R. (1987) 'Women's programmes: Why not?', in H. Baehr & G. Dyer (eds) *Boxed in: women and television*, pp. 96–106, London: Pandora.

Dahlgren, P. (1995) *Television and the public sphere, citizenship, democracy and the media*, London: Sage.

Fraser, N. (1985) 'What's critical about critical theory? The case of Habermas and Gender', *New German Critique*, No 35 (Spring /Summer 1985), pp. 97–131.

Gill, R. (1993) 'Justifying injustice: Broadcasters' accounts of inequality in a radio station', in E. Burman, and I. Parker (eds), *Discourse analytic research: readings and repertoires of texts in Action*, pp. 75–93, London: Routledge.

Günnell, T., Jankowski, N., Jones, S., Lewis, P., Klug, A., Mitchell, C. and Poysko, A. (1999) *Creating community voices: community radio and new technologies for socially disadvantaged groups*, Socrates Programme for Adult Education, Year 1 Report, Sheffield, UK: AMARC-Europe.

Habermas, J. (1974) 'The public sphere', *New German Critique* no. 3.

Habermas, J. (1989) *The Structural transformation of the public sphere. An enquiry into a category of bourgeois society.* Translated by T. Burger, and F. Lawrence, Oxford: Polity Press.

Holland, P. (1987) 'When a woman reads the news', in H. Baehr and G. Dyer (eds), *Boxed in: women and television*, pp. 133–50, London: Pandora Press.

Jallov, B. (1992) 'Women on the air – community radio as a tool for feminist messages', in N. Jankowski, O. Prehn, and E. Stappers (eds), *The people's voice: local radio and TV in Europe*, pp. 215–24, London: John Libbey.

Jallov, B. (1996) *Women's voices crossing frontiers, European directory of women's community radio stations and women's radio production collectives*, Sheffield: AMARC – Europe Women's Network.

Jankowski, N, W. (1991) 'Qualitative research and community media', in K.B. Jensen, and N.W. Jankowski (eds), *A handbook of qualitative methodologies for mass communication research* pp. 163–74, London: Routledge.

Karpf, A. (1990) 'Women and radio' in Baehr, H. (ed.) *Women and media*, Oxford: Pergamon Press, pp. 41–54.

Lacey, K. (1996) *Feminine frequencies: gender, German radio, and the public sphere, 1923–1945*, Ann Arbor: University of Michigan Press.

Lara, M. P. (1998) *Moral textures, feminist narratives in the public sphere*, Cambridge: Polity Press.

Lewis, P. M. (1994) *Community radio – employment trends and training needs. Report of Transnational Survey*, Sheffield: AMARC Europe.

Local Radio Workshop (1983) *Nothing local about it – London's local radio*, London: Comedia.

McKay A. (1988) 'Speaking up: voice amplification and women's struggle for public expression', in Kramarae, C. (ed.) *Technology and woman's voices*, pp.187–206, London: Routledge & Kegan Paul.

McLaughlin, L. (1993) 'Feminism, the public sphere, media and democracy', *Media, Culture and Society*, 15, 599–620.

McLaughlin, L. (1995) 'From excess to access: Feminist political agency in the public sphere'. *Javnost/The Public*, 4, 37–50.

Mitchell, C. and Caverly, T. (1993) *Fem FM 101 – first in women's radio*, University of Sunderland: Fem FM.

Mitchell, C. and O'Shea, A. (1999) 'Gendered practices in radio broadcasting – a critical study of cultures of management and production', paper presented at Critical Management Conference, Cultural Industry Stream, July 1999: Manchester.

Mitchell, C. (2000) 'Short term bursts of inspiration': The development of British women's alternative radio. *Journal of Radio Studies*.

Mitchell, C. (2001) 'Sisters are doing it…From Fem FM to Viva! A history of women's radio stations in the UK', in Mitchell C. (ed.) (2001), *Women and radio*, London: Routledge.

Nye, S., Godwin, N., & Hollows, B. (1994) 'Twisting the dials: lesbians in British radio', in Gibbs. L. (ed.) *Daring to dissent: lesbian culture from margin to mainstream*, pp. 147–67, London: Cassell.

Peruzzo, C. M. K. (1996) 'Participation in community communication', in J. Servaes, T. Jacobson and S. A. White (eds), *Participatory communication for social change*, pp.13–25, London: Sage.

Riaño, P. (1994) *Women in grassroots communication – furthering social change*, London: Sage.

Scannell, P. (1996) *Radio, television and modern life – a phenomenological approach*, Oxford: Blackwell.

Steiner, L. (1992) 'The history and structure of women's alternative media', in L. Rakow. (ed.) *Women making meaning, new feminist directions in communications*, pp. 121–43, London: Routledge.

Suarez Toro, M. (1996) 'Feminist international radio endeavour', in R. Allen, D. Rush, and S.J. Kaufman (eds), *Women transforming communications*, pp. 226–32, London: Sage.

Tuchman, G. (1979) 'Women's depiction by the mass media', *Signs: Journal of Women in Culture and Society*, 3, 528–42.

van Zoonen, L. (1992) 'The women's movement and the media: constructing a public identity', *European Journal of Communication*, 7, 453–76.

van Zoonen, L. (1994) *Feminist media studies*, London: Sage.

Werden, F. (1996) 'The founding of WINGS – a story of feminist radio survival', in. D. Allen, R. Rush and S. J. Kaufman (eds), *Women transforming communications*, pp. 218–25. London: Sage

Woolf, N. (1993) *Fire with fire – new female power and how it will change the 21st century*, London: Chatto and Windus.

Part 3

Women working in radio

In this business, you have to think like a man, act like a woman, and work like a dog!

(Martha Jean Steinberg quoted in Barlow 1999: 153)

The context of gendered employment

Women have always worked in radio but they have been more visible in some areas than in others. In BBC radio in the 1920s and 1930s they mainly worked as entertainers and behind the scenes as secretaries. Some did work as producers, particularly in areas like Children's and Schools' radio. In the 1950s and 1960s there were a few women producers, unseen, unheard but quietly influencing BBC output. Dennis Gifford notes that for the fifties all-woman revue show *Ladies Please* '*even* the producer was a woman' (1985: 147 [my emphasis]). By 1971 33 per cent of radio producers at the BBC were female (Political and Economic Planning 1971: 167). Although briefly presented by a man, since 1946 *Woman's Hour* has been a haven and training ground for women presenters, producers and contributors.

In 1950 Mary Somerville became Controller of Talks at the BBC. However until Monica Sims' appointment as Controller of BBC Radio 4 in 1978, women were virtually absent from BBC management. In Chapter 16, Caroline Millington presents a positive and optimistic view of the way women are 'getting in and getting on' in the BBC as well as offering a critique of why they may not be represented in equal numbers with men in some areas.

The BBC started with an enlightened policy of equal pay and non-discrimination against married women (Political and Economic Planning 1971), however it seems that until the 1960s the BBC frowned upon women working after they married BBC employees and like many employers at that time it had an ambivalent attitude towards women working at all once they married (Shapley 1996). In Chapter 17 Stephen Wells tells the story of how Radio 1 presenter Janice Long was treated by BBC management when she had a baby and was prevented from returning to work six weeks after the birth. A decade later things had improved a bit for female presenters at the BBC. Jo Whiley is said to have organised the music tracks of her programme so that she could breast feed during the news break.[1]

There has been very little recent research[2] in Britain into employment conditions for women in the media industries.[3] In the Republic of Ireland the radio training and policy group Women On Air commissioned research into the independent radio industry. In Chapter 18 Maria Gibbons carefully takes us through the results of this research which highlight how women are still not getting radio jobs even when they have more training and qualifications than their male counterparts and how the new community radio sector is providing management opportunities for women.

Women working behind the mic

'Can you get a job as a DJ if you are a girl? . . . (G)enerally the profession does seem to be rather male dominated' (Rosco and Beerling 1976:103). So says that unreconstructed DJ, Emperor Rosco in his 'DJ Book'. When Radio 1 started in 1967 it recruited a line-up of male music presenters from the pirate stations, stating that men were symbolic 'husband substitutes' for women listening at home (Nightingale 1999).[4] As the BBC expanded to include local radio, male presenters dominated both the national and local airwaves. When the first commercial stations were established in the mid-seventies they also followed the well-established pattern of recruiting men to present music. In Chapter 19, Kim Michaels and I discuss the first piece of detailed British research about how women get into UK music radio. They reveal whether or not women are finally breaking into this 'last bastion' and making their mark as DJs.

Towards the end of the Second World War women were employed by the BBC General Overseas Service to read news bulletins and thereby boost the troops' morale (Barker 1999). Women however were not employed regularly as radio newsreaders until the late 1970s; until then their voices were not considered to be 'authoritative' enough (Ross 1977).[5] Since then they have progressed steadily in both commercial and radio news operations and their voices are no longer missing from news presentation and reporting and women editors have become less scarce. Women currently outnumber men in some radio journalism courses in Higher Education (Currie 2000). In Chapter 20, Janet Haworth looks at the gendering of radio news both in terms of the recent demography of the work force as well as the way that the news agenda has been feminised in response to notions of what the female audience wants from news. Tim Crook notes

> No modern radio journalist will survive in the twenty-first century without a full grounding and understanding of information technology, the power and research potential of the Internet and World Wide Web, and the application of digital systems to radio news text, production and transmission.
>
> (Crook 1998: 21)

In the light of this Haworth charts some of the recent changes in radio news working practices and discusses their implications for women entering and working in the industry of the twenty-first century.

New directions for women's work in radio

Increasingly the study of the theory and practice of radio is integrated within academic media courses which also have a strong vocational ethos. Doubtless many women who read this volume will be interested in working in radio. Women who enter the industry in the twenty-first century can expect a much wider range of jobs in comparison to the BBC that their sisters worked in, and will require very different knowledge and skills. There are now new areas of employment such as: bi media news, independent production, digital radio, Internet radio and multimedia production. The workforce is largely casualised: short term contracts are the rule rather than the exception in commercial radio. In Chapter 21, I introduce case studies of women working in a wide range of BBC, commercial and community radio roles including presentation, production, journalism, management, drama and commercial production. These personal narratives offer information, advice and 'coping mechanisms' designed to be critical and helpful to new entrants to radio.

Women have made their mark in all areas of radio and where once excluded they are now making inroads (although there are unfortunately still some dinosaurs around who believe that women and the technical side of radio do not mix). Anyone with a job in the media industries has to make careful decisions about working in an area with unsociable hours and an increasingly casualised workforce. Women and men with young families or other caring responsibilities still have to fight to maintain a balance of radio work and the rest of their lives. However the future for women in radio is bright – which can only be good for women – and radio.

Notes

1 Although this didn't stop male DJs like Chris Moyles making puerile remarks about her anatomy.
2 An exception is the Political and Economic Planning group's 1971 study of women at the BBC. This contains data drawn from interviews with 22 women and 11 men about BBC entrance procedures, training schemes, career development, 'closed' jobs for women (like engineering and management), reasons why it is difficult for women to move into senior jobs and how women managed working when they had children. It contains some fascinating material about attitudes towards women at the time, including describing the producer's role as a 'mid wife job' and commenting on how women were less tolerant of 'rules': 'I think women are more realistic – they look twice at protocol and see whether it's worth bothering about. I'm always breaking rules that the Administration dreams up. Women come across this protocol less in their formative years. Boy's schools have much more rigid strata. Men are very good at building structures around them – look at the trade unions' (205).
3 One of the only recent studies is Helen Baehr's (1996) comparative study of women in independent television production companies in Britain and the Netherlands.
4 Briggs (1995) says that there was one female disc jockey – Miranda Ward – in the original line up. This is misleading: she reported on music news rather than presenting her own programme.
5 The 1971 'Women in Top Jobs' report by the Political and Economic planning group stated 'Hard news gathering is considered to be a man's job . . . Women it appears are held by editors and producers to lack the qualifications, experience and interest in current affairs to be used in anything other than a fairly junior capacity' (1971: 186–7). Thanks to Dr. Fred Hunter for bringing this report to my attention.

References

Baehr, H. (1996) *Women in Television: A report on the position of women in the independent television sectors of two European Union member states: the United Kingdom and the Netherlands*, London: University of Westminster Press.

Barker, D. (1999) Obituary of Marjorie Anderson, *Guardian*, 18 December 1999.

Barlow, W (1999) *Voice Over: The Making of Black Radio*, Philadelphia: Temple University Press.

Crook, T. (1998) *International Radio Journalism*, London: Routledge.

Currie, J. (2000) 'Broadcast fails to pull the men', *Times Higher Education Supplement*, 5 May 2000: 3.

Gifford, D. (1985) *The Golden Age of Radio*, London: Batsford.

Political and Economic Planning (1971) *Women in Top Jobs*, London: Allen and Unwin.

Rosco, E. and Beerling, J. (1976) *Emperor Rosco's DJ Book*, London: Everest Books.

Ross, M. (1977) 'Radio' in M. Stott and J. King (eds) *Is This your life? Images of Women in the Mass Media*, London: Virago.

Shapley, O. (1996) *Broadcasting A Life*, London: Scarlett Press.

Further reading

Holman, K. and S. Ortiz, (1992) *Equal Opportunities for Short term Contract and Freelance Workers in Broadcasting*, Brussels: European Commission.

Gallagher, M. (1995) *Employment Patterns in European Broadcasting: Prospects for Equality in the 1990s*, Brussels: European Commission.

Goffee, R. and R. Scase, (1985) *Women in Charge: The Experiences of Female Entrepreneurs*, London: Allen and Unwin.

Chapter 16

Caroline Millington

GETTING IN AND GETTING ON: WOMEN AND RADIO MANAGEMENT AT THE BBC

Many years ago Sally Thompson, a BBC radio producer, dubbed the difference of approach between the sexes the Wow! factor. She had noted that women disadvantage their career development by responding to advancement with astonishment and pleasure:

'I've got into the BBC at last! Wow! I'm a producer! Wow!'

On the other hand, she saw that men don't waste time being pleased and amazed. They are much more likely to respond to employment or promotion by looking to their next step:

'Good, I'm a producer. Now, how do I get to be Director General?'

More recently, the BBC circulated an internal document about the conditions necessary to achieve creative and efficient working in the Corporation. The section on management and leadership began:

Women managers in the BBC (although the sample is small) are perceived as better than men at inspiring others, demonstrating personal integrity, providing opportunities for involvement and learning and being sensitive to others. We know from other research that effective managers of creative groups behave in this way, and it may also be true that women are less committed to the status quo.

(BBC 1996:24)

The report painted the following 'likely portrait of the successful team leader or manager in the BBC':

a woman, working in Network Radio or Regional Broadcasting, who has arrived at a managerial position through the technical area she now manages. Her first job, and her previous managers, have had a critical influence on how she now performs. She plays many different roles in the team, often 'giving away' responsibility and power to others in the team. However, there are some things which she, and she alone takes responsibility for: she protects the team from outside pressures, she puts a lot of effort into securing resources (people, time and money) for the team, she is ruthless with poor performance but warm, open, direct and sensitive. She puts things right when they go wrong, takes personal responsibility for 'cock-ups' and constantly seeks to improve the way things get done! She explains things to the team, puts their work in context, sorts out contracts and physical space, encourages personal development and still finds time for personal craft work of high value!

(BBC 1996: 30)

In 1996, women held a number of key management posts in BBC Network Radio. The Managing Director, Controller of Production and Head of Marketing were all women, as were two of the eight heads of production departments (the Head of Features, Arts and Science and the Head of Drama). The General Manager of the BBC Symphony Orchestra was a woman – the first to hold this post. The Controller (and founder) of Radio 5 Live was a woman, working in the BBC's News Directorate. The Deputy Managing Director of the World Service completed the set.

Although by no means in the majority, there were enough senior women working in BBC Radio to demonstrate that glass ceilings can be shattered, and that management cultures are not impossible to change.

Three years later, the picture was different, but still encouraging. In June 1996, the internal structure of the BBC was radically changed. BBC Broadcast (responsible for commissioning, scheduling, marketing, local radio and the Nations[1]) and BBC Production replaced Network Television and Network Radio. Very senior women managers did not always emerge as winners. But by the summer of 1999 Jenny Abramsky had become Director of Radio (although the five network controllers she inherited were all men). The production departments had become multimedia (making programmes for television, and providing content for online services, as well as continuing to make radio programmes), so direct comparisons for Radio-only staff before 1996 are impossible to make. The heads of the huge multimedia departments responsible for Music and Arts, Features and Events, Science, Education, Birmingham and Children's programmes were all women – six out of 15 programme heads. On the whole the people who head up the radio wings of these departments were men, although in the case of Drama and Music Entertainment, where the most senior multimedia managers are men, their radio leads were women.

The female presence at senior management levels may not yet be ideal, but it has improved enormously over the years. How have women in the BBC made the move into senior management, and how do they get on with it once they get there?

There have been three main factors: organisational will and planning; women's own determination to break through cultural and organisational barriers, and a female readiness and ability to cope with the management of change – something that has dominated the Corporation and the marketplace in which it operates for the past ten years.

One major organisational approach was to set employment targets, with dates, across the entire BBC. The figures are published each year in the BBC's Annual Report.

Table 16.1 Proportion of women in management

	31 March 1998	*31 March 1999*	Target for year 2000
Senior executives	29.1%	**30.8%**	30%
Senior managers	32.7%	**33.4%**	40%
Middle management and Senior professionals	36.3%	**37.5%**	40%

Source: BBC 1999a: 63

The Annual Report also gives a clear policy statement:

> Ethnic and gender targets have been set with the aim of ensuring that the BBC workforce reflects the UK nations we serve, and these are supported by a number of equal opportunity initiatives. The BBC has continued to make progress towards achieving these workforce composition targets.
>
> (BBC 1999a: 63)

Following the structural changes of 1996 it's not possible to break these figures down to isolate everyone working in Radio, but it is possible to identify the figures for the different BBC Directorates that may have Radio staff working in them. These indicate that the chances of a woman making it into senior management in the BBC are much higher in Production and Broadcast than in News, and at their lowest in Resources.

The 1999 figures show considerable progress for women in management in quite a short period. The same is not true for black and Asian staff, nor for people with disabilities.[2] The BBC is a founder member of the UK-wide *Opportunity Now* campaign.[3] Its annual benchmarking survey for the Information and Communication sector has measured significant improvement, moving the BBC from silver standard in 1998 to gold standard in 1999 (only platinum is higher). Joining Opportunity Now was seen as important within the BBC not only as a way to measure progress, but also as a means of getting commitment from senior managers to the targets that had been set in 1991. These were challenging.

In 1985 the BBC's Board of Management were all-male, there were no women Directors, and just one female Controller (the Controller of Education).

Table 16.2 Proportion of women in management: 31 March 1999
(numbers of staff in italics)

	Production	Broadcast	News	World Service	Resources
Senior executives	31.8% *85*	35.4% *164*	29.6% *98*	26.7% *30*	11.5% *52*
Senior managers	41.6% *305*	37.5% *251*	29.7% *364*	39.2% *97*	12.9% *132*
Middle managers and senior professionals	52.7% *833*	43.2% *1141*	43% *805*	34.9% *289*	16.1% *989*

Source: BBC 1999b

Table 16.3 Proportion of women in management, BBC 1985

	Total staff	Female
Senior executives	165	3.6%
Senior managers	263	10.3%
Senior middle managers	738	8.0%
Junior middle managers	3115	13.0%

Source: Sims 1985: 5

The most senior woman in BBC Radio fifteen years ago was Monica Sims, number two to the Managing Director. Her last job at the BBC before leaving it was to write an internal report for the Board of Governors. Its members were concerned that few women had become heads of department or controllers, even though women were entering the BBC's training schemes in greater numbers than ever before.

The Sims Report was wide-ranging and made 19 recommendations. It concluded pragmatically:

> It is in men's interests as well as women's to achieve a better balance of staffing at all levels in the BBC and to recognise women as equal colleagues. It is in women's interests to be prepared to take on management responsibilities, even where these do not appear to provide much job satisfaction, in order to achieve quality of life throughout all grades. . . . The BBC has a potent resource in its women staff who are ready to focus attention on their perceived lack of opportunities. Sensitive action by management could channel this vitality into support for the organisation and would reassure those women members of staff who are such effective advocates for the flourishing survival of public service broadcasting.

(Sims 1985: 37)

BBC management took action. Many of the Sims Report recommendations were implemented. One of them was that the numbers of women on Management Training Courses should be increased, and that some women should be sent on women-only courses.

In this spirit, in 1996 the BBC World Service launched a Women's Development Initiative – the WDI – for its female staff. Some 15 women were taken on, and the course proved so successful that another was run the next year. By 1998/9 Production and News had joined the WDI (now involving 36 young women a year), and the course for the years 2000/2001 was supported by four Directorates, Broadcast joining the other three.

The initiative was designed to help women compete effectively within the BBC on equal terms with men, as one way of increasing the proportion of women at senior grades. The 18 month course demands the involvement of line managers, and offers both management training and personal development to the participants. Liz Kennedy, one of the WDI's joint course directors, says the typical participant is:

> creative, quick to learn, possesses a high degree of autonomy, concerned about how she does things, as well as what she does, ambitious with an existing record of achievement and committed to women's development.
>
> *(Source: interview July 1999)*

The participants meet on a monthly basis, and are regularly addressed by senior women from inside and outside the BBC on current management issues, and on how the speakers themselves managed – or in many cases didn't manage – their own careers. There's no problem in attracting senior women to share their thoughts about leadership and managing change. During the 1998/9 scheme they included Jenny Abramsky (Director of Radio), Jana Bennett (Director of Programmes in Production), and Helen Boaden (then Head of Current Affairs, now Controller, Radio 4).

The course challenges the stereotype of an upwards career path as the only route to go. Speakers and participants identify a range of unconventional career models, involving movement across the organisation, between departments, and taking time out for caring responsibilities or to pursue a freelance career.

As an added support, participants are encouraged to find mentors – usually within the BBC – and the majority choose senior women managers, often outside the area in which they currently work.

The WDI is just one response to the current gender representation at senior management levels in the BBC. Not all the targets have been reached. The Women's Development Initiative helps participants, and others involved, to confront organisational cultural problems (the macho culture of News, for example – by no means exclusively a BBC phenomenon), and to debate the need for a culture shift in which leadership skills more commonly associated with women – listening, empathy and openness – are given equal value with their more traditional male counterparts.

The WDI, like the Sims Report before it, has to confront the fact that the BBC is still not a family-friendly organisation in terms of its hours and its culture. Broadcasting is a 24 hour a day, seven day a week industry, and this results in unsocial hours and work patterns. It is a problem facing parents of both sexes. But because it is still more usual for the woman to be responsible for the bulk of childcare and housekeeping, the greater stress is more likely to be felt by her. 'I have no problem being a woman in the BBC', one senior manager told the WDI, 'but I do have a problem being a mother'. Part-time working and job shares, as well as other options for flexible working hours and days, are encouraged. But there's no question that long working days, plus a culture that makes visibility in the workplace seem essential, make balancing the pressures of maternity and career a problem for senior and junior women alike.

The issue of childcare provision has proved problematic for the Corporation. After lobbying by staff and unions in the 1970s, limited workplace nursery provision was made available in some of the BBC centres. In terms of places provided, the BBC in 1998 was second only to the Midland Bank amongst UK employers. But with a workforce of 23,000, provision is expensive, small scale and patchy. Furthermore, some parents do not want to commute to the workplace with small children, they want childcare close to their homes. Others find that the problem is not with babies and toddlers, but with school-age children. They need childcare help between the end of the school and the working day.

By 1999 the solution was to give all employees access to *Family Life Solutions*. This five day a week, 12 hour a day help line is paid for by the Corporation, but made available without charge to staff. It offers good quality information about what facilities are available on a local or national basis for child care, elder care (increasingly recognised as another area of concern) and disability care, and will also advise on what is available from government and other agencies.

Just before the BBC's internal restructuring of 1996, a crude comparison between the number of senior women in BBC Radio, Television and News and Current Affairs showed that radio had the best of it (at the time women accounted for 64 per cent of all radio staff, at every level). Each of the three areas had a Managing Director – but Radio had the only woman. Television had two Channel Controllers, both men, whereas two of the five Radio Network Controllers were women, as were the Controller of Production and the Head of Marketing. At the programme department head level, Radio had two women out of eight, plus an orchestra general manager. Television had 20 programme heads, six of them women (although one had just announced she was leaving the BBC). News and Current Affairs had 12 people at this level – only one of them a woman.

An analysis of the way in which these senior women in Radio had reached their positions revealed no consistent pattern. The Managing Director was appointed from a background in Channel 4 Television and print journalism. The Controller of Radio 2 had joined the BBC as a secretary and worked her way up through production. The Controller of 5 Live had joined the BBC as a studio manager – as had the head of radio training, and Radio 4's managing editor. The Head of the Arts, Science and Features department joined the BBC in the first place as a newsroom sub (from an engineering background), and the Head of Drama had been recruited as a producer from the theatre. The Head of Marketing had come from advertising and independent television; the Controller of Production had been trained as a BBC journalist.

Most, but not all, of these women got their jobs through a system of competitive appointment. Only three of them had children. At least three were not graduates. Some were appointed to their senior jobs in their thirties, others in their mid to late fifties.

This snapshot reveals a lack of cloning. Each woman had a different background and brought with her something distinctive to the job. Seventy per cent had worked for the BBC for most of their working lives, despite the arrival of the 'contract culture'.[4] Many had therefore been the beneficiaries of the BBC's internal training provision, and of its attachment system.

'Attachments' are the BBC's internal secondments, which enable staff to spend six months or longer with another department doing another job, without prejudicing the security of the job back at base. For example, as the Controller of Production for Network Radio in 1994 I had worked on attachment over the years as a reporter and producer for BBC Television in London and Manchester, as a trainer for News and Current Affairs, and as an internal civil servant for a member of the Board of Management, as well as in my substantive jobs as a producer and manager for BBC Radio. I had also received training from the BBC, both at point of entry (as a trainee journalist), and subsequently in craft and management skills, both inside and outside the Corporation.

Institutional advantages such as these are significant for those women ready to make use of them, not only in providing a more attractive c.v., but also by introducing them to a wide range of people in the organisation. This can be invaluable in boosting confidence that might have been dented or undermined by local management or colleagues, and in developing a wide network of contacts and friends. There is a perceptible solidarity amongst many (although not all) women in the BBC. It is not a surprise that despite remorseless workloads, senior women make time to help their junior female colleagues, letting new generations of women benefit from what they have had to learn for themselves. It is generally acknowledged that women network more readily and naturally than men. Within the BBC these informal networks are extensive and often long-lasting.

In 1999 the Director of Education, Jane Drabble, left the BBC after more than thirty years. Her first job had been as a radio studio manager, and her early years had been spent as a producer of radio current affairs programmes. One of the less formal farewell parties thrown for her was a dinner, arranged by a dozen senior women managers, in gratitude for what she had achieved for other women in the BBC. She had, for example, encouraged one pregnant woman to go ahead and apply for a senior job (to which she was subsequently appointed). She had supported flexible working of all kinds. She had been a role model. The dinner was in recognition of the fact that she had demonstrated it was possible to challenge and change the culture of the organisation.

Women seem more ready than men to question fundamental assumptions about the way in which the business is run, and the way its employees behave. There are two reasons for this. Women are not as likely as men to be full – or even honorary – members of what has been, until very recently, the overwhelmingly male club running things. At its simplest, if you are a woman in the BBC there is no cultural expectation that you will wear a suit and tie. An immediate liberation. (A former Managing Director of Network Radio held regular informal lunches for his senior managers at a nearby dining club. An overwhelmingly male environment, the dining area was surrounded by enormous blown-up photos of men playing rugby. Giant thighs loomed over the tables. On one occasion, when the MD was lunching three female heads of department, the owner of the club came over and asked them if they were the Managing Director's personal assistants. Those days are gone, but this event took place less than ten years ago.)

Just as the club uniform does not apply to women, there is no expectation that behaviour generally will conform to the club norms. Women are in the strong position of being expected to behave differently. In practice, this means that if the cultural norm for a manager has been secrecy, and not to admit fault or mistakes, then it is easier for women to begin to shift that culture into one which is more open and less defensive. A culture in which the phrase 'I don't know' is seen as a positive and confident statement, rather than revealing weakness or indecision.

The other strong foundation for individuality and independent thinking is maternity. Although it can be a barrier to the kind of life currently demanded of a senior manager, motherhood can also be a strong motivator in changing organisational custom and practice. Working mothers have overpowering reasons to want to change the balance of time spent in the workplace and at home. Despite covert criticism of their strict time keeping from fellow staff (men and women alike), the strength of the desire to spend time with their children makes it imperative to overcome these unspoken pressures. Managing time well is a challenge for all senior managers. The presence of working mothers who manage to do this well educates every manager they work with, introducing men and women alike to more efficient and sensible ways of working.

At the end of the so-called swinging sixties, thirty years ago, there were no senior women in the BBC. None on the Board of Management, none running Radio, no women Editors in News and Current Affairs. Women engineers were not allowed to wear trousers to work. Part-time women workers were not allowed to be members of BBC staff – they had to switch to short-term contracts – and they were barred from membership of the BBC pension scheme. There were no women newsreaders on Radio 4 because the head of presentation argued that if they were introduced listeners would turn off. 'Particularly women listeners', I remember him saying unrepentantly to both male and female colleagues. The one woman who was held up as evidence that women could make it in the BBC was Grace Wyndham Goldie – she had worked in Television, not Radio, and had retired in the mid 1960s.

If matters have changed for the better in the last 15 years, then they have changed beyond belief in twice that time. But although a genuine organisational lead, in parallel with changes in society at large, has led to a significant increase in the numbers of senior women in the BBC, it has not yet managed to change every attitude, nor all behaviour. And the Corporation has yet to appoint its first female Director General.

Women at all levels, in Radio as in Television, can find their self-confidence surprisingly shaken by the patronising behaviour of a few male colleagues. A casually dismissive remark can prick the bubble of achievement that many senior women quite rightly inhabit.

That's one of the reasons why the women who have made it have not, on the whole, emulated their male bosses and colleagues. Instead they have taken risks, been daring and behaved idiosyncratically – as individuals – rather than following tried and tested career paths designed by generations of men. They have been prepared to be bold; they've stuck their heads above the parapet. And when a sniper's remark has injured them, they have demonstrated their emotional resilience (as necessary as the physical stamina demanded by long days and weeks), brushed themselves down and gone on to prove that they can engineer and cope with change successfully just because they have dared to lead it.

As the critical mass of women at senior levels grows, it is likely that new ways of working and some new corporate values can be introduced that will liberate everyone, men and women alike. There needs to be a shift to valuing the outcome of the work rather than putting all the weight on the way in which it is organised and approached. It may challenge the organisational norm to suggest that it is possible to run an efficient, effective and fully accountable organisation without spending time in long meetings, or writing lengthy position papers. But if it can be demonstrated that schedules can be managed and good programmes made in a variety of less traditional ways by staff who are, as a result, less stressed, less exhausted and more productive, which man or woman is going to argue with this improvement to their lives?

Radio throughout the world is truest to the medium when it is intimate, revealing and passionate – all female characteristics, although not exclusively so. Women in radio management should celebrate these characteristics by showing in the way they run and organise their part of the broadcasting world that they believe in the value of diversity, and are fully committed to delivering it. It is a fully diverse workforce, at all levels, that will provide the best range of quality programmes for an increasingly demanding public.[5]

The majority of the population, and the majority of those who listen to radio is, after all, female.

Notes

1 Nations refers to the broadcasting output of BBC Scotland, N. Ireland and Wales.
2 The BBC also has employment initiatives for ethnic minorities and for people with disabilities. These began later than the gender awareness activities. The Corporation keeps data for the three main groups separately (although clearly for some individuals

there may be some overlap), since the core root of any discrimination is different in each case

3   *Opportunity Now* is a national campaign. It was launched as *Opportunity 2000* in 1991 by the UK not-for-profit organisation *Business in the Community*, and was designed to promote the commercial benefits of women in the workforce. As a first step, the 350 member organisations (including the BBC) voluntarily set their own goals for increasing opportunities for women in the workforce by the year 2000.

4   The BBC has a reputation for casualisation of employment. However, in 1999, 80 per cent of all staff are on continuing contracts. The average of 20 per cent fixed term contracts rises to just under 40 per cent in production areas, where the project nature of some programme genres (in particular Television Drama and Entertainment) leads to industry-wide fixed term contracts. But in Production there is no statistical difference between the numbers of men and women on fixed-term contracts. The picture is different in other broadcasting organisations

5   A Diversity Database was set up within the BBC in 1998, to help journalists and programme makers reflect the full diversity of the UK population in its output. Contacts on the database include experts, individuals and organisations with either a minority or specialist interest in mainstream issues, or expertise in a minority area. Categories covered include: ethnic minorities, women, people with disabilities, older people (especially women), lesbians and gay men.

References

British Broadcasting Corporation (1996) The Necessary Conditions for Creative and Efficient Working at the BBC, Organisation and Management Development. Internal document, London: BBC.

BBC (1999a) BBC Annual Report and Accounts 1998/9, London: BBC

BBC (1999b) Corporate HR Planning (internal report) London: BBC.

Sims, M. (1985) "Women in BBC Management", BBC Internal Report, London: BBC.

Chapter 17

Stephen Wells

THE LONG GOODBYE

From: Wells, S. (1988) 'The long goodbye', *New Musical Express* 23/4/88, p. 19

I don't know if you know this, but when you're a woman and you have a baby, your brain comes out with the afterbirth and you suddenly can't think.

I still can't believe that on one television programme I did I was told to cover up my lump and could I stand at an angle because it looked disgusting. I am not a different person. . . . I haven't lost my capabilities. For God's sake, this is 1988!

There's a buzz going around Commonwealth House. So cool is this, the throbbing heart of London's rock media, that visits by mega-stars are usually studiously ignored. Today's guest is different. With her rugged toy-boy and pink bairn in tow, Janice Long is surrounded by eager hacks, like worker bees flocking to worship their queen.

Janice hosted the only four days a week show on Britain's only national pop station that dared to feature rap and indie bands. She has been the voice of the cutting edge of pop. Then she decided to have a baby. Rumours flew – Janice was for the chop? The *NME*, as usual, was first with the story. Contacts at the BBC suddenly started talking in whispers.

Christ! How did you know that?

'I was asked before I had Fred, I was about six or seven months pregnant, what I wanted to do. I said I wanted to return to work six weeks after he was born and I was told that I must have four months off, I thought that was a bit excessive but I was told that I would probably get post-natal depression and would want to breast feed and how could I possibly want to return to work?

'Then I got a letter – you're probably wonder[ing] where your broadcasting career is going, you will not be returning to your evening show because under Simon Mayo it's taken a new direction . . . They asked me whether I could be a Mum and fit it in with doing a half hour on Sunday.'

Bland ahoy

Everybody in the media, other than mercenary Tory skunks, is worried about the way the wind's blowing. Thatcher may not yet have ushered in a Victorian era but the steady erosion of 'controversial' journalism and broadcasting is seen by many as a return to the 'respectful' 1950s. For pop this means the axing of *The Tube* and *The Whistle Test* - programmes that looked outside the charts.

The 'current affairs' section of the *Janice Long Show* annoyed all the right people.

'After the first programme on AIDS it was about the same time that Anderton made his "cess-pit" speech – I was asked at a press conference what I thought of Anderton and I said that I found him totally unchristian. The next day I was inundated with mail from people telling me that I was leading people astray and I was encouraging people to have sex.

'A guy phoned – "It's about her outspoken remarks about James Anderton. How dare somebody who is barely out of nappies criticise the chief constable of Manchester. I hope she gets AIDS! . . ." and hung up.

'I dedicated "Really Stupid" by The Primitives to Edwina Curry after she said that really stupid thing about people in Northern Ireland eating pie and chips. I said she should concentrate on the NHS and allocate more to buying kidney machines. I was pulled in for that.'

A recent *World in Action* traced the increasing sheepishness of the BBC back to the appointment of reactionary right wing stooges to the Board of Governors. Whilst avoiding a conspiracy theory, their governships are doubtless far more comfortable with the mindless but often racist and sexist 'humour' of the daytime jocks than they ever were with Janice's too-human face.

Thus far, an impartial BBC mole tells us, there has been no pressure on replacement DJ Simon Mayo (27) to drop the politics. Mayo, however, is far more in the mould of the traditional 'balanced' (sic) BBC Presenter that Janice ever was. Mayo was being groomed for the nauseatingly zany *Morning Show*. He was hardly likely to rock the boat.

Nor, says my mole, has the producer Phil Ross – mainly responsible for the show's musical content – yet been given the push. Mayo himself is allegedly 'a massive punk rock fan'.

Janice is certain that the show is still beyond the ken of most people at Radio One.

'What makes me cross is I was watching *TOTP* last week and somebody said – here's a group, The Primitives, that we've been going with for ages . . . And I thought, Hang on, no you haven't, *I've* been going with them for ages. Peelies' been playing them for ages and all of a sudden it's like, here's a new band, come out of nowhere! "That Morrissey chap - he's done awfully well" – somebody at Radio One actually said to me the other week.'

'I think there's an awful lot of people who assume that night-time radio is weird. Night-time radio is actually listened to, it's not just there in the background. The people tune in because they want to hear what's happening, because they want to know if The Primitives have got a new single out, they want to know if gigs are taking place, they want to know what Morrissey's got to say.

'The audience is a lot more intelligent that the daytime audience. That was proved by a survey that we did, we found out that they wanted an element of current affairs, they wanted interviews with bands. The favourite feature was one where I spent an evening on the streets with homeless kids. They wanted to know about South Africa, they read the *Daily Mirror* and they read the *Guardian* and their ages range from 14 to 25.'

'Arrgh! An entire generation weened off taped-up tits, furry dice and Government lies! But even if the format of the show isn't altered, there still remains the attitude of Radio One Controller, Jonathan 'Johnny' Beerling.

'Er um, everybody here thinks he's behaved extremely badly.' squeaked my mole.

DJ wanted: must be a prick

There are over 25 Radio One DJs. Only six are women. Of the 135 hours Radio One is on the air every week, only five are broadcast by women.

Is the station sexist?

'They will say to you that women don't go down well with the audience. Johnny Beerling said that. . . .' claims Janice.

How many of the management at Radio One are women?

'None.'

Doesn't that strike you as absurd?

'Of course it does. But there's this myth, isn't there, that women aren't interested in music. . . . Someone at Radio One came up to me and asked me if I had any real interest in music. I mean what can you say? Can you believe that?

Does being a parent stop you being able to DJ?

'You should ask Steve Wright or John Peel that. I don't think they had any problems. The thing is that they can do what they want because we're all on three month contracts. I'm damn sure the same thing wouldn't happen to a man. . . .'

'I have raised this point and I was told I was being cared for . . .'

Radio One seems to pull its DJs from a bottomless pit of Steves and Garys

'That's true, but there's a massive audience for that isn't there?'

What do you think inspires Radio One's Blandkrieg other that a total lack of taste?

'Figures, I suppose. Going for the lowest common denominator.'

If I ruled the world

If Janice hasn't been plucked out of the way in preparation for a further bland out, then Johnny Beerling's letter must have been telling the truth. She was sacked because it wasn't felt proper for a mum to have a full time job.

The BBC's liberal veneer has been badly scratched. The present atmosphere, with the Alton Bill and Clause 29 festering in the background, has seen a number of spineless functionaries drop the liberal facade they've always been uncomfortable with and come out as the reactionaries they are.

What would you do if you were controller of Radio One?

'I'd fight to broadcast 24 hours a day. I think it's a myth that people are only into pop music. I think you can do a lot more. What's wrong with putting a really good play on? What's wrong with putting comedy on the radio? What's wrong with current affairs, what's wrong with phone-ins? I would scrap the pigeon-holing. I would not have a reggae programme or a heavy metal programme.

'Why can't you have programming that has a hip-hop record next to a heavy metal record net to a Smiths record next to Kylie Minogue? I think at the moment people don't get to hear this stuff so they assume it's going to be weird and offensive but it's not, it's all pop music in the end. I'd take more risks with presenters, I'd have more individuals, more accents . . .'

Are you going to miss doing the show?

'For me it wasn't just one huge ego trip. I felt there was a point at the end of it. That somebody else was going to get something out of it, whether it was Fred Bloggs listening at home who would hear stuff that he wouldn't normally hear because I was the only person playing these little jangly guitar indie bands or for these bands because I'd played a record or a tape or gone to a gig and they'd done a session and perhaps got a recording contract at the end of it.

'Then there was a speech element. You always got a stack of mail after, thousands upon thousands of letters, you could have carried on making programme after programme about the subject. It wasn't just me sat there thinking *Hooray*! I'm a really brilliant DJ and aren't I wonderful . . . and what was the question?'

Janice has already turned down the offer of Radio One's half hour Pick of the Week spot. As yet no major acne cream manufacturers have beaten a path to her door.

Chapter 18

Maria Gibbons

THE NATURE OF GLASS: PARTICIPATION OF WOMEN IN THE IRISH INDEPENDENT RADIO INDUSTRY

Introduction

Like its counterparts elsewhere, the Irish radio industry[1] employs many women. There are prominent and respected women fronting programmes, and making important background decisions in production and in management. Also like its counterparts elsewhere however, the mere presence of women has been used as an argument to suggest that all is well with regards to the female/male balance in the workforce. In point of fact, Ireland is no different from most other European countries in that there are less women than men working in the industry overall, particularly in the higher echelons of influence and responsibility. In addition, women and men tend to be segregated into different types of jobs. This situation has persisted throughout the media industry world-wide despite legislative and apparent attitudinal changes in many countries (van Zoonen 1994). Arriving in the new millennium it is pertinent to question yet again both why and how women are largely excluded from certain positions – in other words, to re-examine the operation of the 'glass walls' and the 'glass ceilings', the invisible barriers to women's progress in this and many other industries.

This chapter will report on the main findings of 'Breaking Glass Walls',[2] a study on gender and employment carried out on the independent Irish radio industry in 1997 (Nexus and Gibbons 1998), which illustrates the complexity of the mechanisms involved, and the challenge facing those attempting to effect a real change in gender relations in the workplace.

Employment patterns: the wider picture

Although the proportion of women in paid work is increasing all across Europe, men still make up most of the general workforce. In Ireland, just about 40 per cent of all employment is now taken up by women (Ruane and Sutherland 1999) and figures are similar across the film and TV production sectors (STATCOM/FAS 1995; RTE 1998; IBEC 1999).

Coincidentally, many of the newly-emerging jobs provide non-standard employment such as contract or part-time work, and women tend to predominate in these, leading to the so-called 'feminisation' of the general labour market. In RTE, for example, women presently constitute only 29 per cent of 'permanent and pensionable' employees, but 58 per cent of 'other', i.e. less privileged, staff (RTE 1998). This pattern is widely repeated across European broadcasting organisations (de Graef 1997).

There are some areas of the media industry that have become more accessible to women. In the US and many other countries, women are now prominent in journalism (Beasley 1989), and there are certain other media jobs such as researcher where women often predominate. (In RTE, women made up 78 per cent of researchers in 1998, compared to 33 per cent in 1981). This phenomenon has given rise to the risible terms 'velvet ghetto' and 'pink collar', and has even generated some concern about the so-called 'gender switch'. Perhaps it is more relevant to query why some areas provide more opportunities for women than others, particularly since it appears that the relative status of the particular medium or job is pertinent. In Ireland, for example, only 25 per cent of RTE television programming staff is female, compared to 48 per cent of its radio programming staff (data from Personnel Dept., RTE 1997). On the other hand, in countries where it remains the primary broadcasting medium, radio still tends to be dominated by men (van Zoonen 1994).

There are two further characteristics of gender-related employment patterns – horizontal and vertical segregation – that commonly occur in the general labour market including the media industries (Gallagher 1996). Horizontal segregation occurs where women and men largely occupy different types of jobs, and vertical segregation where women and men are located at different hierarchical levels of an organisation. Across the board in the media industries generally, men are over-represented in the technical and top management sectors, while women dominate the general administration and production support grades. In the UK, for instance, Skillset has reported that two-thirds of the production workforce in the independent radio sector, three-quarters of the technical and presenter/reporter grades, and almost two-thirds of producers, are men (Woolf and Holly 1994). The Irish audio-visual industry appears to be no different (STATCOM/FAS 1995; RTE 1998; IBEC 1999).

Finally, in addition to being consistently under-represented at senior management level, it appears that female employees tend to get paid less than their male counterparts for the same work, even after controlling for other pertinent factors such as relative experience (Lafky 1989; Abrahamson 1990).

'Breaking Glass Walls' report: the main findings[3]

The study revealed clear evidence that practically all of the common patterns of gender segregation were prevalent in the workforce of independent radio in Ireland in 1997.[4]

Job categories

Women were distinctly under-represented at the top decision-making levels particularly in commercial radio, where only 14 per cent of the members of boards of management were female. While 41 per cent of all paid employees in this sector were women, only 5 per cent of top executives and 39 per cent of middle management were female. In contrast, women made up 77 per cent of the general administration and sales staff.

In community radio, relatively more women worked in the sector overall (women made up 52 per cent of paid staff), and women had achieved better representation at senior levels where 70 per cent of management/administrative staff were female. In addition, 40 per cent of the members of boards of management were women, though this figure was obviously influenced by the imposition of a 40 per cent gender quota on boards of management in community stations by the IRTC.

It is useful for the purposes of this analysis to identify two separate areas of work in the independent radio sector – radio-specific posts which refer to jobs directly involved in programme-making i.e. presentation/DJ, programme production, programme management, executives and technical staff – and administration/sales posts. In both commercial and community radio, women tended to occupy different jobs to men, with women being more numerically prominent in administration/sales, and men more prominent in radio-specific work. Consequently, while 41 per cent of all employees in commercial radio were women, only 26 per cent of programme-making staff were female. Similarly, women made up 52 per cent of the total staff in community radio, but only 33 per cent of programming/technical employees (figures 18.1 and 18.2).

Within the programme-making area itself, men predominated overwhelmingly in the frontline positions of presentation/DJ (constituting 82 per cent of presenters in commercial radio for instance) and in technical areas (men made up 93 per cent of the technical staff in commercial radio, and 77 per cent in community radio), while women predominated in production support roles (85 per cent of researchers in commercial radio were women).

Job status

Most employees in independent radio in Ireland had part-time status in 1997 and, in general, income levels in the industry were relatively low.

In commercial radio more women than men had part-time status (79 per cent compared to 72 per cent) and women overall earned less than men overall (only

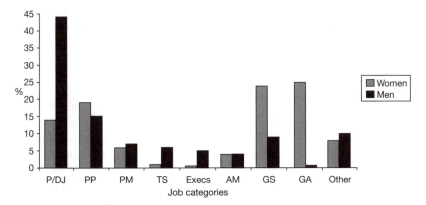

Figure 18.1 Commercial stations – percentages of women and men in different job categories

Key: P/DJ: presenters/DJs; PP: programme production; PM: programme management; TS: technical staff; Execs: executives; AM: administration management; GS: general sales; GA: general administration

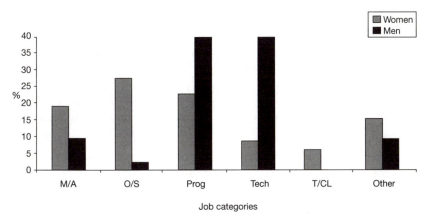

Figure 18.2 Community stations – percentage of women and men in different job categories

Key: MA: management/administration; O/S: office/secretarial; Prog: programming; Tech: technical; T/CL: training/community liaison

5 per cent of the former earned IR£25,000 or more compared to 12 per cent of the latter). While nearly three quarters of all employees earned a gross annual income of less than IR£14,000, women working in administration/sales earned less than both women and men in radio-specific posts (while only 29 per cent of the former earned IR£14,000 or more, 47 per cent of female and 51 per cent of male programme-makers did so). In community radio, similar trends were apparent.

It is unclear from the data whether women were in fact paid less than men for the same work, since other factors such as age, experience and the gendered segregation of jobs also influence income levels.

Staff age and dependants

Independent radio in Ireland employed a youthful staff in 1997, with half of all workers still in their twenties. Female employees in general were younger than males (55 per cent of females were in their twenties compared to 42 per cent of males).

In commercial radio fewer women than men had dependent children aged under sixteen years, and this was particularly so among programme-making staff (where only 14 per cent of women had dependants compared to 32 per cent of their male counterparts). In contrast, more women than men had dependent children in community radio.

Staff education and training

Most paid staff working in the independent radio sector in Ireland in 1997 had obtained the secondary school Leaving Certificate, while about half had acquired higher qualifications, with more women than men doing so. This was particularly the case amongst programme-making staff in the commercial radio sector, where women on the whole had much higher educational qualifications than men. For instance, 82 per cent of these women had a third-level qualification compared to 42 per cent of their male equivalents.

There is a similar gender-related pattern evident in relation to training. For instance, 45 per cent of female programme-making staff in commercial radio compared to 22 per cent of their male counterparts had undertaken training in the preceding 12 months.

Staff skills and experience

In general, a high proportion of employees in independent radio had been in their current job for a relatively short period of time, suggesting an expanding industry and/or a high staff turnover.

In commercial radio, all the indicators suggest that female staff had less accumulated experience of working in the industry than their male counterparts. For instance, women in general had been in their jobs for a shorter period of time than men – 33 per cent of women and 21 per cent of men had been in their current jobs for less than a year. Although women programme-makers had more experience of the industry than other women staff, they still had less experience than male programme-makers. This is also reflected in the fact that less women than men claimed to have acquired skills in the programme-making areas (see table 18.1). These trends may arise in totality because women were younger and/or left their posts earlier than men, particularly those women working in administration/sales posts.

Table 18.1 Proportion of women and of men holding selected programme-making jobs, together with the proportions of each claiming relevant skills or experience (commercial radio)

Job Category	Women *Current Job*	Women *Skills/Experience*	Men *Current Job*	Men *Skills/Experience*
	(%)	(%)	(%)	(%)
Presenter/DJs	1	21	24	65
Researchers	4	48	1	44
Producers	5	25	15	50
Managers	16	18	31	32
Technicians	0	13	3	24
Journalists	9	23	12	35

A closer look at table 18.1 reveals that women appear to have been disproportionately excluded from some areas of programme-making and disproportionately clustered into others, irrespective of their relative skill/experience levels. Consider, for example, the job of presenter/DJ, where the highest proportion of male staff were located in 1997. While 24 per cent of male employee respondents worked mainly in presentation, 65 per cent claimed to have had some skills in this area. So, there was one male working in this area for every 3 male employees with relevant skills. By contrast, there was only one woman respondent working as a presenter/DJ for every 21 women with relevant skills. In other words, there were proportionately less women than men with relevant skills getting jobs as presenters/DJs. Why might this have been the case? The situation was similar with regard to technical and production work, whereas in research, where women predominated, there were proportionately more women than men with relevant skills acquiring jobs. These data suggest that there were pressures operating in some job categories, other than a relative lack of appropriate skills or experience, which served to exclude or include on a gender basis.

Employees in community radio were in general less experienced than those in commercial radio, but there were no striking gender differences apparent. For instance, about one half of all employees had been in their current job for less than a year, 43 per cent of women and 50 per cent of men.

Staff recruitment and career advancement

Informal recruitment practices and informal networking are characteristics of the traditional 'old boy' system. In both radio sectors the most common route into employment was by informal means. In commercial radio, informal contact was particularly associated with the acquisition of programme-making work for both women and men (73 per cent came into their first job this way), while formal contact, i.e. job advertisements, was more associated with the recruitment of administration/sales staff (27 per cent acquired their first post in this manner). Also, it would appear that even though equal numbers of women and men worked as volunteers in the commercial sector, more of those men than women obtained paid employment in radio subsequently (17 per cent of men compared to 5 per cent of women were volunteers prior to their first paid radio job).

In both sectors, pirate radio was a more important route into radio employment for men than for women (figure 18.3). Although community radio was still relatively new in 1997, it appears to have been a more common entry point for women in both sectors.

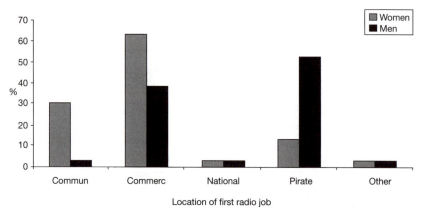

Figure 18.3 Routes into radio employment – location of first radio job of commerical radio employees (who are not currently in their first radio job)

Key: Commun: Community radio; Commerc: Commerical radio

Most of those working in programme-making in commercial radio and the majority of staff in community radio, declared that they had had some difficulty in obtaining employment or advancing their career in the business. In commercial radio, the biggest problems for women were 'lack of contacts' (particularly for women programme-makers – 32 per cent of those who did have difficulties) and 'problems in moving from job to job within a station' (especially for women in administration/sales work – 25 per cent). These, on the other hand, were not major difficulties for male employees.

The findings reflect the difficulties that women in the programme-making area had with the networking system and the informal recruitment procedures which operated in commercial radio, and that women in administration/sales had in moving upwards in the hierarchy or sideways into programme-making.

In community radio, the biggest problems encountered by both sexes were 'lack of contacts' (43 per cent of those who declared that they had difficulties) followed by 'few local jobs' (40 per cent).

Discussion of findings

Gendered segregation in the workplace

The Irish independent radio sector exhibits many of the employment patterns previously identified both nationally and internationally – they are structured significantly in a gendered way. Although there are some notable differences between the community and commercial sectors, men are generally predominant in the industry, and female and male employees tend to be clustered vertically (i.e. at different hierarchical levels) and horizontally (i.e. in different types of jobs) in the workforce.

Vertical segregation is a particular feature of commercial radio. In the community sector, women's overall participation is higher, and women are better represented at board and management levels. The introduction of a 40 per cent gender quota on the boards of management and a greater concentration on training, together with the more participative pervading ethos, would seem to have influenced women's representation in this sector.

Horizontal segregation is a feature of the whole industry. Male employees are almost exclusively working in programme-making while women staff work both in programme-making and in general administration/sales. There is in effect one cohort of men (programme-makers) and two cohorts of women (administrative staff and programme-makers) apparent amongst the staff. Particularly in commercial radio, there is in some ways as much or even more difference between the two cohorts of women as there are between female and male programme-makers. Presumably this is reflective of the different career choices being made by women in the workplace.

Women employed in radio sales and office work

Long and unpredictable work hours are part of the professional practice of radio production – it would appear that many of the women working in general administration and sales ('traditional' female posts) have prioritised a job with regular hours and less demands, which allows them to meet outside needs and responsibilities.

> I would hate to be in a position where my job was taking over my life and my family had to suffer; and that's the way I feel if you're very career-minded and looking for promotion; that's the pattern your life automatically takes.
>
> (female salesperson)

As a result, and not unexpectedly, women in these jobs tend to have more child dependants, lower incomes, less experience of working in radio and less ambition to move on from their station, than do their sisters working on the far side of the wall in programme-making.

Many of these women also expressed relative satisfaction with their jobs.

However, it appears that some, at least, would wish to move sideways into programme-making, but find it difficult to do so, encountering resistance from management in the process:

> Yes, I would have an interest, but the problem is when you're in a permanent job in the structure, its difficult. Unless you go to your employer and give your notice and leave; then go into another area which is difficult. It's almost easier to come from outside.
>
> (female salesperson)

Other women quoted a personal lack of confidence in making the move:

> I would like the area of production too, but I couldn't see myself in production at the same time . . . I wouldn't be confident enough to venture into that area.
>
> (female administrator)

Women employed in programme making

While there are practically no men to be found in general office/secretarial work, they predominate in the programme-making areas. Here both women and men tend to be recruited informally, and are more ambitious in terms of career progression than staff working in general administration/sales. However, there are significant and telling differences between female and male programme-makers too. Women are on the whole younger than their male counterparts, they have far less child dependants, and have achieved far higher educational and training attainments. Women, it seems, are obliged to maximise their educational and training opportunities, and perhaps to minimise their dependants, in order to acquire and maintain jobs in programme-making. These findings reflect the extra pressures bearing on those women attempting to forge a non-traditional radio 'career' with its demanding work hours.

In interviews with station staff and management various reasons were put forward to explain these trends, particularly the lack of women on-air. While undoubtedly containing elements of truth, many of these explanations notably relieved the stations themselves from any responsibility for the unbalanced state of affairs in their workforce. For instance:

> There is a need for female voices but we don't get the level of interest from females in terms of these positions. Historically it was seen as a man's job and now it's changing . . . we have no preference for males over females.
>
> (male station manager)

> With the men they would have done mobile discos, DJs, and that is great experience and that is still relevant. The path from pirate radio was almost all men.
>
> (male station manager)

Women might be just slow to get into radio. Maybe it's the technology thing; they feel they can't handle it . . . it's the man's world.

(female journalist)

I think it's confidence mainly . . . X presents an afternoon programme between 1.30 and 3.30pm, it's news, current affairs, socially oriented, and she is very good; but then if I say to someone like X to present a main news and current affairs programme she doesn't want to. She doesn't feel that she is up to the standard.

(male station manager)

It's the whole culture of the talk shows in RTE always being dominated by males and the fact that maybe management may not want to take a leap or listeners maybe wouldn't like to switch to women.

(female head of news)

This sort of reasoning, whereby the stations themselves tend to be excused from any responsibility, is particularly common amongst station management and has previously been described in British radio by Gill (1993). Some ideas, such as the notion of the listenership preferring male voices, are without any basis in the research literature (Baehr and Ryan 1984).

Among the more realistic explanations, supported by the present data and certainly more challenging to the stations, are the following:

It is a very demanding job, any part of it, so obviously if you are married with children it would present a problem as it's not the type of job that you can plan when you get home in the evenings . . . when people employ women, they think that to themselves she will get married and have kids and leave.

(female head of news)

I do see it as being male orientated in programming and management . . . the directors on the board are all male and it tends to be a kind of buddy system.

(female salesperson)

The finding that women appear to be disproportionately excluded from some areas of programming such as frontline presentation, and disproportionately clustered into others such as research, also points to underlying factors operating to pressurise women in programme-making, and to direct both women and men into different areas. It is not simply a case of women not having the appropriate skills or experience, there are matters of self-confidence, of expectations and attitudes around the roles of women, from both employers and women themselves. The research study also suggests that the historical development of commercial radio from the pirates and the prevalence of informal recruitment practices (both contributing to the 'old boy' network) are factors which may facilitate the ongoing progression of men, at the expense of women, into the programme-making aspects of the commercial radio industry.

Community radio

Patterns are less distinct in community radio, and there are fewer contrasting differences in the profiles of female and male staff. The community sector is much smaller than the commercial radio industry in Ireland, and evolved out of the community development tradition where women are more prominent. This is likely to have contributed to a greater consciousness of gender inclusivity here. It is worth noting, however, that while women are well represented at senior decision-making levels in the sector, yet horizontal segregation is still prevalent where women generally tend to work in administration while men are engaged in programme-making and technical work.

Conclusions

It is now widely accepted that there are a whole range of interacting factors impeding women in the workplace generally. Among those factors are the following: work structures (recruitment procedures, organisation of work hours, informal networking, lack of childcare facilities); training (lack of technical skills, lack of confidence); prejudicial expectations and attitudes, and lack of role models. Significant and prolonged breakthroughs in participation by women will only be attained by analysing and tackling the complex web of factors underlying the process of exclusion, and by adopting strategies of redress that take this complexity into account.

Women On Air, the organisation that commissioned the research, endeavoured to utilise the findings to inform its ongoing work in promoting women's participation in the sector. To this end, Women On Air developed a multi-faceted training programme which, given the short lifespan of the organisation and the apparent difficulties facing female employees, began to focus more than previously on women already working within the industry. Training courses on specific areas where women were under-represented such as DJ and technical work were instigated, along with courses addressing non-radio issues such as personnel and financial management. These courses were designed to increase the skill levels of participants and to encourage the career advancement of middle-management women. Conscious of the finding that female employees did not lack in training generally, Women On Air consulted closely with them in devising and running these programmes, in order to maximise their usefulness for participants in the long term. Women were employed as trainers to provide role models, and most training was carried out in-house within stations so that station management became more directly involved in the process of female staff development.

Because some people might want to go up to that level, to CEO level . . . it was good to do that [workshop in financial matters organised by Women On Air] because when you find you understand it, you have confidence in yourself in an area you thought you weren't so good in.

(female head of news)

Given the difficulties for women with the 'old boy' network, Women On Air always saw the training courses as opportunities for networking among female staff. That this did indeed happen is indicated by the formation of a new Broadcasters' Association for programme-makers in local radio, spearheaded by some participants on Women On Air courses. This new organisation is the first of its kind for staff in the industry, has strong female representation on its steering committee, and will provide alternative opportunities for networking and for the development of training strategies for the industry.

I think it will be very interesting, and because they are senior people, they're not people with a high turnover, these are people who are fairly solidly in there, long-term staff members . . . because they're all women involved at the moment, they're more likely to keep that [EO agenda] up there as well.

(station manager)

In terms of the broader issues around work structures Women On Air has worked closely with the state regulatory and development body for the sector, the IRTC, to develop a 'Diversity Management Strategy' for the industry whereby Equal Opportunities issues would be incorporated into the development of a broad Human Resources framework. This is a strategy often utilised to interest senior managers in general Human Resource Management in situations where they show no inclination to engage with equality issues *per se* (Kandola and Fullerton 1998). By its demise at the end of 1999, Women On Air had initiated, in collaboration with the IRTC, a programme on Human Resources Management training which successfully attracted the interest and support of station managers generally. A working party has been set up to follow through on this initiative, but its survival depends largely on the commitment of the IRTC in the immediate future. There are of course no guarantees for women in the development of a Human Resources Management strategy for the industry, but without the latter in place there is little likelihood of a major change in the attitudes of management towards their female employees as a human resource to be valued.

Women On Air was a small organisation with a short lifespan, and it is too early at this stage to determine whether its efforts to catalyse the independent radio industry in Ireland around the issue of gender equality in its workforce will ultimately prove successful. It does however, provide a good example of an organisation prepared to tackle the issue of equal opportunities in novel ways and at many levels in the industry, and the experience which Women On Air has gained in this process deserves to be widely disseminated.

Notes

1 RTE is still the dominant player in the Irish broadcasting industry. Set up in the1920s on the lines of the BBC, it declares a public service ethos while deriving two-thirds of its income from advertising. In the 1980s, responding to changes in technology and in attitudes to state regulation, the government introduced legislation to cater for radio and television broadcasting independently of RTE. By 1997, the independent radio sector in Ireland consisted of 19 privately-owned commercial stations and 12 publicly-owned community stations scattered throughout the country and employing just under 1,000 people. Most were on air legally for less than 10 years, and were still struggling to establish themselves in a difficult economic climate. All the commercial stations, bar Today FM which broadcasts nationally, are licensed to cover a defined local geographical area, and many maintain staff from previous incarnations as pirate operations. Most community stations have been on air for five years or less, and depend very heavily on government-funded FAS social employment schemes to maintain staffing levels. Commercial stations rely almost exclusively on advertising for their funding, while the non-profit-making community stations depend on grant-aid, local support and sponsorship.

2 The research was carried out by NEXUS Research Co-op and Maria Gibbons PhD, on behalf of Women On Air, an EU-funded body set up to promote women's participation in the independent radio industry in Ireland. Women On Air was a joint initiative between the National University of Ireland, Galway (NUI Galway), the Independent Radio and Television Commission (IRTC) and Connemara Community Radio.

3 The data on which these findings are largely based was derived from questionnaires completed in 1997 by 84% of radio station chief executives, and 23% of the paid staff.

4 A more recent survey of the sector conducted by the IRTC in 1999 indicated that these trends had changed little.

References

Abrahamson, U. (1990) 'Are we nearing the top of the hill?' Notes from a Decade of Working towards Equality in Swedish Broadcasting, paper presented to the 17th Conference of the International Association of Mass Communication Research, Bled.

Baehr, H. and M. Ryan (1984) *Shut up and Listen! Women and Local Radio: A View from the Inside*, London: Comedia,

Beasley, M. (1989) 'Newspapers: Is There a New Majority Defining the News?', in P. Creedon, (ed.) *Women in Mass Communication: Challenging Gender Values*, London: Sage, pp. 180–94.

Gallagher, M. (1996) 'Studying Gender Patterns in Media Employment', *Sequentia* 3(7): 14–15.

Gill, R. (1993) 'Justifying Injustice: Broadcasters' Accounts of Inequality in Radio', in E. Burman and I. Parker (eds) *Discourse Analytic Research, Repertoires and Readings of Texts in Action*, London: Routledge, pp. 31–40.

Graef, V. de (1997) *Radioscopie de l'Emploi a la RTBF: Analyse Quantitative et Qualitative en Termes d'Egalité*, Rapport no. 1, Brussels: RTBF.

IBEC (1999) *The Economic Impact of Film Production in Ireland 1998*, Dublin: IBEC.

Kandola, R. and Fullerton, J. (1998) *Diversity in Action: Managing the Mosaic*, London: IPD Books.

Lafky, S. (1989) 'Economic Equity and the Journalistic Workforce', in P. Creedon, (ed.) *Women in Mass Communication: Challenging Gender Values*, London: Sage, pp. 164–79.

Nexus Research Co-op and M. Gibbons (1998) *Breaking Glass Walls*, Galway: Women On Air.

RTE (1991) *Equal Opportunities for All. Review and Recommendations*, Dublin: RTE.

RTE (1998) *Equality Report 1998*, Dublin: RTE.

Ruane, F. and J. Sutherland (1999) *Women in the Labour Force*, Dublin: Employment Equality Agency.

STATCOM/FAS (1995) *The Independent Film and Television Production Sector in Ireland: Training needs to 2000*, STATCOM Report prepared by FAS Project Team, Dublin.

Zoonen, L. van (1994) *Feminist Media Studies*, London: Sage.

Woolf, M. and S. Holly (1994) *Employment Patterns and Training Needs 1993/4: Radio Survey*, London: Skillset.

Chapter 19

Kim Michaels and Caroline Mitchell

THE LAST BASTION: HOW WOMEN BECOME MUSIC PRESENTERS IN UK RADIO

BBC Radio 1 presenters like Sara Cox and Jo Whiley have high national media profiles. On most commercial radio stations however, it is difficult to find more than one female music radio presenter, let alone one with a high profile. More often than not, the female commercial radio DJ is relegated to a weekend slot or to being the sidekick for a male anchor.

This chapter reports on the first stage of research across the UK radio industry (commercial and community sectors) which surveyed employment patterns and practices relating to female presenters and radio.[1] Our research takes a snapshot of employment of female presenters in the UK; it looks at how women working as presenters are resisting the 'flexible sexism' identified by Gill (1993) and how radio managers are responding to the problem of recruiting women into presentation.

Researching DJs

When Annie Nightingale first applied to the BBC national youth station Radio 1 in 1967, she was told that they did not intend to take on female presenters because the male DJs functioned as 'husband substitutes' to the identified female listeners (Nightingale 1999). From this idea, both BBC and commercial radio DJs built up a culture where it seemed the art of presentation was to flirt with the female listener who was characterised as 'Doreen' the housewife. (Baehr and Ryan 1984) Women seemed to be invisible as 'makers' of music radio until the 1980s. This is partly explained by the background roles that they performed 'off air', particularly as producers – including producing male DJs. This job is far from a secondary role (some would argue it is the key to good radio production), however it was not the *audible* role that listeners could identify with, and thus it could not act as a role model for women entering the profession. Until the early 1990s, women were almost completely absent from presentation roles in UK music radio, which meant that a symbolic and actual absence of female identity developed on the airwaves.

Woods (1994) found that in Ireland there was a similar story. Some female DJs presented a show jointly with a man – often as an assisting 'sidekick' rather than an equal, or presented a programme outside peak listening times. There was a similar pattern in pirate radio. The only station where there was 'gender parity' was the Irish language station 'Raidio na Life' (a community station) where women presented all types of music shows and at all times (Woods 1994). More recent research in the commercial and community radio sectors in Ireland commissioned by Women On Air[2] reflects a general trend: within programme making, men 'overwhelmingly' dominate in presentation or DJ work and technical areas, while women work mainly in research (NEXUS and Gibbons 1997: 2).

What are the reasons that help to explain this gender imbalance? Gill's survey of attitudes of commercial radio programme controllers (PCs) has gone some way to exploring the reasons for this inequality (Gill 1993). She used critical discourse analysis of their many explanations of the inequality to look at the ideological framework in which they interpreted the reasons for a lack of female DJs. She highlighted six different accounts of what she termed 'flexible sexism':

- Women do not apply to become DJs
- Women interested in broadcasting become journalists rather than presenters
- Audience objections: Listeners prefer male presenters
- Women's voices are not suited to radio presentation
- Women lack the skills necessary for radio presentation
- Male DJs are necessary to serve the predominantly female ('housewife') audience

(Gill 1993: 77–89)

She concluded that PCs use these methods to avoid responsibility for the lack of female DJs and at the same time to deflect accusations of sexism (Gill 1993: 90).

How women became music radio presenters in the 1990s

In order to start answering the question of why there were so few women radio presenters we wanted to map out where and how women were employed as presenters in the BBC and commercial radio. (Although the research mainly focuses on the commercial and community sectors the BBC was surveyed to give a comparison as well as a whole view of the industry). We surveyed station web pages to find out the number of women presenters and where they existed in the schedules. Although this method has its downfalls (occasionally programme names hide the gender of the presenter, or web pages are out of date) it is an effective way of collecting recent data. We also interviewed female radio presenters from the commercial and community sectors. The interviews were informal, carried out over the telephone or in radio stations using a structured pattern based on Gill's (1993) analysis of six accounts given by male programme controllers for the lack of women radio presenters (see above). Finally we sent a questionnaire to a small sample of community and commercial radio station managers particularly focusing on employment and recruitment methods.[3]

A snapshot of the industry

We surveyed 225 web sites for BBC and commercial national local and regional radio stations. Stations employed between 1 and 23 presenters, with an average of 9 presenters per station. The sample comprised 98 per cent of all BBC stations – 40 stations in all (405 presenters) and 78 per cent of commercial radio stations – 185 stations in all (1583 presenters). We found:

26 per cent of BBC presenters are women
7.5 per cent of BBC stations have no female presenters
11.6 per cent of commercial presenters are women
38 per cent of commercial stations have no female presenters

If one combines the BBC and commercial sectors to get a picture of mainstream UK radio, 14.6 per cent of presenters are female and 32 per cent of stations have no female presenters at all. Commercial stations aiming at the over 40s were particularly poor and stations promoting particular genres of music (for instance dance or gold) employed mainly men.

We made an attempt to break down which time slots and roles women are undertaking.[4] Of the 11.6 per cent female presenters in commercial radio:

60 per cent are co-presenters
22 per cent are weekenders/specialist music presenters
18 per cent are solo/self driving

The majority of women were working as co-presenters on breakfast. Within this there seems to be a continuum ranging from genuine co-presenters sharing the work of the programme, through to 'sidekicks' reading weather and traffic, to an individual or posse member represented by a 'giggle' or comment, 'off mic.' at the back of the studio.

Of the 26 per cent of female presenters within the BBC:

23 per cent are co-presenters
33 per cent are weekend/specialist music presenters
44 per cent are solo/self driving

BBC local stations, which over the past decade have favoured news-based programming have a better representation of female presenters compared with commercial or BBC national stations. In BBC Radio 1 where presenters have a high media profile, under a quarter of their presentation staff are women.

Our interview-based research used Gill's six categories of explanation as a thematic and methodological base to supplement information provided by the web sites.

'Women do not apply to become DJs'

In our questionnaire 66 per cent of managers said that they would like to employ women presenters but claimed they could not find them, again repeating claims made by Gill's research subjects in 1993. However one interview respondent had moved on from blaming women themselves to looking at possible solutions:

> Recruitment is our industry's biggest problem . . . there are not enough female presenters . . . there are no proper formal routes to get into presentation and this needs addressing.
>
> (female managing director, commercial radio)

> I have encountered negative discrimination from the ridiculous grey suit brigade . . . one said . . . 'you women all you do is have babies . . . I wouldn't employ any woman between the ages of 23 and 30'.
>
> (female managing director, commercial radio)

It is likely that both of the above problems remain in the radio industry today. We were also interested in what routes into music presentation there are and how women use them.

The survey showed that in commercial radio most presenters were recruited through the informal contacts of programme controllers, within and outside their station or group of companies. This is supported in stations by the culture of volunteers working for free and hanging out at stations and then stepping in when a presenter is ill or on holiday. One woman we interviewed had left a further education course in Media Studies in order to 'hang around' a local station and gain the necessary experience. She made the tea and taught herself various jobs in order to become 'invaluable' and felt that this was a better way 'in' than through training. She says:

> I've had more experience in however many years of radio than most people get in a lifetime, and so by saying no to the diploma . . . And actually going in and getting the practical experience, I'm more well versed in the ways that the media actually works and therefore more valuable to prospective employers.
>
> (Local commercial station, weekend presenter)

We found that community stations use a wide range of methods to positively attract women into presenting. Fem FM[5] used local and national publicity to encourage women to put themselves forward. They ran workshops on how to put together demonstration tapes, and held a competition in conjunction with local commercial station group GWR. A North East community radio project, 107 The Bridge, trained a group of thirty women in radio techniques and put them to air for a week during International Women's Week. This gave them both training and experience in radio which could be carried forward into the industry.

'Women who want to be broadcasters become journalists not DJs'

The myth that women do not want to, or are just not able to, become presenters has long been perpetuated by programme controllers (Baehr and Ryan, 1984). All the women we interviewed were conscious of a lack of role models as they were growing up, and acknowledged the importance of women in radio becoming role models and mentors:

> I just thought women can't be DJs. It wasn't until I went to a party and there was a female DJ doing the disco – and she was good – that I realised that women could do it. I thought only men could – 'cos of their egos and their willingness to perform.
>
> (Community radio presenter)

> Just because you're little or whatever and particularly because you're female as well, they think there's some really silly reason why you want to do it. Someone said – 'did you have a troubled childhood?' to me! . . . and 'What makes you so aggressive that makes you want to present rock music?' It's really because so many people didn't agree to women doing it that sparked me off.
>
> (Community radio presenter)

The 'DJ' job is often perceived as relating to 'club culture' and might shed a negative light on the role of the radio presenter (also known as a DJ) compared to the status of say a journalist's role in the radio industry. One interviewee from a regional commercial station highlighted how employed positions such as radio reporters provided more stable prospects for women who had family commitments and needed a regular wage.[6]

'Audience objections – listeners prefer male presenters'

The way audience research is carried out might account for the supposed audience objections to female presenters (Baehr and Ryan 1984; Steward and Garratt 1984). The sexualisation of the DJ's relationship with the female listener – constructing himself as replacing the absent husband in the women's life – extends to fantasising about a relationship with the female listener. Gill shows how this shift is understood by a commercial DJ she interviewed:

I think mid morning radio has always been considered 'housewife radio'. It isn't to the same extent now. Actually in some parts of the morning you have more men listening than women. But I think you still go for a female audience. I mean you flirt with them – that's exactly what you do for three hours. But what you've not got to do, is do it to the extent that it annoys the men listening.

(Gill 1993: 333).

Most of our female DJ interviewees said that they had been told that research showed that listeners, male and female, wanted to hear male voices: this was a perceived 'truth', based on research carried out by an unknown source. A community radio presenter talking about listening to women's voices said: 'women *like* to listen to women – look at how much we like the daytime chat shows hosted by women [.]' (her emphasis). One respondent had encountered identical attitudes that Baehr and Ryan (1984) and Gill (1993) have identified:

He basically said it's proven, research has shown that people don't like to listen to women's voices on radio because they are high pitched and scatty and this that and the other . . . I just thought you haven't got a clue pal. There are as many women who like to . . . listen to women's voices as they do like to listen to men's voices. It's not just a sex/girl thing, they like to relate as well, but also on the other hand . . . women like to hear men's voices because of the sex appeal thing. I'm sure men like to hear women's voices. I would hope so.

(Community radio presenter)

One late night regional radio presenter said that she had worked in the industry for more than ten years and had only recently heard that 'audiences preferred male presenters'. She questioned the idea and wondered how old the research was.

Could it be that the lack of serious female presenters, those in other than 'giggling girl' slots, is preventing female listeners from taking women DJs seriously? This is answered by another interviewee: 'Women should like listening to women but they don't because there aren't the "right" women' (London commercial station, weekend DJ).

This argument is countered by managers who look to both cater for neglected audiences and to bring in new listeners. BBC Radio 1 Programme Controller Andy Parfitt brought in children's television presenter Zöe Ball as a 'side kick' for a male presenter and ended up using her to front the BBC Radio 1 Breakfast show. She was brought in with the intention to:

coax more young female listeners as part of a 'girlification' strategy to redress the balance after the Steve Wright and Mike Read years.

(O'Rorke 1999: 2)

The programme's share of listeners has risen since Ball's appointment.[7] A victory for Parfitt and Ball and a useful point to those who doubt the audience pull of female broadcasters. It is interesting then that a large number of commercial stations use a female at breakfast only as a 'token' figure co-presenter, representing the female 'voice' and only a few 'solo' presenters are on the smaller local stations. As one presenter said:

> Once there are a few more women presenting radio, the audience will not even notice whether they are listening to a male or female, and then maybe we will have more than one woman per day shift, which in turn will encourage more women to enter to the industry because there are more interesting jobs to be had.
>
> (community radio presenter)

Cramer argues that a critical mass of women on air will lead to a change in on air representation. She cites two women who worked in US radio in 1992:

> There are just too many women in radio for women's voices to be an issue any more . . . There are no problems any more with women's voices being too high. There are standards for both men and women.
>
> (Cramer 1993: 165)

'Women's voices are not suited to radio presentation'

Gill's interviewees said that they believed the audience did not want to listen to a woman's voice, and yet our questionnaire found that a 'good voice' with 'warmth' were the most important features. Women's voices are often said to be too high pitched and yet only a sixth in our survey said this mattered. Other features of a good presentation voice were cited as clarity and tone. A large number said that 'personality' and 'suitability to the station style' were important. The latter is problematic because if a station style is based on what is generally heard, and what is heard has usually been a male presenter, then the station's style is based on a premise which excludes women.

Historically women have trained their voices to fit in with a style needed for particular genres (e.g. lower pitch for presentation). What is worth discussion is women's ability to be adaptable. They do this by altering and training their voices to be more like their male counterparts or bubbly 'ladettes' to get onto breakfast shows or developing their 'sexy' voices to get late night slots. The latter is usually in response to the programme controller wanting a sexy late night female voice because it's perceived that more men listen at night.

One female presenter said when asked what was the most important thing for a presenter to have:

> I think rather sadly in terms of the industry it's probably voice . . . most women who have made it are there because they have a really horny voice.
>
> (London commercial station, weekend presenter)

One regional commercial radio presenter said that she had never heard of any problems with the female voice. She said that it is a variety of voices that make listening interesting and that the idea that radio voices need to be deep and authoritative went out decades ago. However we may conclude that women's voices are being accepted only if they are adaptable. How much this is in a limited /gendered range of options ('sexy', 'horny', 'laddette', 'sidekick') needs more research.

'Women do not have the necessary skills for radio'

Women's level of production skills and their technical ability has long been thought to exclude them from radio work. Interestingly the BBC has traditionally had a reasonable number of women working as technical operators because they are trained from scratch through their studio manager's scheme. However women who enter as a DJ often have to learn desk operations 'on the job' and this may be more daunting (see Steward and Garratt 1984). Computer and IT skills are deemed particularly important in contemporary radio where digital production is the norm. Most male and female solo presenters in our survey could 'drive' a desk and do digital editing. However most female co-presenters who do travel and weather work did not have these skills nor were required to learn them.

When we asked how skills were gained three interviewees felt that being taught by men was a barrier to women learning radio technology: 'I think the only problem for women on the technical side is men telling them there is a problem' (community radio leader). One breakfast show presenter felt that any mistakes she made were judged as being because she is a woman and not because she is a human being:

> You can't get away from the fact that if you're a woman in radio, you're gonna get propositioned a lot, . . . you're going to get people saying that your mistakes are because you're a woman but at the end of the day, that doesn't make you who you are.
>
> (Local commercial station, breakfast show presenter)

Another said the reason why there are so few women DJ's in radio is because:

> I still think there are few (women) to choose from because some are put off by the technical stuff . . . Because they're being taught by men and they think 'this bloke's gonna think I'm really crap if I don't learn this straight away', if they were taught by women, they would quickly learn the technical stuff and make it a career instead of a hobby.
>
> (London commercial station presenter)

The community radio sector has been addressing this training issue for some time and there is evidence of women-only and women-taught courses in several stations.

Discussion and conclusions

Female news readers are now accepted as normal rather than the exception in all sectors of UK radio. Our research shows that women are now making inroads into music presentation in a number of different ways and some managers are beginning to address the issue of a lack of female presenters without blaming women themselves. The presence of more female presenters in a high profile station like BBC Radio 1 may mean that an increase in role models should contribute to changes in representation on UK radio as a whole.

There is still a dearth of women in music presentation, particularly in commercial radio. Some commercial radio stations, even whole groups, have long stretches of their schedules (sometimes the whole 24 hours) with no female presenters at all. In the last ten years there has been a significant shift however in the perception within and outside the industry towards women entering it. Because of the high media profile of national presenters like Zöe Ball and Jo Whiley, the public perception of women as presenters is positive. Women are gaining skills and confidence through courses and by volunteering at commercial and community radio stations.

In our questionnaire two thirds of PCs said that they would like to employ women presenters but claimed they could not find them. Some radio managers have moved from the position of 'Women don't apply' to 'How can we get more women to apply?' Some of the myths about women's voices being 'wrong' for radio and disliked by audiences are fading and women are adapting their voices to suit different time slots and station styles. Radio managers are becoming more interested in how they can attract new sectors of male and female listeners – witness Andy Parfitt's call for the 'girlification' of BBC Radio 1. (O 'Rorke 1999)

Women themselves are using a range of strategies to get on air. Some of these – like 'hanging out' at stations until a shift becomes available, getting as many practical skills and voluntary experience as possible – involve appropriating tried and tested methods of entering the industry up to now mainly used by men. In addition they are entering the on air space in new roles – in particular the role of breakfast 'side kick'. Arguably this is an inferior role in relation to the male 'anchor', however it could be interpreted as being used to gain experience and 'visibility' on the most high profile timeslot in any radio station. It can also be used to negotiate further skills training, for instance in how to drive the desk.

In the new millennium we have to ask whether female listeners constructed as housewives and/or pseudo sexual relationship objects, is still a hegemonic force in radio and whether new stereotypes (for instance the husky late night female voice chatting up men in the small hours) are emerging. The political economy of radio advertising related to female audiences, and a study of the symbolic level of representation in this area and new ways of defining audiences as part of audience research needs further study. The case of the short lived Viva! radio,[8] and other stations that target female listeners, could shed light on some of these areas.

The combination of factors influencing managers and presenters explored through Gill's categories (1993) shows that 'flexible sexism' is multi-layered. The women we spoke to felt that competition for potential presenter jobs was made more difficult by there being only a possible number of shifts available for women:

> There is a feeling that there is only one on-air shift for a female going and that's wrong . . . at the moment they're either the late night show or the bimbo co-presenter on breakfast.
>
> (London commercial station presenter)

Could this added competition put off potential women presenters? Those who feel that maybe they do not fit into either category of 'bubbly girlie' or 'sexy late night siren'? Could it also be that women who try for other shifts (in traditionally male areas) and who fail decide to move to other professions instead of compromising themselves? One woman had been offered a position as part of a 'posse' in a commercial station but had turned it down because she wanted her own show:

> It's just the nature of the company . . . I don't think it's because they didn't think I was good enough, they just don't put women in their own shows.
>
> (potential London commercial station presenter)

Clearly women are offered a limited number of role models on air. Personal accounts and research suggest it is difficult for women to enter the profession and that a contributing factor could be a patriarchal institutional culture (and contributing individual attitudes) in the workplace. This is reflected in national/celebrity representations of female DJs, for instance Chris Evans talking about Jo Whiley 'The DJ most likely to give you the horn' (O 'Rorke 1999: 2).

What needs further exploration is the gendered nature of DJ/presenter culture, particularly how it is experienced within radio stations. It could be said that working in a male dominated environment could be difficult for all but the strongest of women. One woman from a London station talked about how you need 'personal character to survive'. She said that a belief in oneself was essential in order to overcome any gender 'knocking' that might take place within the workplace. Another local radio presenter said:

> I would say that the women I've met in radio are more confident than the men . . . They're not arrogant . . . there are some men who perhaps let their egos drive them, they say 'wow, I'm on the radio, I've made it' and I don't think you get the same thing from women.
>
> (Local commercial station, breakfast presenter)

So what does it take to work in radio presentation? Does it take a large amount of ego or assertiveness to work in the industry and how much room is there for acknowledging vulnerability? A community radio respondent said: 'Women are always so keen to get involved but they're always so scared as well, you can feel they're wary about their level of capability'.

Zilliacus-Tikkanen (1997) found in her study of gender and news in Scandinavia, that the proportion of women in an organisation and whether the organisational culture is flexible or rigid are important factors. A higher proportion of women and flexibility makes it easier for women to work in news organisations and promote a gender oriented journalistic culture.

So as we enter the new millennium and the world of digital and Internet radio, which will undoubtedly alter the face of what we now call radio, will institutional and cultural ideas about a woman's role in music radio alter? How do we continue to improve the numbers of women working as DJs in music radio? Can women get equal air-time, with equal shifts and access to both male and female audiences? How can female radio presenters define (and redefine) their roles?

Notes

1 Research is part of a three year programme carried out by the University of Sunderland for the 'Permanent Waves' project UK – funded by the European Social Fund and supported by the Radio Academy, Commercial Radio Companies Association (CRCA) and the Community Media Association (CMA).
2 Women On Air, Galway – National campaigning and training group for women's radio in Ireland.
3 The response sample consisted of 8 commercial and 4 community stations, a 40 per cent return.
4 This is as accurate as possible bearing in mind the limited information provided by websites.
5 Fem FM was a short-term station which broadcast in Bristol in 1992. It was the first women's station in the UK.
6 The relationship between club DJ-ing and gender is summed up by Brewster and Broughton (1999) in their history of the disc jockey where they say, albeit tongue in cheek , '99.9 per cent of DJs have a penis.'
7 Zöe Ball resigned from her breakfast slot early in 2000 to concentrate on starting a family. She continues to produce special features for Radio 1. She was replaced by Sara Cox, another transferee from entertainment TV presentation.
8 Viva! Radio broadcast in London from 1995 to 1996 as a commercial radio station aimed at women. It was bought by Mohammed Al-Fayed in May 1996 and re-launched as Liberty Radio.

References

Baehr, H. and Ryan, M. (1984) *Shut Up and Listen! Women and Local Radio*, London: Comedia.
Brewster, B. and Broughton, F. (1999) *Last Night a DJ Saved my Life. The History of the Disc Jockey*, London: Headline Book Publishing.
Cramer, J. (1993) 'A Woman's Place is On the Air', in P. Creedon, (ed.) *Women in Mass Communication* (2nd edition), London: Sage.
Gill, R. (1993) 'Justifying Injustice: Broadcasters' Accounts of Inequality in a Radio Station' In Burman, E. and Parker, I. (eds) *Discourse Analytic Research: Readings and Repertoires of Texts in Action*, London: Routledge.
NEXUS Research Co-operative and Gibbons, M. (1997), *Breaking Glass Walls, Gender*

and Employment Issues in the Independent Radio Sector in Ireland, Women On Air, Galway, Ireland.

Nightingale, A. (1999) *Wicked Speed*, London: Sidgwick and Jackson.

O'Rorke, I. (1999)' Who do you Fancy for Breakfast? *Guardian*, G2 section, 1/11/99, p. 2.

Steward, S. and Garratt, S. (1984) *Signed, Sealed and Delivered. True Life Stories of Women in Pop*, London and Sydney: Pluto Press.

Woods, M. (1994) 'Where the girls aren't – missing voices on music radio'. Paper presented to WERRC Conference University College, Dublin, March 1994.

Zilliacus -Tikkanen, H. (1997) *Journalistikens Essens I Ett Konspersspectiv* (English summary pp. 151–64) YLE ISSN 1235–092.

Chapter 20

Janet Haworth

WOMEN IN RADIO NEWS: MAKING A DIFFERENCE?

I knew I was having a miscarriage because the spotting had started . . . I just thought, well, I'll try not to bleed on the studio floor. The doctor said there was nothing I could do to stop it anyway, so I went in to work. Afterwards I felt terrible and my partner was very upset, but at the time I just felt I had no choice.

Introduction

There are many more women working in radio news now than a generation ago, (Cramer 1993; Woolf, Holly and Connor 1996) and the effect of this shift in the gender balance on journalistic practices has yet to be fully assessed.[1] This chapter reports on the Haworth study of women radio news editors and the female news agenda (1999).[2]

Dickey (1985) articulated a widely-held view at the time that

The way the media look at women is closely related to the comparative shortage of women working in the media . . . What would the news be like if it was (sic) women who freely selected the stories? The media can never reflect women's viewpoints while the majority of the decisions are taken by men . . . the only real solution is to ensure that there are sufficient numbers of women working in the media at all levels so that they become representative of men and women and serve the interests of both.

(Dickey 1985: 35)

Now the gender balance has changed it is possible to investigate whether the greater proportion of women in radio news has had any effect on the news agenda.

To understand whether and how women are changing radio journalism as a practice it is necessary to analyse the factors which brought them into newsrooms in large numbers in the 1980s and 1990s, the proliferation of media outlets, new technology, media convergence and new ways of working.

The new radio news landscape

At the end of the twentieth century there were many more terrestrial, cable, satellite and digital channels and digital radio multiplexes, 'Sallie'[3] licences, community radio stations, RSLs[4] and Internet radio services. As well as proliferating across the map, radio stations are spreading out across the day – 24 hour live broadcasting is now the norm. The essence of news is its 'liveness' so radio journalists have to be prepared to work long shifts of ten to twelve hours duration and including overnights, weekends and public holidays. The sheer number of different stations and bulletins make radio a very hungry medium in terms of staffing.

The UK Culture Secretary Chris Smith has indicated that all analogue broadcasting signals will be switched off as early as 2006 and no later than 2010, by which time he expects 95 per cent of households to have switched to digital radio and TV (Smith 1999). He argues that, to persuade 95 per cent of consumers to buy digital sets, there must be an explosion of new products (radio stations and news services on multi-media platforms) and a consequent rapid expansion in the job market.

The proliferation of radio news outlets started with the unleashing of market forces in broadcasting under the Conservative Government of Margaret Thatcher 1979–90. It introduced Channel Four, cable and satellite television and a raft of new commercial and community radio stations. It was the Thatcher/Tebbitt employment laws, as much as the Broadcasting Acts, that really freed the market in broadcast news, because they broke the stranglehold of the trades unions in print and broadcast media.

What did this mean for women? Natasha Walter (1998) outlines the many ways in which trades unions have failed women and alienated them. She describes how the unions pursued a male agenda based on pay for the family breadwinner, status, differentials and demarcation. They neglected concerns such as sex discrimination, sexual harassment, unequal pay for work of equal value, training, health and safety, long working hours, paid maternity and paternity leave, job sharing and flexible working arrangements. Insofar as this is true at all, it is less true of the unions representing broadcast journalists: the NUJ and the ABS/ACTT (now merged as Bectu) have a long tradition of campaigning for equality in the workplace and for fair representation in the media of women and other groups. During the 1980s the print and broadcasting media unions were involved in mass pickets at Warrington and Wapping and TV-Am and subsequently robbed of the power to organise in these aggressive ways by new employment laws. O'Malley (1997) argues that this also meant that the unions were less able to tackle gender issues in the workplace:

(the assault on the unions) had implications for equal opportunities policies which became harder to implement in a casualised, underpaid workforce.

(O'Malley 1997: 183)

Employers were free to pay as little as they could get away with. They found that young women were typically more willing and able than men to accept low wages, since they were less likely to be family breadwinners. This state of affairs continues under New Labour, which has not repealed the employment laws of the 1980s.

Deregulation swept away broadcasting as a concept and introduced niche radio or 'narrowcasting'. This created a niche for women's radio. One early example was Viva! in London which failed to gain a significant market share and was bought out by Mohammed al Fayed's Liberty Radio. There were also experiments with non-commercial feminist community radio stations, operating on temporary RSL licences (Fem FM in Bristol, Celebration and Brazen in London). As the market fragmented, some commercial stations began targeting women with spending power who are therefore attractive to advertisers (see GWR lifestyle news below) and women in general, who are important to the BBC's requirement to serve all sections of the community as a public service broadcaster.

New stereotypes?

Media convergence is turning radio into a permanent plank of a journalist's career rather than a temporary stepping-stone in a linear progression from radio to TV. There are jobs now that combine radio, writing for the screen on Internet and teletext services, and television. So young women whose eventual career goal is to become a TV presenter may now choose radio rather than print journalism or drama school as a fast track to their ideal job.

There is also a new kind of journalist emerging in the Nineties to wipe out the Humphrey Bogart stereotype of a white man in a raincoat and a trilby hat with a cigarette in his mouth, according to research by Tony Delano (1997) at the London College of Printing. This research shows how the image of journalists as universally hard-bitten, heavy-drinking, unfeeling, objective, cynical workaholics has changed and most are now non-smoking, driven, introspective careerists who sip mineral water and work out at the gym. The 'New Journalist' represents a certain feminisation of the stereotype, possibly making journalism more attractive to girls and women, and making it easier for a woman to 'fit in' to a newsroom.

Research by Heather Purdey (1999) shows that the ideal new recruit for a UK radio newsroom is defined principally by attitude. Purdey reported that radio news editors place great emphasis on voice and attitude. By 'attitude' they mean a state of mind that is free from moral and ethical judgements and does not approach journalism with the idea of campaigning for a cause. She also reported that many editors felt that young women, rather than young men, were likely to fit this mould.

New technology

My own observation of radio journalists and broadcast journalism students over the past 12 years in various UK higher education institutions is that technology works in favour of women radio journalists in a number of ways. Nowadays most radio news interviews are done over the phone or ISDN,[5] rather than face to face. This method requires a less intrusive, confrontational, stereotypically masculine approach to the interview, which is one of the basic building blocks of radio news. Radio reporting relies more heavily now on short sound bites of five to fifteen seconds in duration rather than extended interviews. Physical presence and proximity to the interviewee or event is less vital nowadays. In the 1980s, a radio reporter would often need to use 'foot in the door',[6] 'doorstepping'[7] or 'media scrum'[8] techniques to get close enough to the interviewee to make a broadcast-quality recording. To succeed in these practices the reporter would need sufficient height, weight and aggression to take on mostly-male rivals and intimidate mostly-male interviewees.

Computers are now a vital tool for radio news journalists. The office computer, granddaughter of the typewriter, is apparently as much a female as a male tool. Perhaps because of women's long history as typists and secretaries, women typically suffer no 'technophobia' (in my experience as a teacher of computer and digital editing skills) when faced with a computer-based task. The downside is that computers have also replaced secretaries and clerks, so these jobs which traditionally provided a 'way in' to broadcast journalism for the previous generation of young women (along with the casting couch!) have been abolished. The industry has created lighter, smaller, more user-friendly portable recording and editing equipment such as MiniDisc and DAT, and lightweight digital cameras which facilitate bi-media working. Twenty years ago the journalist was forced to rely on a studio manager or technical operator (usually male) to physically cut and splice the magnetic tape and 'drive the desk' (operate the controls in the studio) to create radio news. Now she can do it all herself with just a mouse and a microphone.

Multi-skilling however can also have the negative effect of de-skilling the broadcast journalist, forcing her to compromise journalistic quality for the sake of technical excellence. Desktopping[9] liberates women in that it abolishes the old studio-based, purely technical jobs usually held by men with engineering qualifications. Yet desktopping is a form of disempowerment for both men and women, since the journalist is forced to become a Jack (or Jill) of all trades and mistress of none, so her work may appear mediocre.

There is a greater emphasis on processing and re-versioning news, using the vast array of news sources available through networked newsroom systems and the Internet, and a corresponding decline in the number of original stories and exclusive interviews. The BBC newscaster Michael Buerk roundly deplored this trend, saying that the job of reporter is the best job in the world but that reporters are in danger of extinction.[10]

There are health and safety worries, too: possible risk of infertility, increased danger of miscarriage, genetic defects, the potential for back trouble, Repetitive

Strain Injuries, mental illness and eyesight problems, but these must be the subject of another sort of research involving medical experts.

Female voices

A study by Valentine and Saint Damian, quoted by Shingler and Wieringa (1998) shows that female voices are perceived by the listener to carry less authority.

> We can for the purposes of clarity and cogency define the radio voice as (i) refined (ii) masculine and (iii) authoritative whilst the radio voice possesses masculine and feminine characteristics, the ideal radio voice approximates more to male than to female vocal qualities
>
> (Shingler and Wieringa 1998: 48)

Female voices are now acceptable on radio news if they sound deep and powerful (masculine) and refined (Received Pronunciation or without a strong accent). The received wisdom is that a young, high-pitched voice risks sounding too girlish. A mature high-pitched voice is too strident, a voice that is throaty or breathy is too sexy for news (though one radio critic recently wrote in admiration of the BBC Radio 4 newsreader Charlotte Green, describing her voice as 'postcoital'). Regional accents may handicap a female radio journalist's career. John Pickford, head of news and speech at Key103/Magic in Manchester said of one potential recruit

> She's a great reporter, a very good journalist but I couldn't put her on air with that voice. She sounds like a fishwife or a washerwoman.[11]

This chimes in with Valentine and Saint Damian's research, which found the ideal radio voice was more refined than normal. Two respondents in the Haworth survey of radio news journalists (Appendix 1) complained that their working-class accents had prevented them from reaching their career goals. Biology works against women here. However accents can be softened and women can overcome the natural squeakiness of their voices in various ways, using posture and breathing. They strive to make these changes, and institutions involved in training broadcasters actively promote the process of change, in order to meet the employers' demand for 'authoritative' (i.e. mature, masculine-sounding, refined) voices. This demand has led the Broadcast Journalism Training Council to set up a UK-wide network of approved voice coaches for use in training students on the courses it inspects and accredits.

Comparative studies

The UK has followed a similar trend to the Nordic countries studied in Henrika Zilliacus-Tikkanen's research (1996). She finds a marked difference between

Swedish radio and TV newsrooms, where there has been a gender balance for more than ten years, and the Finnish newsrooms where women are only recently joining in large numbers. Tikkanen characterises as 'soft' those news stories that primarily interest women namely human interest, family, children, consumer issues, social politics, education, health, housing and the environment. News stories characterised as 'hard' or appealing mainly to men are categorised as politics, administration, the labour market, economy and enterprise, foreign news, technology, science, crime and defence.

She finds that the Swedish broadcast news contains more 'soft' stories of interest to women and that programmes run by mainly female producers are more investigative and revelatory than those with a mainly male editorial and production team. The Finnish counterparts show less of a difference between male-dominated and female-dominated newsrooms, more hard stories and a more superficial approach.

In the UK a study by Linda Christmas (1997) analysed the results of a growing proportion of female editors in local and national newspapers. Christmas found that female editors she questioned do not have a news agenda that is specifically 'feminine' but that some of them are more likely than their male counterparts to favour stories, and especially photojournalistic features, involving children.

The Haworth survey

This is a survey of senior women journalists in radio newsrooms in BBC and Independent Local Radio stations and networks across the UK carried out in the summer of 1999. Women editors in BBC stations are generally older (age 28 to 52) and more highly paid. They are known as Senior Broadcast Journalists rather than Editors and typically there is a hierarchy of managers over them on higher grades. ILR[12] News Editors are more hands-on, working on-air as well as organising news coverage, assigning reporters to stories and managing the (often very small) budget. Most respondents stated that their sex had neither helped nor hindered their career prospects and that they do not consider radio news to be a male-dominated industry, although those aged over 50 acknowledge that it was certainly anti-women in the 1960s and 1970s.

A significant minority of women surveyed (35 per cent) believed that working in news had adversely affected their relationships and family life. One woman cited the tensions created by her work in news as the reasons for her divorce; another said she had ended a relationship when she moved to another part of the country to take a better job. Only two of the women (10 per cent) surveyed have children, both of them with only one child of below school age.

Most respondents in the Haworth survey believe that women and men have different news priorities. However the respondents explain this in terms of their own life-experience and personality or their station's target audience, rather than as a gendered response to news. The Haworth survey provides a snapshot of attitudes amongst senior female radio news editors questioned in 1999. Twenty respondents completed the questionnaire: this represents around two-thirds of the female radio news editors in UK BBC local and Independent Local Radio stations at the time. It is difficult to be precise about the figures here because BBC and ILR define editorial responsibility differently. What is certain is that the women questioned are all gatekeepers, responsible for filtering incoming news stories and agenda-setters in charge of originating and prioritising the station's news output. Some also have the power to hire and fire journalists, but this varies from station to station.

This is a typical comment from a 48-year-old female news editor with no children:

> A lot of my colleagues who have children are more aware of childcare stories or school issues or stories about child abuse and that gives them different priorities.

In the GWR group[13] there is a deliberate policy of creating a female news agenda to suit the target audience of women aged 25 to 35. This first emerged as a concept called 'lifestyle news'. It does not include any crime or politics or international affairs. The emphasis is on health, schooling, fashion, consumer news, celebrity interviews, relationships, local events and leisure activities. One of the GWR group's (female) news editors says: 'Of course crime and politics have a relevance but they just don't come across well. We give our listeners what they want to hear.'

Where non-GWR editors said they believed in a female news agenda, this was expressed in terms of human interest and an antipathy to sport. Most respondents rejected categories or labels such as 'hard' and 'soft 'news used in the Nordic study by Zilliacus-Tikkanen. (ibid.)

A significant finding where 'femaleness' is positively identified in the Haworth survey is in the approach to the job and treatment of each story:

> Men are interested in facts and figures. Women are more likely to ask why something's happened. They don't take things at face value (ibid.)

The interview is an important building block of radio news and a touchstone for the differences between men and women. For many male journalists the interview is a gladiatorial contest. Female interviewers, according to the women in the survey, are generally less aggressive and try to draw out information, emotions and opinions rather than get into arguments. These points support Zilliacus-Tikkanen's observations about broadcast news programmes in Sweden, where the mainly 'female' programme was less superficial, more revelatory and analytical than the 'male' programme.

The perceived male preference for facts and figures over insights is highlighted in sports coverage, where men are employed just to read out the statistics and women reporters and presenters are still in a tiny minority. One senior ILR presenter of twenty years experience told me that she is still not taken seriously as a sports journalist because she has not bothered to memorise a large catalogue of football scores, cricket batting averages and other numerical statistics which her male colleagues carry in their heads. She knows the history of sport in terms of winners and losers, personalities and events rather than statistics and she believes this is a characteristically feminine perspective.

In war reporting, still predominantly male, one female news editor in the survey perceived a similar difference of emphasis.

> In covering the war (in Kosovo), the men seemed more interested in what planes and helicopters were being used and how many of them, and I thought our listeners would be more interested in what was happening to people on the ground, the refugees and their families.

Here there is almost a literal divide between the earth mother and the sky father of ancient myth. Men's stories glorify air power and fire power; the woman is more concerned for the human impact on the tortured and dispossessed civilian families on the ground.

Motherism: the glass door

As the biological clock starts to tick and the female journalist leaves to have a baby she can be replaced by someone younger and cheaper. Then, with a young baby to care for, she is not likely to resume her full-time job working twelve-hour shifts on a roster that covers 365 days a year. So she can be sidelined or put on a part-time contract, and this reduces her power, influence, authority and promotion prospects. There is not so much a glass ceiling in radio news as a glass door that slides shut behind a heavily-pregnant woman as she staggers out of the newsroom to have her first baby. My research interviews indicate that motherhood can be very difficult to combine with a career in radio news (see below).

To be fair to men it must be pointed out that fatherhood inflicts some cruel dilemmas on male radio journalists, too, but they are not the subject of this study. To be fair to employers, there are some who, like Colin Hancock at BBC Radio 1, aim for gender balance in his newsroom and believe that in order to create and keep a gender balance in newsrooms you need to recruit twice as many women as men.[14] This is to ensure that there will be enough women around to replace those who leave to have children.

To discover what happens to mothers who find it impossible to combine family life with their career in radio news, I spoke to ten mothers who no longer work in radio newsrooms about why they left. These interviews do not form part of the Haworth survey but they are a necessary addition, since they indicate that motherhood is a major factor in influencing women to quit radio news.

One was a senior bi-media political correspondent and then held a management post in the BBC before she left. She has two young children:

> I feel quite bitter because I put off having kids until the last possible minute, thinking that if I was in a secure management job it would be easier to come back but it wasn't.

Another, now a mother of three, left BBC national radio when she found she could not conceive for a second time

> Why do you think there are so many women our age teaching broadcast journalism in higher education? It's not because they want to be lecturers, it's because they want to get home in time to put the children to bed and have fun with them in the school holidays.

A high-profile freelance presenter and journalist tells how she struggled, early in her first pregnancy:

> I knew I was having a miscarriage because the spotting had started, but I was booked to do a presenter shift at Bush House so I just went and did it. I just thought, well, I'll try not to bleed on the studio floor. The doctor said there was nothing I could do to stop it anyway, so I went in to work. Afterwards I felt terrible and my partner was very upset, but at the time I just felt I had no choice.

These responses reflect the reality of life in a twenty-four hour news operation. Money cannot buy the sort of childcare that would fit in with a radio newsroom's demands because news is unrelenting and unpredictable.

The BBC offers all parents on its staff the services of a commercial company, 'Childcare Solutions', which promises (for a price) to solve any childcare problem. Typically this involves 'emergency childcare' when the regular nanny or childminder is ill. So the BBC employee has to pay, often an extortionate amount, and leave her/his children with a total stranger before going off to work a very long shift. A truly family-friendly employer would find a way to replace the working parent with a freelance, and would continue to pay her while she took time off work, as indeed she will continue to pay the sick nanny. However in offering childcare solutions, day nurseries and school holiday play-schemes to staff, the BBC is proving far more family-friendly than stations in the commercial sector. There is scant recognition in the broadcasting industry that childcare is a lifelong commitment.[15] However Baroness Jay (Labour Minister for Women and former BBC journalist) told NUJ women at the 1999 NUJ South East Regional Equality Conference in London that she is about to start campaigning for paid time off for grandparents. She described the difficulties she faced when trying to find quality time in her schedule for her new baby grandchild.[16] It seems that in her case at least the 1970s feminist slogan of 'the personal is the political' lives on.

Conclusions

The results of the Haworth survey and the associated interviews indicate that radio news offers good career opportunities for girls and young women but is ageist, class-conscious and incompatible with motherhood. And if there is such a thing as a female news agenda in radio, it is dictated by the audience, not the women in the newsroom. GWR lifestyle news was created for a notional woman who is younger, more intelligent and more sophisticated than the old stereotype of the unemployed housewife listening at home (the creation of radio advertising executives in the 1980s).

At its best, this type of news informs women while pretending to entertain them, sugaring the tiny pills of information in a reversal of Lord Reith's view that the purpose of radio was to inform, educate and entertain (in that order). Lifestyle news can also be seen as deeply patronising to women, increasing their social exclusion and alienation from the democratic process by depriving them of facts and debate. The suffragettes who struggled and died to win the women's right to vote must be turning in their graves as they consider how today's GWR listeners are going to make informed decisions about how to cast their votes.

Those listeners who have a genuine interest in politics are likely to be listening to BBC stations and networks, but ILR's listening figures far outstrip the BBC's.[17] So most GWR radio listeners are potentially missing news that matters. To use Sir John Birt's phrase, they are in danger of becoming part of the

> information-poor – an underprivileged knowledge underclass, denied access to the quality of information, insight and entertainment enjoyed by the richer members of the community.'
>
> (Birt 1999: 3)

Still the BBC should not congratulate itself too much. It has a recent policy of presenting 'personally useful information' (BBC internal document, November 1998 reported in *Press Gazette*) Since the BBC levies a universal licence fee of £101 from every viewer and listener, it must be seen to be provide what most people want to hear. 'Personally useful information' covers many of the topics that GWR offers its listeners. Some BBC insiders are critical of this definition of news:

> If you want to get a job in the BBC nowadays you've got to specialise in social affairs. Social diseases, we call them. All kinds of surveys of deviance and perversions . . . They squeeze out the real hard news.
>
> (female senior correspondent in the BBC Business Unit)

A senior (male) journalist on BBC Radio Four's *The World Tonight* said:

> We hardly ever send reporters abroad any more, never mind producers and presenters. We're supposed to cover the whole world, but we've got two women News Editors on a jobshare and so we're stuck on the domestic agenda.

'Domestic' in this context does not mean stories about household or family matters, though it is an interesting coincidence that the word is associated with the home, traditionally the woman's place. 'Domestic' here means UK-based stories, as opposed to the 'true' BBC news agenda which is international.

If it is defined as 'lifestyle' or 'personally useful' news, a 'female' news agenda may not necessarily serve the best interests of women as listeners. It omits vital subject areas which are male-dominated at present, but which could be transformed if enough women were well-informed and interested enough to challenge the male hegemony of government, diplomacy and the law courts. Such a challenge requires more than the straightforward increase in the proportion of female journalists called for by Dickey (1985). In radio, the clock starts ticking as soon as a young woman enters a newsroom as a new recruit. It is not just a biological clock that might drive her to start a family by the age of thirty. It is also a very short career ladder with a flattened hierarchy and multi-media modus operandi that might lead to a job with a less 'motherist' atmosphere and a better rate of pay.

From the Haworth survey a picture emerges of women in senior editorial positions who believe that, and behave as though, gender plays no part in their work as radio journalists. According to Heather Purdey's research, they were probably hired because they have a compliant attitude and no strong moral code. They accept and perpetuate the generally masculine culture of the newsroom rather than trying to challenge it or innovate, they will get up early and work late and accept low rates of pay (Purdey 1999).

On the positive side, the Haworth survey suggests a female radio journalist may accept the prevailing, male-dominated culture of the newsroom but will strive to make every item accessible to female and male listeners, rejecting jargon, challenging officialdom and asking questions that penetrate rather then provoke. Beyond 'hard' and 'soft' news, beyond the 'gender agenda' set by advertisers and audience researchers, there is now a large body of women in radio news who can, and will, change the way their profession operates. At present, they are doing it unconsciously, they would say instinctively. In the future they may try to codify their new ways of approaching news, and actively train their staff to adopt new attitudes to news priorities, the language, content and presentation of news. That will only benefit news in general, because after all 'personally useful news' and 'lifestyle news' are relevant to every listener, not just to women. If they can be provided without sacrificing informed debate and reportage of the more sterotypically 'male' aspects of life such as politics, crime, sport and international affairs then we shall all be better served.

Notes

1 Although it is mentioned in Sebba (1994).
2 The Haworth survey is a telephone questionnaire completed by twenty senior radio news editors in BBC and Independent Local Radio stations in 1999 and provides a snapshot of their attitudes to the female news agenda. The 'motherism' research (1999) canvassed the views of ten former radio journalists who are mothers.
3 Sallies: Radio stations licensed by the Radio Authority for eight years in a restricted geographical area.
4 RSL: Restricted Service Licence, 28-day licence for a localised radio station, issued in the UK by the Radio Authority.

5 ISDN a technical device for producing studio-quality sound via an enhanced telephone line.
6 The practice of physically pushing one's way into a room or home in order to get close enough to the interviewee to record a radio interview of acceptable technical quality (with the microphone less than half a metre away from the interviewee's mouth).
7 The practice of waiting on the doorstep for a potential interviewee to emerge.
8 The practice of physically pushing past rival reporters to get close to an interviewee (similar to a rugby scrum).
9 The process by which broadcast news items are sourced, edited, scripted, and sent to air by one person using a networked desktop computer.
10 Buerk, M., Lecture at City University London, October 1999 (in personal capacity as Visiting Fellow).
11 Interview with John Pickford, Head of News and Sport, Key103/Magic 1242, June 1999.
12 ILR: Independent Local Radio.
13 GWR Group of Independent Local Radio stations which owns the national station Classic FM, the London digital radio multiplex and a number of local and regional radio stations.
14 Interview with Colin Hancock, Head of News, BBC Radio 1, July 1999.
15 Radio journalists may equally well need time off to care for frail elderly or disabled relatives or sick partners, friends or pets: care does not begin and end with babyhood.
16 Jay, M. Speech to the National Union of Journalists South East Regional Equality Conference, 1999.
17 Listening figures from RAJAR (radio research body that carried out research for both BBC and commercial radio sectors).

References

Birt, J. (1999) *The Prize and the Price*, The New Statesman Dinner, Banqueting House, Whitehall, 6/7/99.
Christmas, L. (1997) *Chaps of Both Sexes*, London: City University.
Cramer, J. (1993) 'Radio: A Woman's Place is on the air', in Creedon, P.J. (ed.) *Woman in Mass Communication* (2nd edition), London: Sage.
Delano, A. (1998) *The New Journalist*, London: London College of Printing.
Dickey, J. 1985 *Women in Focus*, London: Campaign for Press and Broadcasting Freedom.
Haworth, J.M. (1999) 'Women radio news editors and the female news agenda', (unpublished telephone survey) City University, London.
O'Malley, T. (1997) *A Journalism Reader*, London: Routledge.
Purdey, H. (1999) 'Research findings about journalism recruitment', presented to the Broadcast Journalism Training Council, Preston, UK.
Sebba, A. (1994) *Battling for News. The Rise of the Woman Reporter*, London: Sceptre.
Shingler M, and Wieringa, C. (1998) *On Air – Methods and Meanings of Radio*, London: Arnold.
Smith, C. (1999) Speech to Royal Television Society conference, Cambridge, UK, 18.9.99.
Walter, N. (1998) *The New Feminism*, London: Heinemann.
Woolf, M., Holly S. and Connor H. (1996) *Employment Patterns and Training needs, 1995/6*, Broadcast Journalism. London: Skillset.
Zilliacus-Tikkanen, H. (1996) *Journalistikens Essens I ett Könsperspectiv* (*The Essence of Journalism in a Gender Perspective*) Finland: Rundradions Jämställdhetskommitté.

Chapter 21

Caroline Mitchell

SOUND ADVICE FOR WOMEN WHO WANT TO WORK IN RADIO

At the beginning of the new millennium a large part of British radio is run by women: Jenny Abramsky is in charge of BBC Radio and the Controller for BBC Radio 4 is Helen Boden. Having a female manager isn't necessarily a guarantee for good working conditions; as we've seen in this volume (Gibbons, Haworth, Michaels and Mitchell, Millington,) there is often a complex web of factors relating to personal, institutional and societal pressures that prevents women getting into, and on in the radio industry. It's a sad truth that even when women have a string of appropriate qualifications that they are still not getting as many permanent jobs in production and management as men (see Nexus and Gibbons 1998: 4). Ginny Dougary's interviews (1994) with prominent media women make depressing reading and reveal that the media industry is still run by men, in the interests of male employees and this contributes to a male view of the world represented in programming.

So this chapter unashamedly concentrates on hints, tips and helpful strategies for women who want to get into radio. It's based on the experience of women who have succeeded in different roles in BBC, commercial and community radio sectors. Like all areas of the media radio is a highly competitive employment area. Ask anyone who works in radio about 'how to get in' and they will advise you to get relevant skills, qualifications and work experience. You need persistence, the ability to gather and use contacts in the industry, to be prepared to do anything (often in a low paid or voluntary capacity) and to seize opportunities as they occur.

This chapter does not purport to be a comprehensive guide to every job in radio. There are now several books, organisations and web sites with advice about getting into work in radio, journalism and multimedia (see Contacts section): the BBC web pages and the *UK Media Directory* are particularly good starting places. However I will look at a number of job areas supported by case studies of women who have succeeded in their chosen careers.

The areas are as follows:

Production and programme making;
Writing for radio;
Music presentation;
News, journalism and sports reporting;
Engineering and studio management,
Station management;
Commercial radio sales, production, sponsorship and promotions;
Experimental and Internet radio

Production and programme making

When I was at university in the early 1980s I was told that if I wanted to get into radio production at the BBC then I should 'take the secretarial route'. I wondered how men got in! Women do still use this route enter radio.[1] It is one way of getting to know the different departments and people in what is a huge organisation and one of the biggest employers in the country. However starting off as a Broadcast Assistant (BA) involves research, organisational and production skills and can be a faster track to a careers as a full-time researcher or producer. The people who tend to succeed in this area tend to be focused, keen, and have an abundance of programme ideas.

Profile

Name: Maud Hand

Job: Freelance Producer for BBC Network Radio.

'I have a driving desire to make good radio. The job draws on my interpersonal, technical and intellectual resources. My skills are in teamwork, executing ideas in fresh ways and translating them into radiophonic terms. I have opportunities to learn and talk to people from all walks of life.'

Route in: After working as a primary school teacher and getting experience of programme making and station management with women's radio (she was one of the women who set up Brazen Radio in London), Maud got a place on a BBC production training scheme. She went on to report for and produce programmes like *Kaleidoscope*, and *Woman's Hour* for BBC Radio 4 and *Megamix* for the World Service. For BBC Radio 1 she produced *Jammin in Jamaica*, the acclaimed series about roots of reggae, and *Sound Sirens* about female club DJs. She has also produced drama for BBC Radio 3 and is currently working on experimental productions for an independent production company.

Sound Advice: 'Think seriously about going into this area. To be successful it requires a huge commitment, which leaves little time for a personal life. Assess your own character and skills – self-confidence and awareness is essential if you are to survive. Frank speaking isn't always valued. I've learnt some hard lessons about people taking on my ideas as their own. There is a lack of awareness of black cultural identity in the industry. Coming from Ireland I've been belittled because of my accent and I've had to battle a lot because I allowed myself to feel inferior,'

Hints and tips:
- 'Listen to the radio'
- 'Get to meet people whose work you admire'

Writing for radio

This is an area where women are doing well. Opportunities for writing for radio broadcast of short stories, plays and features are mainly within the BBC. The important things are to listen to the different slots available; find out what the BBC are interested in commissioning at any one time and get yourself, your ideas and your work known to producers. This can be done through contacting producers directly or by going through regional arts initiatives, writer's courses, workshops and competitions (contact your local arts board for further details).

Profile

Name: Julia Darling

Job: Freelance writer, producing novels, stories, plays and some journalism for radio, stage, etc. 'My most useful skills are an obsession with the sounds and nuances of language.'

Route in: 'I have always had an interest in radio, but never did any specific unpaid work relating to it like volunteering in a radio station. I always liked messing around with tape recorders though. I did two training courses – the first in 1988 in Hull with BBC writers and producers which was very inspiring. Then I did *Write out Loud*, a training week for published writers wanting to use sound and radio techniques. It was wonderful, and we all made short programmes. Some of us were able to develop these into broadcast material, and to learn a bit about producing and budgeting for radio. I started off like everyone else, sending unsolicited stories and plays to faceless directors at the BBC. Eventually got to know Kate Rowland, who used to come up to the North regularly scouting about looking for writers. She liked my stories and produced a couple of them. After that I seemed to get to know a few producers and felt it was quite easy to talk over ideas for radio if you had them. I wrote a radio play, and more stories, then did *Write out Loud*. I then produced *Home Truths* a documentary feature about the very old in old people's homes, and worked with an independent company making a series of four stories called *Scraping the Sky* about people working high in the air. When the system changed at the BBC and things got more 'slot led' it seemed to be harder to develop ideas with producers, and a lot of things don't get through, so it's not a linear progression by any means'.

Sound Advice: 'Study the field . . . listen to radio . . . be aware of slots if submitting to the BBC. I create networks of support around me, as it's very easy to get isolated as a writer. When problems arise I tend to talk it through with other writers.'

Hints and tips:
- 'Domesticity and creativity don't go. I go and work in a room that I rent outside my home.'
- 'You need to manage time in order to nourish your ideas. Children of mothers who do this are better off I think.'

Presentation

Presenting and DJ-ing are arguably the most prestigious jobs in radio and there are very few opportunities compared to other areas. (See Michaels and Mitchell in this volume for discussion of why there have been so few women DJs.)

Media attention is usually focused on high profile female DJs working on the major network stations. The BBC web page profiles of star female DJs show that they have worked their way through music journalism (Jo Whiley, Mary-Ann Hobbs), University broadcasting (Emma B) or crossed over from entertainment television presentation (Zöe Ball, Sara Cox). But most of the jobs are in small local and regional radio stations. The best place to get experience is unpaid work in hospital, student, community and local radio stations. There are now more women getting experience as club DJs and then getting radio sessions, often starting on the 'graveyard' overnight shift. In commercial radio, women often get in through casual work in promotions for instance dressing up as 'Easter Bunnies' and handing out leaflets. With some production skills and perseverance you can also get in through making yourself indispensable in production related work, including making up trails and jingles. Another 'route in' is as a side-kick to another presenter (yes, usually male) reading the weather, traffic reports and generally responding to the other presenter's comments. Some women have used this as a way in and have turned the side-kick role into one as a co-presenter. Enlightened programme controllers sometimes pick full-time presenters with this kind of experience.

Making your own luck (sometimes called being in the right place at the right time), is explained by long-time Radio 1 presenter Annie Nightingale:

Hang in there . . . hover about and be on the periphery of what you want to do until the 'you'll do nipper' syndrome comes into play . . . one day someone's gone on holiday and they go erm – you'll do. You're the one who comes to mind because you've been making the tea, you've been helping out, probably working for nothing and being enthusiastic and helpful and turning up every week. Just do that and it *does* work.

(BBC 1999)

The main complaint that programme controllers have made about women in the past is that 'they just don't apply'. In fact most presentation jobs aren't advertised because they are filled by tried and tested people who are already known to the station or network (see above). However programme controllers (PCs) do still listen to demo tapes and it's worth putting together a short well produced tape that shows off your versatility, skills and experience. The most important thing to remember is that PCs are busy people so make sure that you cue up and label your tape/disc properly, and make an impression in the first few seconds – otherwise your tape will go straight into the recycling bin. Some stations are now seeking new talent through competitions, so use any avenue to get your voice heard. When they do advertise most stations use the Radio Magazine (see Contacts).

Profile

Name: Margherita Taylor

Job: DJ at Capital Radio, London. Margherita has presented a range of programmes including night and weekend shifts. She also works on outside broadcasts: 'Working at Party in the Park was a fantastic experience – a live concert/radio show to an audience of 100,000 and millions world wide on TV, 32 artists performed over 8 hours, unforgettable'.

Route in: She did a Media and Communications degree at the University of Central England in Birmingham. After graduating she won a competition on Birmingham's local radio station 94–6 FM BRMB. A year later she went to work for sister station 95.8 Capital FM in London.

Sound Advice: 'Get as much work experience as you can and be prepared for a lot of rejection. It's almost as hard to get work experience as a job, but it all helps. Be determined. Don't give up.'

Hints and Tips: See Margherita's web page: 'So, You Wanna Be a DJ?' at http://www.CapitalFM.com

News, journalism and sports reporting

Over the last ten years women have made huge strides in the area of radio news and journalism. Women now outnumber men on many of the general and specialist degrees and training courses in journalism provided by colleges and universities.

Although good research, writing and reporting skills are essential your voice is still your main asset so getting training and practice in this area is a must. Despite the number of women in radio news there can still be extraordinary prejudice about female voices (and sometimes about regional accents too, although this is less common nowadays). Journalist and presenter Sandy Warr (who is also featured below) comments:

I do feel – as someone who trains broadcasters' voices – that women still have to conform to a much more narrow definition of what is an acceptable broadcasting voice for women. It strikes me (that) men get away with far more imperfections in tone and diction than women. I often hear editors criticising student voices by saying the student sounds too much like a young girl. What else are you supposed to sound like when you are 21?

Profile

Name: Sandy Warr

Job: Presenter LBC Breakfast programme. 'In radio I genuinely believe that progression is down to how fast and accurately you perform the work, your ideas and the quality of your voice. The main useful skills to get in early days: speed – everything is always needed ten minutes ago – and a tough skin to deal with editors losing their tempers. You need confidence in dealing with telephone calls and interviews and as wide a knowledge of current affairs as possible. A working knowledge of sport is always a good idea – especially in the more jurassic newsrooms around the country where they tend to view a woman who can talk football like some kind of performing pet worth showing off to the listeners. Endless enthusiasm, energy, and a willingness to sacrifice your social life.'

Route in: After a degree in English Sandy did a Diploma in radio journalism, then various radio jobs – Radio Mercury, BBC Radio Bedfordshire, Capital Radio, BBC GLR, BBC Radio Sport (mainly Five Live), Talk Radio, and News Direct Radio. 'The list makes it all look very simple – but hides a long trail of applications and rejections that were overcome by sheer doggedness and refusing to take no for an answer from prospective employers! To start with I tried to plan my career with military precision and proceeded to glean an equal balance of BBC and Independent Radio experience. But then companies started contacting me and offering me opportunities that I had previously never considered – so all my planning went out of the window.'

Sound Advice: 'If you really want it – then you will get it. But you have to *really* want it. The industry is famous for dishing out knocks and insults. Arm yourself with a solid sense of humour, a detailed knowledge of the technical equipment, the law and who you really need to impress in any given newsroom. Always make sure you know exactly what you are being asked to provide – how long the piece will be, when it is needed. Always ask for help if you are not sure – better to ask up front than fail to meet a deadline if you were too scared to interrupt someone else.'

Hints and Tips:
- 'You still get stewards and officials at sports grounds asking you when your boyfriend is going to turn up to do the real job . . . My answer has always been to ignore the insult and just do as great a job as possible . . . I like to think my

skills would have had more impact than any bad tempered discussion about their sexist assumptions.'

- 'Never inflate your own abilities – but equally don't sell yourself short.'
- 'When you are starting out in the business spend time nurturing your voice – get some training and get someone you trust in the business to listen critically to what you sound like and help you improve.'
- 'Shift working is seriously bad news for your energy levels and eating patterns and it's really hard to keep a full life outside the job when you are starting out. It gets easier when you become more willing to set the phone to answer phone and not be always available at the drop of a hat to cover someone else's shift.'

Engineering and studio management

The hard end of engineering – putting up transmitters, designing, building and maintaining studios – is still very much a male preserve. The BBC, universities,[2] and schools are making efforts to change the way girls and women perceive engineering as a career. If you haven't had the opportunity at school, some further education colleges offer taster courses which combine skill training and confidence building. The studio manager role (see below) involves a wide range of production, organisational and technical skills.

Profile

Name: Vicki Carter

Job: Senior Studio manager (SM), Europe Team, World Service. Carrying out all technical operations for live and pre-recorded programmes – working with programme producers and continuity announcers. The shifts are often long – she is regularly at work for more than 10 hours – but she also enjoys having days off during the week.

Route in: She started as a theatre electrician and stage manager then took a degree in Women's Studies and Drama. She has also worked as a producer for the Sony award winning *Euromix* for Radio 5 and *A Sunday Outing* – the first lesbian and gay programme for BBC Radio 4. Most of her training came from courses within the BBC.

Sound Advice: 'Get some experience and then bang on doors and ask to trail the job that you think you are interested in – make sure you know what the job is about before you waste time trying to get a job that you may not enjoy. There have always been about 50 per cent women in Studio Management. I am always very open, although I rarely tell people that I am lesbian, they glean it from conversation. The BBC are quite good on equal opportunities, although I think some of my Black women friends would say that sometimes there is racism at work.'

Hints and Tips:
- 'Look out for jobs and trainee schemes in the media sections of newspapers and the BBC website.'
- 'Computing skills are very handy.'

Management

The BBC has made some headway in making institutional changes to lift some of the barriers to women reaching management positions. In commercial radio, although there is still a lack of females in executive positions and at Board level, women are using their considerable experience in areas like radio sales to move into management positions. Small-scale community stations are an excellent place to getting experience, (usually unpaid) of working with a variety of people, financial management, fundraising, programming and marketing.

Profile

Name: Sally Aitchison

Job: Managing director TFM and Magic 1170 (part of EMAP group of commercial radio stations). She manages and leads a team of 55 staff including 28 women. She is responsible for the on air sound of the station, marketing (including developing the station brand in clubs etc), commercial activity, business plans, budgets (including delivering a profit!), creative development, training and staff development.

Route in: She joined the station as a receptionist straight from school. Worked in selling radio advertising over the phone and progressed through the jobs of Sales Executive, Sales Manager and Sales Director before becoming MD.

Sound Advice: 'Women have to juggle and so make better managers – they are better listeners, less hierarchical, more creative and encouraging. At TFM Aitchison encourages a station culture of promoting from within-several staff started on Youth Training schemes and she is committed to recognition and development of staff.'

Hints and Tips:
- Aitchison has two young children and couldn't manage at work and on business trips without having the support of her husband and mum: 'I drop the children off at 7.45am and leave them until 6.30pm.'
- 'I believe that success is not gender based, it is determined by skill, knowledge, ability, talent and commitment. These attributes will always win the day. I have also never tried to compete on a masculine level, I don't believe that women need to lose their femininity or the female qualities that actually set them apart from their male colleagues.'

Profile

Name: Ami Yesufu

Job: Station manager and co-ordinator of Elle FM a women's radio broadcasting project on Merseyside. Her skills include: being enthusiastic and committed to the station, people management, fundraising, broadcasting.

Route in: A Media Youth Training Scheme led to specialist training in radio at the Ariel Trust in Liverpool and work as researcher and reporter for BBC youth programmes on local and network radio/TV. She has presented on pirate radio and worked in a number of jobs including radio training. In 1994 she went on a media management course at Ariel and as a result established Elle FM a women's radio station and training project.

Sound Advice: 'You should always be prepared to 'serve your apprenticeship' down the voluntary route. A lot of opportunities arise from offering yourself about, being noticed fulfilling specific roles. Don't make money an issue if you're trying to get initial experience.'

Hints and Tips:
- 'Get as much experience as possible.'
- 'Don't believe that the BBC is the only thing to aspire to – there are so many other areas of radio/media that will give you the freedom to use your own talents and interests.'

Commercial radio sales, production, sponsorship and promotions

Since 1990 British commercial radio has expanded hugely, with new stations and formats coming on air every month. The industry is increasingly dominated by small stations (and small staff teams) within large radio groups. This means that there are opportunities to get experience of a number of different areas within a station and move around within groups. The downside however is that small stations can be dominated by a small number of people and often the personality and management style of the manager or programme controller determines who is employed and promoted.

Profile

Name: Trisha Jarman

Job: Scriptwriter and producer for radio commercials; voice over artist.

Route in: Degree in English Literature, voluntary experience in hospital and student radio. She started as an advertising agency copywriter, then scriptwriter in a radio station. All her production and voice over skills were learnt on the job. She's done in-house courses in management, accounts and marketing as well as training in word processing and digital broadcast equipment.

Sound Advice: 'As a writer get to know the technical side of the work too – if you're a studio engineer, then vice versa! It helps the quality of your work to have an overall understanding of the process – even though you work in the creative side. Technology and business change constantly. Keep your knowledge and skills up to date. Many voice overs now work from their own home studios using ISDN.[3] If you are trying to get into voicing commercials try to compile a simple demo tape and get the opinions of some producers about your work before investing in equipment. Don't assume it's a job for life. It's a fast developing area and new opportunities are emerging all the time. Think about how you'd next like to use the skills you acquire. Also radio stations are fond of merging, de-merging and restructuring, so be ready for change. You may have to be prepared to operate in a different way to continue doing the work you enjoy.

Hints and Tips:
- 'If you're putting together a CV include two or three examples of your work. If you don't have any, take something you've heard and create a different idea to show how you would've approached the same project.'
- 'You have to be prepared to work late / weekends; there is a high element of unpredictability. There are only few part time posts, so I think life is very demanding for those with children.'

Profile

Name: Jude Mallabar

Job: Promotions and Sponsorship manager Century Radio North-East.

Route in: 'I always listened to the radio. After I left school I worked in a shop – the Cookie Jar at the Metro Centre! I had a child when I was young and at 22 I did a Media A level at night school. Then I did a Media Studies Degree at the University of Sunderland as a mature student and did my work experience in the commercial production office at Century and they took me on as a trainee. I became an executive and now I have my own assistant! The most enjoyable part of the job is working with the client and eventually hearing the end result on air. I want to move in to programming – I want to be a programme controller.'

Sound Advice: 'Get to know your way around the industry – read industry magazines like the *Radio magazine*, *Broadcast* and *Marketing Week*. Some people come in from other media sales jobs – about half have degrees in Business Studies. There are no formal ways in. If necessary, work for nothing until your face is known. You need to be able to cope with presenters with big egos and remember commercial radio is there to make money not programmes. I've used my sexuality to get a sale – men can be silly! It's not ideal but it works!'

Hints and Tips:
- 'Networking is important – make sure people in the radio station and the group know who you are and what you're interested in. Often opportunities for promotion come from hearing about new licences and stations coming on air.'
- 'For childcare I've had support from my family when I've had to work late or at weekends. If my child is ill I've been allowed to work from home – most people have a family and understand.'

Experimental/internet radio

This is the newest area of radio and it provides some fascinating opportunities for people to use sound and the web.

Profile

Name: Kate Rich

Job: Digital sound artist in residence at ARC, Stockton-on-Tees; producer and editor of *Fallout* – the online audio magazine of culture and technology.[4] As technical director and programme co-ordinator of the 'live-stock' webcast event (72 hours of experimental audio online & on local FM radio). Kate oversees the technical side – audio and data: PAs, telecom, streaming software, as well as working with the local community and artists on how to realise their projects in experimental audio. This includes organising introductory training in digital sound techniques.

Route in: Kate did a Radio Production degree in Australia and then worked as a voluntary announcer/producer for the alternative radio station 3RRR in Melbourne. After doing a digital audio training course at SoundLab in San Francisco she worked in a series of positions in multimedia/educational environments producing amongst other things audio-books and museum audio-tours. She also worked at the Bureau of Inverse Technology (BIT) on diverse projects as a sound engineer.

Sound Advice: 'I have a thorough knowledge of computer environment; technical skills with analogue audio and basic familiarity with studio recording techniques'. She enjoys the 'very malleable hours and the non-office environment.' The least enjoyable aspects of the work are 'headphone headache and proximity to humming computer drives.'

Hints and Tips:
- 'Impressive technical skills and being female can be actually demographic advantage!'
- 'How to roll cable and knowing the names for connectors are very influential skills if you need to hold your own in a technician environment.'

Summary of sound advice to women who want to get into radio (and survive)

- Be prepared to do almost anything to get initial radio experience. Be flexible and available. Once you're in be more choosy and focused in picking the kind of work you do.
- Keep a contacts book of people whom you come across in radio/media. This will be the groundwork for getting into networks that that will help to land a job and provide ongoing support.
- Seek out good role models: watch how they work. Get to meet people whose work you admire. Organise a mentor. Make strategic alliances with men and women in the industry.
- Build up your confidence as much as possible. Appearing enthusiastic and confident (even if you are quaking inside) is winning half the battle. Discuss fears or problems with supportive people. Try to get training run by women and men who know what they're doing and who don't patronise. Some women find that a 'women only' course provides a safe and enjoyable space to learn.
- Employers are looking for people who are both 'multiskilled' (doing a million things at once, including good computer, communication and organisational skills) and who have *specialist* interests and skills relating particular jobs. Develop technical competence and IT skills. Get help with production techniques from people you trust.
- Be focused on what area of work you want to enter. Get informed so you can be single minded in pursuit of work.
- Plan how work can fit in with domestic arrangements and social life. For production/journalism are you prepared to work long and unsociable hours? What are the options for working freelance and from home? What kind of arrangements can you make with a radio employer to balance work and family responsibilities?
- Use community radio, hospital and student radio to get training and voluntary experience in a supportive environment. Remember nearly all radio environments are competitive but BBC and commercial radio are particularly so – watch your back!
- Men tend to assume that they will work the controls in the studio. In male–female teams the woman tends to end up on the 'wrong' side of the desk, like a passenger. A woman getting in to radio should make sure she finds out what all the knobs do (or at least be able to bluff it as well as the men do). Otherwise they will remain passive, secondary and, ultimately, dispensable.[5]
- Develop a persistent and pushy side to your personality and use it to get where you want to be!
- Remember having a female manager doesn't necessarily mean that she will give you an easy time. To succeed at senior management level a woman has to be tougher, more organised and better than the men in similar jobs. You cannot be seen to have any weaknesses – and to give and take with women about personal or professional issues can be seen as a weakness.[6]

- Work on strategies to challenge annoying or offensive behaviour – calmly and with dignity. Don't let prejudiced comments get you down or let sexist idiots make you behave like a mad woman!

Notes

1 See Hilary Whitney's article about being a broadcast assistant on Radio 4's Today programme (Whitney 2000: 7).
2 See also organisations like Let's Train Women in Science, Engineering, Construction and Technology (Lets TWIST).
3 ISDN stands for Integrated Services Digital Network. It is a high quality telephone link line often used to relay sound.
4 www.fallout.org.uk
5 Thanks to Brian Lister, MD at Sun FM in Sunderland for this advice.
6 Thanks to Caroline Beck, freelance producer and journalist for this advice.

References

BBC Woman's Hour (1999) Interview with Annie Nightingale by Jenni Murray, 23 April 1999, 10am, London: BBC.

Baker, P. (1995) *Making it as a Radio or TV Presenter – An Insider's Guide*, London: Piatkus.

Brown, L. (ed.) (1998) *Media Careers: Broadcasting.* London: Purple House.

Dougary, G. (1994) *The Executive Tart and Other Myths – Media Women Talk Back*, London: Virago.

Horstmann, R. (1997) *Writing for Radio*, London: A & C Black.

Nexus Research co-operative and Givvons, M. (1998) *Breaking Glass Walls, Gender and Employment Issues in the Independent Radio Sector in Ireland*, Galway: Women on Air.

Russell, F. (1996) *Getting into Broadcasting*, London: Trotman.

Selby, M. (1997) *Careers in TV and Radio*, London: Kogan Page.

Whitney, H. (2000) 'Tuned into her world', Office Hours supplement for secretarial staff, 29 February 2000, page 7, London: *Guardian*.

Part 4

Contacts and resources

UK WOMEN'S RADIO STATIONS, COMMUNITY-BASED TRAINING PROJECTS AND SUPPORT GROUPS

Elle FM
PO Box 426
Liverpool L69 8JG
Tel: 0151 709 8899
Elle FM runs an accredited training scheme in radio for women

Radio Venus
c/o Bradford Community Broadcasting
2 Forster Square
Bradford BD1 1DQ
Tel: 01274 771677
Web site: www.bcb.yorks.com

107 The Bridge Women's Radio
c/o Bridge Women's Education and Training Centre
Columbia
Washington
Tyne and Wear
0191 417 2445

Women's Radio Group (WRG)
Unit 13
111, Power Rd
London W4 5PY
Tel: 020 8742 7802
Web site: www.twiza.demon.co.uk/wrg/
WRG runs a range of training courses for women in London. It has an online directory of women who have radio skills and runs occasional seminars.

Let's TWIST (Let's train women in Science, Engineering, Construction and Technology).
c/o Bradford College
Great Horton Rd
Bradford
West Yorkshire BD7 1AY
Webpage: http://www.bilk.ac.uk /college/extraweb/twistweb/index/htm
Contact: A.Williams@bilk.ac.uk
Campaign and training group for women in non-traditional trades (including broadcast engineering)

UK RADIO AND TRAINING ORGANISATIONS AND PUBLICATIONS

BBC
BBC Broadcast
Broadcasting House
London W1A 1AA
Tel: 020 7580 4458
Web pages for jobs, trainee schemes and careers advice: www.bbc.co.uk/jobs

Commercial Radio
Radio Authority
Holbrook House
14 Great Queen Street
London WC2B 5DG
Tel.: 020 7430 2724
Web site: www.radioauthority.org.uk.
The Radio Authority is the UK's commercial radio regulatory body. It has information about all UK commercial radio stations (including setting up restricted service stations) and fact sheets about careers in broadcasting.

Commercial Radio Companies Association (CRCA)
77 Shaftesbury Ave
London W1V 7AD
Tel: 020 7306 2603
Web site: www.crca.co.uk
The CRCA web site has information about working in radio, work placements, getting into commercial radio. It has produced a report (mainly based on industry interviews and anecdotes) called 'Women in Commercial Radio'.

Community Radio
Community Media Association (CMA).
15 Paternoster Row
Sheffield S1 2BX

Tel: 0114 2795219

Web site: www.comedia.org.uk

The CMA can provide list of radio stations and RSLs (short term licensed stations) in your area as well as details of subsidised radio training courses, conferences and training materials. Provides radio training for minority ethnic and women's groups and raises money for campaigns and radio training. It is one of the partners for the 'Permanent Waves' project – a series of initiatives designed to improve conditions for women working in radio, including stations in the community sector. (see International stations and contacts below)

Radio Studies Network

c/o Peter Lewis

London School of Economics and Political Sciences

Houghton St

London WC2A 2AE

Tel: 020 7995 6494

Web site www.jiscmail.ac.uk/lists/radio-studies.html

The Radio Studies network promotes the study of radio theory and practice. Its email discussion group is an excellent way getting in touch with broadcasters, radio lecturers and students in the UK and abroad.

The Radio Academy

5 Market Place

London W1R 3HG

Tel.: 020 7255 2010

Web site: www.radacad.demon.co.uk

The Radio Academy is a membership organisation for professional broadcasters (not an academic organisation!) It hosts the annual Radio Festival and the Sony Radio awards. It also provides membership facilities for the Student Radio Association. (www.studentradio.orguk/8080/)

Industry publications

The Radio Magazine,

Crown House

25 High St

Rothwell NN14 6AD

Tel.: 01536 418558

Web site: www.theradiomagazine.co.uk

Broadcast

33–39 Bowling Green Lane

London EC1R ODA

Tel.: 020 7505 8014

Both publications contain adverts for jobs in BBC and commercial radio.

UK Media Directory www.mediauk.com/

WOMEN'S RADIO STATIONS AND CONTACTS WORLD-WIDE

Radio Pirate Woman
10, St Brigits Place Lower
Galway
Irish Republic
Tel: +353 91 65 430
Web site www.larkspirit.com/d'arcy

RadiOrakel
Postboks 6826
St Olav's Plass
0130 Oslo, Norway
Tel: 47 22 42 65 60

Feminist International Radio Endeavour (FIRE)
Web site: www.fire.or.cr
FIRE is a Latin American-based radio news agency which distributes international feminist news and information.

Women's International Newsgathering Service (WINGS)
Web site: www.wings.org/
WINGS is a US based-feminist news agency: 'raising women's voices through radio world-wide.' It has a network of feminist reporters and distributes reports via cassette and on line.

Association for Progressive Communication (APC) women's programme
Web site: colnud.apc.org/apcwomen/

AMARC-Europe Women's network
C/o AMARC Europe
15 Paternoster Row
Sheffield S1 2BX
Tel: +44 (0)114 221 0592
Web page: www.amarc.org/europe/women

AMARC is the world Association for Community Radio Broadcasting which promotes, supports and develops community radio stations world-wide. The women's network produces a newsletter, runs courses and conferences and produces training materials and directories of women's contacts and radio programme material for exchange. Partner in the 'Permanent Waves' training project: www.amarc.org/pw

AMARC International
3575 Boulevard St Laurent
Bureau 611,
Montreal, Quebec
Canada
Web page: www.amarc.org
International office for AMARC. Contact for International women's network.

Women On Air (WOA)
Web site: www.woa.iol.ie
Irish campaigning and training group for women and radio. This project was part of the Permanent Waves project and although WOA is no longer in existence it's site is still active and contains resources and policy reports.

Index

Abrahamson, U. 255
Abramsky, J. 210, 262
ABS 251
ACTT 251
Aitchison, S. 269–70
Ali, Y. 187n
amplification 15–26, 52
Anand, A. 193
Ang, I. 153, 160
Annie on my Mind 77–8
announcing 22–6
anti-slavery 11, 18
Any Questions? 75
Archers, The xvi, 2, 66, 72n, 74, 162, 163–4
Ariel Trust, The 270
Asian radio 6n, 104, 182–8
Asian Radio Network 6n
Association for Community Radio Broadcasting (AMARC) 281–2; Europe 281; Women's Network 281
Astor, N. 42, 43, 44, 45, 68
Attachments (BBC) 215
Audience xvi, 5, 37, 60, 64, 67, 69, 70, 75, 88–9, 101, 113–14, 116–201, 141–3, 206, 242–4; research 3, 6n, 70, 113, 115n, 130, 261n
Austin, J. 150

Baehr, H. 4, 95, 96, 129, 134, 135, 137, 207, 242, 243
Ball, Z. i, 243, 248n, 265
Barker, D. 206
Barker, M. 142

Barnard, S. xii, 2, 113
Barthes, R. 151
Bates, S. 130, 132–3
Baumann, G. 187n
BBC 6, 12, 22, 29–40, 41–7, 77, 78, 82, 95, 96, 118, 126–9, 205, 209–18, 219–23, 238, 239–41, 252, 255–7, 279
BBC Light Programme 36, 66, 126
BBC Northern Region 12, 29, 32
BBC Radio 1 xv, xvi, 3, 5, 6n, 95, 114, 130–3, 134,137, 157, 238, 241
BBC Radio 2 xvi, 3, 6n, 131
BBC Radio 3 3, 6n, 76, 155, 165n
BBC Radio 4 3, 6n, 64–72, 74, 78–9, 81, 82, 107, 133, 146, 154, 156–9, 162, 165n, 205, 259
BBC Radio 5 xvi, 13, 70, 77–8
BBC Radio 5 Live 3, 5, 6n, 70, 267
BBC Radio London 13, 84–93, 95, 133, 210
BBC Third Programme 74, 157, 165n
BBC World Service 210, 268
Beasley, M. 225
Beck, C. 274n
Bectu 251
Behrens, T. 49, 53
Benhabib, S. 191
Bennett, J. 213
Bery, R. 94
Bessler, H. 48
Billig, M. 142
Birt, J. 78, 79, 259
Black woman presenter (first) 11

Black Women's Radio Group 96
Blackburn, T. 131, 133, 136n
Boaden, H. 213
Bock, G. 54
Bode, C. 16
Booth, J. xv, 11
Borrect, Mrs G. 22
Bradford Community Broadcasting 98,
    109n, 193, 277
Brah, A. 182
Brainard, Miss B. 24
Brazen Radio 81–2, 94, 98, 100, 101,
    102–5, 252, 263
Bredin, M. 189, 190, 193
Bredow, H. 49
Bremmen, G. Von 54
Brewster, B. 248n
Bridenthal, R. 50
Bridge, The 94, 98, 102, 109n, 193,
    197, 242, 277
Bridson, D.G. 29
Briggs, A. 11, 12
Briggs, S. 12, 14
Brighton Festival Radio 80
BRMB 266
Broadcast (magazine) 134, 271, 280
Broadcast Assistant (BA) 263, 274n
broadcast talk 13, 43, 52, 55–60, 86–7,
    88, 128, 175, 183–4
broadcasting i, xv, xvi, 5, 11, 13–14, 29,
    33–6, 37, 41, 48, 49, 52–3, 60,
    64–72, 74, 75, 76, 77, 78–80, 81,
    94–108, 122–4, 167–81, 182–7,
    193–4, 195, 222
Broadcasting (book) 45
Broadcasting with the Lid Off 34
Brock, Dame D. 38
Broughton, F. 248n
Brown, M.E. 55
Bruce, K. 2
Bukht, M. 135
Butler, J. 192

Call Nick Ross 76
Canal Journey 33–4
capacity building 194
Capital Radio 13, 84, 88–9, 90, 95, 127,
    128, 129, 131, 134, 135, 266, 267
Cardiff Broadcasting Company 96, 129
Cardiff, D. 11, 32, 34, 43, 46, 49, 52,
    118

Carney, M. 47n
Carter, V. 268–9
Caverly, T. 81, 94, 97, 102, 105
Celebration Radio 96, 98, 102, 106, 252
censorship 76, 78, 185
Century Radio 271
Chalmers, S. 65
childcare provision 214, 257–8
Childcare Solutions 258
Children's Hour 32, 38, 122
Christmas, L. 255
Cixous, H. 197
Classic FM 155, 165n, 261n
Clause 28 76, 78, 83n
Clement, C. 197
Clithero Kid, The 1
club culture 242
Collins, N. 36, 66
commercial radio 2, 4, 6n, 11, 14, 78,
    80, 82, 84–93, 94, 96, 101, 103,
    105–8, 109n, 206, 207, 226–37,
    238–49, 270, 279
Commercial Radio Companies
    Association (CRCA) 248n, 279
commercials 52, 61n, 91, 102, 108,
    134, 270
Community Media Association (CMA)
    109n, 248n, 279–80
community radio xvi, xvii, 6, 11, 80, 94,
    95–6, 97–101, 108, 109n, 189–201,
    207, 226–37, 238–49, 279; Europe
    189–201
Connor, H. 250
consumption 152–66
controllers (radio channels) xiii, 3, 64,
    65, 67, 68–9, 71, 135, 205, 210,
    211, 213–5, 221, 243–4
Cooke, Mrs R. 17
Corrick's House 74
Coward, R. 131, 132, 190
Cox, S. i, 238, 248n, 265
Cramer, J. 244, 250
Crisell, A. 3, 11
critical discourse analysis 5, 114,
    137–51
Crook, T. 11, 14, 47n
cultural production 189, 190, 192–9,
    206
Cunningham, W. 24

Dahl, P. 48

Dahlgren, P. 191
D'Arcy, M. xvii, xii, 2, 4, 114, 193, 194, 196–7
Darling, J. 264–5
Davis, A.H. 17
Delano, A. 252
demo tapes 266
deregulation 252
Derrida, J. 151
De Saussure 151
desktopping 253, 261n
Dickey, J. 250, 260
Diller, A. 53
Diversity Database 218n
DJ 2, 4, 5, 7n, 13, 14n, 81, 86, 88–9, 93, 95, 96, 103, 104–5, 113–14, 131, 137–51, 183, 206, 207, 219–23, 226, 229, 232, 238–49, 265–6; club 79, 80, 96, 105, 242, 248n, 263, 265
documentary 29, 32–6
Dolman, F. 17
Doreen 95, 107, 109n, 128, 238
Dougary, G. 262
Dowson, M. 99
Drabble, J. 215
Dream FM 96
Dreyer, E.A. 52
Du Moncel, T. 20
Dyson. F. 115

Elle FM 94, 98, 99, 101, 102–5, 270, 277
EMAP Radio Group 269
Emma B 265
Emperor Rosco 206
equal opportunities 92–3, 97, 135, 137–51, 192–3, 235, 251–2, 268
Equal Opportunities Commission 95, 96, 109n, 129
ethnographic research 5, 109n, 113, 152–66
Euromix 268
Evans, C. 247
Evans, Dame E. 38
Extending Choice 78–9

Fallout 272
Family Life Solutions 214
fantasy 152–66
FAS 225, 236n

Feldman, S. xii, 13, 68, 69, 72n, 77
Fem FM 1, 6, 81, 94, 97–9, 100, 101, 102–5, 108, 193, 195, 197, 198–9, 242, 252
femininity 99, 132, 134, 183–4, 197, 198, 252
feminism 2, 4, 5, 6, 7n, 13, 50, 65, 91, 92, 95, 99–100, 101, 106, 107, 113, 171, 189–92, 193–9, 252
feminist cultural production 5, 189, 190, 192–9
Feminist International Radio Endeavour (FIRE) 193, 281
feminist radio 2, 95, 97–100, 113, 193,
Fenton, N. 7n
Fielden, L. 44
File on Four 76
Fiske, J. 96
F.M. 55
For the People (FTP) 7
Fraser, N. 191
Frauenfunk 12, 48–63
Fullerton, J. 235

Gallagher, M. 225
Galway Women's Entertainment (GWE) 169, 173
Gardiner, R. 72
Garfinkle, H 151
Garratt, S. 242, 245
G.A.Y. 80, 83n
Gay 2 Gay 78
Gay and Lesbian London 79–80
gay radio 13, 77, 78, 79, 96
Gaywaves 96
gender and employment 97, 137–51, 192–3, 209–18, 224–37, 238–48, 250–60
gender and technology xii, 15–28, 116–25, 144, 169, 172, 194–5, 198, 225, 245, 268
gender segregation in employment 137–51, 224–37, 238–48, 257
German radio 2, 13, 48–63
Gibbons, M. xii, 2, 224, 239, 262
Giddens, A. 160–61, 163
Gill, R. xii, 239, 242–3
Gillespie, M. 187n
girlification 243, 246
glass ceiling 210, 224–37, 257
Godwin, N. xiii, 13, 104, 197

Gould, J. 16
Graef, V. de 225
Greater London Radio (GLR) 79–80, 267
Green, M. 64, 68
Greenham Women's Peace Group 96, 169
Greer, G. 64
Griffin, C. 148
Griffith, E. 16, 22
Griffiths, J. 37
Grunberger, R. 53
G-Spot 80
Günnell, T. 195
GWR 256, 259, 261n

Habermas, J. 6n, 191–2, 196
Hamilton, D. 130
Hand, M. 105, 263–4
Harding, A. 29, 30
Harrison, H.P. 16
Hartnell, N. 39
Haworth Survey 255–7, 259, 260, 262
Haworth, J. xiii, 206, 262
Health and Safety 251
Heart FM 5
Heritage, J. 151
Hermes, J. 7n, 102, 153
Higginson, T.W. 18
Hill, M. 67
Hilmes, M. 11, 14
Hitler, A. 53, 57, 60, 61
Hobbs, M.-A. 265
Hobson, D. 114, 131–2, 133, 152
Holland, P. 199n
Hollows, B. xiii, 13, 104, 197
Holly, S. 225, 250
Home Truths 264
Homeless People 35
Hood, S. 49
hospital radio 1, 139, 265
housewife 3–4, 37, 51–2, 61, 67, 74, 90, 88–9, 95, 113, 115n, 120, 126–35, 238, 259
housewife radio 107, 113, 243
Housewives' Choice 37, 124, 126
Hunter, F. xiii, 12, 207n

IBEC 225
ideal radio voice 11
identity xvi, 183–7

In Town Tonight 75
incremental radio stations 97
Independent Broadcasting Authority (IBA) 97, 109n, 128–9, 135
Independent Local Radio (ILR) 78, 129–30, 134–5, 138–51, 255–7
internet radio 14, 108, 207, 248, 251, 252, 272
intimate voice 49, 53, 67
Irish radio 2, 114, 167–81, 194, 224–37, 239
Irish Radio and Television Commission (IRTC) 226, 235, 236n
Irons, E. 44
ISDN (Integrated Services Digital Network) 253, 261n, 271, 274n
Ivieson, A. 66
izzat 184–5, 187n

Jacobson, J. 187n
Jallov, B. 189, 193
Jammin in Jamaica 263
Janis, E. 22
Jankowski, N.W. 189
Jarman, T. 270–1
Jay, Baroness M. 258
Johnson, L. 116, 124
Joint Industry Committee for Radio Audience Research (JICRAR) 130
Joyce, J. 41

Kandola, R. 235
Karpf, A. xiii, 3–4, 5, 74, 96, 106, 129, 137,145
Kearney, M. 72
Kershaw, I. 56
Knowles, W. 65
Kramarae, C. 22, 145
Kuhlman, H. 54

Lacey, K. xiii, 2, 12, 13, 61n, 191, 196, 199
Ladies Please 205
Lafkey, S. 225
Lambert, R.S. 44
Lara, M.P. 191
Lawrence, T.E. 42
Lerg, W.B. 49
Lerner, G. 11
lesbian radio 13, 73–83, 104

lesbian radio drama 13, 74, 75, 77–8, 81
lesbians and Woman's Hour 13, 74–5
lesbians in radio news 76–7
Let's TWIST 274n, 278
Lewis, P.M. xv, 11, 97, 193
Liberty Radio 107, 248n, 252
Lincoln, S. 17
Listen with Mother 39, 124
Listener, The 34, 123
Lister, B. 274n
Local Radio Workshop 2, 82, 95
Locker Room, The 159
London Broadcasting Company (LBC) 13, 84–93, 134, 267
Long, J. 134, 205, 219–23
Loud and Proud 79

Macer-Wright, P. 43, 46
MacGregor, S. 64
McKay, A. i, 11, 15–28
McLaughlin, L. 191
McLuhan, R. 3
Magic 1170 269
Magnus-Unzer, F. 56
Mallabar, J. 271–2
MarBolek, I. 61n
Marx, E. 17
Maternity 65, 90, 207n, 215, 216, 219–20, 221–2, 241, 251, 257–8
Matheson, H. i, 12, 41–6
Mayo, S. 220
Mead, M. 38
Media Studies 4, 6, 113, 241, 266, 271
Megamix 263
Men's Hour 99–100
Men's Minute 100, 103
Michaels, K. xiii, 206, 262, 265
microphone 15, 20–2
Millington, C. xiii, 205, 262
Miners' Wives 35–6
Mitchell, C. xvi, xiv, 81, 94, 97, 102, 105, 184, 262, 265
Mix, J.I. 22, 23–5
Monday Play, The 75
Moores, S. i, xiv, xv, 49, 113, 154, 183
Morrison, T. 16
motherism 257–8, 260
Moyles, C. 207n
Murray, J. 64, 65, 71, 72
Muslim women 182–8

My Word! 75

narrowcasting 252
National Broadcasting Company (NBC) 22
National Union of Journalists (NUJ) 251, 258
New Journalist 252
New Statesman and Nation 45
'new racist' discourse 142, 143
news 32, 76, 90, 103, 142–3, 161, 193, 206, 207n, 220, 246, 250–61, 266–8; lifestyle 255, 256, 259–60
news agenda 43, 193, 250, 259–60; female 106, 255, 256, 259–60
newsreaders 206, 216, 250, 254
Nexus Research Co-operative 224, 236n, 239, 262
Nicholson, H. 41, 44, 45
Night Journey 35
Nightingale, A. 95, 134, 206, 238, 265
Now She Laughs, Now She Cries 75
Nye, S. xiv, 13, 104, 197

Oakley, A. 127
Okokon, S. 11
Old Boy Network 216, 229, 234
O'Malley, T. 251–2
One in Ten 74, 81
Ong, W. 15, 16, 26
Opportunity Now 211, 218n
O'Rorke, I. 246, 247
O'Shea, A. 199n
Our Radio 96
Our Tune 132

Parfitt, A. 246, 243
participatory radio 193, 197–8
Peck, L. 53
Permanent Waves 248n, 280, 282
Peruzzo, C.M.K. 197
Phillips, Mrs A. 18
phone-in 76, 80, 85, 87–8, 128
Pickles, W. 33
pirate radio xvii, 2, 6, 14, 82, 95, 96, 108, 114, 167–81, 194, 196–7, 230, 232, 281
Plauderei (chitchat) 13, 48–63
pleasure xvi, 6, 7n, 122
Potter, J. 137–8, 141, 144–5
praxis 2, 6n, 97, 189

presenters: female xv, 22–6, 37–40,
55–60, 61n, 64, 65, 71, 77, 87,
91, 95, 102, 104, 107, 128, 134,
140, 185, 206, 233, 238–9, 265–6;
male 13, 85–93, 113, 114, 130–3,
206
Private Eye 66, 72
private sphere 4, 11, 48–9, 53, 54–5,
113, 116, 184, 191–2
Programme Controllers (PCs) 114, 130,
134–5, 137–51, 266
propaganda 47n, 55–60
public speaking 11, 15–19, 20–2, 49
public sphere 4, 6n, 11, 15, 18, 48–9,
54–5, 189, 191–2
Purdey, H. 252

Queertalk 82
Quigley, J. 67
Qureshi, K. xiv, 114

Radel, F. 51
Radio Academy 280
Radio Advertising Bureau (RAB) 3–4
radio as a domestic medium 4, 53–5,
113, 120–4, 126–35
Radio Authority 6, 105, 108, 279
Radio Bloke xvi, 3
Radio Broadcast (magazine) 23–5
Radio Donna 193
radio interview 12, 29, 34, 37, 68, 87,
133, 253, 256–7, 260, 267
Radio Joint Audience Research (RAJAR)
3, 6n, 70, 115n, 261n
Radio Magazine 266, 271, 280
Radio na Life 239
Radio Pirate Woman 114, 167–81, 193,
194, 196, 281
Radio Studies 4, 5
Radio Studies Network 7n, 280
Radio Times 71, 72n, 75, 121, 122,
133, 154
Radio Venus 94, 193, 195, 196, 198–9,
277
RadiOrakel 193, 199, 281
Radway, J. 153, 159–60
Rantzen, E. 30
Reeves, W. 142
Reith, Lord J. 12, 30, 42, 44, 45, 74,
259
Restricted Service Licence (RSL) xvi, 6n,

16, 97, 101–5, 106, 108, 182–8,
193, 199, 251
Riano, P. 189
Rich, K. 272
Rider, J. 26n
Roosevelt, Mrs E. 38
Rosebury, A. 17
Rosenberg, A. 53
Ross, M. xv, 4, 115, 206, 145–6
RTE 225, 233, 236n
Ruane, F. 225
Rupp, L.J. 53, 54
Russell, S. 12
Ryan, M. 4, 95, 96, 129, 134, 135, 137

Sachs, J. 20
Sackville-West, V. 42, 44, 46
Sallie licences 251, 260n
Sandford, J. 49
Sappho 76
Scanell, P. 6n, 11, 12, 32, 34, 43, 46,
49, 118
Scottish/Pakistani community 115,
182–8
Scott-Moncrieff, J. 74–5
Scraping the Sky 264
script writing 264–5
Searle, J. 151
Sebba, A. 260n
Selerie, C. 64, 65, 72
sexism: female voice as unsuitable for
radio 5, 15–28, 145–8, 206, 216,
243, 244–5, 254; flexible 238, 239,
137–51, 246–7; male presenters 13,
85–93, 113, 114, 130–3; on local
radio 1, 84–93, 138–51
sexist language 85, 86–9, 91, 92–3, 133,
134
Shapley, O. i, xiv, 12, 29–40, 67, 205
Shingler, M. 254
sidekick 150, 238, 239, 240, 243, 244,
245, 246, 265
Simons, H. 151
Sims, M. 205, 212–3
Sims Report 212–3, 214
Sinn Fein 170, 172, 173
Smith, C. 251
Smith, D. 151
Somerset, Lady H. 17
Somerville, M. 205
Sound Sirens 263

soundscape 165, 197
Spacks, P.M. 55
Spain, N. 75
Spectrum Radio 80
Spender, D. 55, 148
sports reporting 42, 43, 256–7, 266–7
STATCOM 225
station management 197, 269–70
Steinberg, J.C. 19, 26
Steiner, L. 189, 192
Stephenson, J. 54
stereotyping xvi, 4, 88–90, 129–33, 252;
    of lesbians 75–6
Steward, S. 242, 245
Stocks, C. 99, 101
Stuart, S. 94
student radio 107, 108, 265, 280
Studio Manager (SM) 268–70
Suarez Toro, M. 193
Sullivan, J. 3
Sunday Outing, A 78–9, 81, 268
Sunrise Radio 182
Sutherland, J. 225

Tacchi, J. xiv, 108, 114
talk: scripted 12, 41, 43, 59
Talks (BBC Dept) 43–5, 205, 268
Taylor, M. 266
technology 15–16, 20–2, 29–30, 32–3,
    51–2, 116–21, 123, 144, 194, 245,
    253, 268–9
TFM 269
Third Ear 76
Third Reich 49, 52–4, 58, 60, 61
Thompson, J. 151
Today FM 236n
Today Programme 64, 72n, 158
Top 20 1
training 194–5, 198, 199n, 207n,
    234–5, 246, 251, 254, 269, 277,
    278
Tubman, H. 18
Tuchman, G. 189
Tucker, D.G. 22
Twin Peaks policy 64, 69–70

UN Charter of Human Rights 167

Valentine, P. 95, 254
Van Zoonen, L. 5, 7n, 190–1, 224, 225
Venus FM 98, 99, 101, 102

Viva! 5, 94, 96, 105–8, 248n, 252
Von Saldern, A. 61n

Wall T. 114
Wallace, J. 25
Walter, N. 251
Ward, M. 207n
Warr, S. 266–8
Watt, A. 20
WBAI, New York 193
Wear FM 78
Week Ending 158–9
Weimar Republic 48–54, 58, 61n
Welch, D. 52
Welch, E. 11
Weldon, F. 64
Wells, S. 205
Werbner, P. 182
Werden, F. 193
Wetherall, M. 137–8, 141, 144–5
Whiley, J. 238, 246, 247, 265
Whitney, H. 274n
Wieder, L. 151
Wieringa, C. 254
Wilkinson, E. 42
Willard, F. 18–19
Wittgenstein, L. 151
Wogan, T. 2, 131
Woman to Woman 97
Woman's Hour i, 5, 12, 13, 14n,
    36–40, 61n, 64–72, 74–5, 76,
    77, 80, 100, 102, 108, 126, 157,
    205, 263; audience 37, 64, 69;
    brand 68
Woman's Hour Book 14n, 74
woman's perspective on radio news 90,
    103, 250–61
Women in Media xii, 4, 146
Women on Air 194, 195, 234–5, 239,
    282
Women on the Line 193
Women on the Waves 96
Women on Wearside 193, 194, 197,
    198–9
women politicians 68, 131, 220
women reporters 32–6, 80, 92, 95, 206,
    207n, 253, 263, 266–8
Women Without Men 39
Women's Airwaves (WAW) 13, 84–93,
    95, 190, 199n
Women's Alternative Media (WAM) 192

Women's Development Initiative (WDI)
213–14
Women's Feature Service 193
Women's Hour 12, 61n
Women's Liberation Movement 64, 91,
190
Women's magazine programme 78, 97,
102–5, 128, 183
women's magazines 7n, 101, 102,
126–8, 135n, 190
Women's Newsgathering Service
(WINGS) 193
women's programming 5, 48, 50–1,
102–5, 107, 108, 113, 128,
131–3, 134, 169–81, 196–7
Women's Radio Group 95, 106,
277
women's radio stations i, 1, 4, 5, 13–14,

94–110, 113, 167–1, 182–8,
189–202
Women's Radio Workshop 95
Women's Scéal Radio 167–9, 197
Wood, L. 25
Woods, M. 239
Woolf, M. 225, 250
Woolf, N. 198
Workers' Radio Club 61n
Wright, S. 2, 78, 131, 243
Write out Loud 264
Wyndam-Goldie, G. 216

Yesufu, A. 99, 270
Young, J. 2, 130–1

Zerman, Z.A.B. 53
Zilliacus-Tikkanen, H. 248, 254–5, 256